Richard Bernstein

CHINA 1945

Richard Bernstein has been a reporter, culture critic, and commentator for more than thirty years. He was a foreign correspondent in Asia and Europe for *Time* magazine and *The New York Times*, and was the first Beijing bureau chief for *Time*. He is the author of many books on Chinese and Asian themes, among them *The Coming Conflict with China* and *Ultimate Journey: Retracing the Path of an Ancient Buddhist Monk Who Crossed Asia in Search of Enlightenment*, the latter of which was a *New York Times* Best Book of the Year. He is also the author of *Out of the Blue: A Narrative of September 11, 2001*, which was named by *The Boston Globe* as one of the seven best books of 2002. He lives in New York.

richardbernstein.net

@R_Bernstein

Praise for Richard Bernstein's

CHINA 1945

"Elegant and compelling. . . . This thoughtful book moves decisively beyond sterile old debates to demonstrate that in the end, China's fate in 1945 was for the Chinese people, and not Americans, to decide." —*Foreign Affairs*

"Authoritative and engaging." —NPR

"Extensively researched. . . . [Bernstein's] findings about the limits of US influence in China are relevant to more recent American interventions in Iraq and Afghanistan." —*The Christian Science Monitor*

"A fascinating, sometimes harrowing account of an uncertain period . . . pointedly relevant to today's global dilemmas as well." —*Richmond Times-Dispatch*

"Stimulating. . . . A timely analysis that sheds light on the realities of American engagement in Asia." —*Publishers Weekly*

"Thoroughly researched and well argued. . . . Highly recommended." —*Library Journal*

"Immensely readable. . . . A nuanced hindsight assessment that expertly pursues the historical ramification of roads not taken." —*Kirkus Reviews*

"A rich, compelling book told with subtlety and grace. For those interested in understanding how China went Communist in the middle of the twentieth century, it is well worth the read." —*Military History Quarterly*

"Cogent and engaging."   —*Booklist*

"The current rivalry between the United States and China for the dominant role in East Asia is rooted in a complicated history dating back to 1945. Richard Bernstein's compelling and moving examination of U.S.-China relations during and immediately after World War II sparkles with fresh insights into the tragic events and colorful personalities of that era. A model of historical writing for nonspecialist readers, its only fault is that once begun it is almost impossible to put down."
                    —Steven I. Levine, coauthor of *Mao: The Real Story*

"The dramatic events of 1945 continue to shape American relations with China. Mao, Zhou Enlai, Stilwell, General George Marshall—these and other giant personalities come to life in these pages, as we relive the fateful choices events forced on them in a year of nonstop crises. The book offers a thoughtful examination of the roots of authoritarianism in China, the sources of Chinese-American mistrust, and the intractability of history."
                    —Andrew J. Nathan, coeditor of *The Tiananmen Papers*

"Richard Bernstein's *China 1945* is the rare book that underpromises on its title. The author goes far beyond delivering up that pivotal year, providing instead a learned and compelling narrative of the characters and forces that drove China and the United States apart and created today's world."
                    —Howard French, author of *China's Second Continent*

"At the beginning of 1945, America had the chance to forge a good relationship with Mao and his Chinese communist rebels. Richard Bernstein's fascinating and important tale of what happened provides crucial lessons about creative diplomacy that are still very relevant, both in dealing with China and around the world."   —Walter Isaacson, author of *Steve Jobs*

CHINA 1945

MAO'S REVOLUTION
AND AMERICA'S
FATEFUL CHOICE

Richard Bernstein

VINTAGE BOOKS
A Division of Penguin Random House LLC
New York

FIRST VINTAGE BOOKS EDITION, OCTOBER 2015

Copyright © 2014 by Richard Bernstein

All rights reserved. Published in the United States by Vintage Books,
a division of Penguin Random House LLC, New York, and distributed
in Canada by Random House of Canada, a division of Penguin Random
House Ltd., Toronto. Originally published in hardcover in the United
States by Alfred A. Knopf, a division of Penguin Random House LLC,
New York, in 2014.

Vintage and colophon are registered trademarks of
Penguin Random House LLC.

The Library of Congress has cataloged the Knopf edition as follows:
Bernstein, Richard.
China 1945 : Mao's revolution and America's fateful choice /
Richard Bernstein. — First edition.
pages cm
Includes bibliographical references and index.
1. United States — Foreign relations — China.
2. China — Foreign relations — United States.
3. China — History — Republic, 1912–1949.
4. Taiwan — History — 1945–   5. Mao, Zedong, 1893–1976.
6. Chiang, Kai-shek, 1887–1975.   I. Title.
E183.8.C5B439 2014   327.7305109'044—dc23   2014003598

Vintage Books Trade Paperback ISBN: 978-0-307-74321-3
eBook ISBN: 978-0-385-35351-9

Author photograph © Zhongmei Li
Book design by Betty Lew
Maps by Mapping Specialists, Ltd.

www.vintagebooks.com

Printed in the United States of America
10 9 8 7 6 5 4 3 2

TO THE MEMORY OF

Clare Bernstein

For men change their rulers willingly hoping to better themselves, and this hope induces them to take up arms against him who rules: wherein they are deceived, because they afterwards find by experience they have gone from bad to worse.

—*Niccolò Machiavelli*

The whole state apparatus, including the army, the police, and the courts, is the instrument by which one class oppresses another . . . it is violence and not "benevolence."

—*Mao Zedong*

Contents

A Note on Chinese Names and Places

Transcribing names of Chinese people and places is complex, because of the multiple ways in which it has been done over the years, and because some names have changed since the period covered in this book. For place-names, I have mostly used the names that were employed in 1945, and if the name used today is different, I show that in parenthesis after the first mention. The two main instances of this are Mukden, the largest city in Manchuria, which is now known as Shenyang, and Chefoo, present-day Yentai. An exception is Beijing, which means "northern capital." In 1945, the city was known as Peiping, meaning "northern peace." But I render it as Beijing, in the way that has become generally accepted today.

In 1945, the main system used for transcribing Chinese names into the Latin alphabet was called Wade-Giles, and it decreed, for example, that the leader of China's Communist Party was Mao Tse-tung. But since coming to power, the Communists have adopted an alternative system, known as pinyin, by which the aforementioned name is rendered Mao Zedong, and for most names, including Mao's, this book follows the pinyin system currently in use. However in the case of Kuomintang officials, I use the Wade-Giles system still in use on Taiwan. Thus, I refer to the Kuomintang official who negotiated the ceasefire of January 1946 as Chang Chun. The pinyin spelling would be Zhang Chun. The Kuomintang itself would be Guomindang, or GMD, in pinyin, but I have used the old romanization—Kuomintang, or KMT.

Finally, a small number of the names are rendered in a way that does not correspond either to pinyin or Wade-Giles but is still so familiar that it would be confusing to abandon it. The chief example is the Nationalist leader Chiang Kai-shek. In pinyin his name would be Jiang Jieshi, but his name is rendered as Chiang Kai-shek in this book. The names of several Chinese cities are similarly rendered—hence Canton (rather than the pinyin: Guangzhou) and Chungking (pinyin: Chongqing).

CHINA 1945

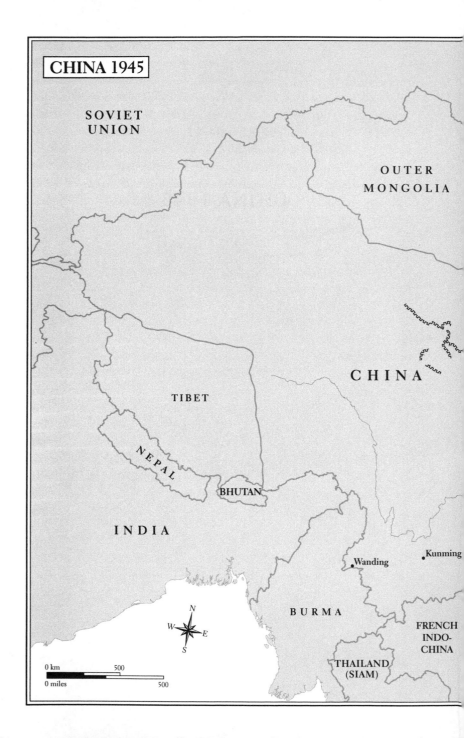

CHINA 1945

SOVIET
UNION

OUTER
MONGOLIA

CHINA

TIBET

NEPAL

BHUTAN

INDIA

Wanding

Kunming

BURMA

FRENCH
INDO-
CHINA

THAILAND
(SIAM)

N
W E
S

0 km   500
0 miles   500

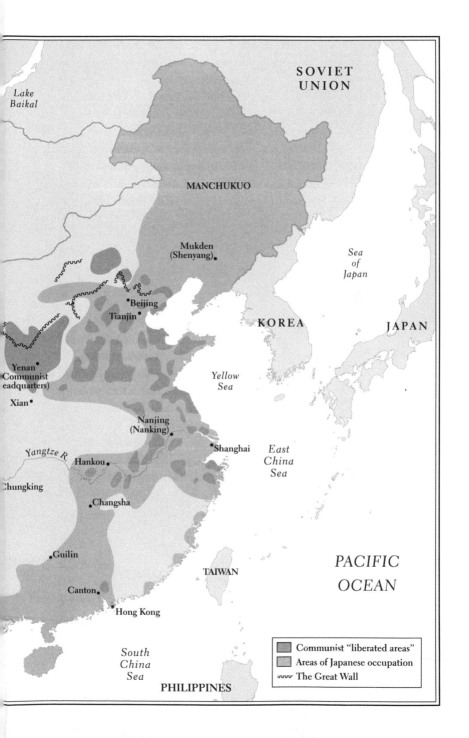

Lake Baikal

SOVIET UNION

MANCHUKUO

Mukden (Shenyang)

Beijing
Tianjin

KOREA

JAPAN

Sea of Japan

Yenan (Communist Headquarters)

Xian

Yellow Sea

Nanjing (Nanking)

Shanghai

East China Sea

Yangtze R.

Hankou

Chungking

Changsha

Guilin

TAIWAN

PACIFIC OCEAN

Canton

Hong Kong

South China Sea

PHILIPPINES

Communist "liberated areas"
Areas of Japanese occupation
The Great Wall

Introduction

Near the end of 2013, something new made its presence known in the waters off the coast of China. It was an aircraft carrier, bought from Ukraine and refurbished in the port of Qingdao. Called the *Liaoning*, it was China's first-ever such craft and therefore, while not nearly as swift or powerful as the American colossi that patrol the world's oceans, a sign of China's growing power and, more important, of its intention to project that power well beyond its shores.

Naturally, this was of interest to the United States, which dispatched ships of its own to observe the *Liaoning* as it sailed with its escort of destroyers and cruisers in international waters. When one of the American ships, a guided missile cruiser known as the *Cowpens*, almost collided with a Chinese vessel that cut closely and aggressively across its bow, there was angry comment on both sides.

The American secretary of defense called China's action "irresponsible." China, through its controlled press, declared that the *Cowpens* had intruded into a "no sail" zone declared by China in the South China Sea, virtually all of which China claims to control, though that claim is not accepted by the United States or by other countries in Asia. The newspaper *Global Times*, an English-language mouthpiece for China's ministry of propaganda, warned that China had a right to defend its territory, and "just because it wasn't capable of asserting its interest in the past doesn't mean it has given up this right."

There were other high-seas confrontations between China and the United States in the early years of the twenty-first century, as China indicated an intention over the long run to supplant the United States as the dominant power in East Asia and the western Pacific.

But for the historian what is striking about the newest phase of Sino-American relations is how closely it echoes the past, particularly actions undertaken by earlier Chinese Communist forces to warn the United States away, to stop it from exercising what it assumed to be its paramount power in Asia. The most important and best-known of these actions took place during the Korean War in 1950, when, for the first and, so far, only time, China and America engaged in large-scale hostilities. But the first armed standoff between the United States and the Communist Chinese took place five years earlier than that along a dusty, tree-lined road between the Chinese port of Tianjin and the ancient imperial capital, Beijing (then known as Peiping) that was being patrolled by detachments of United States Marines.

It was September 1945. The devastating war against Japan, which had occupied much of China for eight years, had ended only weeks before. The United States had sent its marines to China's north coast to help maintain order there and to enable China's central government to retake possession of its previously occupied territory. But the Chinese Communists, who had warmly welcomed American soldiers, diplomats, and journalists during the war, now didn't want American troops on the ground in China at all. And so they embarked on a campaign of harassment and intimidation that was more lethal than anything that has happened in the more recent confrontations on the high seas. Shots were fired in anger, men were killed, and prisoners were taken, including some who were on missions like that of the *Cowpens* nearly seventy years later, to collect information that the Communists didn't want them to have.

The year 1945 in this sense marked the origin of a rivalry between the United States and China's Communists that, like a recurring illness, has always reinstated itself, and has bedeviled the relations between the two sides even after periods of near-rhapsodic warmth and declarations of common interest, during which the suspicions and animosities of the past seem to have been put permanently to rest. It is a strange rivalry in its way, because for all of these decades, China and the United States would appear to have had much more to gain from friendly cooperation than from conflict—gains in trade and investment, cooperation against environmental degradation, terrorism, and nuclear proliferation. In 1945 too, until the clashes that began on the road between Tianjin and Beijing, the United States and the Chinese Communists had not only cooperated in the war against the Japanese occupiers, but they had also talked enthusiastically about major plans for the future, during which American money and technology would help lift China out of poverty.

That didn't happen, of course. The mood that seemed so buoyant at the beginning of 1945 deteriorated, and replacing the banquets and toasts and declarations of friendship that had taken place earlier were armed clashes, mutual accusations, and, especially from the Communists, angry expressions of eternal and inevitable enmity. Not all of the more recent rivalry between China and the United States has its origins in that one year, but the pattern of enmity, which resulted in two devastating wars, first in Korea and later in Vietnam, was established during the months just before and just after the end of World War II in Asia.

Was this pattern avoidable? Could things have been different? The answers to those questions are to be found in the chronicle of events of 1945, the turning-point year for both China and the United States, whose relations in coming years will do more to affect the shape of the planet than those between any other two countries.

PART I

Innocents in China

CHAPTER ONE

A Rare Victory

Nineteen forty-five, the eighth year of the war between China and Japan, opened with a Chinese military success. It was a rare and therefore heartening event in a China that had become perhaps not inured to defeat but well acquainted with it, and with the human devastation that it brought with it.

The victory took place in western Yunnan province along the border with Burma at a place called Wanding, a semitropical customs station that under normal circumstances nobody outside the region would have heard of. Then as now, the town was connected to Burma by a single-lane wooden bridge over a tributary of the Salween River. It was a not-very-charming place of small merchandise markets, customs sheds, and a frontier inspection station set in a breathtaking territory of terraced fields, swift muddy streams, and fingers of mist that crept down an endless succession of far-flung valleys. There, on January 3, 1945, two large Chinese armies, one coming across Yunnan province from the east, the other from the west across Burma, converged on some two thousand weary and hungry but battle-tested and well-dug-in Japanese troops.

Wanding's momentary importance came from its position at the northeast exit of Burma's Shweli Valley. Three years earlier, a Japanese army, using forced marches through the jungles and coordinated air and ground assaults, had seized all of Burma, up to then a British colony, thereby achieving two important goals as Japan sought to extend its sway across all of Asia. One, the eviction of the British from Burma completed the eradication of white European colonialism in East and Southeast Asia. Japan had already chased the British from their possessions in Hong Kong, Malaya, and Singapore, and the Americans from their only Asian colony, the Philippines (Vichy France, allied to Nazi Germany, was still nominally in control of the Indochinese countries of Vietnam, Laos, and Cambodia, but Japan largely dictated terms there too).

The other Japanese goal was to blockade China, in effect, lay it under siege, preventing it from getting supplies from the outside world and thereby forcing it to surrender. When Japan embarked upon its full-scale invasion of China in 1937, its expeditionary armies took control of all the country's ports on its long Pacific coast—Dalian, Port Arthur, Yingkou, Huludao, and Qinwangdao in the northeast; Tianjin, Chefoo (now Yentai), Qingdao, Ningpo, and Shanghai in central China; Amoy, Swatow, Canton, and the British colony of Hong Kong in the south. The Japanese also prevailed upon Vichy France to close the old railroad leading from the Vietnamese capital of Hanoi to Kunming in southwest China, so that former overland route was no more. For the early years of the war, the Soviet Union supplied substantial arms and equipment to China, but that stopped in 1941 when the Soviets became too busy with their own struggle against Nazi Germany to ship much of anything to China.

The result was that China, a continent-sized country with a population of 425 million, was in imminent danger of being entirely cut off from the rest of the world, and therefore cut off from its sources of military supplies. In response, China's government dispatched two hundred thousand laborers from Yunnan to Burma to construct a two-lane, all-weather road that served for five years as the final segment of a very long supply route to China. Goods shipped from San Francisco came by freighter to the Burmese-British port of Rangoon (now Yangon), then inland by train five hundred miles to the town of Lashio in the Shan states of eastern Burma; from there, these shipments went by truck up the steep gradients of the Burmese tribal borderlands and over the Wanding bridge into China itself. The road continued northeast for another five-hundred-mile stretch through the corrugated verdure of rural Yunnan province, crossing a trestle bridge over the deep, steep banks of the Salween River and ending up in Kunming, the provincial capital.

With Japan's conquest of Burma, China's sole connection to the rest of the world was a treacherous, high-altitude air route over the Himalayas from northeast India. Known ruefully to the pilots who flew it as "the Hump," this often fatally dangerous supply line provided China with all the arms, ammunition, and fuel it could get in its desperate war of resistance against the well-armed Japanese. The supply was woefully inadequate. And that is why the reopening of the Burma Road was a constant and, in the case of one commander in particular, obsessively pursued goal. It would be a way of supplying China and thereby helping it to make a greater contribution to the main and overriding objective of the war in Asia, which was the defeat of Japan.

The commander for whom Burma was an obsession was Lieutenant General Joseph W. Stilwell, a legendary figure, much written about at the time, who subsequently served as chief of staff to the supreme Chinese leader, Chiang Kai-shek, and as commander of all American forces in the entire China-Burma-India theater. The only problem with the latter designation was that, with the important exceptions of teams of advisers, some very effective army air force units, and a famous guerrilla battalion known as Merrill's Marauders, there were hardly any American combat forces in the theater. Stilwell commanded Chinese troops almost exclusively, deployed reluctantly by Chiang, who had many fronts, military and political, to contend with, Burma relatively minor among them. In 1942, when the Japanese first invaded Burma, Stilwell had gotten separated from the main body of the Chinese troops he was commanding, and narrowly escaped the pursuing Japanese by walking to India, where he minced no words to the journalists who met him there. "We got a hell of a beating," he said. "We got run out of Burma and it is humiliating as hell. I think we ought to find out what caused it, go back and retake it."

Now, at the beginning of 1945, the United States and China were retaking it, and even though Stilwell, relieved of his command four months earlier at Chiang's insistence, was no longer on the scene, the two armies converging on Wanding had been largely created and trained by him, and they were carrying out his tactical plan. One arm of the pincer, made up of twelve Chinese divisions known as the Y-Force, had moved the five hundred miles toward Burma through Yunnan province from Kunming, commanded for that long march by the Nationalist general Wei Li-huang—aka "Hundred Victories Wei"—but prodded into action every hard-earned mile of the way by American liaison officers who were assigned to every large Chinese unit. Wei, ordered by Chiang to "succeed—or else," began fighting his way through Yunnan in April 1944. He ferried his seventy-two thousand troops, his pack animals, and his weaponry by moonlight across the treacherous Salween, which cuts north–south through central Yunnan province. He fought in torrential monsoon rain and thick fog that turned to sleet in Yunnan's higher elevations, building bridges over innumerable mountain streams, receiving supplies by air drop, and keeping the Japanese on the defensive. Wei got crucial help from the American 14th Air Force, aka the Flying Tigers, the storied unit led by General Claire Chennault, which relentlessly strafed and bombed Japanese troops during the entire Salween campaign. Still, Wei's forces took heavy casualties from an enemy always ready to fight and die rather than surrender. Colonel John H. Stodter, a liaison officer attached to the Y-Force, recalled the Chinese practice of attempting "to climb up through inter-locking bands of machine gun fire," a "sheer bravery" that seemed "sickeningly wasteful."

The other arm of Stilwell's pincer was the X-Force, five divisions of Chinese troops, these under the command of an American, Lieutenant General Daniel I. Sultan, who had spent the better part of a year fighting their way from India over a succession of ridges and valleys across Burma in the direction of China. In November, Wei took Mangshi, a town in western Yunnan that had a landing field, permitting supplies to be flown in rather than air-dropped. On December 1, 1944, Chefang fell to the Chinese. On the other side of the border, the X-Force had taken the town of Bhamo on the Irrawaddy River, just fifty miles as the crow flies from Wanding.

Wei attacked there on January 3. Detachments of the Chinese Second Army climbed the dominant local peak, known as the Huilongshan, which commanded the approaches to the town. Colonel Stodter had a clear view of the action from an observation post, as did Theodore H. White, *Time* magazine's correspondent in wartime China, who described the unfolding battle "as one of those vignettes that mark a turning point."

"It was a long, hot day of mountain climbing," White wrote in his memoirs,

> and it began with American planes circling the peak: a tattoo of three smoke shells from the artillery to mark the Japanese positions on the crest, then American pursuits and bombers peeling off one by one, dropping their napalm, dropping frag bombs, dropping heavy bombs.

Artillery salvos, lasting eight minutes every hour, blasted the Japanese positions, and "after each salvo a rush of Chinese infantrymen to

A convoy of American trucks and jeeps rolls through the Chinese town of Baoshan after the reopening of the Burma Road at the beginning of 1945.

the next height through the shell-shredded trees; then another salvo, and one could see the Chinese in their blue-gray uniforms tumbling into trenches or circling Japanese blockhouses and dropping on them from the top." Afterward, the vultures flew over the slopes of the mountains, where they picked at the corpses of the Chinese and Japanese dead.

White's claim that a turning point had been reached seems a bit hyperbolic, and yet, the successful conclusion of the Salween campaign did seem a promising event in a war that had gone very badly. With their tanks, aircraft, gunboats, and fast infantry, their coordinated attacks, mobility, and firepower, the Japanese had won victory after victory in China. China's territory was vast enough, Japan's supply lines sufficiently long, and Chinese resistance just stubborn enough to deny the Japanese the total victory they sought. They had not conquered all of China, but they had slaughtered hundreds of thousands of China's troops, whose fighting ability earned them little in the way of respect or admiration in American military circles or elsewhere in the world.

The most pathetic element in the Chinese military picture was the Chinese soldiers themselves, for whom being wounded or being killed in action ended the same way, the difference being either a quick death or a slow one. Foreign visitors reported their shock at seeing wounded soldiers by the roadsides, their eyes blank with hopelessness as their wounds went unattended, as if they were street beggars ignored by the passing throng. The dead and wounded were replaced by conscripts dragged unwillingly from their homes, underfed men sometimes literally roped together.

China had striven in the decade before the war began to create a modern military force, using mostly German advisers in its effort, but its armies were still underarmed and underfed, their soldiers often so emaciated that, in the words of one United States Army report, their skin was the "shabby cover of an emaciated body which has no other value than to turn rice into dung." The military leadership was infested with corrupt and incompetent officers. Many of its senior commanders were actually semi-warlords whose allegiance to the central government was shaky, and who followed the custom of putting a portion of the salaries paid to their men into their own bank accounts—which gave them an incentive to pad their rolls. China was backward, inefficient, demoralized, fragmented, unhealthy, and poor. Japan was in every way a modern twentieth-century power, and that's why China's losses were so horrendous.

Despite this poor record, China fought on, and, as we will see later, there was a tendency on the part of foreign observers to stress its armies' faults and to ignore its virtues altogether. The mere fact that China was undefeated for eight years and that it held down a million Japanese troops was itself an important contribution. Still, victories were few, and decisive victories fewer still, and that is what gave the campaign on the Salween its special glow. According to the official American military history, the campaign marked "the first time in the history of Sino-Japanese relations that the Chinese forces had driven Japanese troops from an area the Japanese wanted to hold." As they ended the three-year Japanese blockade of their country, the Chinese also recouped twenty-four thousand square miles of territory in Yunnan province that had been held by Japan. *The New York Times* noted the "savage no-quarter fighting" in "the world's toughest battle-ground, the gorges, cloud-shrouded passes and towering peaks of Yunnan province" and called the victory there "a smashing climax to China's first real offensive of the war."

Nine days after the fall of Wanding, a convoy of American trucks flying American and Chinese flags rolled through the Shweli Valley, passing the terraced landscape of the hill tribe villages on either side of the river, and ground up the steep hill toward China. American correspondents accompanying the X-Force stopped their jeeps to talk with the Chinese soldiers, tied the two countries' national flags to their radio antennas, and then sped away toward Wanding, where their dispatches informed the world that the last Japanese positions on the Burma Road had been "wiped out or driven away." To celebrate the victory, a veritable who's who of Nationalist Chinese and their American advisers arrived in Wanding. China's premier, T. V. Soong, the American-educated brother-in-law of Chiang Kai-shek, flew from the wartime capital of Chungking at the head of a delegation of the powerful and influential. General Albert C. Wedemeyer, who had taken over from Stilwell as American commander of the China theater, arrived from Chungking as well. General Sultan was there and so was Chennault, the 14th Air Force commander who had started air attacks against the Japanese occupiers of China before the Americans were officially in the war, when his air squadron was known as the American Volunteer Group. Some of Chennault's planes now droned above Wanding to guard against a surprise Japanese attack.

The day before, Chiang Kai-shek, speaking on a broadcast to the United States, declared that breaking the siege of China would serve as "a powerful tonic on the spirit of our army and our people" and an "omen of defeat" for the militarists of Japan. For three years, Chiang declared, Japan had proclaimed that the blockade of China would force the country into collapse and give it no choice but to surrender. But "now comes this caravan [proving] to the enemy that neither the will power of China nor the will power of her allies to win the war can ever be shaken." In a gesture of apparent gratitude and admiration to the man whose work, vision, and planning were behind the success, the generalissimo officially named the new highway from India to China "the Stilwell Road," in memory, Chiang declared, of Stilwell's "distinctive contribution and of the signal part which the Allied and Chinese forces under his direction played in the Burma campaign and in the building of the road."

From the vantage point of nearly seventy years, it is easy to be both moved and saddened by the Allied achievement in Burma, the blood, the sacrifice, the cruel immensity of the task, and by what appears now to have been its futility. The high-flown rhetoric marking the beginning of 1945 now seems false and formalistic given how badly that year ended, for the government of Chiang Kai-shek and for American ambitions in China. Despite the enormous sacrifice made to seize the territory and to build it, the road from Ledo in northeast India to Kunming in southeast China did not turn out to be of great significance in the war against Japan. Winston Churchill had long argued against making Burma the focus of a major Allied war effort, saying it would be like eating a porcupine quill by quill. Rebuilding the road, he argued, would be "an immense, laborious task, unlikely to be finished before the need for it had passed." He was right. By the time the road was reopened, the American Air Transport Command, now equipped with big, four-engine Douglas and Consolidated airplanes, was supplying forty-four thousand tons of matériel on the route over the Himalayas, nearly ten times the amount that had been brought over by air a couple of years before and double the highest amounts trucked in on the Burma Road early in 1942, before it was seized by Japan. Planes were now crossing the Hump on the six-hundred-mile route every two and a half minutes day and night, which, as Tillman Durdin of *The New York Times* put it, "is making the Ledo-Burma Road virtually obsolescent so far as the transport of military supplies to China is concerned." In the end, even though Churchill, the supreme colonialist, had advised against the Burma campaign, what the Chinese troops had mainly done was regain for Britain its lost colony. They hadn't done all that much for China itself.

Of course, as the firecrackers went off to welcome the convoy at Wanding, nobody was so impolitic as to say as much. Nobody alluded to the awkward fact that Chiang and Stilwell hated each other, or that for the months before he left, relations between China's government and the Americans sent to the country to help in its war of resistance were tense and mistrustful. It must have left a sour taste in the Chinese leader's mouth to name the Burma Road after the American general. But in winning the battle of the road, the Chinese had vindicated a long-held conviction of Stilwell, who, sometimes almost alone among American leaders, had sustained the belief that Chinese troops could fight with the best of them if only they were given proper supplies, solid training, and good leadership. Now, in an ambitious program code-named Alpha, training camps staffed by American officers were up and running in Yunnan to ready thirty-nine divisions of crack Chinese troops for the rest of the war against Japan.

Wedemeyer had it all planned out. The next step, after finishing the Alpha training, was to take the war to the Japanese strong points inside China itself, drive to the coast, secure a major port, probably near Canton or Hong Kong, and prepare for a landing of American troops. "It is believed," Wedemeyer wrote to Chiang, "that if our operations can be initiated in July, they will catch the Japanese off-balance and probably preclude planned redistribution of their forces." In other words, the Japanese would have no time to redeploy for a defense against an American invasion. After a port was seized, Wedemeyer felt, "the increased flow of supplies in conjunction with victorious battle experience may inspire confidence and create conditions that will enable the Chinese forces to destroy the Japanese on the Asiatic mainland without large-scale American ground participation."

Things, in short, were looking better in China than they had in many years of war. American policy was beginning to pay dividends. Japan would certainly be defeated, the only question being how long it would take and exactly how and at what cost it would be done. The long-term American goal in China—to rescue it from Japanese domination and, once that was done, to foster a united, democratic, and friendly great power—seemed within reach.

The other big subject that nobody thought it politic to mention during the celebrations at Wanding was the dire political situation in China. Where it was not occupied by Japan, the country was divided into two geographic regions each governed by a rival armed political party. One of them, by far the larger, covering most of China west of the Japanese lines, including the rich, heavily populated provinces of Sichuan, Yunnan, Guizhou, and Guangxi, was controlled by the Kuomintang

(KMT), literally the National People's Party, led by Chiang Kai-shek, recognized the world over as China's legitimate president. The Nationalists were headquartered at China's temporary capital of Chungking in Sichuan province, where the entire, large wartime assemblage could be found—the foreign embassies, including the American, the British, and the Soviet; several Chinese universities, which had moved there from their homes farther east; the Chinese government bureaucracy; the international core of journalists covering the Japan-China war; and tens of thousands of refugees living desperately on the fringes, literal and figurative, of the city.

A thousand miles north of Chungking was the other main Chinese force, the Communist Party of China and Mao Zedong, its resourceful, charismatic, and ruthless leader. The Communists had been the sole Chinese beneficiaries of the Japanese invasion, because the war had put a stop to Chiang's effort to wipe them out, forcing him to recognize them as a partner in the national resistance. As such, they had used the chaos of China to recruit a large number of new soldiers to the armies that they maintained in the areas under their control, mostly in the more sparsely populated areas of the north, especially in Shaanxi province, where their headquarters, in an old walled town called Yenan, were situated. After the inevitable defeat of Japan had been achieved, it was highly likely, though far from certain, that a new conflict would break out in China between these two parties and these two leaders, who had been enemies for twenty years. Once this occurred, moreover, the chances were very strong that the new China war would be a duel to the death, with the winner taking the whole prize, which was China itself.

The United States was too preoccupied by the war with Japan and the immense, ongoing task of finishing the war in Europe to be thinking very hard about China's political future. From the standpoint of January 1945, a civil war in China seemed only one of several possible futures. The Americans had managed to arrange matters politically to suit their preoccupation with winning the Japanese war.

Most important from the standpoint of global politics, American relations with the Soviet Union, the most powerful country in the world after the United States itself and the other major future victor of World War II, were cordial and trusting. The American president, Franklin Delano Roosevelt, regarded his Russian counterpart, Joseph Stalin, as a friend and an ally in the ongoing war and a partner in the creation of a new order of peace and stability that FDR intended to follow the war, to be ensured through the creation of a powerful new organization, the United Nations. After all, hadn't the United States through the massive Lend-Lease program essentially given the Russians the equipment they needed to fight Nazi Germany, and wouldn't the trust the two sides had built up during the war endure when it was over? When the Soviet foreign minister Vyacheslav Molotov visited Washington in 1942, he'd been invited to sleep at the White House. "I think," Roosevelt told Churchill in 1942 referring to Stalin, "that if I give him everything I can and ask him for nothing in return, noblesse oblige, he won't try to annex anything and will work with me for a world of democracy and peace." The American president clung to that illusion until his death in April 1945.

Separate from its dealings with Stalin, the United States, over the strong objections of Chiang, was also maintaining cordial relations with Mao and his forces in Yenan. While Chiang's troops were closing in on Japan's forces in Burma and Yunnan, American representatives were talking by candlelight to Mao and his lieutenants about the various forms of cooperation that could emerge in the two parties' struggle against Japan. There was animated discussion of intelligence sharing, of American arms and training for Communist forces, of Communist help to American paratroopers in the north and to a Normandy-style landing of American troops on China's coast, which would require close coordination with the Communist guerrillas who had established themselves behind Japanese lines. Most of all, there were solemn vows to avoid civil war in the future and to work together to promote a united and democratic China, which was the long-standing American dream for the country.

"We would serve with all our hearts under an American general," Mao gushed to an American envoy in the fall of 1944, one of many statements he made about the strength of the Communists' friendly regard for the United States. "That is how we feel toward you."

And then, over the course of the year, it all fell apart. By the end of 1945, pretty much all realistic hope of avoiding civil war, forging a united, pro-western China, and maintaining good relations with a Communist Party integrated into a functioning government had been effectively dashed. The American ambition was still being formally pursued, but it was clear, certainly in retrospect but to many even then, that it was a futile pursuit, a chimera. Japan was gloriously defeated, but the victory won in the Pacific turned out to be only a way station toward a tremendous, unprecedented loss, namely the emergence of a China entirely closed to the United States, deeply inimical to its values, bombastically hostile to its interests, and closely allied to its most menacing rival, the Soviet Union. Within a few short months, the American dream for China evaporated in a cloud of recrimination and accusation.

This, far more than the battle at Wanding, was the real turning point for the United States in Asia. The war to rescue China from the hands of an enemy was won, but China was then quickly lost. The main American goal in Asia unraveled as China slipped into the hands of a dictator allied to a new enemy whose ambitions, values, and practices were deeply inimical to those of the United States. This condition would endure for a quarter of a century. It would lead the United States, in its attempt to prevent history from repeating itself, to fight two costly wars, one in Korea, the other, the most disastrous conflict in twentieth-century American history, in Vietnam. Both of these wars were among the long-range effects of the events that took place in the twelve months and a little more that followed the heartening success at Wanding.

CHAPTER TWO

The Generalissimo and the Americans

Once during the Sino-Japanese War the president of the United States talked with his senior military representative in China, Joseph W. Stilwell, about the possibility of assassinating Chiang Kai-shek. FDR didn't use the word "assassinate," and it seems unlikely that he meant precisely what Stilwell took him to mean, though this confusion could be said to mirror the deep ambiguity and uncertainty of American policymakers as they tried to maneuver throughout the war and after it in the murk and gloom of Chinese domestic politics. Stilwell's version of this matter comes through his chief of staff and most trusted subordinate, General Frank Dorn, who met with Stilwell in Chungking on the latter's return from a conference in Cairo in 1943, attended by FDR, Chiang, and Stilwell himself.

Stilwell and FDR had had a twenty-minute private meeting in Cairo, Stilwell told Dorn, during which, as Stilwell related it, describing the president as if he were a Mafia godfather had told him, "in that Olympian manner of his: 'Big Boy, if you can't get along with Chiang and can't replace him, get rid of him once and for all. You know what I mean. Put in someone you can manage.'"

In Dorn's account, Stilwell instructed him to "cook up a workable scheme and await orders," and Dorn did just that, devising a contingency plan for an assassination that would have been worthy of a Hollywood thriller. The Gimo, or the Gissimo, or CKS, or Cash My Check, or Generalissimo, General of Generals, as Chiang was variously called by Americans, either respectfully or derisively, would be taken on a flight to Ramgarh, India, to inspect Chinese troops being trained there as part of the effort to improve China's backward army. The pilot would pretend to have engine trouble and order his crew and passengers to bail out. Chiang would be ushered to the door of the plane wearing a faulty parachute and told to jump.

"I believe it would work," Stilwell told Dorn.

There was of course no assassination of Chiang, nor did Dorn receive further instructions from Stilwell on this matter. There is, moreover, no other evidence that FDR expressed any desire to have Chiang eliminated, and it seems unlikely that he did, despite the ominous sound of that you-know-what-I-mean uttered to Stilwell. Roosevelt had his occasional bursts of irritation at Chiang, but he also nurtured a certain sympathy for him as a fellow head of state, another lonely man at the top of the unwieldy contraption known as a political system. Roosevelt, whose ancestors on the Delano side had made their fortune in the China trade in the eighteenth and nineteenth centuries, shared that very American wish for China to rise out of the ashes of its recent deplorable condition, preferably by adopting American ways. Unlike, for example, his closest wartime ally, Winston Churchill, who thought American aspirations for China to be silly and wishful, FDR aspired for Chiang to be one of the Big Four of the postwar world, along with Churchill, Stalin, and himself, and he believed that Chiang was the only person with the prestige and standing to lead his afflicted country to a new era of respectability. His remark to Stilwell at Cairo came at a moment of particularly intense puzzlement at what seemed to Roosevelt a combination of evasiveness, deceitfulness, and imperiousness on Chiang's part. At the Cairo conference, speaking to his son Elliott, FDR wondered why Chiang seemed so loath to allow Stilwell to train Chinese troops, why he kept "thousands and thousands of his best men on the borders of Red China," and, above all, "why Chiang's troops aren't fighting at all."

Stilwell has been lionized in histories of this period and in biographies, and, indeed, he was a powerful figure, a brilliant commander much beloved by his troops even when he drove them almost beyond endurance. He was a straight-talker with no tolerance for fakery, deceit, or incompetence, but he was also truculent, indiscreet, stubborn, lacking in sober judgment, and disinclined to recognize his own mistakes— not, in other words, the right man for the job in China, which required fewer prejudices and more diplomatic finesse than he was capable of. He despised Chiang, whom he called "Peanut," not only in his diaries but in his utterances to his staff and superiors, and from time to time he mused aloud on what a good thing it would be if he could be removed from the scene. Even before the Cairo conference or his conversation with Dorn, Stilwell had summoned Carl F. Eifler, the senior American intelligence officer for China, to his office in New Delhi, and, according to Eifler, told him that to pursue the war successfully, "it would be necessary to get Chiang Kai-shek out of the way." Under instructions from Stilwell, Eifler inquired about how to achieve this objective, and he determined that botulinus toxin, which is undetectable in an autopsy, would be an effective weapon. But in May 1944, at a meeting in his headquarters in Burma, Stilwell told Eifler that he'd changed his mind about eliminating Chiang and nothing further was done.

These were outlandish ideas—to throw an allied leader out of an airplane, or to poison him in the fashion of some Roman Empire plot. But the mere fact that it is part of the historical record, mentioned in the memoirs of creditable witnesses and discussed in the serious biographies of Chiang, makes it a gauge of sorts to the dilemma facing American policymakers in China, a poor and divided country, during World War II and right after it, coping with an imperfect leader whom they counted on for more than he could deliver.

It is worth noting in this connection that twenty or so years later, the United States was complicit in the assassination of a supposedly allied Asian leader—Ngo Dinh Diem, the president of South Vietnam from 1955 to 1963—with more than a passing resemblance to Chiang. Diem was killed by local rivals who had gained the approval of the Kennedy administration because his erratic rule and growing unpopularity were deemed by senior officials to be increasingly problematic.

Chiang was a sort of predecessor to Diem, in that he too was the leader of a corrupt rightist dictatorship, though he himself was rigorously honest in the financial sense. Chiang's wife, American-educated Soong Mei-ling, came across to foreigners as charming and imperious— "dragon lady" is the common, racially tinged pejorative; Diem was represented in this sense by his sister-in-law, the glamorous, charming, and vindictive Madame Ngo Dinh Nhu, educated in France and assumed, like Madame Chiang before her, to exercise great influence behind the scenes. Ngo was a Catholic, Chiang a Methodist. Both faced Communist insurrections that rendered them helpless without American aid and goodwill.

But Chiang was never a client ruler in the way that Diem was. He was a man who came to power on the basis of his own intelligence and charisma; he was not put in a gated presidential palace by a foreign intelligence agency. In the decades since World War II, it has become conventional wisdom to see Chiang as one of the great incompetents of twentieth-century history, but at the time, and even subsequently, there was reason to see him in a more sympathetic light, as an effective leader striving under tremendous disadvantages to push his country into a brighter future. Recent biographers, especially Jay Taylor, a former American diplomat, have emphasized Chiang's good qualities rather than his deficiencies, and have portrayed him as laboring under almost impossible circumstances, especially after the ruinous Japanese invasion. Chiang was born in Zhejiang, the coastal province south of Shanghai, in 1887 and educated in part at a Japanese military academy. He became the chief protégé of Sun Yat-sen, the first republican leader of China, the man who led the overthrow of the Manchu dynasty in 1911 and established the Kuomintang, promising after a period of authoritarian tutelage to establish a western-style democracy. Chiang was slender, small, stiff, prideful, and patriotic, imbued with a sense of China's humiliation at the hands of foreigners and determined to do something about it, though following the revolution of 1911, China, far from becoming a powerful democracy, had fallen into fragmentation and chaos, its territory divided up among a group of competing warlords and prone to Japanese aggression.

Among Chiang's great achievements was the Northern Expedition of 1926 to 1928 when the army he led established a fragile sort of unity across the country. He was advised in that endeavor by members of the Communist International dispatched from Moscow, his armies trained by the German officers who had forged the kaiser's forces in the years leading up to World War I. This was a great moment in Chinese history, even if it has taken on the appearance of a brief interlude, lost in the tumultuous events that followed it, great because Chiang, in eliminating many of the warlords and establishing a modern government, embodied the national and nationalist aspirations of a majority of his countrymen. His army was by far the best in China, and it made the heretofore scary private armies of the warlords seem almost quaintly archaic by comparison. The world saw in Chiang a young, competent, visionary leader who would finally, after so many false starts for China, lead his country into the modern world.

But Chiang was never able to overcome the deep divisions in China or the byzantine, sometimes literally murderous politics of rival parties.

In 1927, he mounted a vicious coup against his allies in the reunification drive, the Communists, who he believed, probably correctly, were plotting, with Moscow's connivance, to eliminate him, once he had served his purpose. The Communists, or those not among the thousands arrested or assassinated, were driven out of the cities and set up rural bases under the newly emerging leader Mao Zedong. Meanwhile, Chiang set up the capital of the Republic of China at Nanjing, a former imperial-era capital on the Yangzi River that was in territory controlled by the new government—in contrast to Beijing, which, though China's capital for most of the previous six hundred years, was dominated by one of China's as yet unvanquished warlords. For the next decade, Chiang presided over a promising and resurgent country, one whose economy grew rapidly and that made great progress against its poverty, superstition, and backwardness. In the early 1930s, having expelled the Soviets but advised by his German officers, he undertook several campaigns to wipe out the Communists in their rural bases, and he would likely have succeeded if he hadn't had to address a Japanese threat at the same time.

Chiang did not oppose earlier Japanese aggression in China, especially the conquest of Manchuria in 1931. Chiang felt China was too weak to fight Japan, and he concentrated instead on nation building and eliminating the Communists. It wasn't a stupid decision. Chiang understood that as long as China was divided into warring factions, it was unlikely to be strong. But as Japan continued to press for more Chinese territory, an aroused Chinese public put pressure on him to forgo the effort to eliminate his domestic rivals and to enter into a united front with them to fight Japan, which he did at the end of 1936, though unwillingly and as the result of a comic-opera deception aimed at forcing his hand.

In December that year, Chiang flew to Xian, the ancient imperial capital in China's northwest, where he was to meet with a man known as the Young Marshal. This was Zhang Xueliang, who had seen his share of bloody intrigue in his short lifetime. Zhang's father, Zhang Zuolin, was one of the more picaresque characters of the time when power in China was dispersed among a group of warlords, each with his own army, territory, and ambition to become the ruler of all of China. Known as the Old Marshal, Zhang Sr. was a thoroughly reactionary, antirepublican former bandit who, in good Chinese warlord fashion, liked to appear in a Prussian-style uniform with braids and sashes, oversize epaulets, medals, and a tassel swaying over a brimmed cap. He commanded an army of several hundred thousand men, had five wives, and for a brief time controlled Beijing. But in 1928, as the armies of Chiang Kai-shek advanced northwards in their reunification drive, Zhang was forced to retreat to Manchuria, where Japan enjoyed semi-colonial privileges, including the right to deploy a sizable military force known as the Kwantung Army—Kwantung being a name given to the part of Manchuria east of the pass dividing it from the rest of China. On his way back, Zhang was killed when a Kwantung Army soldier put a bomb under his train. The reason normally assumed for this assassination was Japanese anger at Zhang's failure to stop Chiang Kai-shek's forces from advancing north, but it seems equally likely that Zhang was deemed too independent at a time when Japan planned to turn Manchuria into a puppet state.

Zhang Jr. was a decadent, opium-using womanizer whom the Japanese installed as the new warlord of Manchuria, apparently thinking he would be more pliant than his father. They were wrong. Zhang gave up opium and got serious as a Chinese political figure, supporting the Nationalists. In 1929, he invited two pro-Japanese Chinese officials to a banquet and had them executed in front of the other guests. Chiang named him commander of the renewed effort to cut the Communist cancer out of the Chinese body politic. But as 1936 wore on and the prospect of further Japanese incursions against Chinese sovereignty seemed imminent, Zhang balked at the idea of Chinese fighting other Chinese, and he opened up contacts with the Communists to plot what he would later call a coup d'état.

At the end of November, Zhang told Chiang that his troops in Shaanxi province were close to mutiny at the prospect of fighting fellow Chinese, and he proposed to Chiang that he come up from Nanjing to Xian, a couple of hours by airplane, to talk to them. Chiang agreed to go. Zhang informed Mao of the unfolding plan. Mao called it "a masterpiece."

Chiang arrived with his usual retainers, including his foreign minister and military advisers, staying at a hot springs resort ten miles from Xian. He spent his time talking to the officers of the army organized to march on the Communists in Yenan, telling them that only "the last five minutes" remained to go before victory in that long campaign would be theirs. Then, in the wee hours of December 12, Zhang's bodyguards, wearing the fur caps of Manchurian soldiers, burst into the cabin where Chiang was sleeping. They intended to kidnap him, but Chiang, wearing his nightclothes, escaped out of a window and climbed over the back wall of the compound, injuring his back when he fell. The Generalissimo spent a frigid night with a few loyal aides in a cave at the top of a nearby mountain, and in the morning he was taken into custody by Zhang's troops.

Within hours, Mao, in his more comfortable cave at Chinese Communist Party (CCP) headquarters in Yenan, was informed of the kidnapping. Overjoyed at the news, Mao wanted Chiang and his top generals put on trial and executed. He sent a cable to Moscow asking for advice on the matter from the leader of the global proletarian revolution, Joseph Stalin, expecting no doubt that Stalin would rejoice in Chiang's elimination. Stalin was also the main source of arms and funds for the Chinese Communists, who were only beginning to rebuild their strength after the last attempts by the central government to wipe them out.

Stalin was appalled at the Chiang kidnapping and even more so at the prospect of assassinating him. Here is evidence of a certain pattern in the relations between the cautious Stalin and the more impetuous Mao. The Soviet leader's overriding concern at the end of 1936 was the simultaneous threats of Nazi Germany and imperial Japan. In November, Japan joined with Italy and Germany to form the Anti-Comintern Pact, directed explicitly against the Soviet Union, and this raised the prospect that the Soviets would be attacked by Germany in the west and Japan in the east. For this reason, Stalin had for months encouraged the Communists to make an accommodation with Chiang so that they could be united in the anti-Japanese fight. Stalin therefore saw this threat on Chiang's very life as reckless and dangerous. If Chiang were eliminated, he felt, the road would be open for the pro-Japanese faction inside the KMT to take power, facilitating Japan's ability to roll into Soviet Siberia. Stalin issued strict orders to Mao that Chiang was not to be harmed; having received these instructions, Zhou Enlai, the Communists' suave and skillful chief negotiator, flew to Xian and passed the message on to the Young Marshal, who found himself suddenly abandoned by his Communist ally.

A negotiation spearheaded by Zhou then ensued in which Chiang promised to call off the campaign against the Communists and to join with them in a new united front against Japan, with Chiang recognized as the undisputed national leader. When, on the day after Christmas, Zhou went to see the Gimo, the first thing he did was salute him—"the Red Army's first sign of obedience to the united front commander," Chiang's biographer Jay Taylor has written. In exchange, the Communists got a kind of de facto legalization, or at least Chiang would give up his efforts to destroy them. They would keep their own army; indeed, they'd now have a chance to substantially expand it; and they'd be able to send their representatives to the national capital at Nanjing so resistance to Japan could be coordinated.

News of Chiang's capture and the formation of the United Front quickly spread through all of China, with the result that when he left Xian and returned to his capital in Nanjing, Chiang was no longer just a popular leader; he was, as Taylor has put it, "a national hero," propelled to new heights of popularity and power. China was still poor, weak, and fragmented, but it was stronger, more orderly, more united, and more economically vigorous than it had been at any time since the overthrow of the Qing dynasty a quarter century before, and Chiang was given a lot of the credit for this. The new determination to forge unity in the fight against Japan made him globally and locally recognized as China's man of destiny, the sole figure who could lead his country in its hour of peril. And the luster endured for nearly the entire duration of the Sino-Japanese War, the four years when China resisted alone and the four years after Pearl Harbor when its chief and only real ally was the United States.

For all that time, Chiang enjoyed the almost universal conviction that he was valiantly resisting the naked aggression of a nefarious invader. This image was supported in the United States most of all by Henry Luce, the China-born son of missionaries and the founder of *Time* and *Life*, which were the most influential magazines in America. Over the years, Chiang was on the cover of *Time* ten times, more than Roosevelt, Stalin, Churchill, or anyone else.

Luce was far from the only passionate observer of the scene in China who saw greatness in Chiang's character and leadership. Hans von Seeckt, who had effectively commanded the German army during the Weimar Republic and was Chiang's chief adviser during the Northern Expedition, called him "a splendid and noble personality." Owen Lattimore, the scholar of China who would later be accused, falsely, of

Chinese president Chiang Kai-shek in one of his many appearances on the cover of *Time,* this one in August 1945.

being a Communist agent, called him a "genuine patriot," a "highly nationalistic" figure who was "certainly responsible for holding China together at the critical moment." Claire Chennault, the commander of the Flying Tigers, told Roosevelt in 1943, in Stilwell's presence, that Chiang was "one of the two or three greatest military and political leaders in the world today."

Han Suyin, the novelist who would later become an unabashed acolyte of Mao, was just as unabashed in her admiration for Chiang in the early years of the war. The reunification of China was "due to the genius of one man, a slim, unassuming young Chinese officer" who had realized the goals of the Chinese revolution after "sixteen years of the struggle in the dark," she wrote. Chiang, she continued, in her many-splendored prose, possessed "a will as stern as the Great Wall, as irresistible as the flood of China's rivers." He was "the man in whose hands the fate of our four hundred millions still is laid." In the face of the Japanese onslaught, she continued,

> he is there, Chiang Kai-shek, directing the war with steady, unshaken resolve never to yield, in weakness and cowardice, to armed force. We are strengthened, reassured . . . . Here is the determination that has stirred the whole country, willed China to rise from her torpor, given her consciousness of her past glory and future dignity and greatness. One man, yet not one man alone. A spiritual force, a symbol, an inspiration to us all.

The savior-of-China, man-of-destiny image was reflected in the photographs of Chiang that appeared everywhere — schoolrooms, government offices, public squares, even, for a brief few years after the end of the war, over the massive entry gate to the Forbidden City in Beijing, long since replaced by a photograph of his great enemy, Mao. One of the standard pictures shows him in the military uniform favored by Chinese commanders in those days, with oversized epaulets, golden braids, sash and belt, and a constellation of saucer-sized medallions. His left hand is on the hilt of a sword, his shaved head and trim mustache somehow just a bit too small for all that paraphernalia. One of the covers of *Time*, this one published in 1933, has him on a white horse, in sunglasses, saluting. Other photographs show him in an elegant silk scholar's robe, and in still others he smiles in avuncular, mustachioed fashion, the understanding, kindly, indulgent teacher of the Chinese nation.

The images were all designed to convey a sense of the dignity, wisdom, and command due the leader of China, a spiritual force, as Han Suyin put it, and, if the image is to be believed, a tranquil, confident one. Henry Luce continued to convey this image to the American public until long after Chiang's cause was lost. Other Americans with a more balanced, less rhapsodic vision of Chiang admired him despite his faults, and when a heavy cloud of disillusionment with Chiang took hold of many, perhaps most, in official American circles, these diehard supporters argued that his faults were being exaggerated and his virtues underplayed.

For Albert C. Wedemeyer, who arrived in China late in 1944 as the commanding American military officer in the China theater, the astonishing thing was not how badly Chiang had done in the war but how well. Compared to Britain and the Soviet Union, he wrote, China had gotten only "a trickle of aid," yet "she had managed to survive as a national entity in spite of Western indifference and neglect." Wedemeyer made no secret of his disagreement with his predecessor, Stilwell, about Chiang. "Far from being reluctant to fight as pictured by Stilwell and some of his friends among the American correspondents," Wedemeyer later wrote, China "had shown amazing tenacity and endurance in resisting Japan."

Americans, in Wedemeyer's view, failed to understand the sacrifices that China had made and the degree to which it had fought. The battle for Shanghai in 1937, he noted, was "the bloodiest battle that the world had seen since Verdun." This was true. The battle for Shanghai belied the view that came to prevail later that China essentially had failed from the beginning of the anti-Japanese war to the end to resist the Japanese invasion. As a matter of historical fact, China's resistance had been so fierce as to take the Japanese completely by surprise. At the outset of the war, the Tokyo militarists who pressed for the conquest of China had predicted that the fighting would be over in a few months. They did not predict that nearly eight years later, nearly one million Japanese troops would remain tied down in China. The British colonies of Hong Kong, Malaya, Singapore, and Burma fell to Japan almost without a fight. So did the sprawling Dutch-run archipelago of Indonesia, and ditto the Philippines, which was then an American colony. But China was still resisting, unconquered.

And there was a comparison with Europe as well, in which Chiang emerged in a favorable light. Wedemeyer noted that China could have "followed France's example and let herself be occupied, waiting to be rescued eventually by the United States." But after the Japanese invasion of 1937, Chiang called on the Chinese people to go to the "limits of endurance" and to "sacrifice and fight to the bitter end," a statement that was, Wedemeyer felt, more gallant and resolute than Churchill's famous "blood, sweat and tears" speech after Dunkirk. And China did resist, in complete international isolation, for the four long years before Pearl Harbor, during which the United States, supposedly neutral, continued to supply Japan with such vital materials as oil and iron.

Chiang's American allies supported him in the very areas where he was most criticized by his American detractors, in his military strategy and in his undemocratic rule, which made FDR think about getting rid of him and Stilwell apoplectic. Chiang's military philosophy seemed reasonable to some highly qualified observers who believed that Chiang simply could not do what the Americans like Stilwell were asking of him and also survive in power. "China could hope for victory only by hanging on against superior forces in the expectation that Japan would sooner or later become embroiled in war with the Western powers," Wedemeyer concluded. "The Generalissimo adopted the sound strategy of endeavoring to dissipate Japanese strength and forcing the enemy to overextend his lines." FDR's cousin, Joseph Alsop, who was an aide to Chennault, believed that American policymakers did not understand Chiang's dire situation, in which a domestic force that wanted to overthrow him was growing stronger by the day even as his sole foreign ally demanded that he do nothing about it.

In many ways, Chiang's kidnapping and the united front agreement that resulted from it were a genuine historical watershed for him and for China. Seen at the time as a sort of apotheosis, it was actually the beginning of his decline, the point after which he could no longer be the ultimate victor in China's domestic strife, leading his country down a path of political reform and change strongly influenced by western liberal-democratic ideas. Had it not been for the Xian kidnapping, Chiang would almost surely have completed the "last five minutes" of the campaign to defeat the Communists. His army was not of international caliber, but it was larger, better equipped, and more effective under its German advisers than it had been earlier, while the CCP's Red Army was still a ragged and poorly armed force of perhaps thirty thousand men. Had Chiang undertaken a new campaign against the Communists in late 1936 and 1937, before the Japanese embarked on their full-scale effort to conquer China, Mao and his followers would have taken refuge in Mongolia or the Soviet Union. There, Stalin would have kept them alive, but, needing to confront the great danger to Soviet survival that a Japanese victory in China represented, he would have had little choice but to support China's central government, and he would not have backed the CCP in any effort to overthrow it. Dislodged from their base in northern Shaanxi and chased across the border, the Communists would not have been able to expand their army and territory in the way they did during World War II, growing in those years into a force of more than a million soldiers governing some nineteen "liberated" areas.

But that is not how events unfolded. Under extreme duress, Chiang broke a fundamental rule of civil conflict, which is never to allow an armed force that you do not control into your camp, because surely, when the conditions are ripe, that force will oppose you. The story is told that when he got back to Nanjing from Xian, Chiang was advised by an old friend and senior KMT official, Chen Lifu, to organize a large force and wipe out the Communists in their Shaanxi refuge, but Chiang, as Taylor has written, "bent his head and did not answer."

And with that decision to keep to his word, Chiang helped to establish the conditions that, in the long run, would destroy him.

For the entire war, Chiang remained a hero to many people, both Chinese and foreigners, but for many others a slow disillusionment set in, and in the later stages of the war, no place would his image and reputation be more tarnished than in the United States, Chiang's indispens-able ally. By the beginning of 1945, Chiang's reputation as China's man of the hour, *Time*'s gallant knight on the white horse, became mixed with something close to its opposite, a reputation as a petty-minded, obstructionist, and deceitful dictator. This was Stilwell's frequently expressed description of Chiang, and it slowly came to be accepted as accurate by many American experts on China and by many in the press, even if the public at large was unacquainted with it. On that same day in the Oval Office when Chennault affirmed Chiang's greatness, Stilwell described him to FDR as "a vacillating, tricky, undependable scoun-drel." For many Americans, including some of those who observed him most closely, Chiang turned into a right-wing dictator more like Benito Mussolini or Francisco Franco in those days of ascendant fascist leaders than George Washington, though China in general, many Americans came to feel, had its particular cultural blind spots. "They are great believers in make-believe," Brigadier General John Magruder, a senior adviser to the Chinese army, told the War Department. They ignore reality in favor of "flattering but fictitious symbols," among them the defeats they suffered at the hands of the Japanese that they turned into victories.

Some of this was caused by what the French call *usure*, a slow dull-ing of the sheen due simply to the passage of time, the very length of the war, the sweep of Japan's armies, the casualties, the rivers of refugees, the famine, the malnutrition, the fearsome reach of the secret police, the lines of conscripts roped together and marched off to war without proper clothing, arms, training, and food, the inability of the govern-ment to put a stop to Japanese atrocities—all of these things wore down the once-great leader's standing. The KMT government tried to fight on the morale front. There were marches, songs, slogans everywhere. The government press office put out an endless series of good-news reports about valiant resistance and tremendous Japanese casualties, most of it fictitious, but at a certain point reality becomes inescapable, and when it does, it is the leader who is held responsible. Chiang made mistakes as well. He was repressive of dissent; prominent figures were jailed or put under house arrest. The press was rigorously censored. Chiang's image came to seem more and more bogus, a matter of artifi-cial inflation. Over time more and more of China's intelligentsia, much of it American-educated, the country's professors, students, and writers, shifted their allegiance, sometimes active, often passive, to the Communists, whom they saw as more dynamic, less corrupt, less responsible for the country's suffering, and, in the minds of many of them, more democratic.

This disillusionment was also strong among the Americans in China. "Where is the gallant resistance?" Stilwell asked. "Where is the great guerrilla warfare? Where is reform or even elementary understanding of the problem?" He likened Chiang's government to that of Nazi Germany—"same outlook, same gangsterism." Stilwell once summarized to George C. Marshall, FDR's chief of staff, a conversation he had with Chiang as "one and a half hours of crap and nonsense." In his diary and in his letters to his wife back home, the American commander was even more vitriolic. Chiang, he wrote, was a "stubborn, ignorant, prejudiced, conceited despot." He was a "grasping, bigoted, ungrateful little rattlesnake." He presided over "a one-party government, supported by a Gestapo and headed by an unbalanced man with little education."

All through 1944 and into 1945, the dispatches from the American embassy in Chungking were loaded with outraged complaints against Chiang for holding his forces in reserve while the United States did the fighting and made the sacrifice for him. The American ambassador, Clarence E. Gauss, dismissed the heroic portrayals of Chiang as "rot," noting as early as 1943 that there were no KMT troops north of the old course of the Yellow River and, unlike the Communists, the Nationalists had failed utterly to establish a guerrilla presence there.

"The Chinese strategy is entirely defensive in character," Gauss wrote. "The Chinese soldier suffers such serious deficiencies that from an offensive standpoint he has no value . . . and the Chungking forces are unwilling to use their scanty military resources against the Japanese when they feel the Communist problem still exists, many military and civil officials stating that the Japanese are the secondary enemy and the Communists the primary one."

Upon leaving China in the fall of 1944, the entirely fed-up Gauss told the newly arrived Wedemeyer, "We should pull up the plug and let the whole Chinese government go down the drain."

This disenchantment with Chiang was rooted in the fact that for the Americans and for China's leader, World War II in Asia and the Pacific were very different struggles. For the United States the battle was to defeat Japan, and this came with the sense that some of the American sacrifice in the war was being made for the sake of China, and, in particular, for the sake of China's imperfect and, as Stilwell put it, "ungrateful" regime. In the fall of 1944, having gotten more than an earful from Stilwell, Marshall greeted Chiang's agreement to commit Chinese forces to the campaign in north Burma as "the first time since the war began that the Generalissimo had shown an active interest in the improvement and employment of his Army"—this comment made about a leader whose army had up to that point taken over a million casualties and had for seven years tied down a million of Japan's best troops, most of whom would have been deployed directly against the Americans if China had surrendered.

In his memoir of his wartime service in China, Oliver J. Caldwell, who worked for the Office of Strategic Services (OSS), recounts being approached by a certain Mr. Chen, who claimed to be an emissary of a coalition of secret societies that opposed Chiang, believing that his dictatorial and divisive rule would lead eventually to a Communist victory in China—a view that, as it happens, was shared by some of the best American analysts of China and turned out to be correct. Mr. Chen told Caldwell that his group wanted to replace Chiang with General Li Zongren, China's vice president and a semi-independent military leader with a base of support and loyal troops in Guangxi province.

Nothing ever happened with this plan, and Caldwell didn't raise it again. But from time to time, some anti-Chiang, non-Communist groups would make contact with Americans seeking support for Chiang's ouster. Chiang, of course, knew of these approaches. He knew that he was unpopular among China's intellectuals, especially among those who had been to school in the United States and yearned for greater freedom in China. He also knew that his armed domestic opposition was growing vastly more powerful. By early 1945 the bedraggled remnants of the Communist armies who had survived Chiang's earlier campaigns against them had grown into a large and, by Chinese standards, potent armed force. Mao had built his refuge in the northwest into a de facto independent state with some 90 million people within its informal borders. Chiang's greatest fear was that as soon as the war was over, the Chinese Communists would combine with the Soviet Communists in a concerted effort to overthrow him. This is why he kept four hundred thousand of his best troops on a long front in the north blockading the Communists, to the puzzlement and fury of FDR and many other American observers. But the simple reason for Chiang's behavior was that he didn't have the resources to fight effectively against the Japanese and to contain the Communists at the same time. Those divisions that he kept out of the battle with Japan not only blocked potential Communist expansion to the south and east but also sealed off the main routes north into the Soviet Union via Mongolia, thereby helping to forestall the cooperation that Chiang felt, with good reason, could spell his ultimate doom.

This was the biggest divide between Chiang and his putative American friends. By the middle of 1944, especially with American victories against Japan in the Pacific, both sides in China, the KMT and the CCP, were no longer primarily interested in defeating their common foreign enemy. This, they both knew, would be accomplished by the United States. Both sides were now preparing for the postwar showdown whose ultimate prize would be China itself, and Chiang, who was weak, knew it.

So, for the rest of the war, Chiang walked the narrow path between two incompatible requirements. He was materially weak and his country was effectively sealed off from the rest of the world by the Japanese—but for the cargo-plane lifeline from India. So Chiang needed to do enough to keep the Americans happy and the all-important Lend-Lease supplies coming into the airfields at Kunming. But he could not do so much of what the United States wanted that he would wreck his chances in the postwar struggle to come. Stilwell found Chiang arrogant and ungrateful, but Chiang saw himself as humiliated by American demands that threatened his ruin. He had to maintain a posture of deference. He ingratiated himself, as when he swallowed his pride and named the reopened road from Burma the Stilwell Road, honoring the man whom he probably most disliked among those Americans whose demands, he feared, might in the end destroy him.

The animosity between Chiang and Stilwell went back to Burma in 1942, when Japan chased the British colonial rulers across the border to India, defeated Chinese and American forces, and closed the last overland supply route to China. Stilwell by then had been appointed Chiang's chief of staff, and as such he supposedly had effective command over Chinese troops in Burma, but it was in this campaign that, for the first time, Stilwell experienced Chiang's inclination secretly to direct his commanders to ignore Stilwell's orders, especially the order for them to take the offensive, and Chiang's reluctance to commit troops to Burma ever after remained a sore point.

"The Peanut says he won't fight," Stilwell told Marshall in 1943. He was speaking specifically of Chiang's refusal to commit troops to the campaign that Stilwell wanted to wage to retake Burma after its loss in 1942, but that short, brutal sentence also reflected Stilwell's more general contempt for Chiang. As early as 1937, while on a long inspection tour of China, Stilwell had lamented Chiang's lack of preparation for the fight against Japan that everybody knew was looming, even as Chiang was assuring the Americans that he would vigorously resist the invaders. "He can have no intention of doing a thing," Stilwell wrote in an army intelligence report, "or else he is utterly ignorant of what it means to get ready for a fight with a first class power."

There is more ammunition on both sides of this argument than Stilwell, Gauss, and others angry at the rosy portrayal of Chiang that had appeared elsewhere were likely to admit. From the beginning, it is true, Stilwell always had to beg Chiang to commit his troops and was infuriated when Chiang hesitated, procrastinated, promised to deliver, and then didn't. "He can't make up his mind," Stilwell groaned during that first campaign in Burma, the one that ended with a rout of Chinese and British troops. Stilwell recognized that Chiang had sent some of his best and best-equipped troops, his Fifth and Sixth armies, but it had taken them a long time to move, and Stilwell believed that the delay had "fatally compromised any chance we might have had here in Burma."

But Chiang's analysis of Burma wasn't at all ridiculous. Having fought the Japanese since 1937, he thought he knew something about it. "Resisting the Japanese is not like suppressing colonial rebellions, not like colonial wars," he told Sir Archibald Wavell, the commander of British troops in Burma. "We Chinese are the ones who know how to do it. For this kind of job, you British are incompetent." And while this might seem pretentious in light of Chinese losses in the war and the historical fighting reputation of Britain, in this instance his view is confirmed by the official British history of the Burma campaign, which indicts British commanders in general for "complacency and haughty disregard for their enemy." Both the British and the Americans underestimated the Japanese in this early stage of the conflict, thinking that they were no more threatening than one of those colonial rebellions that Chiang had spoken of and that the British, especially in places like India and Afghanistan, were expert at suppressing. Wavell's "failure to recognize the degree of superiority of the Japanese forces led him into unjustified optimism," a British military historian concluded.

In Chiang's view, Stilwell and other American officers were also guilty of underestimating the Japanese. After observing the battle of Shanghai in 1937, the attaché there, Captain Evans F. Carlson, declared that the Japanese army was "third rate," and later, in 1938, he noted its "inferiority of striking power, poor coordination of transport, poor coordination of airforce and ground troops, inferiority of weapons, poor direction of artillery fire, and lack of imagination and initiative on the part of leaders." By contrast with the supposedly rigid and uncreative Japanese, Stilwell, though lacking in combat experience, was famous in the army for his exploits in field exercises, in which he stressed speed, surprise, and spirit. Just before being sent to China, he had been rated number one of the forty-seven major generals in the United States Army. Burma was his first real experience in combat command, and his plan was characteristically audacious. The Japanese had landed three divisions in Burma in December 1941, and, contrary to what many opposing commanders thought of them, they were proficient in both jungle and off-the-road warfare. They moved quickly, outmaneuvered the road-bound British, and had excellent air-ground coordination. They also benefited from local anticolonialist sentiment, posing—convincingly to some Burmese nationalists—as the local liberators from European exploitation; they quickly won a series of engagements against the British, who, as the local colonial power, were primarily responsible for Burma's defense. Stilwell's readiness to blame Chiang for the 1942 loss of Burma seems, in light of all this, unreasonable.

By the end of February 1942, the main British force, the 17th Indian Division, was backed up against the Sittang River, the final natural obstacle before the Burmese capital of Rangoon. There was only one bridge across the river, a five-hundred-meter-long span that had been planked over to handle vehicular traffic, and rearguard detachments of the 17th, dug in on the east bank of the river, fought to defend it so the main body of troops could get across. But in an extraordinary communications snafu, the bridge was blown up while two brigades were stranded on the wrong side of it. In the melee that ensued, more than half the division was lost and most of its heavy guns destroyed, even as the way to Rangoon was left open and the British were never again able to form a strong defensive line.

Stilwell, in command of Chinese troops at least nominally, believed that the Japanese could be stopped with a swift counterattack, which he planned at Toungoo, a walled town on the main rail line between Rangoon to the south and Mandalay in the north. He sent there the 200th Division, a component of the Chinese Fifth Army, which engaged the Japanese in fierce house-to-house fighting inside the town itself. When Stilwell wanted to send the 22nd Division to Toungoo to help, its commander obstinately refused to go, and the 200th had to cut its way out. The 22nd never got into the fight.

Infuriated with this disobedience, Stilwell flew to Chungking, where, as he put it in his diary, he "threw the raw meat on the floor" and asked to be relieved. "I have to tell CKS with a straight face that his subordinates are not carrying out his orders, when in all probability they are doing just what he tells them," Stilwell complained to his diary. But Chiang had moved his troops to Burma and told Stilwell that he was putting them under the American general's command even though he found Stilwell's plan, which was to retake Rangoon, a risky one, given Japan's control of the entire Bay of Bengal, its superiority in the air, its strength in tanks and artillery, and the demonstrated undependability of the British. Chiang favored a more cautious plan. "Going on the offensive should not be a guiding principle so far as Burma is concerned," he said, thereby articulating his major philosophical difference with Stilwell, for whom going on the offensive was the only way to save Burma. Instead, Chiang favored what he called "defense in depth," placing troops at intervals along the route of the enemy's advance and to making it pay a price, or, as this was also put, to trade territory for time, which is what Chiang had done after the initial devastating months of the Sino-Japanese War.

In 1942 in Burma, Chiang favored falling back on Mandalay, north of Rangoon, and holding an east–west line across the country that would enable a supply route to be built from British-held Assam, India, into China. This was the plan the British favored at the beginning of the second Burma campaign in 1944. But even in 1942, despite his doubts, Chiang yielded to Stilwell, who was aware of the magnitude of that gesture. "It is expecting a great deal to have [the Chinese] turn over a couple of armies in a vital area to a goddamn foreigner that they don't know and in whom they can't have much confidence," he said.

But whether because of Chiang's caution or Stilwell's overoptimism, the 1942 defense of Burma was a disaster. Stilwell decided to try to lure the Japanese into a trap at a place called Pyinmana with both British and Chinese troops, and the Chinese Fifth Army duly got into position there. But the British, fearing encirclement, pulled back, and the Chinese 200th Division resisted Stilwell's orders to rush into the breach. Meanwhile, the Japanese attacked in force from the east, destroying a whole division of the Chinese Sixth Army. On April 29, the Japanese seized Lashio, the terminus of the rail line from Rangoon and the beginning of the truck route to China, which had been built by the two hundred thousand Chinese laborers sent into Burma by Chiang four years earlier.

Chiang now wanted the Chinese forces to concentrate on Mytkyina further to the north. Stilwell agreed, and was determined to join them, but he never made it, choosing to go overland instead of on an airplane sent by Chennault to take him there. With that decision, Stilwell was separated from the troops he was supposedly commanding, and he was forced to lead his staff, a group of Burmese nuns, and a few civilians out of Burma to Assam on foot.

Stilwell's walkout quickly became the stuff of legend, the doughty commander pushing his party of about one hundred soldiers and civilians to safety, some of the injured carried on pack mules and stretchers, getting through without a single loss and then promising, MacArthur-like, to return to Burma another day. Two books were quickly written by Americans who accompanied him, the journalist Jack Belden and Stilwell's loyal chief of staff, General Dorn; these books helped to establish the Stilwell legend and, indirectly, to lend credence to the idea that it had been Chiang's behind-the-scenes interference that had led to the Burmese defeat. At one point in the saga, before Stilwell's separation from his Chinese troops, a Chinese general secretly commandeered a train in order to escape and then caused a two-day tie-up on the rail line when his train collided with another, leading Stilwell to lament that the general hadn't been killed in the crash.

As Stilwell saw it, the Chinese units were never where he ordered them to be, and "Peanut" remained for Stilwell's entire time in the China-Burma-India theater an object of special contempt. Try as he might, Stilwell seemed unable to convince Chiang that what China's armies needed was training, reorganization, and the elimination of all those bungling and corrupt officers whose commission had been granted because of political patronage rather than demonstrated competence.

In mid-April 1942, after the failures at Toungoo and Pyinmana and with the outcome of the Burma campaign still in the balance, Stilwell came across a letter from Chiang, sent from Chungking two thousand miles away from the fighting, ordering that a watermelon be distributed to every fourth Chinese soldier. "When Burma was crashing about his ears—due in large part, as he believed, to the Gimo's other interferences—the watermelon order clinched his contempt for Chiang Kai-shek," Barbara Tuchman wrote in her biography of Stilwell, "and since this ultimately became known, it in turn angered the Generalissimo."

But from Chiang's point of view, Stilwell's plan, pursued in willful disregard of the overwhelming strength of the Japanese, had been foolhardy to begin with and vainglorious in the end. When Stilwell took off for India on foot in April 1942, sending orders to the Chinese to make their way out of Burma as best they could, Chiang was "stunned," feeling that Stilwell "has abandoned my 100,000 soldiers in foreign jungles and headed off to India. Only then does he send me this telegram." While for years Stilwell complained that it was difficult for him to see Chiang, surrounded as the Chinese leader was by an imperial wall of seclusion, Chiang was angry that for days and even weeks at a time he would receive no communication from his supposed chief of staff—until, in the instance of the famous walk out of Burma, he informed Chiang that, having declined Chennault's offer of an airplane, he had become separated from his troops and was making his way out alone.

Largely ignored by Stilwell's supporters, like Belden and Dorn, but of intense concern to Chiang, was the terrible toll taken by Japan's armies on Chinese divisions in the 1942 Burmese debacle, the ones that had been so underestimated by the American command. The retreat from Burma involved many stories of survival and escape, but, aside from Stilwell's, they were untold, or at least Americans never heard them. In all, the Chinese lost twenty-five thousand of their best troops. Some divisions lost a third of their men along with their meager supplies of trucks and artillery. In the tangle of recriminations that followed, the question does arise whether the 1942 disaster could have been avoided had Chiang's recommendation of "defense in depth" been followed, rather than Stilwell's more ambitious but adventurist effort to drive the Japanese out of Burma altogether. Certainly, if that strategy had been followed, as Taylor has written, "the battle at Pyinmana would have been avoided and they would have had a fair chance of success." Moreover, even if the plan had failed, "the retreat would have been orderly and China itself . . . would have been much stronger over the nearly four years of war to come."

Even two years later, Stilwell's victorious return to Burma, though publicly celebrated by Chiang, did not erase his doubts about his chief of staff's judgment. Chiang was generally angry at the Allies for giving priority to the war in Europe over the war in Asia, and he was angry that Stilwell's obsession with retaking Burma gave priority to a secondary theater of the war at a time when the offensive the Japanese mounted in 1944 was seizing whole provinces of China proper—which, in turn, was provoking American criticism that he was refusing to resist. "We have taken Mytkyina but we have lost almost all of East China," Chiang dryly observed to Patrick J. Hurley, FDR's special representative, in October 1944, explaining why he had had no choice but to demand Stilwell's recall. The Burma campaigns consolidated Stilwell's reputation at home, but for Chiang they served to intensify his conviction that, as he once confided to his diary, Stilwell "lacked the virtue and vision of a commander."

It was into this parlous situation that late in 1944 Roosevelt sent Hurley to straighten things out. Hurley, a staunch Republican, was by nature an optimistic man, and he had a great deal of charm, often involving some recourse to his western cowboy heritage. When he first arrived in China, the sitting ambassador, Clarence E. Gauss, expressed the suspicion that Roosevelt wanted Hurley to take over the ambassadorial function. Hurley replied by telling the story of a barbershop out west. While a customer was sitting in the chair having his hair cut, bullets suddenly began whizzing over his head. Naturally alarmed, he made to get up, whereupon the barber said, "Lean back, brother—nobody's shooting at you."

Hurley had succeeded in everything else he had done in his life, as a self-made oil millionaire, as a lawyer to the Choctaw Nation, and as secretary of war under Herbert Hoover. As a soldier in World War I he had earned a medal at the Argonne. When World War II in the Pacific broke out, he ran supplies to the American troops bottled up on Bataan, at least once committing a technical act of piracy by flying the Japanese flag on one of his ships. He had that very American faith that all disagreements can be overcome with a little good sense and tough talk, but in this he was naïve, and he was pigheaded as well, entirely disinclined to take on board views and information different from his own.

Hurley met Chiang for the first time on September 8, the day after his arrival in Chungking, and the two men hit it off. At least Chiang found Hurley "different" from "American officials in the past," by which he must have meant less amenable figures like Stilwell and Gauss. In any event, Chiang agreed to the main American demand, which was that Stilwell be given command over all Chinese armies, including the Communists, in the unlikely event that they accepted Chiang as China's undisputed leader. But things started to sour quickly. Hurley's entry onto the scene came simultaneously with the big Japanese offensive of 1944 — it was called Ichigo, meaning "first" — and the Burma campaign. At a meeting on September 15 with Stilwell and Hurley present, Chiang worried about a Japanese counterattack that was taking place on the Salween front, and he asked that the X-Force at Mytkyina in Burma be moved east immediately to relieve the pressure. Stilwell, who was notorious among his soldiers in Burma for pushing them beyond ordinary human endurance, rejected the request on the grounds that his men needed to rest. In other words, an American subordinate was telling the president of China that he could not use Chinese troops in the defense of his own country.

After the meeting, Stilwell wrote to Marshall calling Chiang a "crazy little bastard" and reporting that he was sabotaging the entire Burma campaign. Stilwell sent a note to T. V. Soong complaining that he had "been delayed, ignored, double-crossed, and kicked around for years" in China and demanding that he be given "nothing less than full power" over all Chinese armies. It was this demand that led, a few weeks later, to Chiang's demand that Stilwell be withdrawn.

In the end, it was a now famous confrontation at Chiang's official residence at the hilltop outside Chungking known as Yellow Mountain that led to the irreparable break between the two men. Roosevelt, who was with Marshall at an Allied conference in Quebec, drafted a note to Chiang with orders that Stilwell deliver it personally. The note was insulting in the extreme. It demanded that Chiang reinforce the Y-Force army in Yunnan "immediately" and place Stilwell "in unrestricted command of all your forces," threatening that if he failed to comply, "you must yourself be prepared to accept the consequences and assume the personal responsibility."

Stilwell, after receiving the note, took a jeep to Yellow Mountain, where Chiang and several of his top officials and military commanders were meeting with Hurley discussing precisely the terms by which Stilwell would take command of the Chinese armies. Chiang, informed that Stilwell was present, suggested that he be invited in for tea, but Stilwell asked to see Hurley privately first. On the balcony of Chiang's residence, he showed Hurley the note from Roosevelt, and Hurley, seeing the offense it contained, asked Stilwell not to deliver it.

"Joe," Hurley said, "you have won this ball game, and if you want command of the forces in China all you've got to do is accept what the Generalissimo has already agreed to." Stilwell insisted on personally handing Chiang the president's note, which he had to know would be an enormous loss of face for the Gimo. Chiang read the Chinese translation in silence. After a few minutes, he inverted his teacup, signaling that the meeting was at an end, and said, "I now understand."

According to the American eyewitness to the event, Joseph Alsop, Chiang burst into "compulsive and stormy sobbing" as soon as Stilwell and Hurley left the room. Later, Chiang confided to his diary that he had suffered "the most severe humiliation I have ever had in my life." Stilwell, though, was triumphant. He had always urged FDR to be tougher with Chiang, in particular to use the threat of withholding aid to get concessions from the Chinese. "Rejoice with me," he wrote to his wife. "We have prevailed . . . his head is in the dust."

That same night, Chiang summoned Hurley back to the residence and told him that Stilwell would have to leave China. The two met again the next day, with Chiang telling Hurley that Roosevelt's message marked a low point in Chinese-American relations. He was especially wounded by the innuendo in Roosevelt's note, which had been encouraged by Stilwell and others, that he had not mounted a fight against Japan. He told Hurley that 30 percent of China's troops had been fighting since 1936, some of them since the Northern Expedition of the 1920s, and these soldiers would not accept the "patronizing attitude" of Stilwell.

Meanwhile, in the days after the meeting at Yellow Mountain, Stilwell was making plans to take over China's armies. He ordered that two hundred tons of supplies be sent to the new commander of the defense of Guilin, the immediate target of the Ichigo offensive, supplies that he had up to then withheld—that is, he had withheld matériel from Chiang's army even as he was complaining that it wasn't fighting. He also drafted a proposal by which the United States would arm five divisions of Communist troops. Finally, he promised Hurley that he would change his behavior toward the Generalissimo.

But it was too late. On September 24, five days after Stilwell handed him Roosevelt's message, Chiang reiterated to Hurley his demand that Stilwell had to go. Stilwell, he said, in a pretty fair assessment, "is a professional, works hard, is resolute, and good at his own military doctrine, which is to attack," but "he has no strategic thinking . . . [or] basic political skills . . . [and] he is very arrogant." The next day he gave Hurley a formal letter asking for Stilwell's recall, while to his diary he confided his pain at what he saw as a betrayal by the man he probably worshipped most in the world, Roosevelt. "My heart is broken," he wrote. "It is difficult to go on." But he also expressed determination. China, he said, could "once again hold out absolutely alone . . . if necessary . . . in four provinces."

Hurley later said that the night Chiang's demand for Stilwell's recall arrived, he was unable to sleep, and in the wee hours he summoned an aide and dictated a message to Roosevelt recommending that the president accept Chiang's demand. "Stilwell's every act is a move toward the complete subjugation of Chiang Kai-shek," he wrote. "You have a choice between Stilwell and Chiang and you have to choose Chiang," he told the president. "There is no other Chinese known to me who possesses as many of the elements of leadership as Chiang Kai-shek . . . . [He] has agreed to every request, every suggestion made by you except the Stilwell appointment."

The divisions sowed by Stilwell's removal were to be deep and long-lasting. Stilwell himself, whom public opinion was accustomed to seeing as honest, straight-talking, and no-nonsense, got in the first blow. After his dismissal but before he left Chungking, Stilwell invited the correspondent of *Time*, Theodore White, and the one from *The New York Times*, Brooks Atkinson, to his office, and, in a remarkable breach of military discipline, gave them not only his version of what had happened but also access to the secret cable traffic involving the Chiang affair. White's account was essentially spiked at *Time*, whose editor in chief, Luce, would not allow Chiang to be seen as corrupt and incompetent, which is how White presented him.

But Atkinson, under no such restriction, accompanied Stilwell on his plane back to Washington, D.C., and his account of the Chiang-Stilwell dispute represented a negative shift in the press coverage of Chiang and his regime. "STILWELL BREAK STEMS FROM Chiang REFUSAL TO PRESS WAR FULLY" ran the page-one headline in the *Times*, which perfectly encapsulated Stilwell's view of the problem. "PEACE WITH REDS BARRED: GENERALISSIMO REGARDS THEIR ARMIES FIGHTING JAPAN AS THREAT TO HIS RULE." Stilwell's dismissal by Chiang, Atkinson wrote, "represents the political triumph of a moribund anti-democratic regime that is more concerned with maintaining its political supremacy than in driving the Japanese out of China." "Relieving General Stilwell and appointing a successor has the effect of making us acquiesce in an unenlightened cold-hearted autocratic political regime."

Hurley said nothing publicly right away. But within a year or so, he was making comments that can only be described as deranged, accusing Stilwell, the State Department officers who agreed with the general about Chiang, and the American press as engaged in a conspiracy to destroy Chiang and see him replaced by a Communist government. He summed up his position this way: "The record of General Stilwell in China is irrevocably coupled in history with the conspiracy to overthrow the Nationalist Government of China, and to set up in its place a Communist regime—and all of this movement was part of, and cannot be separated from, the Communist cell or apparatus that existed at that time in the Government in Washington."

Wedemeyer, Stilwell's replacement, paid his first call on Chiang just five days after Stilwell's departure, on November 2. He had flown to Chungking two days before, then driven out of the afflicted, rubble-strewn city and across the Yangzi River to Yellow Mountain. Chiang, who often appeared in a simple Chinese robe with no insignia, was dressed in his Prussian-style green-brown uniform bearing the emblem of a five-star general. Wedemeyer found him to be a "small, graceful, fine-boned man with black, piercing eyes and an engaging smile."

Chiang was eager to make a good impression on the man who would now be his chief of staff and who would also have control over the all-important Lend-Lease supplies for China, the tons of aviation fuel, weapons, and ammunition that came from India every month. He received Wedemeyer in a spacious reception room adorned with beautiful Chinese paintings and etchings on the walls, rugs on the polished floor, teakwood tables, chairs with marble inlay, and vases with flowers. Servants in long blue robes glided in and out with tea and refreshments. There were so many curtains and screens drawn around the room that

Wedemeyer, no innocent abroad, wondered "how many people might be listening in and noting what we said."

"Please, please," said Chiang, the only English words he spoke, gesturing Wedemeyer to a divan and then sitting next to him on it. It was a gesture of equality. He would not have sat on the same couch with Stilwell. "He seemed shy but keenly alert," Wedemeyer noted, and he constantly and nervously fluttered a fan. Hurley, who had been appointed the American ambassador a few weeks earlier, was present, as was T. V. Soong.

The meeting was an opportunity to exchange pleasantries and to repair the wounds of the Stilwell debacle, but not to get into detailed discussions. Wedemeyer told the Generalissimo he was sure "we would have no difficulties in bringing about an efficient, carefully coordinated employment of American and Chinese forces against the Japanese."

Respectful as he was of Chiang's feelings, Wedemeyer had no illusions about the condition of China's armies. The Japanese were on the offensive, threatening the important cities of Guilin and Liuzhou, both sites of American air bases, yet Wedemeyer found the Chinese to be strangely "apathetic and unintelligent." A bit later, on December 4, in a cable to Marshall, he had changed his mind, but only somewhat. "I have now concluded," he wrote, "that the Generalissimo and his adherents realize seriousness of situation but they are impotent and confounded. They are not organized, equipped, and trained for modern war." Among the problems was "disorganized and muddled planning" that was "beyond comprehension." The Chinese soldier was not only not properly equipped, he was also not properly fed, and Wedemeyer soon realized that this inadequacy, which resulted in malnutrition and disease, "underlay most of China's military problems."

This assessment seemed to correspond with Stilwell's harshest judgments, but in fact Wedemeyer was not only more tactful than his predecessor, an attribute that enabled him to establish a cordial relationship with Chiang, but also more sympathetic, more inclined to give him the benefit of the doubt. While American public opinion was souring on Chiang—or, at least, was now privy to the disillusionment illustrated by the New York Times coverage—and while American diplomats and military officers in China were forming an anti-Chiang consensus, Wedemeyer became convinced of Hurley's assessment that the Gimo was a great man and the only one who could lead China. Others felt that way as well, so that the United States government ended up in a kind of warts-and-all resignation about Chiang, an unenthusiastic acceptance of the fact that, as FDR once said about the Nicaraguan dictator Anastazio Somoza, he may be a bastard but he's our bastard.

At the end of 1944, a young congressman from Montana, Mike Mansfield, who had been a marine stationed in China and had taught Far Eastern history at Montana State University, was dispatched by FDR on a three-month fact-finding mission in China. "Conditions," he wrote to Roosevelt in January 1945, "are really bad." The main problem, Mansfield felt, was the rift between the Nationalists and the Communists, which sapped China's strength in the face of the common Japanese foe. In addition, he wrote, the Nationalists were corrupt and incompetent, their army ill supplied, badly fed, and poorly led. And yet, he concluded, "Chiang is the one man who can make Chinese unity and independence a reality. He and he alone can untangle the present situation because, in spite of some of the things he has done, he is China."

A sort of squaring of circles begins to emerge in views like those of Mansfield and others, in which Chiang was deemed to be a deeply flawed leader, strangely disconnected from the suffering of his people and the abuses inflicted on them by his own government. Yet at the same time these hardheaded, unsparing analyses are accompanied by the judgment that his destiny and China's destiny are one and the same. For the first of several times in its subsequent experience shoring up right-wing dictators against Communist revolutionaries, the United States depended on an Asian leader whose performance was unsatisfactory but who was nonetheless the American choice for the future.

CHAPTER THREE

The Devastated Country

The Sino-Japanese War was devastating and unnecessary. For eight years it raged across China creating an immeasurable degree of death, destruction, and loss—loss in the conventional senses of death and material damage but also the loss of commonality, of humanistic relations among the Chinese themselves, as the struggle to survive overwhelmed the country's capacities for compassion, mutual aid, and fellow feeling.

The main and climactic battles of this war took place between 1937 and 1945, but it could be said to have started in 1895 when Japan, resurgent, implacable, and unrestrained in its pursuit of international prestige—which meant emulating the major European powers in their scramble for colonial possessions—made a colony of the entire island of Taiwan, which had belonged to China for centuries. But Japan's major goal was the possession of Korea and Manchuria, the vast landmasses just across the Sea of Japan that were stepping-stones toward the even larger prize, which was China. China, normally the dominant country in northeast Asia, was weak, in political disarray, and incapable of defending its historic interests in Korea or in its farther-flung provinces, like Manchuria, which became contested territory between Japan and the other powerful nation in the area, imperial Russia.

In 1905, Japan announced itself as a major player in the contest for colonies when it soundly thrashed Russia in a war with the chief characteristic of many colonial wars: the two combatants fought it entirely on the soil of a third country, China, which was not a combatant. The Russo-Japanese War marked the first time that an Asian power had defeated a European one in a major conflict. Japan's armies outfought and outmaneuvered the Russians both on land and, perhaps even more important, at sea. In the decisive land battle for Mukden, the largest Manchurian city (now called Shenyang), the Russians lost ninety thousand men. In the decisive naval confrontation, in the Tsushima Strait between Korea and Japan, the Japanese fleet under the command of Admiral Togo Heihachiro annihilated the Russian fleet, most of which had sailed eighteen thousand miles from its home port in the Baltic Sea. Only three Russian ships escaped. Russia lost all eight of the battleships in its fleet and five thousand men—compared to Japanese losses of three torpedo boats and 116 men. Russia agreed that Korea would be part of Japan's sphere of influence, and Japan seized the whole country in 1910. Japan was awarded the southern half of the Sakhalin Island chain, which had belonged to Russia, and it took over the special colonialist rights that Russia had had in southern Manchuria, including a lease on the port of Port Arthur and control over the South Manchurian Railroad. From that point on, it became a constant Russian ambition to recover these losses, and this, as we will see, was to have major consequences for China and the United States.

As a result of its victory, Japan was the indisputable great power in Asia and the fastest-rising power in the world, a country preparing to move on to the audacious, racially tinged goal of replacing white European colonialism in all of Asia, creating a vast new sphere to be led by Japan. It made modest progress toward this goal after World War I when, as a reward for having aligned itself with the winning side, it was granted the former German possessions in Shandong province in China, including the coastal city of Qingdao, known in the West for the eponymous brewery that the Germans had built there. Japan gave those possessions back to China in the 1920s as the world collectively began to feel some remorse for its violations of China's sovereignty, and Japan, more moderate and accommodating than it later became, felt the need to make a conciliatory gesture.

But then Japan's moderates lost control of the situation to its extreme nationalists and militants bent on realizing the country's pan-Asian destiny, which, they believed, would require an apocalyptic final showdown with western civilization. To dominate Asia, they first had to dominate China, which they despised as flabby, corrupt, and inferior, and to dominate China, they needed to retain control of Manchuria and to build it into a base for expansion.

In 1931 and 1932, the militarists, supported by Emperor Hirohito, gained complete control. Nationalist groups with names like the Cherry

Blossom Society and the Blood Brotherhood League committed a series of domestic assassinations. One victim was the last prime minister who attempted to curb the army's ambitions on the Asian mainland, which wiped out any vestiges of moderation. In 1931, in what came to be called the Mukden Incident, the members of the Kwantung Army, which was the epicenter of armed Japanese nationalism, blew up some railroad tracks on the Southern Manchurian Railway near Mukden, blamed the Chinese for the sabotage, and then used the incident to seize control of all the northeastern Chinese provinces that made up Manchuria. A few months later, they persuaded the last emperor of the overthrown Qing dynasty, Henry Pu-yi, to become the puppet leader of a new, supposedly independent country called Manchukuo. Early in 1932, an angry Chinese crowd beat up five Japanese Buddhist monks in Shanghai—or, as some accounts had it, Japanese officers bribed Chinese thugs to assault the priests. In response, the Japanese sent troops into the Chinese section of the city (the international settlements where most Japanese citizens lived was always off-limits to warfare in Shanghai). When units of the Chinese army, advised by their German trainers, effectively resisted, Japan sent an enormous land and naval invasion force to Shanghai and used both gunboats and biplanes to bomb heavily populated Chinese residential areas, the first such bombing of an urban center in history though it was soon to be followed by many more in both Asia and Europe. The long-term, remorseless, and atrocity-laden effort to conquer all of China had begun.

These aggressions aroused futile protests in the League of Nations. The creation of Manchukuo was deemed to be illegitimate, but no practical steps were taken to punish Japanese aggression. More important, though Chiang Kai-shek's government sent troops in an unsuccessful effort to resist the Japanese invasion of Shanghai in 1932, it acquiesced to Japan's aggression in Manchuria. It was in the midst of its nationalist revolution, striving to forge a "new China," modern, strong, self-reliant, and free of foreign infringements on its sovereignty, and Chiang, the leader of this revolution, understood that the country was militarily feeble and unable to thwart Japanese ambitions. The slogan, before Chiang was kidnapped in Xian and forced to abandon it, was "internal pacification before external resistance."

But Japan's manufacture of "incidents" continued, and each of them was used as a pretext for further encroachments. Beginning on July 7, 1937, when a Chinese patrol killed a Japanese soldier on night maneuvers near an ancient marble span called the Marco Polo Bridge, so named because the Italian traveler was supposed to have crossed it in the fourteenth century, Japan turned to the conquest of all of China. Responding to this new "incident," it sent four divisions of its heavily armed Manchurian-based troops through the Great Wall with the objective of seizing the four provinces of China north of the Yellow River, the old imperial capital of Beijing included. With that move, full-scale war between the two countries broke out, and it continued intermittently, its lulls interspersed with periods of intense fighting, for the next eight years.

By the time World War II had spread to Western Europe, when Germany invaded Belgium, Holland, and France, the Japanese assault on China was three years old, and during those four years, China fought entirely alone, without allies or support, except for some financial and material aid from the Soviet Union and the United States and, more significantly, the efforts of Chennault's American Volunteer Force, which used airfields in the interior of China to make the Japanese pay at least some price for their invasion of the country's northern and coastal provinces.

Like Ethiopia after Mussolini's invasion two years before, China in 1937 appealed to the rest of the world for help, but no help came, not from the League of Nations, which had been set up to make international aggression illegal and of which Japan was a member, and not from the United States. China had a great sentimental importance to Americans, who had been sending their traders there since the late eighteenth century and whose missionaries had been bringing what they ardently believed to be the benefits of Christian civilization to the Chinese for a hundred years. Franklin Delano Roosevelt liked to tell visitors about his Delano ancestors' connections to China. The music room at the family's ancestral home, Hyde Park, was filled with Chinese porcelain and lacquer antiques that the president's ancestors had collected in the eighteenth and nineteenth centuries. But less than twenty years after the end of World War I, the United States was in no mood to intervene in a foreign conflict, whether in Europe or Asia. For most of the first four years of the Sino-Japanese War, the United States continued to supply Japan with vital raw materials, the most important of which was oil, so in a way Americans were collaborators in China's humiliation and despoliation. In 1931, after the Mukden Incident, the headline in the Hearst tabloids provided a succinct summary of the American attitude, wherein its sentimental attachments to China were trumped by China's strategic unimportance. "WE SYMPATHIZE. BUT IT IS NOT OUR CONCERN." The same headline could have been written after the Japanese invasion of 1937, even if the sympathy was greater and the knowledge of Japanese atrocities more immediate.

The United States was brought directly into the war only in 1941 when, on December 7, Japan launched its surprise attack on Pearl Harbor. By that time, China's military and civilian losses were staggering, yet it showed a determination to resist that should have put most of Europe to shame. In contrast to China, for example, France surrendered in six weeks in the face of the German invasion of 1940; it then established an obsequious collaborationist government, and until the D-Day invasion of 1944 remained in a state of noncombative subjugation. World War II also ended quickly in the Netherlands, Belgium, Denmark, Norway, Poland, Hungary, Czechoslovakia, Serbia, Romania, Croatia, Greece, and the other occupied countries of Europe. All of them suffered the heavy hand of the German occupation, including the mass murder of the Jews. The West experienced guerrilla opposition to the occupation and the savage reprisals that the Germans exacted whenever their troops were attacked. Britain, of course, never surrendered and was never invaded. But of the continental European countries only the Soviet Union experienced full-scale war on its own territory for more than a few months. The Soviet Union was at war for a total of nearly five years, the United States for nearly four. China's war, excluding the initial Japanese invasion of Manchuria in 1931, lasted eight full years.

By the time of Stilwell's departure and Wedemeyer's arrival in the fall of 1944, China was exhausted, its armies decimated, its people demoralized, disoriented, and desperate, its economy in ruins, and its government, led still by Chiang Kai-shek, discredited by the depredations it had been powerless to prevent. Tens of millions of soldiers and civilians had died, many millions more were displaced, reduced to penury and desperation. Numerous cities were literally smoldering ruins, the economy of much of the countryside wrecked. Students of the war have estimated property damage at about the equivalent of one hundred billion dollars, which means that the country's industrial capacity was one-quarter of what it had been at the beginning of the war.

Some areas of China, a very big country, were not very adversely affected by the war, or were largely untouched by it, most conspicuously Manchuria and Taiwan, both of which were under Japan's control and had actually benefited economically from Japan's insatiable need for goods. Other areas, especially what was known as the *dahoufang*, consisting of the vast inland provinces including Sichuan, Shanxi, Guizhou, Gansu, and Yunnan, were mostly unoccupied by Japan and not directly touched by the war. Even areas that were more central and that Japan did invade, like Hunan and Henan provinces, saw little actual fighting between the initial Japanese invasion of 1937 and the ferocious Ichigo campaign that Japan initiated in the spring of 1944. In many parts of unoccupied China, the Chinese, resourceful and energetic as always, made do, as people always strive to do even under the worst of circumstances. Human creativity does not grind to a halt even in concentration camps and occupied territories. "When no outside pressure brought terror and wild dispersal, a provincial city seemed able to bumble along in peaceful autonomy just as it had during the centuries of imperial rule," wrote the American traveler Graham Peck, who toured much of China in 1940 and 1941, just before the American entry into the war.

Refugees created new communities. A class of newly wealthy entrepreneurs emerged. Known as "guerrilla merchants," they packed their bags with silk stockings or fountain pens and took them by junk or on horse carts from the cities under Japan's control to the towns and cities that weren't. Traveling in Guangdong and Guangxi provinces, Peck found "boom towns, packed with new restaurants and hotels, noisy all night with gambling and drinking games" where there had been only quiet fishing villages before, bypassed by the river steamboats. The smuggling was technically illegal but was nonetheless taxed by local military commanders and customs officials. A few months later, in 1941 in Henan province, Peck met a former official who had lost his job and become a guerrilla merchant instead. He reported that the town of Jieshou, the busiest smuggling port in Honan, had better restaurants, Chinese or western, than Chungking. Loyang, the provincial capital six hundred miles northeast of Chungking on the Yellow River, "sheltered well over a hundred thousand people, clattering about the routines of Chinese urban life in fair prosperity," almost as if there were no war, and in striking contrast to miserable, overcrowded, rubble-strewn Chungking. The Japanese armies were fifty miles away.

But this semi-prosperity, which existed in spite of rather than because of the activities of China's government, could come crashing to an end at any time. Only two weeks after Peck's arrival, regular Japanese bombings of Loyang commenced—surveillance planes in the morning, bombers at night—and suddenly panic swept the city along with rumors of an imminent invasion. The planes would appear over the Yellow River, which ran just to the north of Loyang, and suddenly thousands who had been engaged in peaceful commerce a minute earlier would be rushing helter-skelter, bumping into each other on the streets, scrambling down steep steps to bomb shelters. "After each lengthening raid, the clean-up squads carried more straw-wrapped bodies through the streets," Peck later wrote. Business died away. The electricity failed. The schools closed. Prices of real estate went down and those of vegetables up. "The city began to have the shabby, disheveled look I had known in Chungking the autumn before, with tangled wires and scatterings of rubble on the streets, posters and paper windows hanging in shreds" and "the big streets . . . deserted from dawn to dusk."

On May 16, 1941, the Japanese sent 110 planes over Loyang, where they dropped over seven hundred bombs. That afternoon,

> the road to the west was filled with people slowly moving away from Loyang afoot or in carts, rickshaws, wheelbarrows, and automobiles. Over the trees by the road, the long straight snake of dust raised by their passing stretched all the miles from the towering smoke in town to the edge of the hills. In the fields a little distant from the road, their shouting, wailing, and cursing merged into a low, quavering, continuous sound, like the moan of a stricken beast pouring out its blood in a long, fatal stream.

After the bombing ended, a semblance of normal life returned to Loyang, as did many of the refugees, and Chinese adaptability was partially restored. But the battles near the city and in the mountains across the river left behind an enduring legacy of anger and distrust. People hated the Japanese, and they lost faith in the capacity of the Kuomintang to protect them. Critics of the government were arrested and sent to prison. Newspapers were censored so the feebleness of the central government's resistance was not publicized, though where it was not witnessed, it was suspected. The government blamed the Communists, whose armies, it said, had failed to attack the Japanese rear, which it was obliged to do under the terms of the United Front. The Communists rejected the charge, but the United Front, never a solid alliance, became ever less united. In the trek out of Loyang, as described by Peck, officers of the KMT army commandeered most of the cars and half the carts, which were "piled with the families, furniture, and files of the provincial capital's great civil and military bureaucracy," and this made no small contribution "to the air of hasty, brutish self-preservation which hung over the road in a miasma as choking as the dust." The prices of food and transport quadrupled; resentment surged as those who could afford it loaded their potted palms on their carts while poorer people carried their necessities on their backs. There were fistfights on the roads.

All of this was taking place before the United States entered the war, when hardly anyone in the outside world was paying much attention. And though they didn't know it, the Chinese people faced four more years of war.

Chinese life was deformed in ways small and big, collective and individual. The heavy toll in casualties taken by the Nationalist armies left the central government severely weakened and depleted and facing a Communist rival that had grown vastly in size and strength during the Japanese occupation.

Beyond the death and economic loss was the destruction of cities, the mass migrations of people, and the decay of the country's elites, its professional classes, administrators, civic leaders, merchants, and financiers. Given the country's poverty and backwardness, many of China's leading citizens, always spread thin over the country's vast territory, had lost their money and their confidence. The civil service was in shambles, the knowledge class not destroyed but dislocated, its leading figures, like the government, in internal exile. The struggle to endure had been intense and had produced an atmosphere of everyone-for-himself hostility, distrust, and cynicism. Traditional China, though poor, had cultivated a certain Confucian and Buddhist social conscience, especially through what were called benevolent associations, where people from a province or city now living in another province or city would offer a helping hand to newcomers from the same region. The Chinese had an expression, *renqing weidao*, meaning the flavor of human feeling, a certain perfume of virtue that cushioned the sharpest edges of life, but the suffering and desperation of the war removed much of the human feeling and left the jagged edges behind.

Perfect virtue, Confucius said, consisted of five characteristics: gravity, generosity of soul, sincerity, earnestness, and kindness. All of these prized characteristics atrophied as a result of the country's long war, so that government exactions, a ruthless exploitation of the weak, the theft of food, banditry, piracy, rape, and usury trailed in the wake of Japan's depredations. This was a phenomenon more noted by foreigners in China than by the Chinese themselves, or at least among those Chinese who wrote descriptions of the war. Peck put it this way: "The difficulty of survival, and the latent panic, encouraged rapacity and dog-eat-dog individualism in all dealings outside the family, the last surviving unit of mutual benevolence and responsibility." Even in the best of times, China, overcrowded and poor, suffered more than most countries. But during the war, the suffering intensified exponentially. "Public spirit, generosity and even honesty were more than most people could afford," the historian of China John K. Fairbank has written. "The strong not only trampled on the weak, they gouged one another."

For all the Kuomintang's propaganda, the patriotic songs it encouraged, the posters it put up in the unoccupied cities, the image it strived to foster of valiant resistance, its constant claims that things were going according to Chiang Kai-shek's plan, the government was held responsible for the failure to drive the Japanese out of China in the first place and for the disorder, the disorientation, the cruelty, the displacement, the sheer inhumanity, that ensued. "You have seen misery you never dreamed of before, dead eyes, sullenness, resentment, hatred, hopelessness, and all this in some of the most beautiful bodies in the world," an American intelligence officer warned the American diplomat John Melby in 1945, who was about to embark on an assignment in Chungking. The officer was speaking of India, but, he added, "It is the perfect introduction to China."

Simultaneous with their invasion of North China, Japan's armies drove up the Yangzi River Valley, and in the first year of the war they seized all the coastal cities of China, from Tianjin in the north to Canton in the south, as well as the great port of Shanghai itself, then Nanjing, the Nationalist capital, and Hankou, the industrial center on the river. Not only was China's land subjected to the shock of the Japanese blitzkrieg but its best German-trained divisions also took terrible casualties, from which the KMT armies never fully recovered.

It was a war without mercy, as the historian John Dower has called it. After the three-month battle of Shanghai in 1937, during which the Nationalist forces put up fierce and, to the Japanese, utterly unexpected resistance, fighting desperate house-to-house battles while under artillery fire from Japanese ships in the harbor, a photograph appearing in newspapers around the world aroused indignation as perhaps no other piece of information from the entire war in Asia did either before or after. It showed an infant sitting upright on some railroad tracks after a Japanese attack, his skin either burned or covered in ash. A pedestrian bridge crosses the tracks just behind him. Jagged shards of corrugated metal litter the ground as if somebody had scattered a deck of huge, half-torn cards. The child's mouth is open. His head seems large for his body. He is strangely upright, his arms at his sides, like a small, battered Buddha, a picture of perfect vulnerability sitting helplessly amid an apocalyptic wreckage, an embodiment of innocent suffering, of the cruelty of the invader, and of Chinese victimhood.

But the world stood by as the massacre continued, and it stood by until the end of 1941 when only the Japanese attack on Pearl Harbor brought the United States and its allies into the conflict on China's side.

Some places in China weren't just damaged; they were destroyed in their entirety, wiped out, depopulated and left in a state of Carthaginian ruin. Changsha, the capital of Hunan province, was such a place. In 1938, it was a city of half a million people, its massive gates and encircling wall testimony to its age and its importance. It lay along the Xiang, or Fragrant, River, a major tributary of the Yangzi in the midst of Hunan's plains and rolling hills, a rich agricultural terrain for which Changsha served as a commercial hub. Its narrow alleys meandered among two-story brick houses with slanting gray-tiled roofs. Its broader commercial thoroughfares were lined by columned arcades and jammed with traffic, rickshaws, donkeys, water buffalo pulling carts, and peddlers chanting the virtues of their spicy snacks. "Everything went on in the streets," a wife of a foreign missionary doctor wrote, "the oiling of paper umbrellas and the filling of cotton comforters, the pouring of candles, and the carving of coffins. . . . Babies were fed in the streets, children spun tops in the streets, and old men dozed in whatever spots of sunlight a wall might offer."

Changsha was famous for its two-thousand-year-old Han dynasty tombs, its many schools, and its Buddhist temples, and also for its experience of the violence of China's recent history. It was besieged during the mid-nineteenth-century Taiping Rebellion, when a charismatic visionary making the unlikely claim that he was the younger brother of Jesus almost overthrew the reigning Qing dynasty. More recently, in 1930, Changsha had been the site of violent clashes between the Communists and the Nationalists. It was, like many cities in China's heartland, a mixture of the charming and the horrible, the elderly men with wispy beards who aired their caged songbirds early in the morning and the beggars who died on the streets in winter. After the Japanese campaign in Shanghai in 1937 and the capture of Nanjing in 1938, three major Chinese universities had transferred to Changsha, so the intramural population had swelled to half a million.

There was also a substantial foreign population, a few hundred or so, including a Jewish refugee from Nazi Germany, a Mr. Lieberthal, who studied and measured the city's monuments and translated its ancient texts. Two dozen idealistic Americans belonged to the Yale-in-China program, whose middle school, hospital, and medical school occupied a twenty-acre compound just outside the North Gate. It was a quiet, privileged campus where the chapel, the dormitories, and the administration buildings were surrounded by chrysanthemum gardens, stands of bamboo, and groves of camphor trees where magpies nested. The more numerous foreign businessmen, with whom the missionaries didn't mingle much, occupied a narrow island in the middle of the Xiang River, where they enjoyed the splendid isolation of foreign traders of those times, with their club (for Caucasians only) and their lives "as foreign eccentrics, with too much money and influence, too easy alcohol and sex."

For the foreigners, Changsha was an example of the kind of Somerset Maugham idyll that China offered during the decades of foreign concessions and extraterritorial rights. There were ten-course banquets featuring dishes from one of China's greatest cuisines; excursions by sedan chair to the not-too-distant Buddhist temple in the mountains, or to famous Han tombs; cocktails, snooker, and gossip at the club. The late 1930s, when the Nationalists enjoyed their few years of political ascendency in China, was the end of the time when China's poverty, disorder, and aspirations provided for exotic slumming, antiquarian aestheticism, and sensual pleasure, a self-indulgent, servant- and banquet-rich style of life that came along with the profits of the China trade.

Even the missionaries had the services of one Chinese servant for every two members of their households; the foreign businessmen enjoyed a ratio of one to one. And it was all so cheap. "In China," one missionary allowed, "we all live like lords and kings on fifty-five dollars a month." But the Sino-Japanese War was crowding in. On Thanksgiving Day 1937, the first of many Japanese bombings occurred. The planes came in the middle of the afternoon and were followed, rather than preceded, by air raid sirens. Within a few minutes Changsha was pockmarked by craters and devastation. Two small hotels packed with refugees from Shanghai and Nanjing suffered direct hits, resulting in a hundred dead. Charred, dismembered corpses lay in the streets. A woman crouched next to the body of her dead husband and wailed. She had already started burning paper money for his use in the afterlife. Three smoldering joss sticks were stuck in the dirt near his feet.

Then, in the fall of 1938, the coastal city of Canton to the south and the industrial city of Hankou in the north, the two connected to Changsha by China's main north–south rail line, had fallen. Refugees were streaming into Changsha and so were the wounded, straining the city's capacity to absorb and treat them. Joseph Stilwell, at the time the American military attaché, came to Changsha accompanied by Jack Belden so he could interview hospitalized soldiers in his effort to find out which Nationalist units were actually fighting the Japanese. They were hosted by Phil Greene, an American doctor in charge of the Yale-in-China hospital.

In late October, as news of Japanese advances up the Yangzi River reached the city, it became clear that Changsha's turn was coming. Late on the morning of October 26 "the arsenal behind the hospital blew up," Greene wrote. "Just one big bang and the whole place was gone." Thirty were killed in the blast and seventy wounded. "It took as long to dig them out as to fix them up." Intensifying the mood of impending disaster, the Nationalist government had ordered that nothing was to be left in Changsha if the Japanese succeeded in taking the city. In Shanghai, Canton, Nanjing, Hankou, and other conquered cities, the Japanese had plundered the granaries and storehouses, stolen livestock and household goods, slaughtered civilians, raped women and girls, and used old men and captured Chinese soldiers for bayonet practice. The Nationalists had made it clear that they would pursue a strategy suitable to a weak but large country fighting a stronger enemy that is far from home. They would fall back into the interior, follow a scorched-earth policy in the invaded areas to deny resources to the enemy, and then counterattack when the enemy was overextended and dispersed.

On November 9, Chiang came to Changsha himself to preside at a military conference, where he spoke admiringly of the burning of Moscow during the Napoleonic wars and said that Changsha should follow that example of noble self-sacrifice. But Chiang's speech and the visible preparations that followed it caused consternation. People began to leave, including people who should have stayed, notably members of the local government. "With the running off in fast time of many provincial officials the panic started," Greene wrote. Changsha became "a deserted and evidently doomed city," its streets empty except for soldiers with rifles and fixed bayonets taking up positions. On the night of November 12, the provincial governor, Zhang Zhizhong, hosted a dinner for the Yale-in-China hospital staff, and after the spicy delicacies typical of the region had been consumed, no doubt with many delicate porcelain cups of warm rice wine, he ordered them all to leave the city by the next day.

But it was already too late. Just after midnight, Greene wrote, the doctor on the British gunboat anchored in the Hsiang River, the SS *Sandpiper*, noticed two fires near the waterfront. Within a half hour he saw three more. No one seemed to be trying to put them out. By 2:00 a.m. he realized that other fires were starting up in the south end of the city. People were desperately trying to get out. The waterfront was ablaze. "Jardines (British shipping firm) going like a bonfire; Defag (German) going hot and fast; a large fire in the center of the city." Before dawn, Greene saw soldiers from the military police headquarters carrying oil-soaked cotton rags breaking down the doors of houses and setting them on fire before opening their windows and running away. There is no report of how these soldiers felt putting to the torch a city that was already ancient at the time of the early Han dynasty of the first two centuries BC. But they followed orders, and by morning the flames seemed to be streaking to the sky, blending with the red of the rising sun, and then, as Greene put it, "the fires blazed and munitions dumps went off singly and together."

The great fire of Changsha burned for three days. Photographs taken at the time show two-story buildings engulfed in fire while outside them men in short silk jackets stand helplessly by. The Communist leader Zhou Enlai, who was living in Changsha, barely escaped when flames began scorching the inside of his apartment. The cultural and commercial center of the city was burned to the ground, leaving behind nothing but rubble and ash.

The fire was a consequence of the fog of war. Local officials, including the chief of police and the garrison commander, were panicked by rumors that the Japanese were outside the city's gates and that its defenses were about to collapse, and so they lit the fires that burned Changsha down. The truth was that the Japanese advance had been temporarily stopped and Changsha was in no imminent danger, but by the time that became clear the city had been torched. Shortly afterward, Chiang flew in to try to make amends. He met with the foreigners and expressed his regret at the havoc and destruction. Soong Mei-ling, evidently trying to exonerate her husband, addressed a letter to the city saying that the intentional burning of the city "was not in accordance with the Generalissimo's orders." Three local officials, including the garrison commander and the police chief, were held responsible for the damage and made to pay the the ultimate price. They were executed. Even though most of the inhabitants had left ahead of the fire, teams sent in to clean up reported taking 20,000 corpses outside the city wall and burying them there. These included wounded soldiers, almost all of whom died in their hospital beds, since there had been no thought of evacuating them ahead of time. More than 21,000 buildings were completely destroyed, two-thirds of all the buildings of Changsha. These included more than 10,000 homes, fifty-five schools, and thirteen hospitals. The city's temples, Buddhist and Taoist, the restaurants, the hotels, the government offices, and the grain warehouses, along with the grain inside them, were all gone. There was enough inside the masonry houses—the furniture, staircases, beams, doors, window frames, and paper windows—to feed the flames. When the wooden roof joists burned away, the heavy tiles that they supported dropped and flattened everything below them like so many falling stones.

"I stood at Pa Ko T'in, the heart of downtown Changsha where the grand silk shops had been," an American missionary later wrote, "and could see virtually without obstruction for a mile in any direction. . . . Several weeks after the fire rice was still smoldering where some of the big warehouses had stood." Changsha "lay flat, wrecked, and totally vulnerable." A person standing at the South Gate could see the silhouette of the chapel and dormitories of the Yale-in-China compound on the other side of the North Gate. Nothing remained between the two to block the view. Greene wrote to his wife, "Hospital running full ward . . . . Most of the city gone." An officer aboard the *Sandpiper*, still anchored in the nearby Xiang River, said, "Changsha, and various industrial points outside, is now completely burned to the ground."

It would have been bad enough if the great fire had turned out to be Changsha's only disaster of the long war, but there were many other wounds inflicted by Japan's invading army and air force. Because of its position on major rail lines and because it was the main depot for the agricultural wealth of Hunan province, Changsha would be a battlefield for the length of the war, and also an emblem of China's will to resist. The Japanese mounted major attacks four times and were repulsed three of those times by Chinese armies under the command of one of the best of the Nationalist generals, Xue Yue, who had studied at the Whampoa Military Academy in Canton when Chiang Kai-shek was the commandant there. The Japanese attempted to seize Changsha in 1939, 1941, 1942, and 1944. In the battle of 1942, Xue, feigning weakness, lured a huge force of Japanese into a pocket and then attacked from all sides even as he sent mobile squads to harass the supply lines behind them. The Japanese retreat was then slowed down by a succession of necessary river crossings, and they were cut down by Chinese firing on them from high ground. It was one of the few clear defeats suffered by the Japanese in the Sino-Japanese War, and it was a costly one. The official account held that 52,000 Japanese soldiers died, and while this is likely among the many exaggerations of China's press department, the losses were certainly considerable.

But when the Japanese attacked in 1944, Changsha, the capital of a territory as large as Great Britain, fell almost without resistance, and by 1945 it typified the devastation that the eight years of war had wrought. It was essentially depopulated, its residents having been slaughtered or driven into exile, its economy, its institutions, and its way of life left in ruins just as much as its houses, stores, and temples. This is a key fact about China as the parties to the conflict—the Kuomintang, the Communists, Japan, the Soviet Union, and the United States—all faced, albeit unknowingly, the final stage of the war and the first stage of the after-war. In large swaths of China, the structures of society and government barely existed.

It is almost impossible to make an accounting of the entirety of China's destruction as the war entered its final few months. The estimate of historians is that twenty to thirty million Chinese died in the conflict, which is an immense number, though in a population of more than four hundred million not proportionately more than the human loss that occurred in the Soviet Union, Poland, or, for that matter, Japan as a result of American bombing. But what added to the devastation of China was not just the length of the war but the poor and fragile state of the country at the conflict's very beginning. For outsiders, Chinese suffering had always seemed expected, almost normal. For a hundred years, it had been a country where wars, famines, and oppression had been continuous and on a grand scale. It was a place whose considerable charm was, as the historian Barbara Tuchman put it, "counterbalanced by the filth, the cruelty, the indifference to misery and disregard for human life." Staggering death tolls were lamentably ordinary in China's history, and they added to such other immemorial Chinese afflictions as famine, official corruption, abuse of authority, forced prostitution, superstition, concubinage, female infanticide, foot-binding, opium addiction, beggary, child labor, warlordism, banditry, onerous taxation, landlessness, overpopulation, illiteracy, domestic violence, the ubiquitous stench of human waste, and astronomical rates of infanticide and infant mortality. "I felt that it was pure doom to be Chinese," the American journalist Martha Gellhorn wrote after trekking across much of China in 1940.

No worse luck could befall a human being than to be born and live there, unless by some golden chance you happened to be born one of the .00000099 percent who had power, money, privilege (and even then, even then). I pitied them all, I saw no tolerable future for them, and I longed to escape away from what I had escaped into: the age-old misery, filth, hopelessness and my own claustrophobia inside that enormous country.

Skinny, sweaty rickshaw pullers strained at their large-wheeled contraptions to provide transportation to the rich. The scenes of nearly naked coolies towing barges up canals and rivers, leaning so far against their harnesses as to be almost horizontal to the ground, were an emblem, picturesque and horrible at the same time, of the unrelenting strain of everyday life in China, as were such other standard images as the women with leathery skin barefoot in the muck planting and weeding, the farmers covered in sweat at the foot pumps along fetid canals or carrying their loads of brick or straw on balancing poles slung over their shoulders or moving slowly and patiently behind water buffalo pulling primitive plows. The fly-specked hospitals, the skinny, crippled beggars, the thousands and thousands of villages made of baked mud whose houses, as one visitor described them, were "smoky, with gray walls and black tiled roofs; the inhabitants, wearing the invariable indigo-dyed cloth . . . moving about their business in an inextricable confusion of scraggy chickens, pigs, dogs, and babies."

Impressive as the stoicism of China was, there was no question of the magnitude of the struggle that tens of millions of people went through every day merely to survive. Theodore H. White wrote in his classic book *Thunder Out of China* that half the people of the country died before they reached the age of thirty. White gives no source for this stunning statistic, and it may be exaggerated, but not by much. In 1949, as the Communists were taking power, the life expectancy in China was 40.1 years. "In war and peace, in famine and in glut, a dead human body is a common sight on open highway or city street," White wrote. "In Shanghai collecting the lifeless bodies of child laborers at factory gates in the morning is a routine affair." The British sociologist R. H. Tawney, who conducted a survey of rural Chinese life in the early 1930s, famously likened the typical Chinese peasant to a man standing neck deep in water, so that "even a ripple is sufficient to drown him." And ripples in the first half of the twentieth century were frequent. "What drove you to settle so far from home?" a peasant was asked in Tawney's presence. "Bandits, soldiers and famine" came the reply. Tawney writes:

> Over a large area of China, the rural population suffers horribly through the insecurity of life and property. It is taxed by one ruffian who calls himself a general, by another, by a third, and, when it has bought them off, still owes taxes to the government. . . . It is squeezed by dishonest officials. It must cut its crops at the point of the bayonet, and hand them over without payment to the local garrison, though it will starve without them. It is forced to grow opium in defiance of the law, because its military tyrants can squeeze heavier taxation from opium than from rice or wheat, and make money, in addition to the dens where it is smoked. It pays blackmail to the professional bandits in its neighborhood; or it resists, and a year later, when the bandits have assumed uniform, sees its villages burned to the ground.

The scholar John K. Fairbank lived in the country in the early 1930s and remembered how he would be greeted in villages by "the barking of ill-fed dogs and the stares of children covered with flies." Scalp and skin diseases due to malnutrition were common. The farmers grew their crops on "strips of dusty farmland" with "few trees and little water." Irrigation was done by hand, "laboriously, bucket by bucket."

If a kind of medieval destitution was normal in China through the first half of the twentieth century, it is not difficult to imagine what the effects of seven and a half years of war on the thousands of poor villages of China would be, not only the wounds inflicted by marauding armies but the foraging for food and supplies of rival bands, the forced conscription, the banditry born of desperation, and the disappearance of able-bodied men. Only a slight disturbance was enough to put the Chinese peasant under water, and the war was far from slight. As one scholar of the period has put it: "The magnitude of the rural misery was completely beyond imagination."

The worst came, paradoxically perhaps, during a relative lull in the fighting, between 1941 and 1943, when one of the twentieth century's worst famines occurred in North China. It was caused by a drought in 1942 and by locusts in 1943 and intensified by the dislocation of war, the destruction of the transportation networks, and by Japanese requisitioning of merchant ships. Three million people died of starvation as a result of the famine while another three million became refugees. White, who traveled to Henan in the spring of 1943, described scenes of sickening horror—children sucking at the breasts of their dead mothers, women who killed their babies rather than hear them cry, people chipping bark off of trees and making a kind of soup out of it, people who survived by eating other people. "There were corpses on the road," he later wrote. "A girl no more than seventeen, slim and pretty, lay on the damp earth, her lips blue with death, her eyes were open and the rain fell on them." The famine was a coup de grâce for the provincial capital, the city of Zhengzhou, which had already been reduced largely to rubble by earlier Japanese bombing. "We stood at the head of the main street, looked down the deserted way for all its length—and saw nothing. Occasionally someone in fluttering, wind-blown rags would totter out of a doorway. Those who noticed us clustered round; spreading their hands in supplication, they cried 'K'o lien, K'o lien' [mercy, mercy] till our ears rang with it."

The famine in Henan was so vast and so terrible that few took notice of a similar famine in fertile Guangdong province, though a million and a half people were said to have died in it. Guangdong, the coastal province bordering on Hong Kong, a British colony then, was a scene of only intermittent fighting, especially after the Japanese seized Canton and tightened the blockade of China. In 1940, two years after the fall of Canton, Graham Peck slipped into Guangdong from Hong Kong in a smuggler's boat that ran the maze of canals at the estuary of the Xi, or West, River. The first real town he saw was Tam Shui Ko, which, though it had not been invaded, was nonetheless "a tomb of a city," most of whose inhabitants, rich and poor alike, had fled in the panic after the fall of Canton. "Weeds and bushes were growing in the little white-colonnaded streets . . . and the windows and doors which were not bricked up gaped upon the blackness of charred rooms or the dazzle of the open sky." Peck remembered anti-Japanese murals and slogans scrawled on the sides of the public buildings, signs of an earlier spirit of resistance, but now "in most streets the only living creatures besides the wild dogs and cats, and strangely tame rats, were a few ragged sidewalk peddlers with trays of flyblown wares," which they hawked clamorously "in rough raincoats of palm fiber, like a herd of shaggy beasts among the ruins."

In 1938, in a desperate effort to stop the Japanese advance in North China, Chiang ordered that the dikes of the Yellow River, not for nothing known as China's Sorrow, be broken. This only delayed the Japanese advance while it created an inundation of the vast North China plain, with two or three feet of water sweeping over whole counties in several provinces. The flooding caused widespread crop failure such that at the worst of it ten thousand starving people each day were gathering in major cities seeking relief. In the end, 800,000 people died either directly of flooding or of starvation. In 1945, five million refugees were still in the places they had fled to.

In her account of China's wartime suffering, the scholar Diana Lary has attributed these actions to a combination of "grandiloquent patriotism at the top and incompetence on the ground." As any war unfolds, especially a long one, constraints are loosened and the wantonness of the destruction increases. World War II marked the era of total war, mass bombings of cities in the West as well as in the East, civilian slaughter on a mass scale. And yet the sheer numbers of the dead and displaced in the Sino-Japanese War suggest an imperial willingness on both sides to accept severe misfortune on the part of the faceless and replaceable masses when the misfortune is deemed necessary for the sake of the national good. After he took power, Mao used to applaud China's cruel first emperor of more than two millennia before, even though his signal achievement, the construction of the Great Wall, not only cost innumerable lives but also failed to stop invasions of the Celestial Empire from the north. On both sides of the Sino-Japanese War, the willingness to accept and even to encourage death on a vast scale bespoke a frenzied, fanatical attachment to the national aspiration, a sense universally shared that death and destitution were always preferable to defeat. Some students of the war have attributed this cult of willing sacrifice to the experience of Japanese military academies, where many future Chinese officers studied alongside their Japanese counterparts in the waning days of the last dynasty and where they were identically imbued with the glory of dying rather than surrendering or being taken prisoner. In any event, there was a striking absence of prisoners of war. Martha Gellhorn attributed this to the ferocity of the hatred the Chinese felt for the invader. "A Chinese soldier," she wrote, "gets one thousand national dollars for any Japanese prisoner captured alive. Despite this huge sum of money, the soldiers shoot any Japanese troops they can lay hands on, as an immediate personal vengeance for the misery of people like themselves in villages like their own homes."

A few weeks after the outbreak of the war, *The New York Times* interviewed Japanese army and navy spokesmen in Shanghai on the complete absence of captured enemy soldiers in a conflict that by then had already involved hundreds of thousands of troops. The army spokesman readily acknowledged that " 'almost no Chinese war prisoners have been taken' and smiled broadly when told of the Chinese claim that one Japanese soldier had been imprisoned."

China's vast size and population have led other rulers besides Chiang to sacrifice vast numbers for the sake of the national purpose, or to see large numbers of dead as an inescapable element of the national experience. The Taiping Rebellion, in which twenty million people were killed, was by far the world's costliest conflict in the nineteenth century, though the American Civil War was a worthy rival for that distinction. Later, after the Communist takeover, Mao used to boast that a nuclear attack on China would cost it much less than a similar attack on other countries because China could afford to lose tens of millions of its people and still be the most populous country on the planet. Mao accepted without any apparent remorse the death of more than forty million people in the famine of 1959–1962, which was a direct result of his economic policies. He was willing to endure the loss of thousands of China's intellectuals, scientists, writers, artists, and technicians in the campaigns for political purity that he waged throughout his time in power. There were always enough people in China for a fresh start. The population was fungible.

There was something of that in Chiang as well, as the Yellow River flood indicated. After appeasing Japan for years on the grounds that his armies were too weak to offer effective resistance, Chiang took on the anti-Japanese fight as a great national purpose for which no sacrifice and no amount of suffering was too great. In the battle for Shanghai, because of furious Japanese bombing of the Chinese part of the city, the population of the International Settlement and French Concession, which were exempt from attack, rose from 1.5 to 4 million. "Tens of thousands of homeless clogged the streets and hundreds of thousands more slept in office corridors, stockrooms, temples, guild halls, amusement parks, and warehouses," the historian Frederic Wakeman has written. "By the end of the year 101,000 corpses had been picked up in the streets or ruins." The Chapei district, the city's largest Chinese residential area, was, as another historian has put it, "the epicenter of devastation." A French journalist arriving in Wusong, a city north of Shanghai, wrote that "the entire town and the villages all round it had been horribly destroyed, burned, and razed to the ground by the bombing." In Wuxi, seventy miles to the northwest, the population dropped from 300,000 to 100,000. The county seat of Jiading, west of Shanghai, was inspected by Kumagai Yasushi, a Japanese officer in charge of what was called pacification for the South Manchurian Railway. "What an awful scene of desolation it was," he wrote later.

Houses had collapsed, roof tiles were scattered over the roads, and snapped electrical wires were strewn about, making it hard just to walk. Here and there were holes probably caused by bombs dropped from airplanes. Oddly enough, the towering pagoda standing in the centre of town was the only thing to survive unscathed. Not a soul was to be seen. All we saw occasionally was a doddering elderly person crawl out from one of the collapsed hovels and then go back in again. A third of the houses

within the city wall had sadly been destroyed. We found ourselves in a city of death, a mysteriously silent world in which the
only sound was the tap of our own footsteps.

To resist the Japanese attack on Shanghai, Chiang ordered whole
divisions to stand and fight, even though it meant that they would be
wiped out, rather than withdraw them so they could survive to fight
again. The resulting losses were ruinous and unrecoverable. The estimates of Chinese military casualties ranged from a low of 187,000
to a high of 300,000, with the main losses suffered by Chiang's best
German-trained and -equipped divisions—a catastrophe that would
directly affect China's military effectiveness for the rest of the war. To
western eyes, this sacrifice was senseless from the military point of view,
even though, as Theodore White put it, "in a political sense it was one
of the great demonstrations of the war," proving as it did "how much
suffering and heroism the Chinese people could display in the face of
hopeless odds."

There were two main periods of intense fighting during the war,
the first in 1937 and 1938 when, following the Marco Polo Bridge Incident, Japan executed its two-pronged full-scale assault on China. One
prong was aimed at seizing the provinces north of the Yellow River and
incorporating them with Manchuria into a Japanese-controlled North
China that would have been larger than Western Europe. The second
prong aimed at the rich Yangzi River Valley. Both assaults involved the
merciless firebombings of civilian concentrations, from Shanghai on
the coast to Guilin in the southwest. Along the way looting, mass killings, and rape were common, as the Japanese pursued a policy aimed
at terrorizing the population into submission and forcing the government to surrender. What has come to be called "the rape of Nanjing,"
in which some three hundred thousand Chinese civilians were killed
and innumerable women and girls raped, was one of the most notorious atrocities of World War II. As a result of the desecration of Nanjing,
some 80 percent of the population was gone, either through death or
escape. Seventy-eight percent of the Chinese population that remained
in the massacred city had no income, and, in most cases, no possessions, not even bedding.

The rape of Nanjing was hardly the only atrocity in China, where,
as we've seen from the example of Changsha, many cities and villages
were left in ruins, virtually without inhabitants. Yanwo was a town on

the slope of a hill about thirty miles southwest of Xuzhou, a railway junction in Jiangsu province north of Shanghai. On May 20, 1938, Japanese troops charged into the town and, within an hour, had killed two hundred people on the streets. "Then they herded 670 men, both locals and refugees, into the courtyard of a house just outside the village," one historian has written. "The buildings around the courtyard were set on fire from outside; men who tried to escape the flames were gunned down by soldiers surrounding the house. All but five of the 670 were killed." In weeks of fighting in the northern railway junction of Taierzhuang, the population of twenty thousand was reduced to seven people, an eighty-five-year-old man and six women, the *North China Herald* reported.

Most places, of course, did not suffer that kind of total devastation, but many places experienced a ongoing, almost routine kind of damage. Gellhorn arrived by air in Kunming one night in January 1941 after twenty-seven Japanese bombers had hit the city during the day. One street on which virtually every house had been struck was

> packed solid with Chinese: men wearing black or faded blue cotton clothes, a few women hobbling along on bound five-inch feet, peasant women in black pants and coats, with their hair in braids down their backs, children caught in the undertow. . . . Gas mains had been hit, and cesspools, and underfoot the street sloshed in water from broken pipes. The miserable houses, suddenly cracked open, let out all their long store of dirt and smell. There was no air to breathe, and any time now these houses sagging sideways on unsteady beams, or balanced against one firm wall, might slip down into the crowded street like an avalanche. . . . All along the side of the street, by candlelight and the light of kerosene lanterns, the people were digging their way back into their bombed and ruined homes and hammering together torn boards to make some kind of roof and some kind of wall, some kind of shelter to live in. There was only the night to work. Tomorrow the Japanese would come back.

When air raid warnings sounded during the day, Gellhorn noted, people just left, because there were no bomb shelters in the city and no protection in the buildings. "They take to the hills and watch the Japanese bombers working over their empty city."

When the Chinese didn't fulfill the prediction of the Japanese commanders that they would quickly surrender, Japan found itself in the kind of quagmire that later became familiar to the United States in Korea and Vietnam, locked into a conflict that couldn't be decisively won but from which it seemed impossible to withdraw. By the end of 1938, after a year and a half of warfare on a vast scale, the Japanese gave up on the idea of a quick victory, or, indeed, on a purely military victory at all. Rather than seek the annihilation of the KMT, they tried to make the Chinese government irrelevant by building up an alternative. They found a compliant former leader of the left wing of the Kuomintang named Wang Jingwei (a name that has lived in universal infamy in China ever since) to head a puppet government installed in Nanjing.

Meanwhile, Chiang Kai-shek moved the government inland beyond the forbidding gorges of the Yangzi River to Chungking, formerly a sleepy, backward city of cliffs and hills. A long period of stalemate ensued, though it was a very sanguinary stalemate. One historian of the period has determined that in the year and a half before December 1942, casualties were nearly 50,000 per month, which are 10,000 fewer than those incurred between the battle of Shanghai and the fall of Wuhan in 1937. According to the Nationalists, there were nine major and 496 minor battles in this period, as well as more than 20,000 smaller clashes.

The year 1940 was an especially bad one. In the winter of 1939, the Nationalists had attempted a general counteroffensive with as many as eighty divisions involved in a nationwide series of attacks. While this took place, the Communists expanded the areas under their control and recruited new troops, both at the cost of KMT strength. But Chiang's troops, to his bitter disappointment, performed badly, their commanders frequently refusing to follow orders to go on the offensive, instead settling down into a treasonous sort of modus vivendi, more often trading with the enemy than fighting it.

From the failure of the winter offensive of 1940 to the recapture of the Burma Road at the beginning of 1945, the KMT never attempted another major offensive. Instead it reverted to Chiang's preferred "defense in depth," hoping that the enemy would exhaust itself through overextension until, finally, a counterattack was feasible. Meanwhile, in 1940, the Japanese advancing down the coast of China toward Vietnam took Guangxi province, tying down more Chinese troops and causing numerous casualties. There were political setbacks as well as military ones. Previously, when the Soviet Union signed its notorious non-aggression pact with the Axis, it freed Japanese troops in Manchuria and Inner Mongolia to concentrate on China. In July 1940, the British, submitting to a Japanese demand, stopped supplies from coming to China through either Hong Kong or Burma. The French, now under the collaborationist Vichy regime, allowed a Japanese military mission to Hanoi. The bridges on the Hanoi-to-Yunnan railroad were destroyed. Even before Japan's actual seizure of Burma, the blockade was virtually complete.

The situation, in other words, a full year before the entry of the United States into the war, was calamitous. By 1940, the Japanese had 1,000 first-line aircraft in China, compared to about 150 second-rate planes for China, which lost both its main flying school and aircraft factory in the conquest by Japan of Hangzhou and Nanchang. All Chinese planes defending Chungking were destroyed months after the Nationalists moved the capital there, and cities including Chengdu, Xian, Changsha, and even Lanzhou, at the gates of Central Asia, were subjected to frequent air assaults. Between May and September 1940, during the supposed stalemate, the Japanese flew 5,000 sorties and dropped 27,000 bombs on Chinese population centers, this despite often effective harassment by Chennault's Flying Tigers. Finally, the Japanese seized the Yangzi River port of Yichang, the gateway to Sichuan province, and a junction for railroad lines going further west. This gave the Japanese a base for its bombing campaigns as well as control of the rice-basket territory of Hubei province.

Though the absolute number of Japanese troops in occupied China seems high, they were actually spread thin in so vast a territory. Japanese policy was to control strategic points, especially along China's railroads, and to set up local administrations by inducing local Chinese to collaborate with them. This made them susceptible to enemy infiltration, resistance, and guerrilla action, in central and south China, by armed bands under Nationalist control and more famously in the north by forces belonging to the Communist Eighth Route and Fourth Route armies. Years after the war, Japanese veterans testified that starting in 1942, in an attempt to cope with this difficult situation, Japan carried out what came in China to be termed the "Three Alls" policy—kill all, burn all, loot all—which meant savage reprisals against villages for harboring guerrillas and against any individuals suspected of opposing

Japanese rule. Japanese scholars have estimated that 2.7 million Chinese were killed as a result of that policy. Herbert Bix, Emperor Hirohito's most recognized American biographer, concludes that the atrocities carried out as a result of the Three Alls policy were "incomparably more destructive and of far longer duration than either the army's chemical and biological warfare or the 'rape of Nanking'" in 1938.

Life was deformed in numerous ways by the war, twisted into strange, unrecognizable shapes, as the Chinese people, like people in occupied Europe, coped in their numerous, various ways. Some became collaborators, or were able to exploit the situation to their economic advantage. Others became martyrs. Thousands of youths from urban areas were drawn to the Communists' headquarters at Yenan, believing that to be the center of real patriotic activity. Millions fled their homes and remained refugees for years. The withdrawal of the central government from big cities like Shanghai left a vacuum to be filled by secret societies, criminal gangs, and black-marketers. "There was nothing they would not do and no evil they would not commit," a Shanghai resident wrote to what was left of the municipal government, "with the result that good people vanished without a trace and bandits arose in great number, committing murders and rapes every day."

"During the resistance," a Shanghai doctor named Chen Cunren wrote in a memoir, "those who suffered suffered all the more; those who were enriched made their fortunes in strange and inexplicable ways." The interactions of collaborationists, patriots, and the vast majority simply trying to survive created pungent tales of helplessness, exploitation, and revenge. In Hong Kong, seized from British control by Japan in 1941, a Chinese policeman named Tse, a squat, fat man who had expropriated the house of an Englishman languishing in an enemy detention camp, formed a partnership with a Japanese gendarme named Nakajima. They arrested Hong Kong Chinese on trumped-up charges and released them on payment of ransom by their families. Naturally, Tse was a feared man in Hong Kong. In one incident, a man of mixed Portuguese-Chinese background, Dominic Alves, disappeared into a private jail maintained by Tse in Kowloon, possibly because Dominic had once bested Tse in a real estate deal. But this story had a fairly happy ending. Dominic's Chinese-Portuguese wife, Miriam, went to the Japanese authorities in Kowloon, where she filed a complaint against both Tse and Nakajima. She was supported by a Japanese colonial official who actually took seriously Japan's claim to have invaded and occupied most of the rest of Asia to liberate the continent from western imperialism and bring about better lives for its people. Miriam's effort brought both a reward and punishment. She was given eight lashes for her temerity in going to the Kowloon gendarmerie. But her husband was released and Tse disappeared.

In some areas that had been the scenes of vicious early fighting but had long been part of the puppet state set up by Japan in 1938, a kind of collaborationist decadence coexisted with extreme poverty and desperation. The historian Frederic Wakeman describes a fancy mansion on the Rue Dupleix in the French Concession of Shanghai "frequented by movie starlets, opera divas, and café society social butterflies" whose cars could be seen parked on the roadway outside. The place was owned by one Pan Sanxing, who had a monopoly on passenger steamers plying the Yangzi River from Shanghai to Hankou about two hundred miles to the west. He maintained Chinese, Japanese, and western kitchens, and the best of Shanghai's prostitutes "ready to be fondled by Japanese officers tipsy after two or three drinks of expensive foreign liquor and looking forward to opium-drugged orgies in the tatami-floor rooms . . . where they were free to stay until dawn." This "collaborationist highlife" included a creative entrepreneurship that exploited shortages and desperation. Dr. Chen writes about a black market in antibiotics, a dose of which could cost as much as a villa, operated by underground gangs that sent runners to Indochina to collect them. Among the best-known of Shanghai's doctors was Ding Huikang, a specialist in tuberculosis who found a clever and profitable way to overcome a shortage of the x-ray film normally used to diagnose the disease. Ding used just one machine, without film. A patient would stand in front of it for a minute while a technician examined the live reflection. The technician would stamp an impression of the patient's lung on his palm with a red circle designating where he thought he had seen a tubercular spot. Then Dr. Ding used a long, thick needle to inject air into the infected spot. He also employed antibiotics for those wealthy patients who could afford them. Ding used the fortune he made during the war to buy rare Chinese antiques and entice women, especially actresses.

But most life under the Japanese occupation was not the high life. By 1945, thanks to the scarcity resulting from the years of conflict, the Japanese had imposed a strict regime of rationing on both the cities and the countryside; in Shanghai, for example, electricity use was restricted to the point that most families had only enough power to burn a fifteen-watt lightbulb for a few minutes a day. And, needless to say, there was censorship of all anti-Japanese sentiment. On the day after Pearl Harbor, the Japanese took over the foreign settlements that had been established in Shanghai a century earlier and where Chinese sovereignty did not apply, and immediately ordered the burning of all newspapers, journals, and books that dealt with contemporary history. There were bonfires in front of every lane. Orders went out for every household to turn in its radios, and all men between eighteen and thirty years of age were required to join local neighborhood vigilance committees and to be part of eight-hour shifts of block-to-block surveillance. Torture of opponents was practiced at police headquarters, and included spraying water in the nose, pulling out fingernails, and something called the sesame roll, where a victim was stuffed into a tightly knotted hemp sack and kicked back and forth.

As Japan became increasingly distracted by its losses in the Pacific and by preparations to defend the home island against an expected invasion, Japanese troops were shipped out of Shanghai and were replaced by collaborationist Chinese troops from Manchuria. These were called "fur hat soldiers" because they wore the clothes appropriate for their cold northern homeland. This happened despite constant Japanese proclamations that triumph was following upon triumph; these successes, some of them no doubt actually occurring on the military front, were sometimes announced on giant propaganda balloons with streamers that floated above Shanghai's racetrack. The Manchurian detachments were, if anything, worse than the Japanese they replaced. They "raped and pillaged their way into Shanghai," according to Wakeman. They demanded that the Japanese create "comfort stations" for them, the wartime euphemism for places of prostitution set up for Japanese soldiers, and when the Japanese replied that there was a shortage of prostitutes, the Manchurians went house to house and rounded up "surviving elderly women for their carnal pleasure."

The assaults on Chinese women were inhuman and innumerable. As they did in Korea and Southeast Asia, the Japanese maintained these "comfort stations" throughout China—officially there were 280 of them throughout the country—so that there could be one "comfort woman" for every forty soldiers. Casual rape took place in occupied districts: village girls simply taken away and used for the pleasure of Japanese officers and lower-ranking men, with disease and lasting shame the consequence for the victim. "They raped many women, including one who'd just given birth three days earlier," a witness to a Japanese raid on Fenglin village in Yongjia District, Zhejiang province, remembered years later. Another witness, a woman named Fu Yang, was a child when the Japanese came to her village, also in Zhejiang. "The Japanese raped 'flower girls,' whether they were six years old or sixty years old," she told an interviewer decades later. "My mother would rub black dirt all over my face every day, dress me in boy's clothes and keep my hair cut short, so afraid was she that the Japanese would take me. Our neighbor, Mrs. Wang, was already sixty, but she didn't escape. The Japanese took her and later burned her to death."

A woman mourns over a boy killed in the Sino-Japanese War, one of the millions of casualties of that conflict, which lasted from 1937 to 1945.

For millions of Chinese who were not direct victims of the Japanese aggression or who were not affected by the actual violence of the fighting, the war brought tremendous hardship nonetheless, along with deep psychological wounds. The Chinese army was plagued by troop shortages for the whole war, in large part because of the heavy casualties, and this created an ongoing affliction for villages throughout the unoccupied zone, such that many peasants felt they were better off under Japanese control than under that of the government. In November 1944, shortly after arriving in China, Wedemeyer explained to Marshall why a country of 425 million people didn't have an impressive number of military recruits. Recruitment couldn't be carried out in Japanese-controlled territory, and Japan controlled the major population centers of eastern China. Beyond that, a lot of otherwise able men were needed in agriculture, or the country would starve, and in industry, working to produce the goods the country needed to stay in the war. Also, Wedemeyer said, "malnutrition, lack of hygiene, poor sanitation and deplorable medical service all contribute to reduce the number of men physically able to perform military service."

"Conscription comes to the Chinese peasant like famine or flood, only more regularly—every year twice—and claims more victims," Wedemeyer wrote after he'd observed America's Chinese ally for a few months. "Famine, flood, and drought compare with conscription like chicken pox with plague." Reporting on conditions in the band of provinces stretching across central China from Shandong to Anhui, Edward Rice, a China expert attached to the American embassy, said, "All but the poorest people are able to evade military service. Conscripts are ill-treated and are given little or no training. Army officers engage in trade and in smuggling narcotics while their soldiers live off the people. Guerrilla units practice extortion against transient merchants and local well-to-do elements," with the result that the people had been aroused to "hostility and opposition."

Other observers, including Theodore White, had reported that conscription in the KMT army was really a kind of kidnapping with supposed recruits literally roped together and marched at gunpoint away from their homes, this while the president of their country lived among whispering servants and ancient paintings.

Many of these unwilling recruits were taken away from wives and children who suffered the loss of their economic support as a result. China was not the United States, where the salaries of troops in the field were paid to their wives on the home front. Innumerable Chinese women were left in poverty as long as their husbands were away, or permanently if they were killed, as so many of them were. The war also brought massive dislocation. Liu Qunying, born in 1921 in Wuhan, told an American scholar that she, her little brother, and her mother became refugees after their home was destroyed in the Japanese bombing of January 1938. Their goal was to reach Sichuan province in China's southwest, where the Kuomintang government itself was to take refuge a few months later.

"A sea of people with their belongings congested the roads and made the movement very slow and chaotic," she said. "We had to stay with the crowd on the major roads, for bandits often attacked straying refugees, especially women and children. . . . During the day, we moved slowly with the sea of people and ate the dry steamed buns we carried with us. At night, we just spread our only comforter on the ground, and my mother and I took turns sleeping for a few hours at a time."

Liu and her mother and brother were part of one of the largest migrations of recent history, the removal of millions of people from the cities and villages invaded, bombed, and pillaged by the Japanese. They moved westward to the unoccupied provinces in search of shelter and work. During the war whole cities, including Changsha, Guilin, and Xuzhou, were essentially emptied of their populations. Huge numbers of people from occupied and desecrated cities like Shanghai, Canton, Nanjing, and Hankou joined the throngs that jumbled along the roads and riverbanks heading west.

Observers at the time marveled at the labor of this dislocation, such as the scene early in the war when seven thousand coolies could be seen along the cliffs above the Yangzi River pulling seven thousand rickshaws loaded with all the manhole covers, sewer gratings, and radiators that could be salvaged from Hankou before the Japanese captured the city in October 1937. A Canadian Catholic missionary, observing the procession south of Xuzhou, wrote, "A long ribbon of ox carts stretches without interruption. This is the whole population of the North in flight. The women and children are on the carts, in the middle of bundles, baskets, sacks, chicks, goats, etc. Many are in tears, the children are crying. The men beat the oxen. Impossible to stop, only to go on. In the middle of all this are incredible numbers of soldiers . . . all is gloom. One only breathes dust."

The American journalist Jack Belden, who covered the four-month battle for Xuzhou, wrote of "oxen, horses, donkeys" all "fleeing along the way."

Some young men were carrying baggage and their household belongings, while others shouldered old men on their backs. Some had children in their arms, some had bedding and some carried their old mothers or their sick wives. Molecules of misery bumping and crowding into each other—an old woman with bound feet, a wrinkled patriarch sleeping in a cart—all fleeing destruction.

At some point along their part of this migration, Liu and her mother met two brothers who were fleeing their home in Anhui province, and they helped them walk the entire distance to Enshi in Sichuan, where Liu's high school had reportedly relocated. In exchange for the help of the older of the brothers, Liu had to submit to his sexual advances, with her mother's silent consent. In Enshi, they discovered that the school had in fact never been established there. The town, near Hubei, was crowded with refugees. Prices were high. "I felt so sad and hopeless. We did not have any control over our lives, and every day we lived in great fear. . . . For our safety, we had to stay with the two brothers. To me, it meant that I had to satisfy the older brother's sexual needs against my will, to endure a painful existence for the sake of my mother and my young brother." From Enshi, the group made its way to Chungking, which was, and is, perched on steep hills overlooking the confluence of the Yangzi and the Jialong rivers. Chungking was itself the site of an amazing story of misery and resistance. The government, as we've seen, moved there at the end of 1938 in order to be beyond the reach of the Japanese invasion. Many universities relocated to the areas outside of the city. Factories that were dismantled ahead of the Japanese invasion were moved piece by piece to Sichuan and Yunnan provinces and reconstructed there. This meant a tremendous influx of government officials, teachers, technicians, factory managers, and others converging on the same backward, inadequate city as the more desperate refugees. The officials had salaries, though they lived in conditions that were spare and difficult at best.

Cecil Beaton, the society photographer who visited China at the behest of the British Ministry of Information in 1944, spoke of the world of "bamboo, mud, and flies," of a China never far removed from the stench of the latrine. The bureaucrats and professors lived in leaky, rat-infested rooms stifling in Chungking's torrid, humid summer and freezing in the dank, wet winter. Beaton called on a professor from Fudan University, removed from its home in Shanghai to Chungking. "He subsists on poor quality rice," Beaton said.

> He sleeps and works in a prison-like cell, with no one to tend him. He possesses no furniture except perhaps a board propped on two dictionaries as a bed, and a case with shelves for the volumes salvaged from his former life. In accordance with the "Oil Thrift" movement, the lamp must be put out early at night.

There was no plumbing, so water had to be purchased from coolies who carried it up on balancing poles from the river. Prices were high, especially toward the end of the war. "Living like peasants," Beaton wrote,

> are the great specialists and experts on French literature or European philosophy; men who have been editors of scientific magazines, who have been the pivot of intellectual life and thought, are stranded here without money for cigarettes, some of them suffering from foot-rot so they are unable to walk, and others from disease caused by under-nourishment and lack of baths. Yet they remain astoundingly cheerful and full of verve.

They also lived with perpetual air raid alarms and, for months at a time, daily visits to shelters dug out of Chungking's steep hills. On the second night after his arrival in Chungking late in 1944, General Wedemeyer was kept awake listening to an aerial bombardment of the city, a reminder, he said, that "China was indeed at the end of the pipeline." As of the end of 1941, out of the $145 million in Lend-Lease supplies that had been promised to China, only $26 million had arrived, and a lot of that was in Burma waiting to be shipped over the Burma Road to China. Wedemeyer noted on that night in Chungking, almost three years later, that from time to time a bomb would land near the entrance of one of the bomb shelters dug out of the city's cliffs and the civilians who had taken refuge there would be buried alive. Even then, six years after the beginning of the war, five since Chiang had made Chungking his temporary wartime capital, there were still no anti-aircraft guns or modern warning equipment and the "Japs consequently could bomb with impunity, particularly just before nightfall." Wedemeyer's conclusion was that "something had to be done about this," but nothing was.

The lives of the displaced officials and teachers whom Beaton met were almost luxurious compared to those of people like Liu or the numberless others who took shelter in shanties that were then torn down by the police, who could get no medical treatment because they had no money, and who were reduced to begging to survive. Many of these people found homes, if that's the word, in the vast shantytown that sprang up in the narrow flats of the two rivers that come together in Chungking. "Humans in the slum co-existed with domestic and wild dogs, cats, mice, and other insects," one former resident of the riverbank remembered, "including fleas and cockroaches. In the summer, the damp riverbank was a breeding ground for mosquitoes. . . . We were miserable all year round."

While on her journey westward, Liu discovered that she was pregnant. She and her mother and brother, along with the two brothers they had met on the way, would walk for a day, then her mother and their traveling companions would find work for a few days to get food for the trip ahead. It took a year to get to Chungking. Liu gave birth to a child who was in poor health from the beginning and died when Liu, running for the cover of some trees during a Japanese bombardment, fell.

"We dug a hole in a field and buried him and moved on with our journey," she said many years later. "My heart was broken. Even today I do not know where he was buried."

When the group arrived in Chungking, Liu married the older brother, who turned out to be a drinker and a philanderer. He frequented brothels. He brought girls home and demanded that his wife cook for them. Eventually her husband left for good, and Liu got a job teaching in the elementary school of the War Relief Bureau in Chungking. Her mother and she did washing and cleaning jobs. The principal at her school helped himself to part of her salary. She had another child, a daughter, who fell ill with pneumonia, but there was no money for medicine, and "she died in my arms."

In April 1944, having failed to force a Chinese surrender and facing the likelihood that the United States would use Chinese territory for an invasion of the Japanese home islands, Japan brought the period of stalemate to an end, launching the Ichigo campaign to secure the provinces of Henan, Hunan, and Guangxi. This was the second period of prolonged and intense fighting of the eight-year war as the Japanese attempted to achieve two goals. One was to open a land route to Indochina, which Japan had seized in 1940, in order to move troops and supplies on the rail lines from Haiphong harbor all the way to Manchuria and then by ship to Japan itself. The second was to destroy the numerous airfields used by the American 14th Air Force to bomb Japanese targets both in occupied China and in the Pacific. It was in this campaign that Changsha was finally taken.

The Ichigo campaign has never received much attention in the West, in large part because it came simultaneously with other important engagements in the war, including the Allied landings in Normandy.

Still, stretching out over the entire second half of 1944, it was the single largest Japanese offensive of the war, involving half a million men in seventeen divisions, some of them moved from Manchuria and the Japanese home islands. On the Chinese side were an equal number of men, many of them, as always, malnourished and underequipped and fighting with their usual inconsistency, running away at times, standing and dying at others.

The destruction and dislocation that ensued from Ichigo were terrible, and the casualty totals astronomical. Refugees choked the roads. The Japanese, hampered by their overextended supply lines and the harassment of the American bombers, were forced to live off the land, looting what they could, shooting or bayoneting those who resisted. Cities that had been bombed in 1938 and 1939 but then more or less left alone in the interim were bombed again. Guilin, the site of a major American air base, was burned to the ground and essentially depopulated, while, as we have seen, Changsha, the largest city of Hunan province, was left a depopulated ruin.

"I watched every disaster that struck Guilin with a heart of hatred," the Chinese novelist Ba Jin wrote in a wartime diary.

I saw how those bombs destroyed the houses. I saw how the bombs exploded into flame, and I saw how the wind added to the fire, twisting two or three plumes of smoke together. On Yueya Mountain, I saw half the sky filled with black smoke, flames blazing across all of Guilin City. The black smoke was streaked with red flashes and huge red tongues of flame. The great fire on December 29th burned from the afternoon late into the night. Even the city gates fell and burned like matches. Countless cloths were burnt through next to the city walls, glazing red in my eyes like bundles of straw paper. Maybe there was a cloth factory's warehouse or something there. . . .

From these simple reports, you can understand the situation of this city in distress, and from this city you can imagine many other Chinese cities. They are all in distress. But they grit their teeth under the suffering, and they will not surrender. I see no hint of a shadow over those cities' appearances. The life I live in those places is not one of gloom and despair. Amid their suffering I even see the glee and laughter of China's cities. China's cities cannot be bombed into fear.

Simply to endure, to keep the hatred alive, was already a victory of sorts, at least a kind of redemption. But to fight back was better, and the group that was perceived to be doing so most bravely and tenaciously would win the admiration of China's people. Chiang did fight back far more than many American observers and subsequent historians have realized. What was often more visible to these observers, who were not allowed to go to the front, was the nonmilitary resistance. Unoccupied China was the scene of posters, marching students singing patriotic songs, propaganda movies calling on the people to endure. Chiang made frequent speeches that were duly reported in the press; his glamorous wife, Soong Mei-ling, traveled the world, especially the United States, advertising China's brave resistance and lobbying for help. The newspapers and official government press office reports were laden with accounts of victories won by China and ruinous losses suffered by Japan.

As we'll see, there was an irony in this. The government's claims were propagandistic exaggerations, which came to be widely disbelieved. But actually the government resisted far more than the Communists, who resisted very little and whose losses were a small fraction of those suffered by the KMT's forces. And yet, both at home and abroad, Chiang came to be perceived less and less as a heroic fighter. More and more, it came to be the Communists who were deemed to be waging the good fight, the main force of Chinese resistance. While China's misery eroded the prestige and legitimacy of Chiang and his government, the Communists were able to turn it to their advantage.

CHAPTER FOUR

Mao, Zhou, and the Americans

On July 22, 1944, eight American diplomats, soldiers, and spies boarded a United States Air Force C-47 cargo plane in the wartime capital of Chungking and flew to the Communists' headquarters at Yenan. The route was almost due north over the six hundred miles that separated one political and geographical China from another, over the semitropical green mountains and terraced rice fields of Sichuan province to the ancient Chinese capital of Xian. The Americans made a brief stop there before proceeding across the Yellow River, a broad, corrugated band more mud brown than yellow. To the south was government territory; east was the Japanese-occupied puppet state officially known, like the government-controlled China, as the Republic of China. About two hundred miles due north was Yenan, which one American visitor around that time described as an "eroded, lumpish plateau" where the Communists, having barely survived their Long March, had established their base area almost a decade before.

As the plane approached, a whitish nine-story Ming dynasty pagoda, famous as a Yenan landmark, loomed up on a nearby brown and treeless hill. A large crowd, some of its members giving hand signals to tell the pilot where to land, became visible on a field below. The plane descended close to the face of some cliffs "in which were dug caves where the Yenan elite snugly resided, safe from enemy bombing."

Disaster almost struck after the C-47 landed on the grassy runway. One of its wheels sunk into an old grave, causing the aircraft to dip to the left. The still-turning propeller hit the ground and separated from its shaft, causing it to shear through the fuselage at the front of the plane, narrowly missing the pilot. After a bit of confused milling about by passengers and bystanders, Zhou Enlai, the urbane external face of

Chinese Communism, strode across the field and shook hands with the head of the delegation, Colonel David Barrett, a tall, stout, genial former military attaché who had spent the better part of the previous decade in China and spoke Chinese well.

A half dozen or so of the American group worked for the Office of Strategic Services, the wartime predecessor of the Central Intelligence Agency, which was eager to get information about the Communist movement but also information from the Communists about the occupying Japanese army and the forces of the Chinese puppet government. Among these agents was the former *Wall Street Journal* reporter Raymond Cromley, who had been stationed in Japan and was an expert on Japan's military. There was Charles Stelle, a veteran of a guerrilla commando squad who had seen action in Burma and who would choose Japanese targets in North China. Another recruit, Brooke Dolan, had traveled widely in China and Tibet on bird-collecting expeditions sponsored by the Philadelphia Academy of Natural Sciences and was deemed familiar with the Communist-dominated areas.

The ranking civilian was thirty-six-year-old John Stewart Service, who, like his friend John Paton Davies, the political adviser to Stilwell, had been born in China of missionary parents. Service was smart, articulate, sophisticated, good-looking in a very American, Jimmy Stewart sort of way, and one of a group of extremely bright and brave young Chinese-speaking Foreign Service officers whose fates came to be bound up in the treacherous domestic politics of China and America.

The welcome was warm, as could be expected of people who had waited a long time for the arrival of a group of desired guests. The Communists had been trying for years to establish their own relationship with the United States. Zhou Enlai had suggested that a delegation be sent to Yenan in 1943, and Davies had officially proposed exactly that to the State Department. "With the Chinese Communists looking so ominously on the horizon, the American Government was urgently in need of first-hand information about and contact with them," Davies wrote later.

And it was certainly true that, aside from the cordial exchanges between Americans and the Communist representatives in Chungking—Zhou and his aides—the American government had had almost no direct knowledge of a movement that, by early 1944, controlled an area with a population of nearly 100 million people. Were the Communists really fighting the Japanese, as they claimed? Were they ideologues subservient to Moscow and bent on world domination, as the Kuomintang insisted, or were they nationalists whose social and political program, as Stilwell believed, went no further than some benign land reform?

Information on these questions came secondhand from ambiguous sources. One official dispatch written by an American diplomat at the embassy in Chungking conveyed impressions about the Communist movement as if it were on another planet, identified its sources as "a French national who was in Communist-controlled territory," a "Belgian Eurasian who recently travelled through that territory," and "an American airman who crashed in an area controlled by Chinese guerrillas." The White House formally asked Chiang's government for permission to send American military observers to the Communist headquarters in February 1944. Chiang replied that he would "facilitate" this plan, but he stiffly resisted it.

Chiang's resistance was understandable, since the American request amounted to an unofficial recognition of the Communists and their state within the larger state of China. And yet the KMT probably did itself no favors in blocking American contact with the Communists or, for that matter, in its overall propaganda about them, which the American ambassador, Clarence Gauss, termed laden with "obvious untruths," "hardly credible," and "slightly ludicrous." And it was, though it wasn't all wrong either. The official portrayal of the CCP, given by chief of staff Ho Ying-chin to Stilwell's chief of staff, Major General T. G. Hearn, in April, was this: Its aim was "to prolong China's war of resistance as long as possible . . . in the hope of creating a state of general confusion in the Far East [in order to] seize the political power in China to serve as a stepping stone towards a World Revolution." As for Communist troops, Ho said, they were "only an unorganized and undisciplined and untrained horde" that was collaborating with the Japanese, not fighting them. The Communists, moreover, according to Ho, were deeply unpopular in the areas they controlled because their policy was to "terrorize them into submission," but because "there is always the possibility of an armed revolt on the part of the Chinese Communists against the Central Government," it has been necessary to "maintain a certain number of troops in that region." The Americans estimated that about 400,000 government troops maintained a blockade of the Communist area and were unavailable for anti-Japanese combat.

Ho's communication was more a caricature than an outright falsehood. The Communists were indeed a greater long-range threat to Chiang's rule in China than the Japanese, and a "World Revolution" masterminded from Moscow was their ultimate goal, though a much more distant and theoretical one than Ho believed. Under the circumstances, a public relations campaign to prevent any favorable view of the Communists from gaining traction in American policymaking circles was deemed essential to the KMT's survival, and the policies it pursued directly reflected this goal. Western reporters in Chungking suffered a heavy censorship that didn't exactly enhance the government's credibility, nor did the frequent press briefings, which, as Ambassador Gauss put it, consisted largely of the "mouthing of homilies." Unfortunately for the KMT, the foreign press and diplomatic corps came simply to disbelieve the reports put out by the Government Information Office, with its impressive accounts of Chinese victories and staggeringly huge and suspiciously precise figures for Japanese casualties. No detail was overlooked. For some time the authorities banned the use of the word "inflation" from western news reports—this at a time when just about every person in Chungking was suffering from rapidly rising prices.

Needless to say, under the circumstances, no verifiable picture of the Chinese Communists was available in Chungking, where western reporters were based, and, indeed, these reporters were banned even from mentioning the Communists in their dispatches except, as Harrison Forman of the *New York Herald Tribune* later noted, "to quote the Generalissimo and other high government officials when they accused the Communists of 'forcibly occupying national territory,' of 'assaulting National Government troops,' or of 'obstructing the prosecution of the war.'" The foreign reporters' requests to be allowed to visit the Communist areas were entirely unwelcome, and they became more numerous as impatience with censorship increased. Chiang himself worried aloud that the "young and naïve" members of any American observer mission would "believe the CCP's propaganda" and pass along their credulity to "senior officers in Washington."

Chiang was caught between the perceived need to manipulate opinion and the need to maintain a degree of credibility among the foreigners. In addition, by the spring of 1944, the government was getting mauled by the Ichigo offensive in Honan province and was threatened by an attack in Shaanxi, making it more than ever dependent on American Lend-Lease supplies. Chiang also nurtured a certain hope that, contrary to his fears, if western reporters and military observers visited the Communist headquarters in Yenan, they might come to understand the dictatorial and deceitful nature of the Communists. In April, Chiang replied to a formal request submitted by the Foreign Correspondents' Association, whose president was Brooks Atkinson of the *Times*, saying that the government would allow a visit to Yenan—provided the Communists would "guarantee full freedom of movement and investigation during [the] trip in Communist areas."

A few months later, a press delegation consisting of a handful of American and British correspondents left for Yenan, accompanied by both KMT and Communist officials—"minders" in current journalists' parlance. Shortly after, Chiang relented on the request for an official military observer mission and what soon came to be known as the Dixie Mission—because it would be based in rebel territory—was born.

On the day of the observers' arrival in Yenan there was a lunch with Zhu De, commander of the Communist armies, and with Zhou Enlai, who didn't wait to show off his skills at personal diplomacy. "Captain," he said to Jack E. Champion, the pilot of the damaged C-47, "we consider your plane a hero. Fortunately, another hero, yourself, was not injured. Chairman Mao has asked me to convey to you his relief that you came to no harm." Mao himself helped to set the affable tone, writing in an editorial in *Liberation Daily* that the arrival of the mission was "the most exciting event ever since the war against Japan started."

Very soon, Service and Barrett were lunching, dining, and drinking tea with the men who would, four years later, become the leaders of the People's Republic of China, and they liked them. Their dispatches describe the Communist leaders as direct, unpretentious, full of Eagle Scout vigor, and, above all, cordial, accessible, unguarded, and open— these latter qualities were in unspoken contrast to Chiang Kai-shek, who lived in imperious seclusion in his antique-laden hilltop residence outside Chungking, dubbed Peanut's Berchtesgaden by Stilwell. Years later, Mao and other senior Communists were to occupy a garden compound adjacent to the Forbidden City in Beijing surrounded by high walls and a moat and as forbidden to ordinary people as the palace next door had been. But in Yenan they impressed their American visitors with the simplicity of their lives, residing in caves fitted with wooden doors and paper-lined window frames, furnished with rustic desks and tables, as well as a stand for an enamel washbasin. This was not Berchtesgaden; this was more akin to Valley Forge.

The caves themselves were an impressive sight, cut out of the loess cliffs in levels, connected by a geometry of steep zigzag paths. Each cave had an arched entrance, a narrow terrace in front for a small vegetable garden, and perhaps a chicken coop or pigpen or a children's play area. The impression was of a sort of desert encampment on a grand scale, like the children of Israel in the Sinai, or the Roman legions in the Middle East. There was no indoor plumbing. The latrines were located a good distance away. The caves were dimly lit with kerosene lamps and heated by charcoal braziers that emitted a dangerous amount of carbon monoxide; one of the mission members, Melvin A. Casberg, a doctor from St. Louis, warned his colleagues to keep the cave doors open for ventilation when the heat was on. The Communist leaders wore padded cotton jackets and pants unadorned by any insignia of rank, and they said they longed for friendship with America, which, they insisted, they admired for its democratic nature. To Forman, who had been to Yenan a few months before on the journalists' guided tour, the whole scene was "a magnificent symbol of the tenacity and determination of the Border Region people."

After just six days in Yenan, Service reported to the State Department on his initial first impressions, which were "extremely favorable," very much like Forman's. One enters an area like Yenan, he said, "with a conscious determination not to be swept off one's feet," to remain aware that things couldn't be quite as good as they've been described by previous visitors. And yet, he continued, "All of our party have had the same feeling—that we have come into a different country and are meeting a different people."

Among the elements in the picture that impressed Service and, he says, the other members of the observer group were a few absences—"of show and formality, both in speech and action," of "bodyguards, gendarmes and the clap-trap of Chungking officialdom," and of "beggars" and "desperate poverty," both of which were inescapable elsewhere in China. "Mao Zedong and other leaders are universally spoken of with respect (amounting in the case of Mao to a sort of veneration) but these men are approachable and subservience toward them is completely lacking," Service reported. As for the fight against the Japanese, "morale is very high. . . . There is no defeatism, but rather confidence. There is no war-weariness." At the same time, "there is everywhere an emphasis on democracy and intimate relations with the common people." He found himself in agreement with one of the western journalists already there who observed, "We have come to the mountains of North Shaanxi to find the most modern place in China." Most important perhaps, Service ruminated on the likelihood that the KMT would fail in the long run and that the Communists would succeed. "One cannot help coming to feel that [the Communist movement] is strong and successful, and that it has such drive behind it and has tied itself so closely to the people that it will not easily be killed." In this he was entirely correct; this view came to be shared by a majority of the State Department's China experts.

A month after his arrival, Service was received by Mao for a meeting that lasted eight hours, during which the Communist Party chairman pleaded with this junior American diplomat, a mere second secretary from the embassy in Chungking, for long-term cooperation. Mao said he wanted an American consulate to be established in Yenan and to remain there after the end of the war, because, Mao said, the end of the war would mean a withdrawal of the military observers, and an official American civilian presence would deter a Kuomintang attack. Mao requested that the Americans pressure Chiang to undertake democratic reforms, so that the Communists could participate in the government. He worried aloud that if the Kuomintang didn't reform itself, there would be civil war, and then American arms would be used against the Communists. To forestall that prospect, Mao asked that American aid go to all forces fighting the Japanese, including the Communists. He told Service that the Chinese considered Americans to be the "ideal of democracy" and a restraint on the repressiveness of the KMT.

In September, Davies arrived for talks with Mao, Zhou, and others, and his presence in Yenan, where he joined his childhood friend Jack Service, must in its way have been a moving and even portentous event for both men. Like Service, Davies had been born in Sichuan, where his parents were among that evangelical Christian cohort striving to bring the light of Jesus to China, though neither Davies nor Service grew up sharing their parents' proselytizing mission. Instead, they joined the U.S. Foreign Service, and after the United States entered the war, both ended up as political advisers to Stilwell. Davies was headquartered in New Delhi and traveled frequently to China, to Washington, D.C., even to Moscow and to Cairo in 1943 (for the summit among FDR, Stalin, Churchill, and Chiang), where he assessed such questions as British and Soviet aims in the war and how they differed from both China's and America's. He gained a reputation for independence of thought, straightforwardness, and an uncommon ability to ferret out the delusional wishful thinking that was common during the war, especially among Americans.

Some, for example, worshipped Churchill and felt it entirely normal that Britain and America developed a special relationship during the war and that the United States agreed to give the war in Europe priority over the one in Asia, so that bombers needed in China went to Britain instead. But Davies warned that, in Asian eyes, British-American intimacy made it appear that "we have aligned ourselves with the British in a 'white-ocracy' to reimpose western imperialism on Asia." In another report of prophetic accuracy, he warned against taking "steps committing us to colonial imperialism lest we find ourselves aligned with an anachronistic system in vain opposition to the rising tide of Asiatic nationalism, possibly enjoying Russian support." In other words, don't get swept up in Britain's goal of reestablishing its colonial empire in Asia (or France's similar desire) and don't allow Stalin to champion a new order in Asia, while the United States remains attached to the decaying remnants of the past. This was excellent advice, though it wasn't followed a generation later in Vietnam, where another nationalist-Communist revolution was forming.

Davies also understood the tendency of Americans, schooled in the optimistic creed that "all things are possible provided that you have the guts, grit, gumption and go," to overestimate the possibilities of sheer goodwill, especially in the face of the indelible and conflicting ambitions of Asia. "One of our major mistakes," he said in 1943, commenting on the American demand that Chiang put Stilwell directly in charge of his armies, "is attempting the impossible—command over the Chinese." What Davies and Service both understood, and what many of their superiors—including, in this example, Stilwell—didn't, was that to reform China's national armies, Chinese politics would have to be reformed first, and reform would be taken by Chiang Kai-shek as a grave threat to his autocratic regime.

The two men formed the core of a group inside the American embassy in Chungking that had arrived at a realistic assessment of the true nature and prospects of the government of China. They saw the corruption and unpopularity of the Chiang regime at a time when more senior Americans believed in Chiang and his cohort as the indispensable embodiments of China's future. They were convinced that the official American policy of forging a coalition between the KMT and the CCP was bound to fail, because neither party could accept the conditions of the other and survive. Under the circumstances, they were

John Paton Davies poses for a picture with Chinese Communist leaders in Yenan in October 1944. From left: Zhou Enlai, the Communists' chief contact with foreigners; Zhu De (commander in chief of the Communists' army); Davies; Mao Zedong; and Ye Jianying, Zhu's chief of staff.
Reprinted with permission of the University of Pennsylvania Press

utterly convinced that the United States needed to find a way to build relations with the Communists, while maintaining its paramount relationship with the central government and without waiting for that halcyon day when China would be united. The first reason for this was utterly in line with American policy—to gain Communist support in the war against Japan. Everything that the United States did in China, from training and equipping new divisions of Chinese troops to encouraging the KMT and the CCP to bury their differences, was directed toward this aim.

But Davies and Service had a second aim, much less widely accepted—indeed, never accepted as official American policy—but one that indicated a good deal of sympathy for the appeal that Mao was making to them. Like a majority of the China hands actually based in China, Davies and Service had been coming to the conclusion that the war against Japan was going to be followed by a civil war in China and that the Communists were going to win it. To be sure, the Kuomintang was portrayed in the press, and was believed, with some misgivings, by senior policymakers, FDR in particular, to be not just the legitimate government of China, but also a valiant and indispensable party, the inevitable future leaders of an emerging great power.

This was the conventional wisdom that Service, Davies, and the other China hands actually on the scene in China were coming fervently, urgently, to disbelieve. The KMT had lost its revolutionary élan, they felt. It was becoming unpopular among ordinary Chinese and even more so among the intellectual and cultural elite. Its ranks were full of cynical petty tyrants; it was ineffective and, most important, beyond the possibility of reform, which meant that the Communists, who had not lost their revolutionary élan and were using the war to set up numerous base areas behind enemy lines, were going to come to power.

"The lines of future conflict are being formed by the course of the present one," Davies wrote in 1943. "We can now be assured of further war and revolution in our time." After his visit to Yenan, Davies asked the key question: Were the Communists going to take over China? His answer was unambiguous: Yes. Chiang's only chance to survive after the war, Davies wrote, depended on an American "intervention on a scale equal to the Japanese invasion of China," but there was no chance, Davies knew, that the United States would send a million troops to fight in a Chinese civil war right after it had brought its armies home from Europe and the Pacific. And that's why, Davies wrote weeks after his visit to Mao in Yenan, "The Communists are in China to stay. And China's destiny is not Chiang's but theirs."

Davies's hope and expectation was that forging a working relationship with the inevitable future rulers of China would further American interests because only that might induce the Communists to lessen their dependence on the Soviet Union. The United States could get the kind of help in the war against Japan that it found hard to get from the central government, and it could give the Communists options at the same time. By talking with the Communists about military cooperation, Davies wanted to encourage them to think that they might have a friend in the United States after the war. "I hoped that my show of interest might help a bit to keep alive the thought that there perhaps could be an American alternative to war-ravaged, necessitous solidarity with the Soviet Union," he wrote later.

Just how good a possibility that was for the United States depended on just how red the Chinese Communists were, how ideologically committed they were to the global triumph of the international proletariat. In the estimate of Davies and the China hands, they weren't really all that red or all that ideologically committed. In subsequent years, many of the China analysts admitted that the view they had of this matter during the war was tinged with more than a bit of wishful thinking. "I obviously underestimated the commitment of the Chinese Communist ruling party at that time to ideology and the dexterity with which Mao and company manipulated it," Davies was to write. "As I see it now, in the clear light of hindsight," David Barrett confessed in 1969, when Mao's China was engulfed in the vast purge known as the Cultural Revolution, shouting venomous epithets at the United States, "the mistake I made in 1944 was in not considering the Chinese Communists as enemies of the United States. . . . Communism as a political doctrine was just as much anathema to me then as it is now, but I was naïve to the extent that I thought the Chinese members of the Party as Chinese first and communists afterwards."

Davies's belief that the Communists were going to come to power no matter what American experts thought of them meant that nothing would be lost in the attempt to woo them from the Soviet embrace, even if the attempt failed. And if it succeeded, there was a great deal to be gained. His conviction, as he put it later, was that "belief in a creed is susceptible to withering, decay and perversion," which meant that the Chinese Communists might be "backsliders." They "would return to revolutionary ardor only if driven to it by domestic and foreign pressure." This was not the view of such bastions of public opinion as Henry Luce's Time Inc., which burnished the reputation of Chiang for the entire war even as it warned of the dread consequences of a Communist takeover of China.

But among the China experts, the journalists, and many of the military advisers in China, starting with Stilwell, two trends developed over time. One was the disillusionment and irritation with Chiang and the KMT that we've seen taking hold among Stilwell, the professional China hands in the State Department who advised him, and among some of the journalists; the other was a hopefulness directed toward Mao among many of those same people, an admiration of the Communists for not sharing Chiang's alleged traits of hypocritical inactivity and excuse-laden passivity toward the Japanese.

"China is in a mess," Second Secretary Service wrote in a State Department dispatch in March 1944. "No military action on a significant scale is in sight. . . . Internal unrest is active and growing. . . . For the sorry situation as a whole Chiang, and only Chiang, is responsible." A month before the start of the Dixie Mission, the American ambassador, Clarence Gauss, cabled Secretary of State Cordell Hull that a "general gloom and a discouraged and somewhat defeatist attitude is becoming prevalent at Chungking in Chinese official and other circles." The Kuomintang-led government, Gauss said, had failed to "offer any appreciable resistance" to the Japanese in Henan, which was at the time the main target of the Ichigo offensive. Chinese peasants, afflicted by their own "deplorable conditions," were turning on Chinese troops, while in China's urban centers "there is covert and fearful criticism by officers, intellectuals and others of Generalissimo Chiang; of his complete concentration of all power and authority in his own hands . . . of his present capricious, suspicious and irascible attitude on both domestic and foreign problems . . . of his attitude of suspicion of Soviet Russia and his irritation that he has not been able to infect the United States with such suspicion."

In retrospect, it is easy to see that Chiang's apprehensions regarding the Soviet Union and his wish to persuade the United States of his view were understandable and justified. But at the time, Stalin was the brave ally who was taking the brunt of the Nazi attack at Moscow and Stalingrad, and it was not in the American character to be overly suspicious of such an ally. The American view was encapsulated by Roosevelt, who assured Churchill in 1942 that he could "handle Stalin better than your Foreign Office." Warned by some of his advisers that Stalin would devour whole countries after the war, Roosevelt's feeling was that "Stalin is not that kind of man." It is not clear what kind of man Gauss thought Stalin was, but his generally sour view of Chiang seems to have led him to dismiss him even when he was right.

And that was the mechanism by which many Americans in the field (the perceptive and hardheaded Gauss not among them) grew enchanted with the Communists as their contempt for the Nationalists intensified. The American press was not monolithic in its portrayals of China either, and, indeed, for many reporters based in China, as for most Americans, the Chinese Nationalists remained valiant resistance fighters against the Japanese occupier. But here and there in 1944 and increasingly in 1945, the gloomier views of Chiang and his government got through to the American public, and Chiang himself was aware of it. "American public opinion toward China is becoming increasingly critical in the U.S. . . . . If we have a failing, we must correct it," he told his closest advisers in March, around the time that Service was blaming him for China's "sorry situation."

The increasing skepticism regarding Chiang was well summed up in a 1943 *New York Times* analysis by Hanson Baldwin, a highly respected military analyst who had earlier won a Pulitzer Prize for his coverage of the battle of Guadalcanal. All those earlier reports of Chinese victories over Japan were incorrect, he wrote. "China is unquestionably losing most of her battles with Japan," whose soldiers "can go anywhere they please in China at any time since the Chinese defenses against them are weak." There was, Baldwin wrote, a misunderstanding of Japanese actions in China, encouraged by the tendency of the official communiqués of the Chinese government to misinterpret them. Unlike the Germans in Russia, the Japanese were striving to police and administer the vast areas of China they already held, not to seize new territory, Baldwin wrote. Their troops went out on forays so as to "dislocate Chinese offensive preparations," and they sometimes suffered casualties in the skirmishes with Chinese troops before they withdrew to their original positions, and these skirmishes were magnified by the official communiqués into "battles and the usual Japanese retirement to their original positions into major strategic 'retreats.' "

Baldwin amplified his view, adding more detail, in a companion piece published in *Reader's Digest* whose title was "Too Much Wishful Thinking about China." But despite his clairvoyance on the military situation, Baldwin's own thinking retained some elements of wishfulness regarding Chiang and the KMT. While China's armed forces are "weak," he said in his *Times* analysis, the "will of Free China to resist, symbolized by one man—Generalissimo Chiang Kai-shek—is still a major determinant in the affairs of the Orient."

Davies and Stilwell, who believed this to be claptrap, didn't shy away from back-channel efforts to influence public opinion. The two were in Washington in 1943, and Davies arranged several meetings for Stilwell, including one with more than a score of reporters at the home of Eugene Meyer, the publisher of the *Washington Post*, during which Stilwell got his views of Chiang across.

———

In this atmosphere, it was perhaps not surprising that diplomats, military officers, and journalists alike would see in the Communists a hopeful alternative, an idea that had been fostered for years by a group of pathbreaking journalists, most conspicuous among them Edgar Snow, the keen, young, adventurous, and leftist China expert whose book *Red Star over China,* published in early 1938, gave a glowing, novelistic introduction of the Communist movement to the American public. Snow had spent about four months with Mao and his cohort in 1936, not long after the Communists had escaped the KMT's encirclement campaigns against them and set up a new base area in Shaanxi province. Mao granted Snow many long nights' worth of interviews, and the resulting book sold out its first edition of 4,800 copies the day after it was published, and it remained a best-seller for months afterward.

Red Star was enormously influential. After living in a haze of legend and rumor, the "Chinese Soviets," as the Communists were commonly called, were suddenly famous, presented to the western public in a brilliantly written, credible first-person account describing them as the heroes of a glorious and thrilling adventure story. Here were the men, and a few women, who had survived Chiang Kai-shek's persistent attempts to annihilate them, who had endured the grueling, death-defying trial by fire of the Long March, and were now fighting a clever, scrappy, and courageous guerrilla campaign against the reprehensible Japanese invaders.

"If the book has been correctly interpreted," the reviewer in *The New York Times* intoned, "the significance of Red China is not that it is red but that it is Chinese and that it may portend the long-predicted 'awakening' of the Chinese people and the ultimate frustration of Japanese imperialism." The reviewer, one R. L. Duffus, does not fail to mention the "treachery, venality, and incompetence" of the leaders of the central government of Chiang Kai-shek, along with the horrors of what he called China's "pagan medievalism," and, of course, Japan's effort to reduce the country to "imperialistic serfdom." The Duffus review quotes Snow himself to the effect that it was "no wonder, when the Red Star appeared in the northwest, thousands of men arose to welcome it as a symbol of hope and freedom."

Red Star over China was and still is a journalistic classic, but it was also a carefully planned and brilliantly executed public relations coup engineered less by Snow himself than by the Communists, who chose him to break their story to the world. Mao and the CCP wanted to garner attention for themselves in the western press at a time when the Chiang regime had banned even the mention of the Communist movement in China's newspapers. The evidence is strong that they identified Snow as the right person to invite to their mountain stronghold. While he leaned to the left politically, he had a reputation for independence—unlike the fellow traveling journalists who made no secret of their preference for the Communists—and he would thus have the credibility they wanted in their effort to end their isolation from world public opinion.

Snow had come to China in 1928, an ambitious young man eager to make his mark. He started in Shanghai, where he was befriended by both Agnes Smedley, the rebellious, feminist, pro-Communist, anti-KMT writer, and Soong Qingling, the widow of Sun Yat-sen, who, in contrast to her younger sister Mei-ling, Chiang's wife, had become an opponent of Chiang and an influential, virtually untouchable critic of his "white terror." By 1935, Snow was living with his wife in Beijing (called Peiping at the time) and writing about China for the *Saturday Evening Post*, which had the second-largest circulation among magazines in the 1930s. He also wrote articles for the *New York Sun* and the *London Daily Herald*, which had named him a special correspondent.

In Beijing, Snow and his elegant, glamorous, equally ambitious wife, Helen Foster Snow, known also by the pen name Nym Wales, had befriended students in Beijing and helped them organize mass demonstrations in late 1935 against Japan and against the KMT's policy of fighting the Communists rather than the Japanese. Not long after the demonstrations, the Snows were approached by a young man who went by the name David Yui—Chinese name: Yu Qiwei. He was an agent in North China of the Comintern, the Soviet-led organization that helped, advised, inspired, financed, and often controlled Communist parties outside the Soviet Union. Yui was a well-placed man of twenty-four. The Snows knew him to be a Communist, the only one they socialized with in Beijing, where the Communist apparatus was almost nonexistent. Among Yui's contributions to the Communist revolution was his recruitment of his Shanghai girlfriend, the actress Jiang Qing, into the party, the same Jiang Qing who would soon go to Yenan, become Mao's fourth wife, and, years later, serve as a radical firebrand in the Cultural Revolution of 1966–76.

Snow wanted to visit the Communist base area, which at the time was in the old walled town of Bao-an, north of their future home in

Yenan. It would be, he wrote to an editor, "a world scoop on a situation about which millions of words have been written, based only on hearsay and highly colored government reports." He expressed his wish to Yui, who seems to have helped broker an invitation from the Communist leadership. Snow also got help from Soong Qingling, whom he visited in Shanghai and asked to use her influence with the Communists to secure their permission for his trip.

The trip was thus at Snow's initiative, but in the months before the Xian Incident ended Chiang's campaigns against them, the Communists were thinking along the same lines. Specifically, Stalin, like Mao, was looking for ways to force Chiang to end his anti-Communist offensive and to fight Japanese aggression instead. As we've seen, Stalin was deeply worried that Japan would secure an easy victory in North China and then be free to strike across the border into Soviet Siberia. Mao's parallel worry was that Chiang would make peace with Japan, thereby freeing him to pursue his campaign of annihilation against the Communists, whose forces had been depleted by the campaigns in Jiangxi and by the Long March. "To change this situation," one historian has written of Snow's pathbreaking visit, "and force Chiang to drop his bloody fixation, required, as Stalin saw it, and as Mao came to agree, some dramatic public relations campaign that would give the revolutionists validity in the eyes of the world as a legitimate popular Chinese political movement."

Snow and Mao perfectly matched each other: the former, as one of his biographers has put it, was "a romantic adventurer in search of a literary grail," while the latter saw himself as a reincarnation of the bandit heroes of *Romance of the Three Kingdoms*, the swashbuckling classic that Mao had read in his youth about a time of turbulence in China's long history. The stories he told Snow of guerrilla warfare in Jiangxi, the dangers and hardships of the Long March, and his patriotic, anti-Japanese ardor perfectly fit Snow's own hatred of Japanese and western imperialism, his identification with China's struggle, his dislike of Chiang and the KMT, and, perhaps above all, his yearning to write an epic story.

Snow's evident partiality to the Communists was amply reciprocated in their treatment of him. Escorted on a trip with the Eighth Route Army, he was greeted at the entrance to one town he visited by a banner reading "Welcome the American Internationalist to Investigate the Soviet Regions." Bugles rang out as he entered through the gate in the town's ancient wall, while troops from three Red Army divisions lined up singing songs, shouting slogans, and saluting as he passed. "I felt," Snow noted in his diary, "like a generalissimo with his prick out." In one place, he played tennis every morning with three members of the Northwest Branch Soviet Government. He taught the wives of the Bao-an elite to play gin rummy. When he left Bao-an on October 12, the entire Communist leadership, except for Mao, who famously slept late, came to see him off, shouting "*Shi Lo Tungzhi Wansui!*"—Ten thousand years to Comrade Snow!"

Comrade Snow! Snow didn't give himself this honorific. Still he was no neutral, much less a skeptical observer. He was a talented and enterprising young man with abundant literary talents enacting the historical role of *l'homme engagé*, as the French put it, the man participating in the great cause of his time. Snow was not a Communist himself. Zhou Enlai was not just covering for him when he told the American China expert Owen Lattimore in 1941 that Snow would never understand what Marxism was. He was indeed quintessentially American, a choir boy in his youth, an Eagle Scout, a believer in democratic freedoms who had discovered one of the great stories of the twentieth century. And yet his identification with Mao, perhaps his vested interest in the position he staked out on the Chinese revolution, led him unwaveringly to champion Mao and the Chinese revolution long after it had become clear that Mao himself was no believer in democratic freedoms. In doing this, Snow became an apologist for a dictator. He suffered for this. Later in his life he found it almost impossible to find work as a journalist or writer in the United States, because he was viewed as partisan, an advocate for a discredited cause, which he was.

Snow was not the only one. He belonged to a group of people who were dismissive of the Nationalists and favorable toward the Communists to varying degrees—from rhapsodic championship of their cause to more sober appraisals of the chance they were more nationalistic and democratic than ideological and hard-line. There were diplomats, military officers, and journalists in this amorphous group, which in the end formed one side of what was to become a bitter, irreconcilable division in American life, in which their advice would go ignored, their careers be ruined, and China and the United States become enemies.

Some of this group, especially the Foreign Service China experts, had gotten to know each other in Beijing in the early to mid-1930s, when they were young, drawn to the romance of China, and imbued with a dislike of both the Japanese imperialists and the KMT for what they saw as its repressive nature. Among them were Chinese-language officers at the American legation, Jack Service, John Davies, Raymond Ludden, and, Snow's best friend in Beijing, O. Edmund Clubb, all of whom were to occupy important positions as diplomatic experts on China, and all of whom, like Snow, were later to be shadowed by the charge that they had been, at best, naïve and, at worst, treasonous in their portrayals of the Communists. It was Clubb who urged Snow to undertake his trip to Shaanxi, wanting like his colleagues at the American legation to break the KMT's blockade of information about the Communists, to know who they were, and to be able to report accurately on them to the State Department.

A few of the old Beijing crowd were together again in 1938 in Hankou, where they were joined by a few others who were to play significant roles in the ferocious later debates about China. Hankou, the industrial center on the Yangzi, was the temporary KMT capital for a few months following the Japanese seizure of Nanjing and before the KMT's more permanent move farther up the river, past the great Yangzi gorges, to Chungking. Davies was there as a Foreign Service officer. Stilwell was the military attaché, accompanied by his closest aide, Captain (later General) Jack Dorn, known as Pinky to his friends. A few journalists covering the Sino-Japanese War in those years before the United States got into the war had also moved to Hankou, Snow, newly famous as the author of *Red Star*, among them, along with his wife and some other left-wing journalists, including Agnes Smedley; Freda Utley, who was English; Anna Louise Strong; and Jack Belden of the United Press, a frequent traveling companion of Stilwell, who later accompanied him on the famous walk out of Burma in 1942. Evans Carlson, a Marine Corps officer, was in Hankou also. He had been able to observe the Eighth Route Army in North China even before Snow made his trip there. Carlson left the Marines when he was forbidden publicly to express his admiration for the Communists.

They called themselves the last-ditchers, the dozen or so Anglo-Americans in Hankou, a city that everybody knew was directly in the path of the Japanese juggernaut moving inexorably up the Yangzi Valley. The war was near, as Davies put it, in the form of "air raids, troop movements, wounded soldiers arriving from the front, Soviet 'volunteer' airmen and German military advisors in the streets, hordes of dazed refugees fleeing before the oncoming enemy, students rushing about the city pasting patriotic posters on walls and calling on everyone to resist the foe, and finally the Communists planting dynamite in key buildings to greet the invaders with a scorched earth." The diplomats and journalists and others used to gather for meals and conversation, always about Japan and its unforgivable brutality, about China, the Nationalists and the Communists, at Davies's apartment, which was in the stately Hong Kong and Shanghai Bank Building, or at a restaurant called Rosie's.

The last-ditchers liked each other, and according to the *Times*'s Tilman Durdin, there was "close collaboration and friendship between correspondents and American officials in Hankou." The common thread was what Durdin called their "deep sympathy" for China and its suffering under the Japanese. Among them, Smedley, Strong, and the Snows were unabashed admirers of the Communists and, almost by definition, opponents of the KMT. The more hardheaded analysts like Davies viewed these rhapsodic pro-Maoists with wry detachment, and the notion that the Communists represented a dawn of freedom and hope was not universally shared; even some of Snow's friends chided him for writing a pro-Mao rhapsody rather than an objective, skeptical report. Still, the body of work produced by the journalists in the group was favorable to the Communists and disparaging of the KMT. As early as 1934, Agnes Smedley had published *China's Red Army Marches*, an impassioned account, based on interviews with Communist commanders, of the early effort led by Mao to create a Soviet-style republic in Jiangxi province in south central China. Smedley later published two more books full of glowing descriptions of the Communists, *China Fights Back* in 1939 and *Battle Hymn of China* in 1943. Anna Louise Strong's *One-Fifth of Mankind: China Fights for Freedom*, published in 1938, is in the same political genre. Not to be outdone by her famous husband, Helen Snow also traveled to the Communist area and in 1939 published, as Nym Wales, *Inside Red China*, which, like Snow's *Red Star*, was enthusiastically pro-Mao. More than a few other young Americans looking for adventure went to China in the late 1930s, and some wrote books that, while forgotten today, enhanced the portraits of the heroic Communist guerrillas and the vicious Japanese occupiers alike. *Humane Endeavor: The Story of the China War*, by Haldore Hanson, a young man who traveled with Communist troops behind enemy lines, was heralded in 1939 in the *New York Times* as "a thrilling description of a world within a conqueror's world, living its own life with the shadows of bayonets over it, but at times paying the ultimate penalty meted out by the Japanese with their Punic vengeance." It is difficult to say exactly to what extent these portrayals of China's revolutionaries seeped into the public consciousness or formed the background to the later views of diplomats. The books of Snow, Smedley, and others were counterbalanced by Luce's mass-circulation *Time* and *Life*, whose portraits of the Nationalists were almost as favorable as the leftist portraits of the Communists. Yet it is striking that, in their more sober ways, many other analysts who were in no way leftists or pro-Communist romantics adopted positions, mostly expressed in official government communications, not all that different from those of Snow and Smedley. Stilwell, a registered Republican and a political conservative all his life, believed that the Communists' goal was "land ownership under reasonable conditions." Frank Merrill, who commanded Merrill's Marauders, told Mike Mansfield during Mansfield's inspection of China at the end of 1944 that the Chinese Communists "were not allied to Moscow but were primarily a Chinese agrarian group interested in land and tax reforms."

Mansfield's own conclusion about the Communists: They are "a force to be reckoned with," having 90 million people under their control under "a system of government which is quite democratic." As for the Kuomintang, it

> is hated more every day and this is due to fear of the army and the attitude of tax collectors; and is proved by the revolts of the peasantry, the party criticism by provincial leaders, students [*sic*] revolts against conscription and the fact that many Chinese will stoop to anything to get to America and, once there, to stay there. It is corrupt. It speaks democratically but acts dictatorially. The worst censorship in the world is located in Chungking and there is one detective assigned to every ten foreigners. . . . Meetings of Liberals are invaded by Kuomintang toughs, spies are everywhere and people are afraid to talk.

This was a vision both of themselves and of their KMT rivals that the Communists themselves did their best to foster in what, especially after the American entry into the Pacific war at the end of 1941, became a creative, multifaceted campaign to influence American public opinion and to gain support from the American government. The remarkable person, the glowing personality, the diplomatic genius, who both masterminded and embodied this effort was Zhou Enlai.

Zhou's contact with American diplomats and journalists began during the brief Hankou period, when, under the terms of the United Front, which was in its early phase of goodwill, he was the official Communist representative in the KMT capital, and he made himself readily available to the American and British diplomats and journalists who were stationed there, a practice that he continued in Chungking for the entire war. In May 1942, Zhou gave a letter to Edgar Snow, asking him to pass it along to Lauchlin Currie, one of Roosevelt's chief White House aides, in which he enumerated the Communists' military successes against the Japanese and, for the first time, asked the United States to give some of its China aid directly to the CCP. Zhou soon proposed what eventually became the Dixie Mission, and he expanded his journalistic charm offensive from well-known leftists like the Snows and Agnes Smedley to the more neutral members of the mainstream press whose numbers had increased in Chungking after Pearl Harbor and who, Zhou knew, were becoming increasingly disillusioned with Chiang and the KMT.

Only a few years before, Zhou had been a man with a high price on his head. Now, because of the United Front and the supposed alliance between the CCP and the KMT, he lived mostly in Chungking, where he maintained an active social calendar, mixing comfortably at dinners and receptions with American diplomats and journalists, explaining China to them, striving to reassure them of the reasonableness of the Communist movement, the treachery of the Kuomintang right wing, and the contribution the Communists could make in the fight against Japan, if only the United States would allow them to. Zhou was so smooth, so articulate, so sophisticated in his analyses, so worldly, cultivated, and seemingly sincere, that he was viewed less as a partisan for one of the two main armed and competing parties in China and more as a friend, as some of the journalists called him, and a reliable source.

"Zhou Enlai had an amazing mind, for detail as well as for synthesis, a memory that could with ease recollect dates, quotations, episodes, incidents," Theodore H. White, the *Time* correspondent in Chungking from 1941 to 1945, later wrote, saying that he had "become friends" with Zhou early on in his China sojourn. White, who was one of the best and most famous journalists of the middle decades of the twentieth century, was veritably worshipful of Zhou, who, he wrote, "was, along with Joseph Stilwell and John F. Kennedy, one of the three great men I met and knew in whose presence I had near total suspension of disbelief or questioning judgment." Later he understood Zhou to be "a man as brilliant and ruthless as any the Communist movement has thrown up in this century," but he "had a way of entrancing people, of offering affection, of inviting and seeming to share confidences. And I cannot deny that he won my affection completely."

It was the ruthlessness that was well hidden, that and Zhou's total devotion to the cause that defined his life. Zhou was complex. He was in style, family background, and education more like the urbane, humanist intellectuals who founded the Communist Party in the early 1920s than the callow and shallow, semi-educated zealots who took over the party in its later, radical phase. He came from a family of scholar-officials of the sort who, having passed the Confucian exams, had staffed the imperial bureaucracy in bygone days but had fallen into obscurity as the Manchu dynasty collapsed. Zhou went to the Nankai Academy in Tianjin, which was an ultra-elite Chinese high school, a kind of Asian Eton or Harrow, modern, reformist, and public-spirited. He studied English, was editor of the student newspaper, acted in plays, and finished at the top of his class. Then, like many of China's brightest young people, Zhou spent a couple of years in Japan before returning to China at the end of World War I.

There, in the northern port city of Tianjin, he joined the secretive "Awakening Society," one of the many study groups that opposed the warlord-dominated government of China and discussed competing visions of national revitalization. Like many such students, Zhou studied Marxism and even met a few of the intellectual-scholar types who, inspired by the success and the promise of the Bolshevik revolution in Russia, founded the Chinese Communist Party in 1921. He spent from 1921 to 1924 in Europe, traveling to London and Berlin but staying mostly in Paris. It was there that he joined a Communist cell and became a leader in the overseas branch of the fledgling CCP, then, under close Comintern supervision, allied to the KMT in the first United Front.

When Zhou came home, he was already well connected and highly regarded in the movement that was going to remake China. Though only twenty-six years old, he was appointed political commissar of the Whampoa Military Academy down the Pearl River from Canton, a school created to form a modern, skilled Chinese officer corps. The academy was led by another man of China's future, the lean and hungry Chiang Kai-shek. Zhou's job was to instruct cadets in the ideology of the KMT, which at the time was, like the CCP, a revolutionary party being advised by a Comintern agent.

The United Front, as we've seen, lasted until 1927, when Chiang carried out his preemptive coup against the Communists, and from that point on, Zhou was in opposition. And being in opposition meant total engagement in the clandestine and brutal life-and-death struggle with the KMT agents whose task was to hunt down Communists and kill them. This is the part of Zhou's history that was undetected by his American friends later in Chungking. Zhou, living underground in Shanghai under assumed names, switching from safe house to safe house, never appearing in public, was the founding head of the Communists' secret police force, the *Teke*, which included a platoon of assassins known as the Red Squad. In 1931, one of Zhou's agents, a certain Gu Shunzhang, was arrested by the KMT police and after being tortured provided information that led to the capture and assassination of some Communist operatives in Shanghai. In retaliation, Zhou ordered the Red Squad to assassinate Gu's entire family, some fifteen people, and this order was scrupulously carried out. Shortly after that, another of Zhou's agents was seized when, disobeying Zhou's orders, he spent the night in a hotel with his mistress. The agent, tortured before being killed, gave away Zhou's cover, which forced him to leave Shanghai for Mao's rural base area in Guangxi province, a wanted man.

This history suggests an essential element in the Chinese picture. The partnership known as the Second United Front, formed to combat Japan, theoretically made the two biggest parties in China friends and allies, but the depth and deadliness of their recent struggles with each other left behind a residue of hatred and distrust that was ineradicable, especially in a culture with no experience or tradition of peaceful political competition. And so here was Zhou Enlai, who had a few short years before been engaged in a game of murder and revenge, set up in the Kuomintang's temporary capital, engaging in the gentle arts of political socializing and persuasion, meeting regularly with foreign journalists and diplomats and trying to persuade them that the Communists were reasonable and trustworthy. He lived with his staff of half a dozen in a ramshackle old compound deep in a Chungking alley, which became ankle-deep in mud whenever it rained. There was a reception room with a few chairs and a couch all covered "with the same coarse blue cloth worn by Chinese peasants and workers."

Except for Mao, the elite of the Chinese Communist movement, including Dong Biwu, one of the founders of the party—"no one could have seemed milder, frailer, kindlier," White said of him—was made available there for American callers. The casual modesty of Zhou's headquarters, especially compared with the forbidding formality of Chiang's, made a favorable impression, similar in its way to the Valley Forge–like encampment in Yenan.

It was a seduction literal and figurative. One of Zhou's assistants— "his personal favorite and mine," according to White—was a certain Gong Peng, who, White adds, "was the most beautiful Chinese woman I ever encountered." Gong used to give the daily Communist briefings to the foreign press, carrying carbons of the latest Radio Yenan broadcasts to the downtown Press Hostel and distributing them to the various foreign journalists who lived there. She was, White says, the daughter of a "warlord" and, as an anti-Japanese guerrilla fighter from the revolutionary mecca of Yenan, "a true pistol packing heroine." This enhanced her appeal for White, who was a romantic at heart, prone to unreciprocated infatuations, though there seems to have been some exaggeration in his description of Gong, who wasn't a warlord's daughter and never packed a pistol. She did nonetheless exemplify the sort of young person who flocked to the Communist cause in those years and who helped to give it its allure of fashion and political chic.

Gong's father had gone to the same Japanese military academy as Chiang Kai-shek, and he played a prominent role in the overthrow of the Manchu dynasty. His stories of that event later thrilled his daughter, who loved reading Chinese Robin Hood fiction as a girl. Three years into the new republic, its president, a former imperial military commander named Yuan Shikai, declared himself a new emperor, and when Gong Peng's father wrote a manifesto condemning Yuan for this imperial pretention, he was obliged to escape China to save his life. He took his family to Yokohama, where Gong Peng was born in 1914. Her birth name was Gong Cisheng, a Buddhist phrase meaning "compassion for all living beings."

A few years later, Yuan died amid nationwide resistance to his rule, and the Gong family moved to Shanghai. There, Gong Peng and her older sister attended St. Mary's Hall, a selective all-girl institution founded by Episcopal missionaries in 1850 where Chinese middle-class families sent their daughters. After graduation in 1933, the Gong girls went to Yenching University in Beijing, another elite institution founded by Protestant missionaries, where there was an active Communist cell. She was a leader in the anti-Japanese student demonstrations in 1935. In 1936 she joined the Communist Party. While in Beijing, she became close to Edgar and Helen Snow. After Snow's return from Yenan in 1937, she and a group of her friends met at the Beijing home of Randolph Sailor, an American psychologist, who showed them the original typescript of *Red Star over China* along with a short film that Snow had made during his stay in Shaanxi province. Thus it was through a foreign journalist's account that Gong and other left-leaning Chinese students became acquainted with Mao's thrilling revolutionary movement. "On the tiny screen of the Snow family," Gong's daughter wrote years later, "Mom first saw the liveliness of Yenan and its soldiers and how energetic and vigorous Mao Zedong, Zhu De, and other revolutionary leaders were, and it was almost as if she could breathe in the atmosphere of Yenan."

Thus inspired, in 1938, with Shanghai under Japanese occupation, Gong Peng joined the youthful throngs who went from China's most advanced cities to the Yenan hinterland, traveling in the company of a couple of friends—"their young and aspiring hearts full of passion," her daughter later wrote. Once, while taking a walk along a local stream, she encountered Mao himself. He asked her name, which while at Yenching University she'd changed from Cisheng to Weihang, meaning "sustain the voyage." In Yenan she'd changed her name again, to Gong Peng, after a revolutionary martyr named Peng Bai. Mao told her she had made a good choice, and after that, she regularly attended his lectures, sitting in a front row and taking notes. She would be a devoted pupil of Chairman Mao for the rest of her life.

She married in Yenan in 1940, and after her husband was sent off on a mission, she was transferred to Chungking, where her fluent English made her useful on Zhou's staff. Two years later she learned that her husband had been killed, and three years after that, she married another Zhou protégé, Qiao Guanhua, a gifted, handsome young graduate of Qinghua University who edited *The Masses*, a Communist magazine. (According to John K. Fairbank, who knew them both, their meager wardrobe was stolen by a thief who inserted a pole with a hook on it through a window grating, whereupon Fairbank gave Qiao one of his Oxford tailored suits.) Qiao became foreign minister of China in the 1970s but was purged during one of China's later factional conflicts.

In Chungking, Gong achieved a kind of celebrity status with the foreign press corps, now hundreds of journalists strong, many of them young men charmed by the slender, comely, twenty-eight-or-so-year-old woman who spoke to them in perfect English and evidently believed fervently in what she said. In that, she offered a pleasant contrast to the glib press officers of the Kuomintang, with their daily fabrications, the regime of censorship, the atmosphere, as Ambassador Gauss put it, of the "slightly ridiculous."

Fairbank, then an OSS officer whose job was to collect Chinese and Japanese written materials for the Department of War Information, was sufficiently taken by the Gong Peng phenomenon to note it in a letter to his wife, Wilma, back home, describing her as "the official appointee for contact with barbarians" with "a taming effect on everybody I know," mentioning Brooks Atkinson of *The New York Times*, the broadcast journalist Eric Sevareid, Chennault's aide Joe Alsop, and "part of the British embassy" as especially smitten. According to Sevareid, she was less an object of sexual desire than a kind of unattainable beauty, inspiring a sort of courtly devotion. She was, he later wrote, "the leading spirit" of Zhou's headquarters, "a tall-stemmed flower." She was "graciousness, urbanity, but she was also the fresh, trusting decency of open-faced youth. . . . In her presence the male-female feeling all but disappeared, replaced by a sexless awe and admiration. . . . More than a few foreign correspondents and diplomats fancied themselves in love with her—but it was a little too much like falling in love with Joan of Arc."

While the press's relations with the KMT press office were tense and formal—Sevareid, for example, described it as "a place of mockery and make-believe, solemnly repeated day after day"—the inclination of many of the American journalists was to sympathize with Gong Peng, and to believe her. Also contributing to her favor among the foreigners was the general image of the Communists, formed, not by their headquarters in Yenan, but by Zhou's modest establishment in Chungking, whose members were constantly under secret police surveillance and perpetually worried about arrest. "The CCP in Chungking was still an isolated group of underdogs and no sense of menace attached to them," Fairbank recalled. In that atmosphere, he wrote later, Gong was "the voice of dissidence in a city of yes men and time servers. She was the spokesman of the outs, whose ideals of betterment exposed the evils of the ins," though Fairbank recalls the one-sidedness of her role. "What she put forward was a liberal bill of particulars against the KMT—its assassinations, press suppression, smashing of printing plants, railroading of liberal critics, refusal to permit demonstrations, denial of the right to strike, and so on," he wrote to his wife—all "civil liberties that the CP also denied." And that the Communists, once in power, have denied ever since. Still, few of Gong Peng's admirers noted this inconsistency. Severeid, normally as hardheaded and perceptive as a journalist can be, bemoaned what he called her "heartbreaking life," trapped in Kuomintang-controlled Chungking, where she was kept under constant watch by the government secret police, a life that "only a woman of soul and exalted vision" could have endured. Once, speaking to Sevareid, Gong expressed her longing to breathe the air of freedom, by which, no doubt, the Americans assumed, this alumna of two missionary schools meant American-style freedom. "If only I could be for a little while in a place where there is freedom," she told him once, "just to see what it is like again for a little while."

The press corps used to try to concoct schemes by which Gong could go to the United States on some sort of scholarship. Meanwhile, they watched over her. Severeid talks about a "silent conspiracy" among the correspondents and foreign diplomats that if she ever disappeared into the swamp of the KMT's secret police, they would call it to the

Qiao Guanhua, an aide to Zhou Enlai at the Communist wartime delegation in Chungking, and his wife, Gong Peng, Zhou's press secretary, in 1943. Gong especially inspired a powerful fascination on the part of numerous western diplomats and journalists

attention of the world, make it a diplomatic incident. Once she came down with dysentery. Fairbank told Atkinson that she was sick, and he arranged for her to be seen by an American navy doctor, who cured her with sulfa drugs. On another occasion, Gong contacted John Service to tell him that her husband, Qiao, was sick and needed a blood transfusion. Service volunteered to donate some of his own blood, and though in the end Qiao recovered without his doing so, his gesture showed something a bit more than purely professional interest in Gong. Still later, after the war, another journalist, Barbara Stevens, who had gotten to know Gong Peng in Chungking, transported the infant son she'd had with Qiao to Gong's family in Shanghai.

It's tempting to see something sexually intentional in Zhou's choice of Gong Peng to be his press secretary in Chungking. The Chinese Thirty-six Strategems, an ancient compilation of adages about how to prevail in war and politics, includes "the beauty trap," the dispatch of a woman to the enemy's camp to induce its soldiers to neglect their duties, allow their vigilance to wane, and perhaps to fight among themselves for her favor. Certainly the attitude of much of the American press corps toward Gong Peng bespoke the feeling they had toward many of the Communist revolutionaries they encountered in Chungking, so likable and attractive in real life, so different from the prevailing image of the Communist, the Red, the Bolshevik, the Marxist-Leninist. "She was not only young and beautiful," a Chinese journalist wrote of Gong Peng in Chungking during the war, "but was very well-mannered and wore a *qipao* [a close-fitting dress with a slit up one thigh] and sat on a chair and looked very sincere, which made all the journalists stare at her, and because she spoke fluent English, she became an archetype of beauty and revolution."

It's telling in this regard that a few years later, after the Communists had taken power, there were a few instances when Gong Peng, now a senior official in China's Ministry of Foreign Affairs, crossed paths with some of the reporters she had charmed back in Chungking. She had become a Communist bureaucrat, distant, severe, and unapproachable. In the early months after the "liberation," before American reporters were expelled from the country, she snubbed the old friends who encountered her, or she crossed the street to avoid them. In the 1950s, she became the head of the information department of the foreign ministry, in charge of handling the very few foreign journalists, mostly from Africa or Asia, who went on highly controlled visits to China.

When the Canadian journalist William Stevenson saw her in China in 1956, she reprimanded him for taking pictures of ancient monuments rather than showing the country's revolutionary progress. She went with Zhou Enlai to Geneva in 1954 during the conference that ended the French war in Indochina, and some of the Americans covering the event who knew her back in the Chungking days tried to renew the acquaintance, but were rebuffed. At a banquet, she objected when a newsreel photographer took her picture while she was lighting a cigarette. She made no further public appearances, despite the fact that she was supposedly Zhou's press officer. She remained, in the words of one journalist present, "in seclusion at the Beau-Rivage Hotel, a brooding, grave-faced woman in a filmy blue dress."

The Communist seduction didn't work on everybody. Tillman Durdin, the *New York Times* correspondent in China in the days right after the war, told one friend that "Zhou overwhelmed you by the force of his personality and his clever arguments. But after hearing him month after month and year after year, you can't trust what he says." Still, the Communists' effort to present themselves in a favorable light, including Zhou's part of it in Chungking, was an amazing success, even if some of that success came not so much because the Communists seemed so good but because the KMT was so bad. "It was so utterly hopeless in free China," Durdin said, explaining the common attitude about both the KMT and the CCP in China. "The graft, the misery, the lack of will to fight any more. Even I felt that it could not be worse and must be better in Communist China."

Favorable press coverage of the Communists reached an apex during the reporters' trip to Yenan when it was finally allowed by Chiang in the spring of 1944. It was a remarkably successful venture for the Communists and a public relations fiasco for the KMT. Israel Epstein, a Polish-born Jew whose family had gone to Asia in 1920 to flee anti-Semitism, reported on the trip for the *Times* and other publications. His dispatches were chock full of startling contrasts between the bold and democratic Communists and the corrupt, decadent, repressive KMT.

In his first dispatch for the *Times*, he wrote about Xian, the government-controlled city that the delegation passed through on their way to the Communist headquarters. "The police state features of Xian were evident at every step," he wrote later, noting that the street on which the Communists' Eighth Route Army office could be found "was empty of people—such was the [KMT] surveillance that anyone daring to walk there might be suspected of secret contact with the Communists."

In Xian also, the KMT minders produced a deserter from the Eighth Route Army, but this initiative became a propaganda flop when it turned out he had escaped from a CCP area because he refused to work clearing land and planting crops, which was one of the Eighth Route Army's duties. He was caught twice trying to escape, but said he wasn't jailed or beaten, only "criticized"—so much for the KMT accusations of "savagery" on the part of the Communists.

On the Xian part of the trip, Harrison Forman of the *New York Herald Tribune* wrote in a book published in 1945, "We learned later that special rickshaw-men, who insisted that we make use of their services, were assigned to the Guest House. When we refused to ride, they followed us wherever we went." Once, as Forman was returning to the Guest House, somebody handed him an envelope. Inside it was a dissenter's proclamation denouncing the Kuomintang tyranny and informing Forman of the extraordinary precautions that had been taken by the government "to deceive you, to blockade you, and to watch you." A fund of $5 million had been appropriated, the document said, involving hundreds of agents who will be in the guise of "translators, ushers, servants, and roomboys." The writer identified himself as "a lodger and citizen of Xian" fighting for the "cause of freedom." He also expressed confidence that Communism can never control China because "any party who wants to have the whole power, and thus deprive the other of his rights and liberty, will sustain a crushing defeat."

From Xian, the journalistic party crossed the Yellow River "on a huge barge-like wooden boat," Epstein recounted, rowed by sixteen men squatting on their haunches and singing the "Yellow River Cantata," a patriotic hymn composed in Yenan in 1939. Now the journalists were in "another world." There were "no flags, no banners, no regimented people jumping up and down with joy as though we visitors were Roosevelt and Churchill combined." Their first night was spent in a cave village where they were met by an unpretentious Communist general—"so different . . . from the tailored-uniformed and white-gloved officers of the Kuomintang." The next day they headed off on horseback for a visit to their first Communist troops—"sweaty, sun-bronzed boys with toothsome smiles" armed with captured Japanese weapons slung over their shoulders, reinforcing the idea that the Communists were waging spirited, full-scale, successful guerrilla war against the Japanese. The land, Epstein reports, had been transformed by the CCP leadership, specifically by Wang Zhen, the general who was escorting them. "Every once-barren hilltop and terraced slope seemed to be cultivated with millet or beans or flax or cotton." Epstein, who had never before traveled to the region and therefore had no firsthand knowledge of what it was like before the Communists arrived, wrote: "There was no cotton here at all before the blockade and people dressed in rags for a couple of years, but not any more." All these "newly fruitful lands" would be turned over to the people, Epstein wrote, who didn't have to pay any of their crops in taxes to support the soldiers.

In Kulin, the first town the reporters reached, they met the local magistrate, a man, Epstein reported, who was illiterate before the Communists came but was now able to write simple reports. A sixty-year-old labor hero was "trotted out," a formerly landless man who told the reporters how much his life had improved. He noted that the magistrate had carried manure out to the fields in the last planting season, "and who had ever heard of a magistrate in the old days doing that kind of work."

There is something almost laughable in an American journalist praising the Communists for having "no regimented people jumping up and down for joy" and failing, in books he published long after the Communists took power, to note the ceremonies of mass fealty to the deified Mao that became a standard aspect of life under Chinese Communist rule. China became a place where factory workers literally did a "loyalty dance" at the beginning of every day, a bit of choreography performed before a portrait of the "Beloved Chairman," where mass rallies of teenagers took place in which they held up copies of a little red book of Mao quotations in a sort of salute, where factories produced hundreds of millions of badges printed with Mao's image to be worn by virtually every person in the country. But Epstein remained a Communist supporter all his life, working for years in the People's Republic of China as the editor of one of the country's main propaganda journals, *China Today*. He was a member of the Chinese Communist Party and seems never to have been bothered by a blatant double standard.

But if some of the journalists who wrote about Mao and Yenan were fellow travelers, most of them, including Edgar and Helen Snow, Jack Belden, and Harrison Forman, and most of the others on that 1944 press tour, weren't. Among them were Maurice Votaw, who, while working for the Associated Press, was an employee of the central government's information office, and Gunther Stein of the *Christian Science Monitor.* "Everything is open and above board," Forman wrote in the *New York Herald Tribune,* "with absolutely no control or restrictions on movements, discussions, interviews, visits, and photographs." Stein struck what was becoming a common theme when he wrote, "The men and women pioneers of Yenan were truly new humans in spirit, thought, and action . . . in a brand-new well-integrated society that [had] never been seen before anywhere."

The notion that the "Chinese Soviets" were not all that red and only sought a higher degree of democracy gained currency among other shrewd, discerning analysts who were not the sort to fall for political fairy tales. Yet they did. In 1942, two years before the beginning of the Dixie Mission and only a few months after Pearl Harbor, John Davies was referring to the Chinese Communists in dispatches as "agrarian democrats" while John Service wrote that the CCP, which, he said, was seeking simple democracy, was "much more American than Russian in form and spirit."

It became something of a trope in State Department reporting on China to refer to the Communists as "so-called Communists," or to Yenan as the "so-called Communist area," as Secretary of State Cordell Hull himself did in a memo to Ambassador Clarence Gauss in June 1944. Even Patrick Hurley, no opponent of Chiang and certainly no leftist of the Smedley or Epstein stripe, used this locution. In a letter to Roosevelt shortly after his arrival in China, Hurley, brimming with confidence that he could bring the two Chinese sides together in a coalition government, dismissed Chiang's concerns about "so-called Communists," passing along to the American president an assurance that Soviet foreign minister Vyacheslav Molotov had given him in Moscow, namely that while some impoverished Chinese called themselves Communists, "they were related to Communism in no way at all."

Molotov's characterization echoed that of Stalin himself, who told the American ambassador in Moscow, Averill Harriman, that the Chinese were "not real Communists" but "margarine Communists," though, Stalin added, they were real patriots and wanted to fight the Japanese. It may have been strange for Americans to pick up this vocabulary from the likes of Stalin and Molotov, but, after all, Stalin was an ally and there was an inclination to believe him.

Mao and company also gave credibility to Stalin's description of them. They never appeared to be ideologues, true believers in a revolutionary doctrine. They were friendly, relaxed, and good-humored with their American guests, dining with them, talking late into the night, drinking what they called tiger bone wine (distilled whiskey made from sorghum soaked, in the absence of tigers, in beef bones), putting on plays that Brooks Atkinson, who had been the *Times* drama critic before going to China, praised highly. Some members of the Dixie Mission went on regular hunting expeditions deep in the mountains with Zhu De, who was always given the first shot. On Saturday nights, there were al fresco dances when the weather was warm—a legacy of Agnes Smedley and the dance lessons she gave Mao—held in a grove of fruit trees called the Pear Orchard, during which Mao and the other Communist leaders moved around the floor with pigtailed local girls while scratchy music played on an old phonograph.

In his book, Forman describes a visit to the Lu Xun College of Arts and Literature, the main cultural institution in Yenan. Lu Xun was China's most famous twentieth-century writer, an iconoclast and free-thinker and the leading figure in Shanghai's League of Left-Wing Writers, which was close to the Communists and opposed to the KMT. Lu died in 1936, and it is a matter of intense debate whether he wouldn't have despised Maoism at least as much as he did Chiang Kai-shek.

At the Lu Xun College of Arts and Literature, Forman found some three hundred artists and writers happily creating plays, stories, and songs under Mao's beneficent guidance. "The Communists take their culture seriously," he wrote. "Artists, writers, musicians, educators, dramatists, and newspapermen meet regularly, to discuss their poems frankly and criticize each other and their work." But it wasn't always this way, Forman informs his readers. Most of the artists and writers came from Shanghai, and "their highly westernized culture was pretty far from peasant folklore of hinterland China," which made it "almost impossible for them not to look down upon the ignorant peasants, the workers and soldiers, who retorted by rejecting them."

"Far-seeing Mao Zedong observed this and decided that it was no good," Forman says. "Calling a meeting of all cultural workers, he flayed them for their high and mighty airs, warned them of retrogression and decay if they persisted." Forman concludes that "Yenan's literati took

Mao Tze-tung's words to heart with amazing good results," adjusting to "new conditions, a new society . . . created by and for the peasant, the worker, and the soldier." As for Mao himself, Forman concluded, after interviewing the chairman, he "is no unapproachable oracle, not the sole fount of all wisdom and guidance, his words unquestioned law." His words are just "taken as a basis for discussion and final approval by a committee of Party leaders who are certainly no rubber-stampers."

Mao assured Forman of the CCP's democratic aspirations and its admiration of western values. "We are not striving for the social and political Communism of Soviet Russia," he told him. "Rather, we prefer to think of what we are doing as something that Lincoln fought for in your Civil War: the liberation of slaves." Mao may have been aware of Snow's use of the word "Lincolnesque" to describe him in *Red Star*. Mao further assured Forman that "we believe in and practice democracy," in contrast with what Mao called the "one-party dictatorship as practiced by the Kuomintang today."

The Dixie Mission had closer relations with senior Chinese military officers than any Americans have had with the Chinese Communists command before or since. There were regular meetings with virtually all the men who would lead the People's Liberation Army in the civil war against the Kuomintang and against American troops during the Korean War. Among them was Zhu De, the Communists' commander in chief, who always impressed visitors with what Davies called his peasant shrewdness and "tremendous character." Among the other future senior military leaders who rubbed shoulders with the Dixie Mission Americans was Lin Biao, who was, until his death in a mortal struggle for power with Mao in 1971, the chairman's closest comrade-in-arms, the man who propagated the *Little Red Book* of Mao quotations and put the military behind Mao's Cultural Revolution. Before that, he was one of the principal commanders of Communist troops in the civil war and a planner, with Peng Dehuai, whom the Americans also got to know in Yenan, of the surprise Chinese offensive in the Korean War that inflicted one of the worst defeats ever experienced by American forces in any war. Colonel David Barrett was deeply impressed by Lin, who, he said, "could not but make a strong impression on anyone who met him." He was polite, Barrett remembered, but among the less openly affable of the Communist leaders, smiling little but clearly "a first rate soldier" whom "I would have been glad to serve under . . . except of course in fighting against my own or a friendly country." Davies draws a verbal portrait of the three top leaders, sitting on stools and talking for two or three hours in Zhou Enlai's cave. Mao was obviously the leader, the authority, the first among equals in Yenan, "big and plump with a round, bland, almost feminine face." Davies spoke of "the incandescence of his personality" and the "immense, smooth calm and sureness to him." This description is so strikingly similar to Henry Kissinger's twenty-two years later, when he met Mao not in a cave but in the inner recesses of a new imperial city. In Kissinger's description, Mao "dominated the room—not by the pomp that in most states confers a degree of majesty on the leaders, but by exuding in almost tangible form the overwhelming drive to prevail."

Zhou Enlai, who spent his life as Mao's number two, impressed Davies with his "mobility, his anger, his earnestness, and his amusement fully set forth in his face," while "Old Zhu," as he called Zhu De, was "the shambling, slow, shrewd peasant."

Members of the Dixie Mission were taken on foot or horseback from Yenan headquarters to the front on expeditions lasting weeks or even months. Among them was Raymond P. Ludden, one of the Chinese-language officers who had socialized with Snow in Beijing a few years before and who, like Davies, was now assigned to Stilwell's command. Ludden spent four months traveling through Shaanxi province, observing the Communists' administration of villages that were theoretically under Japanese control. His conclusion was that the Communists had the support of the local population, that they had done a good job mobilizing the peasants, and that the Communist leadership was "the most realistic, well-knit, and tough-minded group in China."

One important reason for the American impulse to like the Communists was illustrated by the experience of a thirty-year-old American pilot, George Varoff, and the ten crew members of a B-29 Superfortress bomber that took off from Shaanxi province on December 7, 1944, the third anniversary of Pearl Harbor, to bomb Japanese targets in Mukden in Japanese-controlled Manchuria. Varoff had been a track star back home, the world record holder in the pole vault for a time, having jumped fourteen feet four and five-eighths inches at a 1936 meet in Princeton, New Jersey, so his situation attracted attention in the newspapers. On January 3, 1945, *The New York Times* reported him missing in action. Two weeks later, the paper announced that Varoff was safe and had been returned to his air base in China. The paper provided no details about what had happened to him or how he had been rescued, because that information involved a network run by the Chinese Communists and their American friends that had to be kept secret.

Varoff's mission had been to hit an arsenal and airplane factory in Mukden, but at twenty-two thousand feet his B-29, which was the most potent bomber in the American airborne arsenal of the time, was so cold that ice built up on the cockpit windows, making it difficult for Varoff to follow the lead plane in his formation. His aircraft's tail gun, manned by Sergeant John P. Quinlan, failed to function. As he neared the target, Japanese fighters attacked from all directions, streaking through the American formation and pursuing the American planes that had dropped their bombs. Varoff's plane was hit, forcing him to turn back toward Shaanxi. Two other planes from the American formation peeled away from the rest of the convoy to serve as escorts.

Varoff descended to twenty-four hundred feet in an effort to keep his engine running as slowly as possible, but when it became clear that he wasn't going to make it, he ordered the entire crew to bail out, and then he jumped himself. Buffeted by the cold, heavy winds as he dropped, straining to pull his parachute's shrouds so he could maneuver to land in a valley, he watched as his plane crashed into a mountain peak in a ball of fire. The two escort planes circled overhead, marking the position of the downed Americans before they turned west toward base. Varoff fell into the side of a rugged hill and lost consciousness when his head hit a rock. He woke up to find the snow stained by his blood.

The odds of survival for Varoff and his crew were not good. The eleven Americans, scattered by heavy winds across several of the region's rugged mountains, were in Hebei province, which was controlled by Japanese troops who, having seen the planes, would start searching for them right away, and who would surely execute any Americans they captured. But within minutes of the B-29's crash, Chinese peasants were combing the several square miles of forest and crag trying to reach the downed American airmen first. Whole mountainsides were speckled with the light of torches as the search went on through the night, and within two days, the Chinese had found all eleven airmen and brought them to a Chinese Communist guerrilla outpost belonging to what the Americans called the *Balus*, for *Balujun*, or Eighth Route Army. Two of the Americans were badly injured and had to be carried to shelter on the backs of peasants. One, William Wood, who operated the plane's radar, was knocked unconscious when he landed, and when he came to, he saw that local people had already carried him to a dwelling. The *Balus* fed the Americans, tended to their wounds, and assured them that they would be escorted to safety. For more than a month, they moved the airmen from one location to another, keeping them out of the hands of the Japanese, and, as the Americans later reported, treating them as heroes. Chinese peasants scavenged for eggs, peanuts, and fruit and gave them to the flyboys. Banquets were held for them by the villagers who harbored them, all under the threat of discovery and retaliation by the Japanese, who were looking for them. The *Balus* sent word up the chain of command that they had custody of the airmen, and American military officials were informed of their whereabouts. After several weeks of constant moving about, the Communists carved a runway out of a stretch of isolated mountain road and an American plane was able to land. On a cold winter day in January of the new year, the men of the *Balujun* watched as the captured Americans met the Americans who arrived in the rescue plane and then flew them back to their base.

In all, about sixty downed American airmen were saved in this way, some by the Nationalists but most by the Communists, who had the more extensive network behind Japanese lines and were estimated to have suffered some six hundred fatalities fighting off Japanese troops in these rescue operations. Saving American airmen involved great bravery by the ordinary Chinese like those who combed the mountains of Hebei looking for Varoff and his crew, because they surely knew the Japanese would have had no hesitation in executing anybody they caught doing so. Wartime censorship kept these rescue operations from being known to the American public, but the members of the Dixie Mission certainly knew about them, and they were just the sort of thing to promote an atmosphere of common purpose and good feeling.

While Barrett was in Yenan, he witnessed the return of one John Baglio. After going down not far from Beijing, Baglio was guided by a local farmer to the *Balus*, who passed him safely from one area to another on a thousand-mile trek, giving him a party at every stop, until he arrived in Yenan. Barrett noted that "Baglio was one American who couldn't have cared less about the political beliefs of the Chinese Communists. All he knew was that they had saved him."

The next time American pilots bailed out into the hands of Communist troops was in Korea about five years later, and the reception this time was imprisonment and torture, which makes the level of wartime cooperation all the more amazing and the decline of the relationship into enmity all the more shocking and costly.

These rescues did not happen spontaneously. They were the product of close coordination between one of the members of the Dixie Mission, First Lieutenant Henry S. Whittlesley, born and raised in China, and the representative of the Air-Ground Aid Service in Yenan, and his counterparts in the Eighth Route Army. Whittlesley, who died in 1945 in a Japanese ambush (the Communists named one of their airfields after him), collected information on the best places for American fliers to bail out—meaning the places where the Communist guerrilla presence was strongest—and that information was passed along to pilots in their briefings.

The Americans carried "blood chits" in their bags, pieces of cloth inscribed with Chinese characters that identified them as friends and asked for help. They packed "pointy-talkies," bilingual phrase books that enabled either side to communicate by pointing to phrases in their own language. Those men with a bit of linguistic aptitude learned a few Chinese phrases, like *Meiguo Feidi*, American flier, and *Balujun*. All of these devices were put to good use by Varoff and his crew on the day they parachuted into Hebei, Varoff's first words to the first Chinese he encountered being *Meiguo Feidi* and *Balujun*. It was this sort of cooperation that fed the mood of goodwill, along with the bracing clean air and the sense of a new type of person emerging from the revolutionary cauldron, all in great contrast to steamy, ruined Chungking with its reek of pretention, corruption, and incompetence. Years later, Barrett summed it all up in a single crisp sentence: "The Chinese Communists are our bitter enemies now, but they were certainly 'good guys' then, particularly to the airmen who received their help."

CHAPTER FIVE

The Dark Side

A merican and other foreign visitors to Yenan met many people. They interviewed Japanese prisoners who had been captured by the Eighth Route Army, treated well, and persuaded to join the Japanese People's Emancipation League, which called for the overthrow of the militarists in Tokyo. They met George Hatem, a Swiss-educated American doctor who had thrown in his lot with the CCP years before and was in charge of Yenan's hospitals. Hatem had escorted Edgar Snow to Bao-an for Snow's famous expedition to the Communist base area, and now he served as a kind of friend to subsequent American visitors. A couple of Soviet journalists (actually intelligence agents) were at Yenan, and if the Americans weren't exactly friendly with them (they kept to themselves), they knew they were there. They had more contact with Michael Lindsay, a radio expert working for the Chinese Communists in Yenan whom everybody believed to be a British spy.

One person the Americans did not meet was Wang Shiwei, a thirty-seven-year-old literary figure; the translator of Engels and Trotsky as well as of works by Eugene O'Neill and Thomas Hardy and one of thousands of idealistic Chinese who, inspired by tales of the revolutionaries' heroic anti-Japanese exploits, and by Mao's welcome to the "patriotic bourgeoisie" and "intellectuals," had traveled to Yenan to join up. These people, including well-known artists, writers, and scholars exhilarated by the idea of a new China rising out of the ashes of the war, did not simply show up at Yenan and get accepted into the revolution. The chief Chinese scholar of the Yenan experience, Gao Hua, a Nanjing University historian, has described the careful organization and process of interrogations by which new arrivals were screened for membership in the Maoist revolution. To gain access to Yenan at all, newcomers had to have letters of recommendation obtained from the underground CCP organizations in China's major cities. The bearers of these letters were kept in interrogation centers outside Yenan and only admitted into the inner sanctum when they had been properly vetted. From there, to get a taste of the Spartan hardship that awaited them, they were expected to walk to Yenan, a distance of about three hundred miles, which took nine or ten days. Once in Yenan, the new recruit underwent further questioning until, finally, he or she was assigned a job by the Central Organization Department.

Wang Shiwei was one of these young intellectuals, though older than most of them. He was from Shanghai and a veteran of the CCP, having joined the party in 1926. He arrived in Yenan in the very early days after the Communists' arrival there, in 1936, and was assigned, as befits a budding theoretician, to do research in the Academy for Marxist-Leninist Studies. He was, by the accounts of those who knew him, a poetic and passionate individual who wrote essays about "how bloodthirsty and evil and filthy and dark old China was." But he was also disillusioned by some aspects of the Yenan adventure, and his disillusionment was shared by many others who, during their time in China's revolutionary headquarters, had firsthand experience of the gap between the seductive theory of the place and the realities of naked privilege and power.

This is important. If the movement created by Mao was to eradicate the "disease," as Wang called it, of China immemorial, it needed to eradicate both the cruelty of Stygian authority and the blind, automatic obedience to it as well. The revolution could not simply replace one unquestioned authority with another, and Wang dared to question the unquestioned authority of Mao as well as of international Communism itself, at whose apex was Joseph Stalin in Moscow. There is a seeming paradox in this, because Mao made various ostentatious verbal gestures in favor of independent thinking; he brandished an intolerance for stale ideas and dogmatic attachments, though in reality he was prosecuto-rially intolerant of criticism directed against himself. His main rivals in the Communist movement were a group of men, led by a power-ful party official named Wang Ming, who had spent years in Moscow under the auspices of the Comintern and whose aura of authority came from their previous proximity to the headquarters of the global revolu-tion. In the late 1930s and early 1940s, Mao used political campaigns to silence this Moscow faction, whom he accused of blindly applying a set of rigid principles to Chinese circumstances, and to become the undisputed top leader of the Chinese Communist movement. Mao could get away with it. Wang Shiwei, who went treacherously far in his questioning of Stalin's authority, could not. Among the received ideas challenged by Wang were Stalin's ways of getting rid of his opponents. He doubted the honesty of Stalin's show trials and his persecutions of Soviet leades like Karl Radek and Grigory Zinoviev. He wrote essays exploring the dividing line between the "truly great politician" and the leaders who advance "their own reputation, position, and profit and thus harm the revolution."

Wang was encouraged to express these views. A few years earlier, following one of Mao's iconoclastic injunctions, the Central Committee had issued a proclamation inviting party members to "discuss everything," since "no matter what opinion, right or wrong, all should be raised without reservation." Wang, who was not naïvely idealistic, knew that this appearance of openness to diverse opinions was going to be limited at best, and in one of the first statements that got him into trouble, he described it as a sham. He wrote of a "certain comrade" who had written a critical wall poster and afterward been so severely "criticized and attacked" that he became "partially demented." Still, Wang said, "I will dare to follow that certain comrade and speak on egalitarianism and hierarchy."

This was his main concern and his main offense, calling attention to the difference between the egalitarian ideal of Yenan and its actual hierarchy. Contrary to the impression garnered by foreign visitors, an elaborate system of perquisites and privileges had developed in Yenan that seems remarkable given the Communists' theoretical emphasis on material equality and the informality, the lack of insignia or pretension, that so impressed the Dixie Mission members. Of course, the senior Chinese communists, many of whom had lived or studied in the Soviet Union, knew that a hierarchy of privilege was firmly encrusted into Stalin's supposedly classless society, and perhaps that's why they believed it to be normal and acceptable to enjoy a similar hierarchy themselves. In Yenan, the privileges began with the ambulance, donated by the Chinese Laundryman's Association of New York, that was reserved for the exclusive use of Mao and was the only car in the entire Communist encampment. Nobody seems to have thought it odd that the party chairman should have his own vehicle. More bothersome were the everyday distinctions made—three kitchen levels, for instance, by which people at different ranks got significantly different food, high-level cadres served better food in what were called "small pots"; the nannies and special kindergartens of section and department heads to which they sent their children; and preferred access to hospitals for giving birth and getting scarce medications. Various people had different cigarettes, candles, and writing paper. Everybody in Yenan seemed to dress the same, but some people received underwear made of imported cotton softer than the underwear available for the rank and file. Above all, there was a certain hypocritical arrogance to these ranking bureaucrats who called on those below them to accept revolutionary austerity while rejecting it for themselves.

Mao, like the Central Committee, urged revolutionary cadres with complaints to speak out. In speeches to the Central Party School in 1942, he had presented himself as a kind of freethinking iconoclast, comparing dogma to manure and empty, theoretical talk to "the foot-bindings of a slattern, long and foul-smelling." It's easy to see now how this earthy pose of intellectual libertarianism actually produced a deadening authoritarian effect, how it magnified the power and glory of Mao himself, who could somehow appear to be at the same time both an avatar of bold thinking and a tyrant requiring absolute obedience. It was also "fiendishly clever," as Mao's biographer Philip Short has written. His mixture of contrarianism and authoritarianism enabled him "to modulate the progress of an ideological campaign to accommodate his political needs, to change direction at will, and to lure real or presumed opponents into exposing their views, the better to strike them down."

In 1956, seven years after taking power, Mao, in a notorious reenactment of this fiendish cleverness, called for "a hundred flowers" to bloom and "a hundred schools of thought" to contend. This bracing call for freedom of expression was followed by the brutal repression known as the Anti-Rightist Campaign, in which tens of thousands of China's most thoughtful, educated, and loyal citizens who had expressed dissenting views were herded into concentration camps for what was euphemistically called reform through labor.

Something very similar, a sort of foreshadowing of what was to come, took place in 1942. In the old walled town of Yenan, much of it reduced to rubble by the Japanese aerial bombardments of 1938 and 1939, there was a district where the many artists and writers who had been drawn to Mao's standard put up what had always been a unique Chinese mode of expression, the big-character poster or wall newspaper. This is a large placard with an opinion on it that anybody could stand and read right there and, presumably, talk to others doing the same thing. The wall newspapers had titles like *Arrow and Target, Light Cavalry,* and *Northwest Wind,* on which the Yenan cultural elite took Mao up on his call for intra-party debate. Wang Shiwei argued at meetings that the writers of wall newspapers should be protected by anonymity, but this notion was rejected.

Wang did not make his famous criticism of hierarchical privilege on a common big-character poster but in the pages of *Liberation Daily,* the party newspaper, in March 1942. One of the characteristics of Yenan, unremarked by Snow, Davies, Forman, Epstein, and the others, was its isolation from outside influences. Between 1937 and 1940 or so, the Yenan population had increased twentyfold, but among those tens of thousands of people, including thousands of urban intellectuals like Wang Shiwei, there were almost no radios, no newspapers from outside. Those big-character posters and wall newspapers weren't so much an index of intellectual ferment but rather of how extremely limited was the space allowed for unsupervised expression of opinion. In that context, *Liberation Daily* wasn't just another newspaper. It was essentially the sole regular source of information, which meant that the publication of Wang Shiwei's views on CCP hierarchy and privilege was more than simply an individual view, like an op-ed article in an American newspaper. A leading figure on *Liberation Daily* was a writer named Ding Ling, celebrated for her stories about young women struggling to gain control over their own bodies and lives (and a future winner of the Stalin Prize for literature), who encouraged the paper to publish Wang's essay.

It was called it "Wild Lilies," after a flower that grew in the hills around Yenan and that Wang saw as a "pure and noble image." The essay began by reporting that "the youth of Yenan seem dispirited and are apparently harboring some troubling discomfort. Why?" Some people, he continued, might attribute the discontent to the absence of nutrition, or perhaps to the male-female ratio of eighteen to one, which meant not much of a sex life for most of the males, except, though Wang doesn't mention this, for the senior party and army leaders to whom the few women were distributed. But those were not the primary reasons, since young people didn't come to Yenan to have lives of ease and enjoyment. What bothered people most was the system of rank and privilege. "I am not an egalitarian," he wrote, "but the three classes of clothing and five grades of food are not necessarily reasonable and needed—this is especially true with clothes." The "unreasonable perks" that some "big shots" get, he continued, lead "subordinates to see their superiors as belonging to another species."

It was at this point that "far-seeing Mao" held the event that Harrison Forman referred to in his 1945 book as a salutary reform of culture, one aimed at bringing arrogant and supercilious urbanites from Shanghai into line with the cultural needs of peasants, and that had "amazing good results," the sort of results that a professional theater critic like Brooks Atkinson could praise. The event in question was the Yenan Forum on Literature and Art, one of the central initiatives taken by Mao in the larger political upheaval given the name Rectification Campaign, that Mao engineered in Yenan and that was designed both to indoctrinate the thousands who had flocked to Yenan and to eradicate his opponents inside the party. The long-range effect of this famous meeting was to reduce the magnificent art and culture of China, historically one of the greatest contributions to global culture ever made, to standardized, officially approved propaganda. But the immediate, drastic effect was on the artists who had come to Yenan hoping to break away from Kuomintang oppression and the constraints of the Confucian tradition and to create a new culture befitting the new China, only to find that they were under suspicion and under attack.

Mao used the forum to attack Wang Shiwei personally. He was labeled a "petit-bourgeois individualist," which was a capital offense. Mao's loyal followers held weeks of criticism and struggle sessions against Wang. He was called "Comrade Shit-stink." The poet Ai Qing, who himself had complained about Mao's demand "to describe ringworm as flowers," made up for his transgression by calling Wang a "reactionary," and Ding Ling, the fiercely feminist writer who had brokered Wang's essay in *Liberation Daily*, made up for this error by joining the mob. As Philip Short has written, "It was not enough for Wang merely to be purged. His fellow writers had publicly to humiliate him. His 'trial' marked the beginning of a practice of collective denunciation that would remain an essential part of the Chinese Communists' treatment of dissidents for decades to come."

The Rectification Campaign lasted for two years. Mao, in the sort of comment he did not make to visiting foreigners, articulated the psychological theory behind it. "The first step is to give the patient a powerful shock," he said in February 1942 as the campaign was just beginning, even before Wang Shiwei wrote his fatal article. "Yell at him, 'You're sick!' Then he'll get a fright and break out in a sweat. At that point he can be put on the road to recovery."

Mao has been excused by some historians for being different from Stalin in this regard, for wanting to cure the patient rather than do what Stalin did during his purges in the Soviet Union, which was have them executed, and this is true. Mao was a believer in reeducation rather than elimination, though in practice reeducation was not a gentle process; when it meant imprisonment for years in primitive work camps with substandard food and no medical treatment, it was tantamount to elimination. "Party meetings are fixed by an order from above," Pyotr Vladimirov, supposedly a TASS News Agency correspondent in Yenan and an agent of the GRU, Soviet military intelligence, wrote in his diary,

> the chairman of a cell points out who is to be criticized at each meeting and for what. As a rule, one Communist is flogged at each meeting. Everyone takes part in the flogging. He has to. The flogged one has only one right: to confess his "mistakes." But if he doesn't and thinks himself innocent or if he hasn't "confessed" enough . . . flogging is resumed. Meetings are numerous. Speeches are long, high-sounding, and roughly of the same content.

As the campaign unfolded, the shock treatment took the form of accusations of membership in a spy ring working for Chiang Kai-shek. The underlying purpose of this, some historians believe, wasn't only a general thought remolding in the context of a revolutionary struggle, where, after all, a certain ideological discipline might be warranted. Rather, it was more importantly a way of establishing Mao's absolute power by branding any dissent not just wrong but an act of espionage for the enemy—in other words, disloyalty, treason.

The movement was notable in this sense for the rise of one of the more sinister figures of Chinese Communist history, Kang Sheng, Mao's chief enforcer. Kang perfectly illustrated a particular archetype spawned by the totalitarian movements of the twentieth century, one also embodied by Stalin's secret police chief, Lavrenty Beria, or the Nazi Heinrich Himmler, all of them ruthless guardians of the revolution and loyal protectors of its semi-deified Great Leader, whether Hitler, Stalin, or Mao. Kang had earlier belonged to the Moscow faction of the party, having spent four years in the Soviet Union with Mao's great rival in the party, Wang Ming, whom he was in the habit of calling "a genius leader." But when he came to Yenan with the rest of the Moscow group, he cleverly switched from one genius leader to another, joining Mao, who was always leery of possible plotting against him by colleagues and subordinates and needful of a figure whom he could trust absolutely. It didn't hurt that when Mao decided to marry the Shanghai actress Jiang Qing, who had not been fully accepted by most of the senior leadership, only Kang and Mao's personal secretary, Chen Boda, gave their enthusiastic approval.

Over time, Kang became an easily recognizable figure in Yenan, though he appears to have been invisible to the American visitors of

Mao with Kang Sheng, the chief of his secret police and the principal organizer of his ideological purges.

1944 and 1945: they never mention him in dispatches that are full of descriptions of other senior Communist leaders. "Kang always wore Russian jackets and knee-high boots and he went around with a big dog," one ranking party member, Shi Zhe, who was Mao's Russian interpreter, has written in a memoir. "He was followed by four security guards whenever he went out, and he looked very confident. He was already the most frightening figure in Yenan. He was like a faithful dog always ready to follow his master's [Mao's] command and attack his master's enemies." Pyotr Vladimirov saw a lot of Kang, who, he said, spoke Russian, albeit "with an accent, without conjugating verbs," and with a "very poor vocabulary." As if to illustrate the inequality that Wang complained about, he lived in a big house with its own peach orchard that formerly belonged to a landlord. He has, Vladimirov wrote,

> a shrill and hissing voice. . . . Kang Sheng always smiles. It seems that the smile has been glued to his thin, bilious face. When he listens, he inhales the air noisily, in a Japanese manner. . . . [He is] gnarled of features and energetic in a nervous way. The impression he gives of himself is that of a wooden puppet suspended on strings.

It was in the Rectification Campaign of 1942 that Kang, with Mao's evident approval, perfected his technique, which was to find some exemplary target, make a plausible accusation, and then pressure him into an admission of guilt as an example to everybody else — or, as the Chinese proverb has it, to kill the chicken to frighten the monkey. Confessions were extorted in the fashion that became standard in China — a combination of extreme isolation, mass denunciation rallies, a newspaper campaign, wearying interrogations, torture, and a vow to the accused that a full admission of guilt and a self-criticism would lead to lenient treatment while stubborn insistence on non-guilt would be punished severely. All of this took place as a sort of perverse group therapy, in which first destabilizing a person with "a powerful shock" and then getting him on the "road to recovery" were the key ingredients. The Rectification Campaign was a cure for thinking independently, or, as the Chinese journalist Dai Qing said of the Wang Shiwei case, it enacted "the ugliest nightmare in human history — the smothering of dignity and freedom of thought in the name of revolution." It had, in addition, that particular Orwellian element that distinguishes the psychological methods of twentieth-century totalitarianism: the goal was not simply to make the thought-control target admit his errors and flaws but to so thoroughly destroy his sense of autonomous individuality that he feels gratitude and love for the leader who restored him to the correct path — Chairman Mao.

An early example of the method involved a nineteen-year-old man named Zhang Keqin, who was a student at what was called the Xibei, or northwest school, set up by Kang precisely to train agents for the job of internal intelligence. Zhang was a handy target because, in 1942, someone he knew from Chungking sent him a pro-Kuomintang magazine. His father, a doctor, had treated Kuomintang officials, which was taken as evidence of a special relationship with the enemy. In addition, Zhang had been denounced as a Kuomintang spy by one of the young men who had come to Yenan with him. There was no evidence to support this accusation, but Zhang, still a teenager and, no doubt, terrified, was unable to prove that it was false. Kang Sheng ordered him arrested and interrogated. He was questioned for three days and nights in a method called *chelunzhan*, literally "cartwheel war," in which interrogators replace each other in a nonstop bombardment of questions during which the suspect has no respite and no sleep. In the end Zhang, unable to endure any more, admitted to the charge against him.

Zhang's case contained all the elements sought by the engineers of what the historian Gao Hua has called "this live show." With tears streaming down his face, he manufactured a story that fit the Communists' preferred narrative of betrayal and redemption. He said that he had become a secret agent, joining a Communist cell that was actually set up as a kind of decoy by the KMT. He fingered others who were secret agents among the friends who had journeyed to Yenan with him, including the person who had initially fingered him, and then he expressed his gratitude to the party for saving him from his errors and making him a new person. Having demonstrated the perfect functioning of the system of confession and reform, Zhang was then dispatched by Kang Sheng to lecture to other students at the Xibei school. His example, psychological torment followed by treatment as an ideological model, induced others in Yenan to manufacture stories of shortcomings, misbehavior, and ideological errors and of their need for thought reform so that they could become models also. "Once you confessed, you had a better life," Shi Zhe wrote in his memoir, "and if you didn't confess you were tortured and stayed in prison. The more stories you made up the better you were treated."

In 1944, after two years in the hands of the Yenan security apparatus, Wang Shiwei was ushered out to be interviewed by some Chungking-based Chinese reporters (no foreigners were ever given access to him). One of Wang's crimes had been to express the view that Stalin's show trials of the 1930s were "dubious." Very likely he knew that after months or years in detention the falsely accused would be expected to make

full, abject public confessions, admitting to thoughts and deeds either
that they never had or that were in no way criminal. The Czech writer
Milan Kundera spoke of the moral inversion produced by Stalinist persecution in which the disoriented person desperately searches his life
in order to find crimes to admit to. This seems to be what happened to
Wang Shiwei. When first accused, Wang refused to admit any guilt, but
now, brought before the Chungking reporters, looking, one of them
said, like he was "reciting from a textbook," Wang became what he had
most despised. "I deserve to be executed," he said. "But Mao is so mag-
nanimous . . . I am extremely grateful for his mercy."

Wang Shiwei remained an object of public vituperation for the duration of the Rectification Campaign. He was, the propaganda intoned,
the inhabitant of a "counter-revolutionary shit-hole." He was a member of an "anti-party gang" that had "sneaked into the party to destroy
and undermine it." A mob of other writers obediently wrote articles in
which they drew the mandatory lessons from Wang's ideological errors;
these articles had titles like "Thoroughly Smash Wang Shiwei's Trotskyite Theories and Anti-Party Activities" and "The Literary and Artists
Circle's Correct Attitude and Their Self-Examination Regarding Wang
Shiwei," which was by Ding Ling. Wang was locked up in a Yenan
prison unknown to members of the American military mission, and in
1947, as the CCP evacuated Yenan in advance of KMT troops, he was
hacked to death and his body dumped into a well in a village near the
Yellow River.

Twenty-five years later, with Mao ensconced inside what Beijing residents didn't dare call the new forbidden city, a talented and renowned
essayist and playwright named Wu Han, who was also a deputy mayor
of Beijing, wrote a historical allegory called *Hai Rui Dismissed from
Office*. It was about a just official in the Ming dynasty who had been
punished for speaking truths to power, and it was an unmistakable reference to Mao and his practice of cashiering old revolutionary comrades
for daring to criticize his autocratic rule. Wu Han's play was performed
and published in 1961, and it took five years for Mao to find the political backing he needed to launch a counterattack, which he did in 1966
when one of his radical henchmen, Yao Wenyuan, accused Wu Han of
wanting to "replace the state theory of Marxism-Leninism with the state
theory of the landlord and bourgeoisie." In such a way did the Great
Proletarian Cultural Revolution, which lasted for ten sanguinary years
and produced the ultimate apotheosis of Mao, begin with a campaign

against a writer and his impure thoughts. Wu Han was imprisoned for having created a work of literature, a play. In 1969, he was beaten to death. The Communists, as Harrison Forman put it, "take their culture seriously."

Does it really matter that the members of the Dixie Mission were ignorant of the Rectification Campaign, that some journalists said some ridiculously worshipful things about Mao, or that most of the American travelers to Yenan in the final months of World War II missed the essential nature of Maoism, its ruthlessness, its cruelty, its repressiveness, its Orwellian manipulation of the truth? The United States has had cordial relations with numerous dictators over the years, including dictators like Chiang Kai-shek. Once the Cold War broke out, it was not a country's domestic arrangements that determined its relationship to the United States; it was whether it aligned itself with the Soviet Union and put itself in the service of Soviet goals. In the long stretch of time since the months of the Dixie Mission, numerous observers and scholars have forcefully argued that there was nothing inevitable about Chinese enmity toward the United States. If Washington had constructed a separate, cooperative relationship with Mao and his cohort in the final months of the war, rather than giving one-sided support to Chiang Kai-shek, then, as Service has put it, we might not have ended up with "the close friend and ally we once hoped for," but we would at least have had something better than "bitter enmity." Most important, Service and numerous other scholars and observers have argued in later years, we would not have ended up backing the losing side in a harsh and bloody civil war, and therefore "Korea and Vietnam would probably never have happened."

And yet it was important to Davies, Service, and Stilwell that the Communists were potentially democratic; that they seemed more American than Russian; that they sought nothing more radical or revolutionary than a reform of rural taxes; that they would go their own vigorously independent and nationalistic way rather than the way of Stalin and the Russians. To say that they were wrong is not to condemn them or to find them negligent in their duties. These were brave, intelligent, honest, and admirable men trying to puzzle out the truth in murky circumstances, and, moreover, they were more realistic than their adversaries inside the very divided American government and their policy prescriptions were more reasonable. Very few people placed in their complex and difficult situations would have done better than they did. But they made mistakes, and the main one they made was to overestimate the compatibility of Chinese Communism with American values and aspirations. Perhaps there was an element of self-delusion in this, of wishful thinking, because though the China hands were realists, they were also believers in the American mission of fostering democracy in the world, and it would have been more difficult proposing closer ties to Mao if they had been clearer about the profoundly illiberal, destructively totalitarian regime he would establish. This is where their ignorance of the Rectification Campaign becomes significant. In later years, many have contended that Mao and his cohort were driven into radicalism because they were first thrust into isolation and insecurity by the West. But the Rectification Campaign shows that this is incorrect. What the Americans in Yenan did not see or understand was that the elements of Mao's rule that would become visible after the Communists took total power in China were already in place years before that occurred, and that included the adoption of all the methods of twentieth-century totalitarianism.

An argument exactly opposite to the one made by Service and the other China experts in the Foreign Service has also frequently been made; it was made by the new American emissary, Patrick J. Hurley, by Henry Luce, by General Wedemeyer, by the members of what came to be called the China Lobby, and by the congressmen and senators in Washington who later conducted a witch hunt for those they believed responsible for "the loss" of China to the Communists. This argument was that the Foreign Service officers' rosy view of Mao coupled with their denigration of Chiang led to an erosion of support for the KMT, and if that support had not eroded, the Communists would not have come to power, and so the wars in Korea and Vietnam would never have occurred.

The events of late 1944 to early 1946 show that both arguments are wrong, the argument that it was a mistake not to cooperate with the Communists and the argument that more support should have been given to Chiang Kai-shek. Both positions are based on the notion that it is for the United States to shape the world to its specifications and that, if it takes the right actions, it has the ability to do this. As we'll see, American policy was bungling, inconsistent, and improvised; it was not the product of a well-thought-out strategic plan. There are lessons to be learned from this, among them the importance of establishing reasonable goals and pursuing them sensibly, rather than suffer the loss of prestige and self-confidence that comes from loudly announcing unrealistic goals and then failing to achieve them. But it was not American policy that determined the outcome in China. It was the forces on the ground over which the United States, with its vast but not unlimited power, never exercised decisive control.

PART II

Seeds of Animosity

CHAPTER SIX

The Wrong Man

The cry rang out over the grass airstrip and the bare brown hills of Yenan, and Chairman Mao and General Zhou, as Mao Zedong and Zhou Enlai were known to foreigners at the time, didn't quite know what to make of it. "I shall never forget the expressions on their faces," Colonel David D. Barrett, the commander of the Dixie Mission, wrote later.

John Davies called the utterance, made by FDR's special representative in China, Patrick J. Hurley, "a prolonged howl." Barrett said it was an "Indian war whoop." Mao and Zhou, despite the indisputable richness of their experience and the adventurousness of their lives, had never encountered anybody quite like Hurley, who was to charm them at first, disappoint them later, and, ultimately confound, perplex, and infuriate them, while vindicating their ideological predisposition against capitalist and imperialist America.

Mao and Zhou were not the only ones who had never encountered anybody quite like Hurley. The political officers at the American embassy, and those attached to General Wedemeyer's staff, didn't know what to make of him either, and in the end, a conflict broke out between them that was to open up an ugly episode in which malicious and reckless accusations were made, careers were destroyed, and the United States lost the possibility of a reasoned debate on China.

Hurley arrived from clammy, rubble-strewn, death-infected Chungking into the bracing, crisp, fresh air of Yenan aboard an American army C-47, which was on a periodic shuttle run carrying mail and supplies to the Dixie Mission members. The date was November 7, 1944, nearly two months after Hurley's arrival in China. He'd had meetings with the Communist representatives in Chungking during his few weeks there, as he plunged into the task of reconciling the two antagonistic armed parties to each other, so they could dedicate their united energies to fighting the Japanese, but he'd refused Communist invitations to visit Yenan, even ignoring a personal letter from Mao himself, since he wanted to be sure of Chiang's acquiescence in his diplomatic enterprise. But even after he felt himself ready to meet the senior Communist leaders in their own lair, he hadn't let them know in advance of his trip.

Because any American plane arriving at the Yenan airstrip was an occasion, Barrett was on hand when Hurley arrived, and so was Zhou Enlai, who didn't know who the tall, gray-haired man emerging from the C-47 was, even though Hurley did everything he could to make a compelling first impression. He wore what Barrett described as "one of the most beautifully tailored uniforms I'd ever seen," with three rows of campaign ribbons (leading Barrett to quip: "General, you've got a ribbon there for everything but Shay's Rebellion"). Zhou asked Barrett, who was wearing a blue padded overcoat, the identity of the resplendent new arrival. When he was told that it was Roosevelt's special emissary, he "disappeared in a cloud of dust" to fetch Mao. Soon the Chairman appeared in his beat-up ambulance. An honor guard was assembled, bugles blared, Hurley saluted, and it was at this point that he let loose his Choctaw whoop, which, while it surprised the Communists, was typical Hurley. He strove to make the most of his rough-and-ready cowboy background, his "boisterous goodwill," as the historian Barbara Tuchman described it. It was his way of breaking the ice. Pressing the cowboy metaphor, the historian Herbert Feis said, "He tried to corral both sides [KMT and CCP] within a fence of general principles, and turn them into a committee for law and order." Despite his stumble on the Stilwell front, Hurley remained optimistic that his good intentions, persuasive charm, and plain common sense could overcome the obstacles of mutual animosity and conflicting ambitions of China's two armed parties.

After the welcoming ceremonies, Hurley, Mao, Zhou, and Barrett climbed into the ambulance and bounced off toward the walled town of Yenan, all of the participants in this scene surely touched by a sense of historic possibility.

For Mao and the Communists, the presence among them of a special representative of the president of the United States was a milestone in their long climb back from the near annihilation they had suffered at the hands of Chiang only a few short years earlier. In 1937, after the

Long March and a brief stay at their first refuge of Bao'an, the Communists had seven thousand men left of the one hundred thousand that had begun the trek a year earlier. Now they credibly claimed to have nearly one million men in their army, plus an estimated 2.5 million men in part-time militias serving as a reserve force. The Communists controlled territory with a population of about ninety million people spread out across North China in both occupied and non-occupied areas.

They had achieved this remarkable growth by dint of vigorous and brilliant organizing aided by a skillful self-presentation to China's domestic audience, but it was the Japanese invasion that had been crucial to their success, because it forced Chiang to defer his military campaigns against them and gave them a patriotic pretext for building up their own armed forces—whose purpose, they could pretend, was not to take power and impose a proletarian dictatorship but to defeat the hated invader. Years later, in 1972, when the Japanese prime minister Tanaka Kakuei apologized to Mao for Japan's aggression, Mao reportedly told him that no apology was necessary. "If imperial Japan had not started the war," he said, "how could we Communists have become mighty and powerful?" Even if this story is apocryphal, Mao's comment would have been true.

Hurley quickly tried to establish a sense of common ground with Mao, with whom he shared a rural background and a predilection for earthy language. They passed a man herding some sheep, and Mao told Hurley that he'd been a shepherd in his youth. Hurley said he'd been a cowboy. When the Sino-American party crossed the Yan riverbed, Mao informed his guest that the river rose in the spring and dried up in the summer. Hurley told Mao that the rivers in Oklahoma got so dry in the summer that you could tell where the fish were by the dust they raised. The ambulance passed a Chinese farmer having trouble with a balky mule, and Hurley shouted out, "Hit him on the other side Charley." Barrett translated this somewhat mysterious remark (Charley?) for the puzzled Mao and Zhou, a task made even more difficult by "the saltiness of the General's remarks and a manner of discourse that was by no means connected by any readily discernible pattern of thought."

Hurley had an earthy, picaresque quality that transcended national boundaries, but he was an amateur when it came to China, and it was to become clear in the weeks ahead that he was in over his head on what had become his main task, achieving KMT-CCP unity and cooperation. He wasn't in this sense the only amateur to take over American China policy at that time. Among the others was Edward Stettinius, FDR's new secretary of state and a figure who has not occupied a very prominent place in the annals of American foreign policy. He was, like Hurley himself, an almost serendipitous appointment. He just happened to be available in a moment of need, an awkward contrast in this sense with his counterparts on both the Chinese Nationalist and Communist sides, respectively the wily and well-connected T. V. Soong and the consummately shrewd, deeply experienced Zhou.

Stettinius had grown up on an estate on Long Island and been an executive at General Motors and U.S. Steel before he became Lend-Lease administrator in 1941, then, in 1943, deputy secretary of state. He was evidently a capable man, but his experience, including his role as chairman of the War Resources Board, was entirely domestic, though he had dealt with foreign affairs in a limited way as the administrator of the Lend-Lease program. Historians have described Stettinius's appointment as secretary of state in 1944 as an indication of Roosevelt's intention to bypass the State Department and to run his own foreign policy. On China specifically, the president tended to communicate with Chiang through his trusted adviser Harry Hopkins, who maintained close contact with Chiang's brothers-in-law, H. H. Kung and T. V. Soong, who were often in Washington.

The ambassador to China during most of the war, Clarence E. Gauss, whose feelings about Chiang and the KMT pretty much matched those of Stilwell, had always been kept out of the loop, and, unlike Hurley, he enjoyed no direct access to the American president. Also unlike Gauss, Hurley was disinclined to listen to the views of the China hands like Service, Davies, and Ludden, who were technically political advisers to Wedemeyer and continued to send their reports to him. "If I haven't been given American policy, I shall make American policy," Hurley announced on arriving in Chungking. And he did, following his own whimsical course, getting support from the president when he needed it and essentially silencing alternative government views.

The professional China hands, most of whom had been in China for a decade or more and served in several different postings around the country, were instantly skeptical of the new special emissary's chances of success. There was too much animosity between the Nationalists and the Communists, too much past bloodshed, and, most important, too many irreconcilable ultimate goals for Mao and Chiang to come to any sort of durable compromise, the China hands believed. By coincidence, on the very day of Hurley's arrival in Chungking, John Davies, already there, composed a cable to the State Department in which he'd laid out in highly realistic terms the conflicting ways in which the two major parties in China viewed each other and the United States.

For the Communists, he wrote, "the United States is the greatest hope and the greatest fear." On the one hand, they "recognize that if they receive American aid [which would be their reward for making a deal with Chiang] they can quickly establish control over most if not all of China, perhaps without civil war." This was because, in Davies's view, once the CCP had an American imprimatur, many of Chiang's officers and bureaucrats would desert him, and Chiang of course understood that. Correspondingly, the Communists' greatest fear was that the United States would give aid only to Chiang, and the more aid he got, Davies wrote, "the greater the likelihood of his precipitating a civil war and the more protracted and costly will be the Communist unification of China."

Put another way, Davies's argument was that for either Mao or Chiang to accept the terms of the other would mean his own destruction. Both parties wanted to emerge on top in the civil conflict they both knew was coming once Japan was out of the way. Both parties also wanted to avoid appearing intransigent before Chinese and international public opinion, being the party that refused to talk and preferred civil war instead, and that common desire is what gave Hurley his opening.

And so, despite the small chance of success, the United States kept on trying to work out a deal. The effort to bring about peace in China arose from the deepest historical mission of the United States, which was to advance its commercial and strategic interests by nurturing free-enterprise, liberal-democratic values throughout the world. It was to make the world safe for democracy, as President Wilson phrased it, or, as later generations had it, to see the progress of human rights. In China in the months before and after the end of World War II, America saw the possibility of a modern liberal society rising from the ashes of its wartime devastation, and this vision exerted a powerful influence. And in fact, even though Hurley didn't realize it, his arrival in China marked the last chance that the world's most populous country was going to have to forge itself into a modern, democratic state, one whose citizens enjoyed the protections and rights that it has always been the American goal to make universal.

The American scheme worked in Germany and Japan, the defeated powers, but China, with its flawed government and powerful Communist opposition, was to prove a more difficult terrain, and the smarter observers of the scene understood that. "Hurley arrived at Yenan thinking that to bring Chiang's Kuomintang and the Communists together was not much different from persuading Republicans and Democrats to accept bipartisanship in a time of national crisis," Davies remarked years later. Hurley never understood Davies's point. Arriving in Yenan, he told Barrett that he'd once settled a bitter and highly publicized dispute between the Sinclair Oil Company and the government of Mexico, and, moreover, that he'd gotten a fee of a million dollars, and he seemed to suppose that if he could handle that negotiation successfully, he could handle the Chinese one as well. Barrett wondered if the two sides in the Mexico-Sinclair dispute weren't a good deal more anxious to reach an agreement than the two sides in China.

Hurley was born in 1883 in what was then the Oklahoma Territory, and he'd had a hard, colorful, gritty, up-from-the-boondocks life very different from all those Ivy League easterners he would meet in his career overseas. He helped support his family by working in a coal mine in Choctaw Indian territory, starting at the age of eleven. His mother died when he was thirteen and, according to his very admiring official biographer, he continued to work delivering coal or breaking horses or taking whatever odd jobs he could find even as he read voraciously and dreamed of becoming a lawyer. He went to a newly opened night school in the town of Phillips, in Choctaw territory, while during the day he worked as a mule skinner in a coal mine (driving the animals as they carried coal out of the pits), then as a cattle herder for a local butcher. He was an outdoor kid, a friend of young Choctaws (to whom he remained loyal and sympathetic all his life), a rider of horses across the Oklahoma scrubland. He was scrappy, smart, and audacious.

In 1898 with the outbreak of the Spanish-American War, Hurley tried to become one of Theodore Roosevelt's Rough Riders, but he was rejected because he was only fifteen. He finished high school in a year, then attended the Indian University, the only white boy in his class at a school created to serve Choctaw and Chickasaw Indian boys. He had many interests. He played the French horn in the school orchestra, was on the football and baseball teams, and led the school's undefeated debate team. He graduated with a BA in 1905, worked for a while in the Indian Service in Oklahoma, and then went to Washington, D.C., where he was admitted to the National University Law School (which was later absorbed by the George Washington University School of Law). While still in law school, he went unannounced to the White House, barged his way into the president's office, and, on the grounds that he had almost been a Rough Rider, asked him for a government job. Roosevelt, the story goes, refused on the grounds that if he had a government job, Hurley would become a lazy drunk. Better to go to Oklahoma and make something of yourself, the president told him.

Within a year, at the age of twenty-five, Hurley had his law degree. Three years later, when he was just twenty-eight, he was president of the Tulsa Bar Association.

Mostly he worked for oil companies. He made $50,000 on one case alone. In another, he was paid with a parcel of prairie territory, which was soon enveloped by the expanding city of Tulsa. He was expert in the law governing Indian territory, and that involved him in cases having to do with land claims and mineral rights. Once, in a case involving an illegal transfer of land, his opponent's lawyer complained to the judge that Hurley was failing to stick to "the fundamental law."

"Counsel asks for the fundamental law in this case," Hurley replied. "It is very simple and not subject to misunderstanding. It was handed down to Moses on Mt. Sinai. It is *Thou shalt not steal.*"

Someone like Hurley was bound to get into politics, and he ran for the state senate as a Republican in a heavily Democratic district, narrowly losing. When he was a boy, one of his best friends was a quarter-blood Choctaw named Victor Locke Jr., a Republican who, despite his English-sounding name, could speak the Choctaw language and was appointed principal chief of the Choctaw Nation by President Taft. Locke named Hurley national attorney for the 28,000-member tribe, in which post he won 115 of the 118 cases decided during his tenure, one of which saved the Oklahoma Choctaws from bankruptcy. His arguments before the courts and Congress were eloquent statements about the historical mistreatment of the Indians and both the moral and legal need for redress. In 1916, when the newly elected Democratic president Woodrow Wilson reappointed Hurley the Choctaw national attorney,

Wilson wrote, "Patrick Hurley is one of the few men who have held a position of trust for the Indians without using it for his personal benefit."

Hurley served in the American expeditionary force to France in World War I, attaining the rank of colonel. After the war he became secretary of war in the Hoover administration. During 1939 and 1940, having resumed his career as an oil company lawyer, he achieved national attention in the Mexican expropriation case that he recounted to Barrett in Yenan. Mexico's action provoked a furious, nationalistic response in the United States and an equally firm refusal on Mexico's part to bow to American pressure. For months, as Hurley negotiated on behalf of Sinclair, the newspapers predicted that there could and would be no deal. But Hurley, fighting the nationalistic hard-liners on both sides, negotiated an agreement in which Mexico compensated Sinclair for the appropriated properties. Virtually alone among the American actors in the drama, Hurley had accepted Mexico's sovereign right to take over the Sinclair holdings. "He was a realist," the American ambassador to Mexico said at the time, "and knew that the interests of his company depended on the policy of give and take."

He was also an adamant and outspoken opponent of the New Deal, once telling FDR to his face, "You know, Mr. President, I'm against everything you stand for politically," but in the circumstances of the war, he was too good a man not to be put to use.

His first assignment came right after Pearl Harbor, when FDR summoned Hurley to the White House and told him, "We're looking for a man with a little piracy in his blood." The Japanese were in the process of overrunning European and American colonial possessions in Southeast Asia and had imposed a blockade of the Philippines, where General Douglas MacArthur was pinned down on the Bataan peninsula with 76,000 American and Filipino troops. Hurley was being asked to find ways to break the blockade, and he accepted the mission. He went to Australia, hired ships, and ran ammunition and other supplies to the beleaguered soldiers. In at least one instance, as noted earlier, he camouflaged his blockade-running vessels by having them fly the Japanese flag, which was a technical act of piracy—FDR got what he asked for. Had Hurley ever been captured by the enemy, the Japanese could have executed him as a criminal rather than accord him the rights due to a prisoner of war. "We were out-shipped, out-planned, out-manned, and out-gunned by the Japanese forces from the beginning," he said later, ruing the fact that for every ship that slipped through the Japanese encirclement, two were lost. Eventually, after MacArthur escaped to Australia, the Americans surrendered and were forced on the notorious Bataan death march to prison camps.

In 1943, Roosevelt sent Hurley on his first trip to China, to prepare Chiang Kai-shek for his appearance at the upcoming Cairo conference, where the American president was to meet Churchill before moving on to Tehran for meetings with Stalin. A year later, Hurley was back, as boisterous and optimistic as ever, ready to undertake his new job as FDR's special representative in China.

Hurley's arrival in China coincided with a mood of crisis over matters other than KMT-CCP relations. The gravest one was caused by the continuing Ichigo offensive and the Chinese failure to stop it. "It was obvious to me when I first arrived that Jap objective was our base at Kunming and this was also the opinion of the Generalissimo," Hurley said in an early cable to Stettinius. "Our situation here is desperate and if we do not stop the Japs before Kunming all the protestations we may make will have no effect on the verdict of history. America will have failed in China. For that reason I think that you should use all of your power to give Wedemeyer what a victory requires."

On the same day, December 6, as Hurley's "consternation" cable to Stettinius, George Atcheson, the gifted, experienced, and knowledgeable number two at the American embassy in Chungking, wrote to Stettinius: "We do not wish to be alarmists, but it seems clear to us that the time has come to take precautionary measures and prepare as best we can for such contingencies as may arise"—i.e., the possibility that Japan would bypass Kunming and advance directly on the government's temporary capital in Chungking instead. Atcheson recommended that non-essential American personnel be evacuated, that an alternative temporary capital be chosen, perhaps in the remote Chinese far west, and that all confidential files plus the cores and the rotors to the code machines at the Chungking embassy be destroyed. Atcheson thought of everything, even asking Washington to provide "a considerable reserve supply of American currency . . . since Chinese currency is likely to become useless."

Alarm over the consequences of continuing, unresolved Chinese division in the face of Japanese aggression was also raised by General Claire Chennault. The situation, he had told FDR directly at the end of September,

> is extremely grave, since imminent loss of East China will mean loss of any airfield from which vital points in Japanese military structure can be attacked. It will also mean great reduction in Chinese military power and corresponding increase in power of Yenan regime. There is obviously grave danger of civil war in China. Furthermore, if there is civil war in China, the Yenan regime has an excellent chance of emerging victorious, with or without Russian aid. But Russians also surely will give aid. I know that ties between the two are denied; but I cannot altogether forget the suggestive fact that the Yenan leaders took the rigid Communist Party line at the time of the Russo-German pact. I need not point out the extent to which the establishment of a government in China closely tied to Moscow would upset the balance of power in the Pacific, or what this might mean to us in the future.

Roosevelt's response to these alarms was to increase the pressure on Chiang to do exactly what Chiang couldn't do. On September 16, during a meeting with Churchill in Quebec, he fired off a lengthy letter to Chiang warning him that while "we are rolling the enemy back in defeat all over the world," and while "our advance across the Pacific is swift," it could all be "too late for China." Needed now is "drastic and immediate action on your part" or the consequence will be "military disaster." Specifically, FDR demanded that Chiang do two things: spring into action on the Salween, so the land route to China could be reopened, and put Stilwell in "unrestricted command of all your forces." Only by doing these two things, Roosevelt implied, could Chiang keep American aid flowing. "I have expressed my thoughts with complete frankness," Roosevelt concluded, "because it appears plainly evident to all of us here that all of your and our efforts to save China [will have been wasted] by further delays."

Here is the president of the United States, having sent millions of his fellow citizens into mortal danger in war, doing what he must, which was to insist that the beneficiary of the American sacrifice shoulder its share of the burden. And Roosevelt's advisers had been telling him that if China lost Kunming, it would essentially be knocked out of the war, and then "at least an additional year and possibly several years of additional warfare . . . would be required to defeat Japan and liberate China." But in truth, as it turned out, the alarms of Hurley, Atcheson, and Chennault turned out to be exaggerated. There was no Japanese run on Kunming or on Chungking, no need to evacuate the embassy. Chiang's "defense in depth" strategy was in this effective. Meanwhile, Chiang believed that in tying down a million Japanese troops in China, he was already shouldering the burden of the war, and what, he could have asked in any case, did the American president mean by "our efforts to save China"? China had survived for eight years, four of them before Pearl Harbor, while the United States was supplying Japan with strategic raw materials. What reason was there to think China couldn't go on for a few months or even years more now that the United States was "rolling the enemy back in defeat all over the world"? Was it wrong of him to believe that saving China meant not fighting Japan, which was nearly defeated anyway, but making sure that a Communist dictatorship didn't position itself to take power once Japan had been disposed of by the valiant Americans?

This was the fundamental incompatibility of the priorities of Chiang and Roosevelt, the one striving to preserve himself, the other to save the lives of his nation's soldiers. For the United States, getting the government and the Communists into the same "corral," as Feis later put it, became a panacea, the solution for China. And everybody, including those who disagreed with each other about almost everything else, supported this solution. Even Chennault, Chiang's best friend among the Americans, told Roosevelt that what was needed was "true unification between Chungking and Yenan," so that the civil war that Chiang knew was looming in the future wouldn't take place. That was where FDR's personal representative needed to play his historic role.

And so Hurley bent himself to the task. In his initial meetings with Chiang and with the Communists in Chungking, the outlines of a deal had begun to come clear, at least to Hurley. It would be a five-point plan in which the CCP would essentially gain recognition as a legal party in exchange for agreeing to place its army under a centralized command. Chiang and the KMT were ready to accept this arrangement, and why not? Legal recognition of the CCP would be a small price to pay if the party's leaders were willing to give up independent control of their armed forces. Chiang must have been extremely skeptical that Hurley would persuade Mao to agree to this formula.

Hurley's first formal meeting in Yenan was on November 8. Hurley dominated the opening session, which took place in the morning, presenting a written version of the five-point plan to Mao. This document called on both parties, the KMT and the CCP, to "work together for the unification of all military forces in China for the immediate defeat of Japan and the reconstruction of China." In a passage clearly written by Hurley and redolent of the effort made over the decades to remake China in the Christian and democratic image of the United States, the document further called for both parties to work for "a government of the people, by the people, and for the people." Then came the paragraph in which the central government would regard the CCP as a legal party.

Mao was in command during the afternoon meeting. He began with what Barrett called a bit of "polite persiflage," and then plunged into an angry denunciation of Chiang, on whom he put the blame for China's disunity. What was needed, Mao said, was not simply a central military council but an entirely reorganized government consisting of the KMT, the CCP, and the other political parties. In other words, Mao insisted on much more than mere legal status for the Communists. His demand was for a coalition government in which the KMT and the CCP would have equal status, though he doesn't seem to have provided any specifics as to how exactly this government would function. Mao was ominously confident of his chances should there be no agreement on a coalition. Hurley's assumption seems to have been that the central government was overwhelmingly powerful and that the Communists would gratefully accept its offer of legal status. His five-point proposal specified that the Communist troops would get "the same pay and allowances" as Nationalist troops, the implication being that this would be an improvement for the ragtag Communist troops.

Mao bluntly pointed out to Hurley his mistake on this point, saying (as reported by Barrett), "the National Government armies were no longer able to fight." The government had nearly two million men in its army and 779,000 of its men were blockading the Communists, while the rest of the government armies simply ran away when the Japanese were there. The best historians of this period estimate that 400,000 government troops were blockading the CCP, half of Mao's figure but still a high proportion of Chiang's forces. As for equal pay and allowances,

Mao pointed out what many of the American China hands had already noted in their dispatches to Washington, which is that, in Barrett's summary, "Chiang's men were starved and miserably clad, and many were so sick and weak they would scarcely march even for short distances." Barrett agreed on this point, writing: "I had myself seen soldiers topple over and die after marching less than a mile." The Communist armies were the ones who were well fed, well clothed, and in good physical condition.

Hurley's reply to this was to point out that, so far from running away, China had won recent victories in Burma and on the Salween, and, moreover, that Mao's tirade against Chiang contained the words that any enemy of China might use, somebody who wished to see China "continue to be divided against itself." This was nonsense, and Mao knew it. "General," he said to Hurley, "what I have said about Chiang Kai-shek and the Kuomintang has already been said by President Roosevelt, Mr. Churchill, Doctor Sun Fo [Sun Yat-sen's son, an influential member of the KMT's liberal wing], and Madame Sun Yat-sen. Do you consider these persons the enemies of China?"

Hurley changed the subject. Chiang, he said, genuinely wanted to come to terms with the Communists and, as evidence of this, he was willing to give one seat on the National Military Council to the CCP.

Mao was contemptuous of this offer.

Hurley: Well, it's a foot in the door.

Mao: A foot in the door means nothing if your hands are tied behind your back.

Hurley: Membership on the Council would give the Communists full knowledge of all military plans and operations, including, presumably, any contemplated against the Communists themselves.

Mao: The Military Council is a powerless body whose current members are kept in the dark; it is so unimportant that it hasn't bothered to meet in a long time.

"Chairman," Hurley countered, "if you do not think the terms offered by the Generalissimo are fair enough to induce you to join in a coalition government, on just what terms would you be willing to do so?"

Mao spent a day conferring with his cohort and the next day made a counterproposal to Hurley that led to agreement between him and the Communists. When agreement was reached, as Barrett put it, the Communists were "greatly pleased," and no wonder. The agreement gave the Communists everything they wanted, including a "Coalition National Government embracing representatives of all anti-Japanese parties and non-partisan political bodies." This last category consisted of the small, non-armed democratic parties that had emerged in the shadow of the KMT dictatorship, the largest of which, the Democratic League, was the main party of China's left-leaning intellectuals, many of whom had been schooled in the United States. In such a way did the proposal essentially do away with the one-party dictatorship that Chiang had headed since 1927 and that he clearly felt was essential for his continued rule as well as for the future of China—though, as we will see, he did slowly relent on that point under American pressure.

The deal struck in Yenan also included an expansion of Hurley's earlier "of the people" language to a full-fledged elaboration of America's most liberal aspirations for China. "The Coalition National Government will pursue policies designed to promote progress and democracy and to establish justice, freedom of conscience, freedom of the press, freedom of speech, freedom of assembly and association," even "the right of writ of *habeas corpus*," which had never existed in any form in China's three-thousand-year history, and wasn't to exist in its future either. These phrases were obviously inserted by Hurley, who spent an afternoon and an evening fiddling with the text before the final meeting on the morning of November 10. Hurley's political differences with Roosevelt did not stop him from tossing into the text a couple of Roosevelt's most ringing phrases. The new government of China "will also pursue policies intended to make effective those two rights defined as freedom from fear and freedom from want."

The movement Mao controlled had no free press, no free speech, and no rights of assembly or habeas corpus. But he and his lieutenants were happy to sign an American-style bill of rights since they had no intention of honoring it if they ever came to power. They had simply accepted an unalterable principle of political life, which is that the party out of power has more to gain from demanding democratic freedoms than the party in power. This was especially the case in China in late 1944, when disaffection with the KMT, but not with the remote, largely unknown Communists, was growing, and the government's response consisted of the very repressive measures—imprisonments, press censorship, and bans on demonstrations—that the Communists themselves would make permanent features of their rule.

The American attempt to mediate between the two main Chinese armed parties did not lead to the collapse of the Kuomintang and the empowerment of the Communists, but it inevitably helped the Communists with Chinese public opinion. Mao could, without embarrassing himself with the evident expediency of it all, feed the hunger in China for liberal freedoms, portraying the KMT as freedom's enemy and himself as its champion, though the paradox is that the greater long-range threat to freedom in China was Mao himself.

On Hurley's last afternoon in Yenan, the two sides engaged in what Barrett called "a love feast, with everybody in a happy mood." Later, outside the meeting hall, Hurley said to Mao, "Chairman, I think it would be appropriate for you and me to indicate, by signing these terms, that we consider them fair and just," and so they placed the documents on a flat stone and each man in turn scratched out his signature—Mao signing American-style with a pen rather than Chinese-style with a waxed seal. Just before leaving for the airfield, Hurley did add a caveat. "Chairman Mao," he said, "you of course understand that although I consider these fair terms, I cannot guarantee the Generalissimo will accept them."

The optimistic Hurley, though, seems to have anticipated no problem getting Chiang to agree to the revised document. Hurley himself had signed it, after all, and he enjoyed the weight and prestige of the United States, which wanted a deal and whose support Chiang desperately needed. He had had close consultations with Chiang before he turned up in Yenan, so surely he had some idea of just how far Chiang would go. For these reasons, the Communists probably felt that Hurley knew what he was doing. As a sign of that, Zhou and a secretary accompanied Hurley on his plane to Chungking, where, presumably, Zhou would handle any further necessary refining of the text.

As soon as Hurley landed in Chungking on November 10, he sent the Hurley-Mao document to T. V. Soong, intending that it be passed on to the Gimo. An alarmed Soong rushed to Hurley's quarters. "The Communists have sold you a bill of goods," Soong said. "Never will the National Government grant the Communist request."

What was this bill of goods? The exact terms of the coalition envisaged by the Hurley-Mao agreement were never spelled out, though presumably they involved some sharing of power and authority, a certain number of government portfolios going to the Communists while Chiang remained president of the republic. But Soong believed that

Hurley had been taken in by Mao on this point. It was obvious to him and to Chiang that the Communists would be able to use their presence in a coalition to strengthen their hand in an ultimate contest for total power, to win from within. In other words, the very reason the Communists were happy with what Hurley had wrought was the reason Chiang couldn't accept it. When confronted with reports of American discussions with the Communists, Chiang commonly expressed the worry that, once again, the Americans would be "fooled" by the Communists' hypocritically heartfelt expressions of love for the United States and for democracy, and of selfless determination to do whatever they could to help defeat Japan. Now Hurley, whom he had counted on for understanding, was repeating the pattern. Despite Chiang's warnings to the contrary, Hurley continued to believe the Molotov-Stalin description of Mao and his followers as "margarine Communists" rather than radical Marxist-Leninists whose goal was both total power and a total transformation of Chinese society. This belief formed the basis for his negotiating strategy. In Hurley's frequently reiterated view, the Soviets would not back the CCP, which meant that if the pressure on the Communists remained strong and consistent, they would eventually have no choice but to accept a weak role in a KMT-dominated government.

But Chiang knew better. He knew that Mao was a real revolutionary, and that there was a deep ideological connection between him and the Soviets. As we'll see, Chiang hoped that by fostering good ties with Moscow he could prevent the Russians from giving all-out backing to the CCP, but he nonetheless found himself warning Cassandra-like of the Communists' nature as fully red, while the Communists for their part encouraged the United States in the belief that they were radish-like.

On the airplane back to Chungking, Barrett sat next to Zhou, and he asked him whether he thought the United States or the Soviet Union to be the greater democracy. "We consider the Soviet Union to be the greatest democracy in the world," Zhou replied, but, he added, "we know it may take a hundred years for us to attain this state of democracy. Meanwhile we would be extremely glad if we could enjoy the same sort of democracy you do in the United States today." Never mind the ominous naïveté, or the willful ideological blindness, in believing Stalin's Russia to be history's greatest democracy. What Americans always took away from a comment like that one of Zhou's was the benign and reassuring message that Communism was an ideal to be achieved in some distant future and that in the very long meantime, the Communists could be friends of the United States.

Given Chiang's large armies, his reputation abroad as the savior of China, and the recognition he enjoyed from other countries, including the Soviet Union, as the only legitimate ruler of China, why should Chiang have felt that a deal with the Communists was a path to disaster? The answer to that question has to do with the chief difference between the United States and China, allied countries that could nonetheless not find common ground: It's what the historian Tang Tsou has called American simplicity versus Chinese complexity. For Americans, the singular goal was the defeat of Japan, and since that was also the Chinese goal, Americans couldn't understand why Chiang seemed so hesitant about measures that would help to achieve it, such as a reform of the Chinese armed forces, the firing of incompetent commanders, the consolidation of ramshackle, underequipped, and badly led divisions into a smaller number of disciplined and effective troops. For Americans like Stilwell this military reform was simple good sense. It would help defeat Japan and, along the way, equip Chiang with the kind of army he'd need in the future confrontation with the Communists.

Similarly, Hurley must have felt that the KMT would welcome a chance to compete peacefully with the Communists in American-style political contests, in which everybody has his say, the party with the most votes wins, and the losing party will wait for another chance to win in the next election. But what was simple for the Americans was infinitely complex for Chiang. Chiang's power rested on a network of personal relations among China's military chieftains that went back to his days as commander of the Whampoa Military Academy and, in some key instances, to his days in Japan when he was a young military academy cadet. The armed forces were not simply an army; they were a network of power bases, some loyal to Chiang and others (often the more effective of them) independent of him, potentially even rivals to him. Chiang needed to keep commanders loyal to him in charge of their armies, even if it meant tolerating the way they padded their rolls with nonexistent soldiers so as to receive their salaries from the central government, even if they lined their pockets by trading strategic materials with the Japanese, even if they were ineffectual commanders. Chiang refused to fire the commanders who owed allegiance to him. Moreover, during the war, he refused to supply able commanders in combat who did not owe allegiance to him, because in China's quiltwork of personal military relations, they were not part of his personal network.

Chiang faced a similar problem when it came to political reform, a rather abstract, shorthand phrase whose practical meaning was allowing the Communists into the government as a legal party and then competing with them for popular favor. For the United States, political reform would give the Chinese government legitimacy, broaden its popular support, and quell the incubating dissatisfaction and disillusionment among students and intellectuals. The coalition would give Chiang the stronger portfolios, and he would continue to be commander in chief of the armies, an ally of the United States, and the president of his country.

Chiang, however, was convinced that political reform is what would destroy him. For him, the Americans, with all their goodwilled naïveté and gullibility, failed to take into account the reality of Chinese political culture, in which to be conciliatory, to be forced to grant legal status to an erstwhile bandit gang, would be interpreted as weakness, and to be seen as weak was to invite defections to the other side. The Communists themselves would enjoy a tremendous surge in popularity, prestige, and stature. This was the reason for Davies's prediction that many of Chiang's senior officers would desert him once the Communists had an American imprimatur, because in China's winner-take-all political system there is no profit in sticking to a loser. Centuries ago, Machiavelli warned that the prince who invited powerful rivals into his principality, hoping to disarm them and weaken them, was paving the way for his own loss of power. Chiang Kai-shek probably didn't read Italian Renaissance political theory, but he nonetheless understood that his own power depended not on making a deal with the vigorous and durable Communists but on not making a deal with them and, instead, on destroying them, lest they destroy him.

Hurley's negotiation was the most visible and conspicuous American initiative in China but far from the only one. The others were less visible and less conspicuous. Many American agencies operated in China in the last stages of the war, including several different intelligence agencies. Among these was, for example, the innocuous Office of War Information (OWI), which collected Chinese and Japanese written materials and disseminated American government propaganda to the Chinese press. It was headed for much of the war by John K. Fairbank, the Harvard historian who had first gone to China in 1932 and had an unparalleled network of contacts among Chinese intellectuals, many of whom had studied in the United States. Another important group was known as AGFRTS, for Air and Ground Forces Resources and Technical Staff, which had been put into operation in the spring of 1944. Based in Kunming, it collected information on the weather and on the movements of Japanese planes, troops, and ships—information indispensable for Chennault's 14th Air Force, aka the Flying Tigers, with its many airfields scattered about unoccupied China from which it attacked Japanese targets.

AGFRTS was staffed mostly by agents seconded from the Office of Strategic Services, among them Julia McWilliams, who later became the famous cookbook writer and television personality Julia Child. Another highly regarded AGFRTS agent, a man who set up a dozen or so information-gathering centers behind enemy lines, was an impressive, highly capable captain named John Birch, who, as we will see, would later command a dangerous and fateful mission in Communist-held territory in Shandong Province.

Groups like OWI and AGFRTS were, as Davies later wrote, "among the more civilized elements of OSS." But, Davies continued, "there were others not so nice," and among these first and foremost was a secret organization headed by Captain Milton Miles, the American naval attaché in Chungking. Miles fought constant turf battles with other American agencies in China, especially the OSS, which tried and failed to put him under its command. He was the American closest to one Tai Li, a former cadet at the Whampoa Military Academy who had been a close and trusted aide of Chiang Kai-shek's ever since. In the early 1930s, Tai was made head of a clandestine outfit known as the Blue Shirts, which had been created by another of Chiang's former Whampoa cadets, Ho Ying-chin, whom Chiang made his chief of staff and then minister of war after the Japanese invasion. The name Blue Shirts suggests that they were inspired by the Brown Shirts and the Black Shirts, the paramilitary enforcers used by the rising fascist leaders of Italy and Germany to intimidate their opponents, but it was also a kind of traditional Chinese secret society formed by the Whampoa clique that supported their leader, Chiang, to whom they took an oath of loyalty. When war broke out, Tai Li was named head of Chiang's secret police, officially and euphemistically called the Bureau of Investigation and Statistics, or BIS, the most feared institution in China.

The association between American intelligence and Tai is one of the troubling aspects of the Sino-American relationship, precisely because it was close and cordial. William "Wild Bill" Donovan, the corporate lawyer who was the founding head of the OSS, came to China twice, in 1943 and 1945, and had cordial meetings with Tai that were followed by epistolary exchanges so fulsome as to seem almost parodies of themselves. "Your Honor, General Donovan," Tai wrote in one, "my ever longing for you through the stretching distance is like the endless rolling billows and floating clouds in the sky."

His maudlin efforts at ingratiation notwithstanding, Tai was a tough and exceedingly unsentimental operator who insisted on total control over American intelligence operations in his territory. His closest American associate was Captain Miles, who was known as Mary, because when he was at the Naval Academy, class of 1922, Mary Miles Minter was a famous Broadway star. "Mary" Miles was a gregarious and charming naval officer who had been sent by Admiral Ernest King, the chief of naval operations and a close Roosevelt adviser, to China as the attaché at the American embassy in Chungking, charged initially with monitoring Japanese shipping on the China coast and collecting information for an eventual American landing there. Fairbank recalled him as "a youngish man in khaki shorts and shirt" whose "face was not only handsome but actually rather pretty, producing two dimples when he smiled."

Miles, whether pretty or not, enjoyed the backing of the powerful Admiral King, and this gave him a bureaucratic status that enabled him to expand his operations from uncontroversial information gathering to very controversial forms of cooperation with Tai. He was uncontrolled either by the American embassy or by the American military commander, Stilwell first, then Wedemeyer. The ambassador before Hurley, Clarence Gauss, once complained that Tai was the head of a Chinese "Gestapo," and he wanted the embassy to be "freed of all official relationship to Army and Navy officers who may have connections with General Tai," by which he specifically meant Miles. But King, knowing of the State Department's unhappiness with Miles, had him promoted to commodore and made him the head of the new U.S. Naval Group, China, which would be directly under King's command. This made Miles free to do what he wanted, and together with Tai, he established a new organization for "special measures in the war effort against Japan." It was known as SACO (pronounced "socko") for Sino-American Cooperative Organization, among whose thirty-four separate areas of activity were sabotage, assassinations of Japanese and puppet officials, and a school for intelligence agents—Fairbank called it a "sabotage training center"—at a secret location known, with more than a touch of irony, as Happy Valley, about twelve miles west of Chungking along the Jialong River. "It's a tight little kingdom," one naval intelligence officer, Lieutenant Charles G. Dobbins, wrote of Happy Valley, "where at every entrance and cross path sentries armed to the teeth stand twenty-four hours a day."

The creation of SACO was the kind of thing that happens in war. It was aimed at helping to defeat Japan, not at becoming involved in internal Chinese matters. But Miles's close association with Tai, who was the director of SACO, with Miles the deputy director, put the United States on intimate terms with a man known to the expanding cohort of Americans in China as J. Edgar Himmler. His BIS had tentacles reaching into Japanese-occupied cities. He had an extensive network of guerrillas in south and east China that operated behind enemy lines and escorted American intelligence officers on clandestine trips to the coast, where they watched Japanese shipping.

But BIS was known also to keep tabs on Chinese dissenters and, worse than keeping tabs—or so many Americans believed—to arrest and execute them. Tai and the BIS were in this sense the counterparts of Kang Sheng and the Communist intelligence network, though the Americans in China had much less awareness of Kang than they did of Tai. The two services competed against each other in a vicious, ongoing undercover war that began in the late 1920s and continued in the early 1930s, when the KMT, having split with the Communists, tried to wipe them out, and the Communists strove to survive.

In February 1942, Tai Li discovered that a seven-member Communist espionage ring had penetrated his organization, including the man in charge of the radio sets used by Tai's agents throughout China. "This Special Party Branch served as a dagger, stabbing right into the heart of Tai Li's Bureau of Investigation and Statistics. . . . The secret tasks of several hundreds of radio stations and several thousands of operators were all in the hands of our party," according to an official Communist biography of the head of the ring, Zhang Luping, a young and attractive woman.

Captain Milton "Mary" Miles reviews Chinese trainees at Happy Valley, the headquarters of SACO, the Sino-American Cooperation Organization, outside Chungking.

The discovery of these moles inside the BIS alarmed Tai and is one of the incidents that impelled him to seek cooperation with the Americans, who were presumably more expert in counterespionage. All seven Communist agents were arrested, tortured, and, two years later, executed. The Communists only admitted in 1983 that the BIS spy ring had even existed; previously, Mao hadn't wanted to give credibility to the accusations of KMT intelligence.

There is some uncertainty about just how repressive Tai actually was. The conventional wisdom among Americans in China was that he was responsible for a great deal of wrongdoing. Davies's word for him was "unsavory." Davies said that Tai's "main function was to hunt down individuals suspected of being anti-Chiang, though he also had networks in Japanese-occupied territory where he mainly tried to keep track of the Communist underground." Joseph Ralston Haydon, a former chairman of the political science department at the University of Michigan who rose to the senior ranks of the OSS, warned Donovan against being associated with Tai Li because his methods were "assassination by poison and dagger and subtler methods." Even Wedemeyer, no bleeding heart when it came to Chiang's domestic methods, found the Miles-Tai relationship troubling. He practically pleaded with the War Department to withdraw from SACO and terminate Miles's relationship with Tai. Tai Li, Wedemeyer wrote,

> is mainly preoccupied with collecting information on Chinese and on foreigners within unoccupied China. His interest in the Japanese is purely secondary. His methods of operations closely parallel those of the Gestapo and the OGPU [the Soviet secret police]. Continued association and connection with him and his organization by the US has injured America in the eyes of liberal, right-thinking Chinese and has raised doubts as to our motives and the sincerity of our expressed purposes in fighting this war.

And later, with SACO and Miles still in operation, Wedemeyer wrote again:

> If the American public ever learned that we poured supplies into a questionable organization such as Tai Li operates, without any accounting, it would be most unfortunate indeed. Miles has been Santa Claus out here for a long time.

Lieutenant Dobbins, who compiled a report on Tai for the American Military Intelligence Division, wrote, "Hundreds of Tai Li's victims have been killed, thousands languish in prisons and concentration camps not knowing why they are there or for how long."

What is curious is a certain abstract quality to these summaries of disappearances, tortures, and executions that are alleged to have taken place during the war. Some victims of KMT repression are known — including, for example, Ma Yinchu, an American-trained economist and a regular critic of Chiang. Ma was kept for much of the war under house arrest, which, of course, was a repressive measure, but he was not killed, nor was he sent to a concentration camp or a harsh prison; as we will see, when he was released from house arrest, he immediately began making heated anti-KMT speeches. Before the war, in the 1930s, Tai's Blue Shirts carried out several assassinations, including those of at least two liberal critics of the KMT regime, Yang Xingfo and Shi Liangcai, the editor of the Shanghai newspaper *Shi Bao*. In addition, a Blue Shirt publication boasted of the executions of some forty "traitors" in Wuhan, that is, Chinese who were collaborating with the Japanese enemy—this in the years between the Mukden Incident in 1931 and the Marco Polo Bridge Incident six years later. There were also executions of Chiang's rivals for power, including members of a group of young generals whom Tai Li suspected of plotting to arrest Chiang late in 1943. In 1944 Chiang had one of his favorite generals, Zhang Deneng, shot when, instead of defending Changsha against the Japanese, Zhang evacuated the city with trucks allegedly crammed with his own possessions. Chiang, as Jay Taylor has written, would not have stopped himself from ordering large numbers of executions if he had felt his regime was threatened, but there is no clear evidence that he actually did.

The KMT secret police and Tai most assuredly did not observe the niceties of due process. It can be assumed that beatings and torture of prisoners were common in China then, as they are in China now. But the BIS was neither the Gestapo nor the OGPU, not in its efficiency, its thoroughness, or its documented wholesale murderousness. China under the KMT was not a democracy, nor was it a fascist regime meriting comparison to Nazi Germany or Stalinist Russia; indeed, given the conditions of the war, the atmosphere of suspicion and intrigue, the existence of a rival puppet government, and a Communist opposition, the surprise may be not that its misdeeds were many but that they weren't more. The reports on Tai compiled by Americans in China contain virtually no names of anti-Chiang dissenters who were executed or who disappeared, and this absence of specifics suggests the possibility that some of the reports of abuses by BIS and Tai were based on hearsay, or stemmed from a tendency, encouraged by Tai's reputation as a kind of Nationalist Fu Manchu, always to believe the worst that was said about him.

There were Americans on the scene at the time who believed this. Captain Miles defended Tai, arguing in a memoir that his malfeasance was simply assumed, more imaginary than real. Similarly, in January 1946, an Office of Naval Intelligence (ONI) report by one J. C. Metzel noted that ONI had received "numerous adverse reports on Tai Li," but all of those that Metzel investigated, he wrote, "have proved to be misleading, most of them being false and the others distorted."

The chief of ONI, Thomas B. Inglis, writing about Tai Li at the end of the war, concluded that Tai, while tough, had to be judged by the practices of China, not America. "As head of the National Police in wartime, it has been his duty to deal with traitors and criminals under laws and customs definitely cruel and barbarous by our standards," Inglis wrote. Tai's secret police function, he continued, had "made his name feared in broad elements of Chinese society, not only among the actual criminal classes, traitors and collaborationists, but among the multitude who are basically loyal and respectable." These were the people "who are loud in complaints about his power to arrest and detain without warrant, and his description as hatchet man for the political reactionaries," but Inglis concluded, Tai had "simply carried out wartime duties by methods customary in his country."

The problem, however, was that Tai appeared to be an unscrupulous thug in the mold of Himmler or Beria, Stalin's secret police head, even if the comparison was exaggerated. Tai Li's secret police had the outward attributes of a Gestapo or an OGPU, operating in the shadows in a secret guarded compound and answerable only to one man with the peremptory title Generalissimo. It was known to exist, and therefore it inspired fear, and since nobody knew exactly what it was doing, it inspired even more fear.

By contrast, as we've seen, the sprawling Yenan regime also had its secret police and its shadowy commander, Kang Sheng, who was answerable only to the man known as the Chairman. And yet the observers at the time, the Americans and even the Chinese, seem never to have compared Tai to Kang, and this is telling. The CCP's security apparatus was so entirely closed, so utterly opaque, that it did not come to widespread public notice, and therefore it inspired hardly any fear at all, except among those who, like Wang Shiwei, fell under its boot and disappeared, with no brave reporter to reveal to the world what had become of him.

The lesson is this: The party that stands caught between dictatorship and liberal democracy gives away a strategic advantage to the parties that stand solidly in either one camp or the other. The KMT, whose faults could be known, fell under a certain inescapable and damaging opprobrium; the Communists, whose faults were hidden by distance and propaganda, were given the benefit of the doubt.

Conspiracy theorists would see in such a thing as SACO proof of the underlying goal of the United States, which, as the Communists believed of the American "reactionary clique," was to keep China safe for imperialist exploitation. But notable about the operations of the various intelligence agencies in China in the weeks and months around the end of the war was how ad hoc they were, how uncoordinated and unattached to any central plan or central strategic concept. Miles and SACO, while officially approved by the American government, operated almost independently of any central control. Nobody was in charge of everything, not even Wedemeyer, though he gradually tried to put the espionage activities under his control. "One outstanding weakness in Allied war efforts in China is the fact that there are so many different agencies operating independently and uncoordinated, running at cross purposes," Wedemeyer wrote to Marshall in a top secret cable at the end of 1944.

Thus Hurley was only one of the American protagonists of the Chinese drama. He was ignorant of some of the activities of the others, which would have grave consequences, as we shall see. Hurley's focus, his obsession, remained the attempt to forge a KMT-CCP deal, and he was constantly optimistic about succeeding in this endeavor despite the accumulating evidence that he wasn't and probably couldn't. For a while, after Chiang's rejection of the Hurley-Mao five-point plan, he seemed willing to blame the national government for the ensuing impasse. On November 13, he told Davies that he thought the plan was reasonable, adding that he suspected that the KMT's intransigence was coming from T. V. Soong, whom, to Davies, he called a "crook." Chiang, he declared—this to Davies's great surprise; it was the first time he'd heard of it—had promised to make a deal with the Communists in exchange for the dismissal of Stilwell, and now, he believed, Soong was sabotaging that arrangement.

But Hurley didn't stick with this position for very long. Soon, somewhat inexplicably, he adopted a strikingly pro-Nationalist position. He came to anchor one pole of the American debate about how to deal with Chiang, the other pole being a quid pro quo camp that felt nothing should be given to Chiang, whether Lend-Lease aid or moral support, without getting specific commitments from him in return, especially commitments regarding political reform and the streamlining of his armies. Frank Dorn, Stilwell's aide-de-camp, had made this argument crisply and succinctly. Only dealing with Chiang on an "ultimatum basis," he said, could push China away from its political sclerosis.

Hurley rejected this approach, and in doing so he joined the consensus of the senior American leadership, which had never had much stomach for a quid pro quo policy. This view emanated from the president himself, who, as a fellow head of state, one who knew the loneliness of power, had a natural sympathy for Chiang. "The Generalissimo finds it necessary to maintain his position of supremacy," FDR wrote in a letter to Marshall. "You and I would do the same thing under the circumstances. He is the Chief Executive as well as the Commander-in-Chief, and one cannot speak sternly to a man like that or exact commitments from him the way we might do from the Sultan of Morocco."

Hurley later explained to Roosevelt the reasonableness of Chiang's view that to accept a deal with the CCP would be viewed as a victory for them and a defeat for him, and a defeat for him would be fatal. Moreover, the deal signed by Hurley and Mao on that rock in Yenan skirted the basic question: How was power to be shared in a country that in its three-thousand-year history had never once witnessed a peaceful struggle for power? Hurley, in making his deal with Mao, had failed to understand, as Davies put it, "that the concept of a loyal opposition did not exist in China and that Chiang's system of balancing off a variety of competing opportunists would not survive the introduction of western democracy with its free-for-all popular participation, particularly when one of the competing forces would be a dynamic, proliferating, disciplined organization determined to destroy that system and seize power." Hurley's near-unconditional backing of Chiang was his response to Davies's analysis, but it was exactly the opposite of what Davies, a firm member of the quid pro quo camp, would have had him do. "By December," Davies told an interviewer years later, "General Hurley began to assert, without confirmation from Washington, that American policy was one of unqualified support of the National Government of China and the Generalissimo." It was a policy, Davies continued, that Hurley insisted on enunciating so forcefully and with such an absence of any nuance or willingness to compromise "just at the time its validity . . . had become questionable."

Hurley's support was no doubt welcome to Chiang, but it did not relieve him of his predicament. Chiang firmly believed that democratic reforms, especially allowing a coalition government, would do him in, but at the same time he couldn't simply reject the goal of a deal with the Communists without endangering the goodwill of Hurley and Roosevelt. So the KMT replied to the Hurley-Mao plan with a counterproposal that it must have known would be rejected by the Communists. It had three points, compared to the Mao-Hurley five, but the gist of it was that the central government would agree to recognize the Communists as a legal party if in exchange the Communists would "give their full support to the National Government in the prosecution of the war of resistance, and in the post-war reconstruction, and give over control of all their troops to the National Government."

Shown this counterproposal in Chungking, Zhou, not surprisingly, turned it down, saying there was no point in even carrying it back to Yenan. That established the unalterable pattern between the two Chinese sides and the United States for the next two years of strenuous American attempts at mediation. Mao wanted legal recognition, and of course he could, like the French and Italian Communist parties did after the war, compete peacefully for power in democratic elections, though such a solution would have been unprecedented in China. Mao wanted to be part of a coalition government, but he saw giving up control of his own army as tantamount to suicide. Both sides made paper concessions to satisfy the Americans as well as to court Chinese public opinion, which wanted a deal between the two parties, but the goal of both parties remained the same: power—in the KMT's case to keep it and in the CCP's case to seize it.

Nonetheless, Hurley still believed that his efforts would bear fruit. "We are having some success," he wrote to Secretary of State Stettinius in December, though it is difficult to find any success at all in the historical record. He was meeting daily with Chiang, he said, and Chiang had been persuaded that "in order to unite the military forces of China and to prevent civil conflict it will be necessary for him . . . to make liberal political concessions to the Communist Party and to give them adequate representation in the National Government."

This was the situation in Chungking in those last few weeks of 1944 and the first few of 1945. Chiang remained in his secluded villa, surrounded by his antique porcelains, catered to by silent servants, surrounded by his closest aides, who tended to tell him what he wanted to hear. Zhou lived on his modest lane in Chungking, watched over by the secret police (who occupied space in the same building), lunching and dining with American journalists and diplomats, exuding his usual charm and his aura of reasonableness, providing his assurances that all the Communists wanted was to defeat Japan and to install a democracy in China. Hurley shuttled quixotically between them, striving for common ground and nonexistent common ultimate goals. On December 4, he, Wedemeyer, and Robert B. McClure, Wedemeyer's chief of staff, visited Zhou, and together they tried to convince him to accept what was now the Hurley-Chiang three-point plan, to no avail.

On December 7, Barrett and Zhou flew back to Yenan, Zhou because there was nothing further to talk about in Chungking, Barrett because Hurley wanted him to convince Mao to accept what Zhou had rejected. This initiative produced a remarkable confrontation, one in which Mao spoke with furious incisiveness, telling Barrett why he would never accept Chiang's proposal but at the same time assuring him that he wanted to be friends with the United States, even while expressing supreme confidence that whatever happened in the talks Hurley was brokering, the future belonged to him. It was an impressive performance and an impressive sight, this shrewd peasant Communist in his padded clothing holed up in a cave in China's northwest speaking passionately to an American colonel and almost exactly predicting the future.

Zhou was also present at this meeting, during which Mao, in Barrett's account, more than once "flew into a violent rage." At one point, when Barrett told him that Chiang saw the Hurley-Mao five-point plan as a way of forcing him out of power, Mao leaped to his feet and shouted, "He should have left the stage long ago." Chiang's days may not be numbered, Mao argued in effect, but his years certainly were. And if, Mao said,

> on his record, the United States wishes to continue to prop up the rotten shell that is Chiang Kai-shek, that is its privilege. We believe, however, that in spite of all the United States can do, Chiang is doomed to failure. . . . We are not like Chiang Kai-shek. No nation needs to prop us up. We can stand erect and walk on our own feet like free men.

Mao reaffirmed his earlier vow to provide support for an American landing on China's coast, offering to do what Chiang had so hesitated to do with Stilwell: put his troops under an American commander. "We would serve with all our hearts under an American general, with no strings or conditions attached," he told Barrett. "That is how we feel toward you. If you land on the shores of China, we will be there to meet you, and to place ourselves under your command."

Barrett's impression, as he left this discussion, was that he had "talked in vain to two clever, ruthless, and determined leaders [Mao and Zhou] who felt absolutely sure of the strength of their position." He tried to argue with them, but their answers were of the self-confidently defiant kind. By refusing to accept a deal, Barrett said, Mao would "give Chiang Kai-shek an excellent opportunity to claim that all he has been saying about the Communists being traitors and rebels has been proved beyond contention." Mao's reply: "He has been calling us rebels and traitors for so long that we are accustomed to it. Let him say what he pleases."

Barrett: "If the Japanese are turned back from Kunming and Kweiyang by the forces of the Kuomintang and the United States, you are going to look very bad."

Mao: "Should this happen, no one will cheer louder than we will."

And, finally, Barrett: "If the Generalissimo is defeated and you have done nothing to help him in his hour of need, the United States may withdraw her forces from China altogether [and leave the Communists to fight the Japanese on their own]."

Mao: "The United States cannot abandon China."

Mao was also angry at Hurley, and because the feeling was soon to be mutual, there was a quick unraveling of the cordial atmosphere that had prevailed on Hurley's visit to Yenan. Mao understood, he told Barrett, that Hurley had warned him he couldn't force Chiang to sign the five-point plan they'd agreed to, but "after Chiang Kai-shek refused these fair terms we did not expect General Hurley to come back and press us to agree to a counter-proposal which requires us to sacrifice ourselves," he said. "If General Hurley does not understand this now, he never will." Moreover, Mao warned, "there may come a time when we feel we should show this document, with the signatures, to the Chinese and foreign press."

Mao did not release the document with Hurley's now-embarrassing signature on it, but his mere threat to do so had a deep effect on Hurley, who, in Davies's words, "raged that Mao had tricked him." "The motherfucker!" he exclaimed to Barrett. At the end of 1944, having refused to renew the negotiations, Zhou and Mao laid down four new conditions for a deal: (1) that Chiang release all political prisoners, (2) that he withdraw the government forces surrounding the Communists, (3) that he abolish all "oppressive regulations which restricted the people's freedom," and (4) that he end all secret police activity. Hurley was infuriated. The Communist leaders had to know that these seemingly very pro-democratic demands would make it even more difficult for Chiang to accept a coalition, since, as the historian Herbert Feis put it, Chiang had to regard them "as equivalent to allowing the Communists to carry on their revolution without opposition or hindrance." The Communists, moreover, had no intention of observing the principles involved in the territory they controlled. Mao, with his just-completed two-year purge, had eliminated all opposition, choked off independent views, and tightened control of his own propaganda machinery, which was the only permitted medium of communication.

If Hurley was upset with Mao, he was to be even more upset with members of his own camp, including Davies, Barrett, and even for a time, Wedemeyer, over a series of actions and gestures toward the Communists that merely perpetuated the contacts and conversations that had been taking place between Americans and what some liked to call the Yenan regime since the beginning of the Dixie Mission several months before. Hurley willfully misunderstood the contacts that, coincidentally, were taking place as his negotiating effort was falling apart, and this misunderstanding was to lead to an effort to purge the American embassy of much of its expertise on China.

On December 15, 1944, Barrett went to Yenan again, and Davies, who was making preparations to leave China, went along with him. According to Davies's later account, he was in Hurley's office when the ambassador received a phone call from Barrett, who, he presumed, mentioned the imminent trip to Yenan. After Hurley and Barrett spoke, Davies got on the line with Barrett and "with Hurley standing close by," the two men discussed over the phone their Yenan plans. "It was a routine trip made as a member of Wedemeyer's staff," Davies later wrote. His purpose was "to get a quick last impression of the Communist oligarchy before going to Moscow," a purpose that would seem entirely logical and innocuous for a diplomat about to be posted to the Soviet Union.

But Hurley had been developing suspicions that plotting on behalf of the Communists was taking place behind his back, and he saw Davies's trip as part of the plot. In fact, Davies and some of the others on Wedemeyer's staff did like the Communists and felt comfortable with them, and since they believed the Communists would take power eventually, they felt it was in the American interest to build relations with them, beginning with military cooperation. "The Chinese Communists were going to win," Arthur R. Ringwalt, a political analyst at the embassy in Chungking, said later, summing up the consensus among the China hands, "and what was the use in opposing a movement that was almost unopposable." They also disliked the Kuomintang and made little secret of it. All this led Hurley, befuddled and insecure in an alien political world, to embrace his suspicions.

He was encouraged in this by Foreign Minister T. V. Soong, Hurley's main point of contact with Chiang's government. After Davies's departure for Yenan, Soong called Hurley to tell him that his agents had informed him that Davies was there, and Hurley, who seems genuinely not to have known—despite the phone calls in his presence—told him the report was untrue. When Hurley found out that Davies had indeed left for Yenan, he had to call Soong to assure him he hadn't tried to deceive him. "The Foreign Minister had evidently succeeded in the age-old ploy of putting someone on the defensive through imputing dishonorable motives to an innocent mistake," Davies wrote later.

When Davies returned to Chungking, he explained what had happened; Hurley appeared to be "mollified," Davies thought. But he wasn't. Earlier, in speaking with Davies, Hurley had referred to Soong as one of the "reactionaries" who was blocking a KMT-CCP deal; now he assumed that Soong was a more truthful man than Davies, one of the brightest and most dedicated officers the Foreign Service has ever known. Soong passed along what he claimed to be a reliable intelligence report from his agents in Yenan to the effect that Davies had advised the top Communists to pay no attention to Hurley because he was "an old fool." The fact is that there were more than a few professional Foreign Service officers posted to the embassy in Chungking who believed that to be the case. Some of the career officers, speaking among themselves, began referring to Hurley as a figure of "crass stupidity," as "a stuffed shirt playing at being a great man," as "Colonel Blimp," or, borrowing from what they knew to be a Chinese epithet for him, *dafeng*, or "Big Wind." When one of the American career diplomats, Edward Rice, who'd been in China for a decade, met with Hurley to give him a briefing, he was able to say "Hello" and "Good-bye" but nothing else during what he described as an incomprehensible monologue by the ambassador. "Hurley may not have been insane," another of the American professional diplomats, Philip Sprouse, later told an interviewer, "but at routine staff meetings he would invoke the Magna

Carta, the Declaration of Independence, and the Gettysburg address, with such passion that at the end of his spiel you always felt like saying, 'All right, I'll vote for you.'"

Davies shared this unfavorable assessment of his boss, but the accusation that he had told Mao that Hurley was an old fool lacked all credibility. There was no evidence, apart from Soong's unconfirmed, unsourced, and evidently self-interested intelligence report, that he had done anything of the kind.

At this point in the history of American relations with China, after more than four years of desultory Chinese effort in the war against Japan, four months after the dismissal of the revered Stilwell, and even less time since the scare that the Japanese would move against Chungking, the mood inside the American embassy was, as the newly arrived John Melby put it, "poisonous." The "principal occupation," he wrote in his diary, "seems to be eavesdropping and ducking around corners. Those who hew the line with Ambassador Hurley swagger. Others are mostly evasive."

The disagreements inside the embassy echoed the incoherence of overall American policy, or, as Davies put it at the time, the unlikelihood that "American policy can be anything other than a vacillating compromise between realism and wishful thinking." Hurley pressed the Communists to resume the talks he had come to China to sponsor even as he expressed his growing disillusionment with the "Yenan regime" and his increasing insistence on sticking with Chiang, all the while cultivating his suspicion that his American subordinates were undermining his efforts. At the same time, these subordinates sent a thick file of reports and opinions describing a fateful weakening of Chiang and making clear their view that Hurley was wrong about . . . everything. He was wrong about the degree of support for the Communists. He was wrong in assuming that only Chiang could lead China. The China hands were proposing that the Communists be supplied with arms while Hurley was heading angrily in the opposite direction.

At the end of the year, the embassy held its annual Christmas party, the first since Stilwell's departure, Hurley's arrival, and the Ichigo offensive, and the last that would be attended by Davies, who was due to leave for Moscow within days. "Hurley lifted a glass to me and boomed, 'Here's to you, John,'" Davies remembered. Then, wearing a sprig of evergreen behind his head like an Indian feather and letting loose a succession of Choctaw war whoops, Hurley led a snake dance around the room. At the end of the party, he told Davies that he would stop harassing him. "And you do the same with me."

Before he left China, Davies wrote his cable arguing that the American unwillingness to engage in realpolitik, by which he meant recognizing the Communists' strength and the Kuomintang's weakness, could end up handing the Soviets "a satellite in North China." He sent a copy to Hurley. Five days later, Davies called on Wedemeyer and Hurley to say good-bye, making bold to compliment Hurley on his distinguished career and saying it would be a "deplorable culmination" to get "entrapped by Chinese intrigue in case his negotiations failed."

"Hurley flushed, then turned florid and puffy. He would break my back, his Excellency roared," Davies wrote. Davies leaves his account at that, but Wedemeyer describes an extraordinary ensuing scene, with Hurley making the reckless and slanderous accusation that Davies was a Communist and was trying to undermine the government of China. As Davies heatedly denied the accusation, tears came into his eyes. The next day, Davies left for Moscow, and soon thereafter Hurley tried to break his back.

CHAPTER SEVEN

The Rage of an Envoy

On January 10, 1945, Major Ray Cromley, who had been living in a limestone cave in Yenan since the previous July, sent an urgent, secret message to General Wedemeyer in Chungking. "Yenan Government," Cromley wrote, sitting most likely at a wooden desk lit by a kerosene lantern, "wants to dispatch to America unofficial rpt unofficial group to interpret and explain to American civilians and officials interested the present situation and problems of China."

Cromley, the former *Wall Street Journal* reporter who had worked in Japan, was a member of the military observer group in Yenan, and, as such, he mingled with the senior Communist leaders—at the Beijing operas that were performed al fresco there, at the Saturday night dances, and at the other informal gatherings at which American intelligence officers met Chinese Communist leaders. At least once he'd even danced with Mao's wife, Jiang Qing, the grade-B actress from Shanghai once known as Lan Ping (Blue Apple), who failed to conceal her touch of coquettish glamour beneath her padded cotton clothing.

Cromley told Wedemeyer that none other than Mao and Zhou "will be immediately available either singly or together for exploratory conference at Washington should President Roosevelt express desire at White House as leaders of a primary Chinese party." Mao, who had never been outside China, who had spent the past decade and a half as a sort of bandit chief, a Chinese Robin Hood, or a Chinese Lenin (depending on your point of view), was asking to visit the White House!

Mao's request to meet Roosevelt is similar to requests from another Asian revolutionary leader, Ho Chi Minh, the father of today's Vietnam, who, long before the United States went to war against him, requested American help against French colonialism, not once but twice, and was ignored both times. The idea that the two top leaders of Chinese Communism might, in 1945, have gotten on an airplane and flown to Washington for a meeting with Franklin Roosevelt suggests the main question of the entire twentieth century bedeviling America's relations with Asia: Was there a colossal opportunity the missing of which caused incalculable losses in lives and treasure?

The request Mao and Zhou sent via Crowley came twenty-seven fraught years and two American wars in Asia before Mao actually did meet an American president, Richard M. Nixon, not in Washington but behind the walls of a well-guarded palace in Beijing, and not as a revolutionary brigand but as the semi-deified leader of the world's most populous Communist dictatorship who had spent many of his years in power calling on the world proletariat to crush American imperialism. Could the breakthrough of 1972 have happened a generation and a half earlier? If it had, might the Chinese Communists never, as Mao later put it, have "leaned to one side," meaning the side of the Soviet bloc during the tense era of the Cold War? And if China had not leaned to one side, might the wars in Korea and Vietnam, both proxy conflicts fought by the United States to halt an expansion of hostile Communist power, never have been fought?

There are two views of this. One is that American leaders missed the chance to side with the tremendous forces in Asia that were yearning for change, and that had it remained at least neutral toward those forces rather than posing as their chief global enemy, the history of the twentieth century would have been infinitely more peaceful and happy. The other view is that the revolutionary forces that came to be led by Communist parties, inspired by the example of the Soviet Union, were bound to take a radical, anti-American path that would inevitably put them into conflict with the United States, no matter what.

The message passed on by Major Cromley used the word "unofficial" no doubt to enable the United States to accept a Communist delegation without violating the principle that only the government of Chiang Kai-shek could officially represent China. In that spirit, Mao and Zhou had also requested that the special representative of President Roosevelt in China, Patrick J. Hurley, not be informed of their secret initiative. By then, even though Hurley was attempting to get the CCP and the KMT to join forces in a coalition government that would together fight the Japanese, the Communists had identified him as an adversary who would block their efforts to go over his head to the American president directly. In this they were right. Wedemeyer ignored Mao's request to keep their letter a secret, and, following protocol, he passed the cable on to Hurley, who impounded it. The proposal was never passed on to Washington. The future leaders of Communist China received no answer to the query they had initiated.

Their belief that Hurley had turned against them could certainly explain the timing of the Mao-Zhou initiative. It's not difficult to imagine what the two Chinese leaders would have said to FDR in early 1945, because it would surely have been the same thing they were telling Hurley, the members of the Dixie Mission, and the American journalists who were able to visit Yenan around that time. The Communists wanted the United States to put pressure on Chiang Kai-shek to make what the Communists called "democratic reforms," that is, to allow them into a "unity government" with all the anti-Japanese parties of China without requiring that they give up control of the large armies they had built up during the war against Japan. But what the Communists most wanted from America was bullets and guns. Mao no doubt would have asked for those things as well, to be provided directly to the Communists, who, he would have said, were bearing the main burden of the fight against Japan.

Mao would have told the American president that he would happily place his troops under an American commander in the common fight against Japan. In early 1945, when nobody could have imagined that the atom bomb would bring an end to the war in the Pacific in August of that year, the universal assumption was that the war would go on for at least one or two more years. In order to defeat Japan, it was thought, the United States would have to invade the Japanese home islands, and one option on the table for doing so was to land troops in eastern China, which would serve as a staging area for the final assault on the enemy's territory. The other option, which was gaining strength among military planners, was to continue the ongoing island-hopping strategy and to use close-in islands like Okinawa as staging areas for an invasion. Nonetheless, Mao urged the Americans he met in Yenan to employ his troops to protect what might have been hundreds of thousands of American soldiers arriving on Chinese soil, no doubt to fierce Japanese resistance, and he would have repeated that offer to Roosevelt.

Beyond that, Mao would almost certainly have tried to persuade

FDR that the Chinese Communists were not Communists in the Soviet sense, that is, a party determined to exercise the dictatorship of the proletariat, to eliminate private enterprise, imprison its detractors, or to collectivize agriculture—all of which the Chinese Communists did within a few years of coming to power. Mao, as we've seen, had compared himself to Lincoln when interviewed by Harrison Forman in Yenan a few months before, and he would no doubt have talked to Roosevelt as he had done to Forman about "the liberation of slaves," meaning China's impoverished peasants, "improving their livelihood by means of agrarian reform," not, as in the Soviet Union, the brutal elimination of class enemies—though putting landlords in front of howling mobs of landless peasants and executing them in furtherance of class struggle was exactly the model approved by Mao after he took power. Along these lines, Mao might even have spelled out for Roosevelt the grander meaning of his movement, which is that it represented a massive Asian upheaval, something entirely new, a tidal wave of yearning and determination for what the Communists later called "liberation." He could have given Roosevelt, who was an instinctive anti-colonialist, a choice: to ignore this primal new force, or to ally America with it, and in so doing befriend the behemoth that was ascending, whether Roosevelt liked it or not.

It is extremely unlikely that Franklin Roosevelt would have accepted the Mao-Zhou request to visit him in Washington even if it had been passed on to him by Hurley. The president of the United States was not going to give prestige and legitimacy to the leaders of a Communist insurrection against an allied government. Nor would he have agreed to the condition they insisted on before they joined a coalition government: to keep the million-man army they had built up in their "liberated" areas. Hurley's confiscation of the Mao-Zhou request thus does not loom as a lost opportunity. The significance of the Communists' gesture lies much more in Hurley's reaction to it, because their request to Crowley that Hurley not be informed of it was clear and irrefutable proof to him that some of his subordinates were attempting to help the Communists by undermining his peacemaking program.

Hurley had been trying strenuously to get the stalled talks going again. On January 6, he wrote to Mao asking him to send Zhou back to Chungking. On that same day, Edward Rice, the consul in Xian, explained one of the reasons Mao was not anxious to do so: the areas of Communist control were continuing to expand. Most recently, he wrote, the Communists had taken advantage of a central government defeat in Henan "to create a large new strip of Communist territory in that part of north central China frequently spoken of as the Central Plain": Shandong, Jiangsu, Hubei, and parts of Henan. Rice's point was that when Chiang's government lost an area, it did so in two ways: "the main cities and transport lines are lost to the Japanese and control of the country districts is lost to the Communists."

Not surprisingly, on January 11 a letter for Hurley arrived from Yenan. In it, Mao rejected renewed negotiations on the grounds that the KMT was showing "not the least sincerity." Three days later, vexed by Mao's refusal, Hurley fired off a long cable to FDR in which he recounted his negotiating efforts of the previous months, starting with his trip to Yenan in early November. Hurley told Roosevelt that he had been on the verge of success when, suddenly and inexplicably, "the Communists walked out on us." This "drastic change of position of the Communists," their refusal to resume talking even when Chiang was making such significant concessions, Hurley now informed the president, was due to "certain officers" of Wedemeyer's command who had been offering the Communists pretty much everything they wanted from the United States without requiring them to agree to a deal with the KMT. "These American officers had formulated a plan for the use of American para-troops in the Communist-held areas. The plan provided for the use of Communist troops led by Americans in guerilla warfare. The plan was predicated on the reaching of an agreement between the United States and the Communist Party, bypassing completely the National Government of China, and furnishing American supplies directly to the Communist troops."

Hurley said he'd had some inkling of this plan earlier, but "I did not know it had been presented to the Communists until that was made apparent by the Communists applying to Wedemeyer to secure secret passage for Mao Zedong and Zhou Enlai to Washington for a conference with you. They asked Wedemeyer to keep their proposed visit to you secret from the National Government and from me."

Hurley wasn't all wrong about the bare facts. Where he was disastrously wrong was in his accusation of sabotage and disloyalty against these "certain officers of Wedemeyer's command," when what happened merely illustrated the overall incoherence of American China policy, the actions of all those agencies operating more or less independently. Davies's verdict on Hurley, while no doubt self-interested, seems true. It was, he wrote to his wife at the time, that the ambassador was "a little confused by the maelstrom of intrigue in which he finds himself." And one of the main initiators of intrigue was "Wild Bill" Donovan, the head of the OSS in Washington.

Donovan was eager for cooperation on intelligence matters with the Communists, as he was with Tai Li and the central government. The Communists had guerrillas and agents all over occupied China and were clearly in a position to provide the United States with a vast amount of information. The Communists, moreover, made clear in their talks with the OSS agents inside the Dixie Mission, Cromley in particular, that they welcomed and encouraged this interest. The Communists needed equipment, especially radios, that their troops and agents could use in their far-flung archipelago of "liberated" areas. They also wanted technical training for their intelligence agents. In September 1944, the OSS agreed to provide radios for fourteen Communist-held areas, and by April 1945, something like fourteen thousand pounds of American equipment, mostly lightweight radios and spare parts, had been flown to Yenan, and more was in the pipeline. There was enough OSS activity with the Communists for Willis Bird, the deputy director of the OSS in China, to be assigned to deal with Yenan full-time.

Bird was not the only American official talking to the Communists about military or quasi-military cooperation. In early November 1944, just four days after Wedemeyer's arrival in China, Ye Jianying, a Long March veteran who was chief of staff of the Eighth Route Army, responded to an American idea, presented by Davies, that the United States might carry out a Normandy-style landing at Lianyunkang on the Shandong-Jiangsu border. This would be supported by the Communists in what would have been a major joint operation, similar in scope to American operations with government troops in Burma and Yunnan province. Ye suggested that the Communists contribute fifty thousand troops to support five divisions of Americans; this support would include disrupting Japanese communications and tying down Japanese troops to keep them away from the arriving Americans. Davies understood right away the underlying Communist goal: to get American arms that it would later use against the KMT. He knew also that an American landing on the China coast would draw American forces away from the south and west just at the time of Japan's Ichigo offensive, which would leave Kunming and possibly even Chungking much less protected.

Still, he favored Ye's plan, and for good reason. If the United States did land troops on the China coast—and American military planners at that point assumed this would be necessary to defeat Japan—Communist help would be needed. Zhou told Davies that if an invasion took place, "they would mobilize the population within a two hundred mile radius of the landing to provide labor and foodstuffs for the American forces." The Communists, in other words, "offered all of the cooperation within their power to give," Davies confided to his journal, clearly thrilled at the prospect that was manifesting itself, and believing it to be of possibly historic dimensions. "For who can say," he wrote later, "how the orientation of the Yenan oligarchy would have developed had the United States . . . accepted Mao's invitation to cooperate?"

It was to support his view of the breathtaking possibilities that Davies wrote his three visionary papers on the Communists and sent them off to Washington. In them, he played down their Communist aspects and emphasized instead their nationalist qualities, and he favorably assessed the likelihood that the Chinese Communists could be "captured" from Soviet domination—an opinion that he later acknowledged "underestimated the influence of ideology on Communist behavior." But at the time, he was clearly under the influence not just of the prospect of military cooperation but of the warmth and good humor of his reception in Yenan, those affable Saturday night dances, the church-social informality of it all, his inner conviction that the Communists did genuinely yearn for friendship with America. After all, it made sense. Friendship with America would have brought them so much more benefit than closeness to Russia. "They have now deviated so far to the right that they will return to the revolution only if driven to it by overwhelming pressure from domestic and foreign forces of reaction," Davies wrote at the end of 1944. As for such matters as the Rectification Campaign, Davies wrote later that he was "aware" of it but "I did not inquire into it. My attention was fixed on the issue of power, and what the United States might do to attract Yenan away from the Soviet Union."

There is a bit of willed ignorance in this, and what Davis ignored is how much the Rectification Campaign made the Chinese Communists seem very much like their Soviet counterparts. Still, under the circumstances, it is hard to imagine anybody seeing matters more clearly than Davies did at the time.

At the end of 1944, Donovan of the OSS dispatched his man in China, Lieutenant Colonel Bird, to Yenan to talk over further cooperation with the Communists. Bird was accompanied by Barrett, who was told by General Robert McClure, Wedemeyer's chief of staff, to go to Yenan to explore the possibility of stationing American paratroopers in Communist-held territory. They left on the same flight as Davies, who, as we've seen, was taking his farewell Yenan trip. In his memoirs, Davies claims to have had only a vague idea of the nature of Bird's and Barrett's missions. The three landed in Yenan on December 15. The next day, Bird and Barrett went to see Mao and others, and over the next three days, they drew up an ambitious plan for possible future American–Chinese Communist cooperation, which included the stationing of American Special Operations agents with CCP units to "generally raise hell and run," as Bird put it in a memo. More important as an institutional commitment, the plan envisaged American equipment being provided for up to twenty-five thousand Communist guerrillas. In exchange for this, as Bird put it, the United States would "receive complete cooperation of [the Communists'] army of six hundred fifty thousand and people's militia of two and a half million when strategic use required by Wedemeyer."

It is easy to see why the Communists would have agreed to this idea: equipment for twenty-five thousand of their ill-equipped soldiers. It is also easy to see that the KMT would have violently resisted it for the same reason, and so, in fact, nothing came of it. It was just another of those schemes thrown out there by somebody with authority in one of the many agencies that proliferate in war, Donovan in this case. Bird's offer, however, had a permanent effect on Hurley, who, from that point on, was the implacable enemy of the Foreign Service China professionals who, he insisted on believing, had intentionally ruined his mediation attempt. Whether because of bureaucratic deviousness, especially on the part of Donovan, or because of some less sinister motive, Hurley was not informed of Bird's extraordinary mission to Yenan. He would surely have vigorously opposed it had he known what was afoot, because Bird's proposal of cooperation promised substantial help to the Communists without the bother of making a deal with the KMT. At the same time, Hurley assumed the most nefarious possible motives on the part of all three of the emissaries who had gone to Yenan at the end of 1944 — Bird, Barrett, and Davies. His cable to Roosevelt was the opening blow of his long campaign to dishonor both the Foreign Service China experts who labored under him and the military officers in Wedemeyer's command, and not only to dishonor them but to purge them from the service.

FDR took Hurley's cable seriously enough to pass it on to Admiral William D. Leahy, the president's chief military adviser, who gave it to the army chief of staff, George C. Marshall, who sent it on to Albert Wedemeyer. Wedemeyer, at the time, was in the field striving to get the government forces to renew their offensive on the Salween front. Wedemeyer, asked by Marshall for an explanation, replied at first that there had been no "disloyal scheming" by any of the men under his command. Wedemeyer was angry at Hurley for having sent off his accusatory cable to the president without his knowledge. The men Hurley had accused of misbehavior were, after all, on Wedemeyer's staff, including McClure, his chief of staff. Hurley was upset at Wedemeyer's dismissal of the charges. Matters became so strained between the American ambassador to China and the commander of China theater headquarters that they didn't speak to each other for days—while sharing a house in Chungking! "It was most embarrassing, since we had to sit together at meals," Wedemeyer later wrote, until "Pat Hurley came into my room one evening while I was propped up in bed reading. He sat on the edge of my bed, clasped my right hand in both of his, and said that he was sorry for his behavior toward me."

When Marshall pressed for more details, Wedemeyer looked deeper into the matter and discovered that, indeed, Hurley's account had been largely true: some officers, namely Bird and Barrett, the latter under orders from McClure, had indeed talked to Mao. Given McClure's role, it is hard to believe that Wedemeyer knew nothing about the initiative, but never mind. In a cable to the War Department, he apologized for the "unauthorized loose discussions" that had taken place between the Communists and "my officers employed in good faith by General Hurley," and though he disagreed that this had been the cause of the breakdown in KMT-CCP negotiations, he admitted that it "could have strongly contributed to [Hurley's] difficulties in bringing about a solution to the problem." Doing his part to further this reconciliation, Wedemeyer held a press conference in Chungking where he announced that all American officers had sworn henceforth to give no assistance to anybody in China other than the Chungking government—a clear if unspoken repudiation of the McClure-Barrett initiative.

The result of all this was that Hurley, the only actor in the matter who had direct access to Roosevelt, felt vindicated in his suspicions of disloyalty on the part of his subordinates. If he ever learned that the matter had originated with Donovan and that Bird and Barrett were simply following orders, he never acknowledged it. It is, of course, entirely possible that, as Hurley believed, the Communists were emboldened to back out of the Hurley negotiations by the prospect that they could get American aid without a deal with Chiang. But if they felt that way for a few weeks at the end of December and in January, they were soon disabused of that notion, and negotiations did resume.

Meanwhile, an event was taking place thousands of miles away that gave Mao far more reason to believe that matters in China were moving his way than some inconclusive conversations with American military officers ever could have, and this event soon made almost everything that had already taken place between the United States and the Communists irrelevant for the future.

CHAPTER EIGHT

A Moral Compromise

Early in the New Year, Mao Zedong became one of the first to know that something of historic significance was soon to take place along the wintry shores of the Black Sea at a place that few outside Russia had ever heard of called Yalta.

There, from February 4 to February 11, 1945, the Big Three—Franklin Roosevelt, Winston Churchill, and Joseph Stalin—were to meet and to decide among themselves on fighting the war's final battles and shaping the balance of power afterward. The meeting was held under conditions of strict wartime secrecy. Until it was over, the American press and people didn't even know that Roosevelt had left the United States. But the circumstantial evidence strongly indicates that Mao knew about the meeting shortly before it began, and almost certainly it was Stalin who informed him, using a secret radio connection that the two maintained to keep in close touch for the entire anti-Japanese war of resistance in China.

On February 3, the day before Yalta's opening session, Mao cabled Zhou Enlai that "Stalin is meeting Churchill and Roosevelt," and that Stalin would be in touch about the results of the meeting later. Given the overall secrecy, there was no way for Mao to have known that the fateful Yalta Conference was about to start unless Stalin had told him.

Zhou was in Chungking at the time, having gone there on January 22 after Mao acceded to Hurley's persistent entreaty that he resume the stalled KMT-CCP negotiations. But the news about Yalta evidently persuaded Mao that the talks should be postponed, and he ordered Zhou to return to Chungking right away. Mao reasoned, as the leading scholar of this episode has concluded, that the news of the imminent meeting at Yalta meant that, sooner or later, the Russians would come into the war in Asia, and that "would certainly increase the weight the CCP carried in China's politics." Mao's decision therefore was to defer the talks with Hurley for a while "in order to take full advantage of the increasing Soviet influence in the Far East after Yalta."

This would seem to be the cause of the harder line adopted by the Communists in the Hurley-sponsored negotiations, whereas Hurley, as we've seen, had blamed Bird, Barrett, and McClure for this, along with the wider effort, as he saw it, by the China hands, led by Davies, to sabotage his mediation. There is no indication that Stalin actually reported to Mao on the results of his meetings in Yalta, but he didn't have to. Mao and his lieutenants would have known that the strategic picture was changing to their advantage. Stalin would want to get into the war against Japan, in part to achieve the long-standing goal of recovering the territory Russia lost to Japan in its humiliating defeat of 1904–05, and that could not be bad for the Chinese Communist cause. The day after the secret protocol was signed at Yalta, Mao was communicating to Party members in Yenan that the Communists' policy of the previous few years—support for Chiang and a hand of friendship to the United States—was shifting in a more radical and combative direction. A few weeks before, Mao had been on the dance floor in Yenan's Peach Garden encouraging the Dixie Mission members and special emissaries like Barrett and Bird to whirl around with Chinese girls. Now Mao called on all Communists to be prepared for bloodshed against "Mei-Chiang," the derogatory Communist shorthand for the American-Chiang alliance. (Mei is the short version of meiguo, meaning America.)

This was a big rhetorical shift. Mao was friendliest when he felt most threatened, and for much of the war he felt threatened by the prospect of an American-backed attack on Yenan, which would have come when Stalin was overwhelmed by his war with Germany and unable to come to the rescue. Now, feeling less threatened, he told party members, "Do not be afraid of [the Americans'] anger, and their loud accusations." At the same time, Mao persisted in what some historians have called his charm offensive toward the Americans, who continued to see him in Yenan, to talk about possible cooperation in gathering intelligence, to rescue downed American pilots, to assume what Mao called the inevitability of an American presence in China. Mao did not let on to the Americans he met that his discourse inside the party ranks was shifting toward the Soviet Union. But something had shifted. Something new about his prospects of taking total power had entered Mao's mind when he heard about the meeting at Yalta, and this was never going to change.

Mao wasn't the only one who was reconsidering the situation at the time of the Yalta Conference. W. Averell Harriman, Franklin Roosevelt's ambassador to the Union of Soviet Socialist Republics, was thinking deeply disturbed thoughts about Stalin and the Soviet Union as the war entered its final months. He was, as the later expression went, getting mugged by reality. A banker's son who grew up in a forty-bedroom mansion on Long Island on an estate with its own polo field, Harriman had spent more time with Joseph Stalin than any other American. During most of his encounters, Harriman had been a supporter of his president's grand vision of the postwar world, in which the coalition of great powers that would triumph over the Axis would perpetuate their friendship and alliance into the future, thereby ensuring global harmony and peace.

The warm feeling toward the Soviet Union that wartime cooperation had brought about is hard to visualize six decades later, after the Cold War and the voluminous documentation of Stalin's destructive villainy. Now it is clear that in 1945 the world was heading toward a collision not just of powers but of values and ways of life, that the very notions of individual freedom, limited government, and protections against abuses of power were being challenged by an unscrupulous and illiberal giant. But at the time, a year before Winston Churchill's "Iron Curtain" speech, before "containment" of the Soviet Union became official American policy, and years before the advent of the nuclear balance of terror, the tremendous victories that the Russians had achieved over the Germans dominated the mood. Roosevelt, as we've seen, nurtured a cordial trust with regard to Stalin right up to his death in April 1945, especially his trust that he and his Soviet counterpart would perpetuate their alliance after the war.

Near the end of 1944, FDR attended a mass rally of twenty thousand people at Madison Square Garden in New York, one of several held around the country to celebrate the eleventh anniversary of the establishment of diplomatic relations between the United States and the Soviet Union. The Soviet ambassador, Andrei A. Gromyko, was present in the legendary amphitheater; so was the conductor Leopold Stokowski, who conducted an orchestral part of the program. Dwight D. Eisenhower, supreme commander of allied forces in Europe, was there to speak of "the great Red Army." Secretary of State Edward Stettinius talked of an "opportunity—such as the world has never known before—to advance the freedom and well-being of all mankind." Roosevelt, who was accorded a prolonged standing ovation, evoked the "ever-growing accord" between himself and Stalin "to establish a peace that will endure."

In Moscow, Harriman was losing his faith in just this beatific vision, and the reason was Stalin's aggressive behavior, the growing sense during the brass-knuckles talks with him and his representatives that he envisioned a very different sort of world than the one Americans had in mind. On April 4, 1945, he sent a blistering cable to Washington complaining that the Russians operated "from the standpoint of their own selfish interests." They were censoring the press "to prevent the facts becoming known." They "will relentlessly strip the enemy countries they have occupied of everything they can move." Most important, Harriman recognized something deeply malevolent in Stalin's goals. The Soviet dictator, he realized, was not the man Roosevelt thought he was, who would respond to generous treatment in reciprocal fashion. "We must clearly realize," Harriman wrote, "that the Soviet program is the establishment of totalitarianism, ending personal liberty and democracy as we know it."

China does not seem to have been much on Harriman's mind during this period, though he did worry about Soviet intentions there too. On April 21, nine days after Roosevelt's death, he warned that the Soviets could well "cause further trouble" in "Macedonia, Turkey, and especially China." If Chiang, he said, doesn't come to an agreement with the CCP before the Soviet occupation of Manchuria, the Russians "will certainly establish a Soviet-dominated Communist regime in those areas and then there will be a completely divided China." Harriman in this statement makes the same wishful assumption of other American officials, which was that, somehow, if only Chiang could draw Mao in a unified government of China, there would be no malicious Soviet interference in China, but events would show this assumption to be very wrong. Still, China was much less a preoccupation for him and the other postwar planners than Europe was. In the weeks after the Yalta conference, it was rather Poland that was sticking in the collective American craw, for it illustrated the incompatibility of American and Soviet goals, practices, and values.

Soviet designs on Poland had gone unmentioned during all but the final few months of the war. It had been deemed unproductive, impolitic, a faux pas, to bring up the events of six years earlier, when Stalin and Hitler, in a raw and blatant act of aggression, had divided Poland between the two of them. In 1939, the two dictators had watched as their foreign ministers, Vyacheslav Molotov and Joachim von Ribbentrop, signed a non-aggression pact, a secret protocol of which provided for Stalin and Hitler to wipe out Poland as an independent country and to create a new Soviet-German border at the Vistula River, which runs through Warsaw, Poland's capital. A week after signing the pact, on September 1, Germany, in the first of its massive and devastating blitzkrieg attacks, invaded Poland and quickly seized the western half of it, provoking Britain and France, which had treaties with Poland stipulating they would come to its defense in the event of German aggression, to declare war.

When the Soviets followed up with their own invasion of Poland two weeks later, there were no British or French declarations of war, in part because there were no defensive treaties aimed against the Soviet Union and in part because to have gone to war against both Germany and the Soviet Union at the same time would have been a preposterous impossibility. In any event, the immediate threat to Western Europe and its freedoms was the one posed by Hitler. After signing the pact, Germany was free to turn its attention to the invasions of France, Belgium, and the Netherlands, as well as its bombing campaign against Britain, all of which took place a few months later in 1940.

Meanwhile, in the Katyn Forest in Russia, the Soviet secret police, in an operation approved by Stalin, murdered more than twenty thousand Polish citizens, including eight thousand army officers taken prisoner in the 1939 invasion. It was a preemptive attack, organized by the Soviet secret police, the NKVD, and its utterly ruthless leader, Lavrenty Beria, aimed at eliminating any independent Polish leadership for the foreseeable future. The Soviets pinned blame for this signal and unforgivable atrocity on the Germans, an audacious lie that was believed around the world for decades. In January 1941, half a year after the Nazi invasions of France and the Low Countries, Hitler and Stalin furthered their cooperation with a German-Soviet Border and Commercial Agreement, which provided for the exchange of Soviet raw materials and German industrial machinery.

As allies between 1939 and 1942, Stalin and Hitler both committed the mass murders of enemies (to go with the murder or imprisonment of large numbers of their own citizens) unhindered by any moral restraint when it came to the advancement of their interests. Germany rampaged through Belgium, Norway, the Netherlands, and France, and geared up for its genocidal persecutions in the East, while Stalin gobbled up the eastern half of Poland, the three Baltic states of Latvia, Lithuania, and Estonia, and the provinces of northern and eastern Romania (Bessarabia, Moldova, and northern Bukovina). Stalin also invaded neutral Finland, though, unlike the others, the Finns were able to put up a partially successful resistance, losing some territory but never succumbing to Soviet control. All of these countries and territories were within what the Germans had recognized as a Soviet "sphere of influence"—that is, as one scholar has noted, a zone of occupation.

Then this nefarious and cynical German-Soviet alliance collapsed. In June 1941, a year after the German invasion of France, Hitler launched a massive three-front blitzkrieg against the Soviet Union, thereby virtually overnight transforming Stalin from a co-conspirator into a bitter enemy. Hitler's treacherous act ruined Stalin's earlier plan to dominate the entirety of Eastern Europe, and it opened up an alliance of necessity with Britain and the United States, who followed the age-old principle that the enemy of my enemy is my friend. Now at Yalta, nearly four years and many costly Soviet victories over the German armies later, Stalin was determined to secure from his wartime allies the sphere of influence/zone of occupation that he had failed to get in the collapsed deal with Hitler, except bigger this time.

He made no secret of this. The conference at Yalta was the second wartime meeting of the three leaders, the first having taken place in 1943 in Tehran, where Stalin had already made his intentions clear. He hadn't been very anxious to meet again, insisting that the next summit be held someplace close and convenient for him or not at all. This required that Roosevelt travel by train from Washington, D.C., to Newport News, Virginia, then spend ten days on a navy cruiser to the Mediterranean island of Malta, where he met up with Churchill. After that came a seven-hour flight to Sevastopol, the American plane taking off at 3 a.m. to avoid possible German air attacks. Finally, the party had to travel by car on a ninety-mile switchback route through the mountains to Yalta. But such was Roosevelt's wish to come to some understanding on the shape of the postwar world—including, most importantly from FDR's standpoint, Soviet agreement to participate in the United

Nations, which was at the center of Roosevelt's grand and idealistic scheme for the postwar world—that he complied with Stalin's demand, at great risk to his own health.

Stalin was not especially anxious to meet because the facts on the ground favored him, and he had no wish to subject himself to pressure from his allies to roll back from his victories. By February 1945 his troops had overrun the Baltic states and Poland, along with Hungary, Czechoslovakia, Romania, and Bulgaria, and he had no intention of relinquishing control.

With regard to Poland, the American delegation, which included Roosevelt, Harriman, and Secretary of State Stettinius, was stunned by the Soviet leader's unabashed double-talk. A "free, independent, and powerful Poland was essential for Soviet security," Stalin assured his western allies. But, Stalin continued, because Germany had invaded the Soviet Union through Poland, the Soviet Union "had to dominate that state [Poland] completely."

The leaders of the Big Three spent days arguing about Poland, though politely and with no mention of the Soviet annexation of half the country in 1939. Roosevelt and Churchill supported the non-Communist Polish government-in-exile that had been set up in London when the war started, and they pressed for an arrangement that would enable it to compete for power with the Communist group sponsored by the Soviets, presumably in an election, but the Soviets did everything they could to foil this objective. A few months before the meeting at Yalta, in August 1944, the Polish Home Army attempted its famous uprising in Warsaw, fighting house to house and street to street for more than two months in an effort to expel the Nazi occupier. The uprising was timed to the arrival of the Soviet army just on the other side of the Vistula River from the center of Warsaw, but there the Russian troops remained, Stalin watching and waiting while the Germans wiped out Poland's non-Communist armed resistance and then leveled Warsaw. Stalin was happy to see those Poles eliminated who might form an independent opposition to Soviet influence.

By the time the three leaders met at Yalta, the Russians had already installed in Warsaw what was to become the puppet government of Poland, and there wasn't much that Roosevelt and Churchill could do about it. There was a euphonious agreement pledging the Soviet-supported government to hold free elections in the future and, more generally, assuring the liberated peoples of Europe their rights to "to

restore their sovereignty and to establish their own democratic governments." But, as George Kennan, second in command at the American
embassy in Moscow and later the chief architect of containment, put
it at the time, these words amounted to "the shabbiest sort of equivoca-
tion." When the Polish Communists failed later to hold the promised
elections, the western allies could do nothing about it. Later in 1945, the
British and the Americans recognized the Soviet-controlled Polish government, which, in exchange, took in a few non-Communist members.
Soviet domination of Poland became an accepted fact for the foreseeable future.

Given the Soviet Union's ambitious goals and its actions in Eastern
Europe, one might expect there to have been some concern that Stalin
would want to do something similar in China. In fact, there was very
little thought at the top echelons of the American government about
the possibility that Soviet aims in Europe and Soviet aims in Asia might
be similar. Roosevelt's immediate goal at this meeting was to get the
Soviet Union to enter the war against Japan once the war in Europe
was over. Stalin had secretly agreed to that in principle during the Big
Three meeting in Tehran in 1943 and in his meetings with Harriman,
but now Roosevelt wanted to nail him down on specifics, like the number of troops he would contribute, and when exactly Soviet participation would begin.

There was some difference of opinion within the American government on whether a Soviet front in the Japanese war was necessary or
desirable. The State Department on balance was opposed to a deal with
the Russians on this. John Davies, recently departed from Chungking
and on his way to his new posting in Moscow, had wisely prophesied
around the time of the Tehran conference (without knowing about the
secret pledge Stalin had made to Roosevelt there) that the Russians
would open a front in Asia "only in order to be able to participate in
dictating terms to the Japanese and to establish new strategic frontiers."
It made little sense to Davies and others in the State Department to
defeat one enemy, whether Germany or Japan, only to invite a menacing future strategic rival to occupy the very territories that the defeated
enemy had been driven out of. Moreover, there were senior military
officers, namely Admiral Ernest King, the second-highest officer in the
American navy, and five-star general H. H. "Hap" Arnold, commander

of the U.S. Army Air Force, who believed the war in Asia could be won by enforcing a blockade of Japan alone.

Marshall and the Joint Chiefs of Staff insisted that a massive invasion of the Japanese islands themselves was going to be necessary to defeat the Japanese, for whom, they firmly believed, mass collective death in resistance would be preferable to surrender. American military planners estimated that the expected invasion would cost anywhere from 100,000 to 350,000 dead and wounded among the American forces. By entering the war in Asia, the argument went, the Soviets would tie up the million-man Japanese army in Manchuria, which would otherwise be deployed to the home islands to fight the American landings. Douglas MacArthur, who would have commanded the invasion of Japan, urged Roosevelt to get the Russians to commit sixty divisions, or more than half a million troops, against the Japanese army in Manchuria.

Roosevelt also wanted to advance a separate goal at Yalta, the paramount goal of American China policy, which was Chinese political unity. Earlier in the war, a basic assumption of American military planners was that China was an essential base of operations for the war against Japan, in part because a final attack on Japan itself could only be mounted from Chinese territory. By early 1945, China's poverty and the abysmal condition of its armed forces had led to the abandonment of this idea. "By the time of the Yalta Conference," the historian Tang Tsou has written, "leading American officials clearly recognized that China would not emerge as a great power at the end of the war." Nonetheless, Roosevelt wanted China to be unified so it could make more of a contribution to the anti-Japanese fight, and he knew that the Soviets were in a position either to help achieve that goal or to hinder it. Roosevelt had heard all of Stalin's and Molotov's assurances that the Chinese Communists were not real Communists and, in any case, that the Soviet Union would not meddle in China's internal affairs. He wanted to believe that these assurances were true. And if the Soviets could be brought into a formal accord with China's Nationalist government, they might be deterred from throwing their support to the Chinese Communists, thereby wrecking the chances of political unity during the final Japanese campaign, or provoking a civil war once the battle against Japan had been won.

It was with all of this in mind that on February 8, 1945, FDR went to Stalin's study at Yalta to talk about Soviet entry into the war against Japan. There were four people in the room besides the two heads of state—Molotov, Harriman, and two interpreters. To a great extent, the meeting was a formalization of the informal agreement that the two sides had already made more than a year earlier at Tehran, but this formalization was important.

Roosevelt began by asking Stalin if the United States could build air bases in Siberia for use in bombing raids against Japan, and Stalin agreed to allow two such bases in the Amur River region near China. FDR then gave a memo to Stalin asking for joint planning of Far Eastern operations, and Stalin said he would give orders to that effect. This was a breakthrough because Stalin was moving from an abstract promise of help in the Pacific theater to concrete planning. But before he was willing to talk about the military details, Stalin said, he had some political conditions.

First, he wanted to restore Soviet "rights" to the territories Russia had lost to Japan in 1905, namely the southern part of the Sakhalin Peninsula and a few islands in the Kurile chain north of Japan, which blocked Soviet access to the Pacific Ocean. Regarding China, Stalin wanted some big advantages in Manchuria, which Russia had also lost to Japan in 1905. It demanded control of the railroads there, a permanent lease on Port Arthur, a warm-water port at the southern tip of the Liaodong Peninsula, and control over the nearby port city of Dalian; and it wanted recognition of the status quo in Outer Mongolia, which though theoretically independent was a satellite state dominated by Moscow but, having once been part of the Qing dynasty, was claimed by China.

In other words, in exchange for taking part in the war against Japan, Stalin would resurrect the colonial privileges that Japan had taken for itself in northeast China and that the European powers had enjoyed in the treaty ports since the Opium War, though they had formally relinquished those privileges a year or so before the Yalta meeting, which meant that, aside from British control of Hong Kong and Portuguese control of Macao, only the Soviet Union would retain semi-imperialist status in China. Nobody at Yalta was so impolite as to point this out.

Stalin's demands put Roosevelt in a difficult position, stuck as he was between his military's eagerness for the Russians to invade Manchuria and the awkwardness of publicly agreeing to a Soviet sphere of influence in East Asia. To navigate this diplomatic shoal, Roosevelt told Stalin that he'd be amenable to a deal, but only if it could be kept secret. To inform the Chinese would be the same as informing the whole world, since the Chungking government was incapable of keeping a secret. Roosevelt would get Chiang's assent to the deal at the appropriate moment.

Harriman didn't like it. Among other things, he objected to a startling phrase in the final text, worked out between the two sides after Roosevelt and Stalin had met for the half hour devoted to China, to the effect that "the preeminent interests of the Soviet Union shall be safeguarded" in Manchuria. The phrase "preeminent interests" was both vague and imperial in tone, while the secrecy of the deal, in which two powerful countries disposed of the interests of a less powerful one without even informing the less powerful one of the arrangement, echoed that of the Molotov-Ribbentrop non-aggression pact of just a short, violent six years before. Roosevelt had demanded and gotten time to get Chiang Kai-shek's agreement to the arrangement, but this would be a mere formality.

Roosevelt, of course, was striving to save the lives of tens of thousands, perhaps hundreds of thousands, of American soldiers that he thought might otherwise be lost, not a priority easily dismissed. But strangely, Roosevelt also trusted Stalin, demonstrably one of the most untrustworthy major figures of the twentieth century. He wanted to trust him. He felt that his vision for the postwar world depended on Stalin's reliability as a partner. Or, as John Davies explained it later, the entire edifice that the president imagined for the postwar world depended on Stalin's cooperation and goodwill. "The prescription for this," Davies said later, expanding the view to Asia, "was open-handed generosity in granting aid to the Soviet Union, no bargaining for reciprocal advantages, and support of certain territorial and other claims that Stalin told Roosevelt he wanted fulfilled." We've seen Harriman try to disabuse Roosevelt of that trust and to warn him that Stalin's objectives were incompatible with American interests, and Harriman was not alone. Kennan warned that Stalin's goals—he was talking about Europe— were utterly at variance "with the happiness, prosperity or stability of international life on the rest of the continent."

Kennan knew that Stalin sought total postwar mastery of Eastern Europe and that any belief to the contrary was wishful thinking. Moreover, while many have attributed FDR's blind spot on this subject to his feebleness in his last few weeks of life, he had engaged in this wishful thinking for the entire war. His own ambassador to Moscow, Admiral William H. Standley, who served in the Soviet Union before Harriman took over in 1943, used to complain about all the special emissaries FDR sent to Moscow who "leapfrog over my top-hatted head and follow the Rooseveltian policy—do not antagonize the Russians, give them everything they want, for, after all, they are killing Germans."

There are three tremendous ironies here. One is that, eager for advantages in East Asia, the Soviets would surely have invaded Manchuria in any case, precisely to get a place at the table when the postwar terms were dictated to a defeated Japan. It had never been necessary to go to Stalin as supplicants seeking favors or to consent to his conditions in exchange for something he was eager to do anyway.

Second, the United States believed that in giving Stalin what he wanted in Manchuria, it was creating conditions that would strengthen China's central government and weaken the Communists, when, as it would turn out, exactly the opposite was the case. To be sure, there were Soviet vows to leave Manchuria and to turn it over to the Chinese government, and many believed that they would, and that this would pave the way to a treaty between Moscow and Chungking that would exclude the Communists from power. "Russia promises nonintervention in Chinese affairs," Henry Luce wrote in a *Life* editorial after Yalta, "thus pulling the rug out from under the Chinese Communists and deflecting their recently ballooning claims of equality with the government of Chiang Kai-shek." But to believe that Stalin meant what he promised in China was simply naïve. In the end, Stalin did give up Manchuria, half a year late, not to the central government but surreptitiously to the Communists, providing Mao with control over a territorial base from which he could never be dislodged.

And third, as it turned out, of course, the atomic bomb brought about an abrupt Japanese surrender, and the American land invasion for which Russian help was believed essential never took place, even as the high price for that Russian help was paid.

World War II had all along involved a tremendous moral compromise, cooperation with one of the twentieth century's worst dictators, Stalin, in order to defeat another such dictator, Hitler. We were too "weak," Kennan said, "to win [the war] without Russia's cooperation," and this cooperation had been "masterful and effective." To recognize this and to accept that Stalin would be getting as a reward the domination of Eastern Europe that Hitler had been denied was the essence of realpolitik.

At Yalta, the moral compromise was extended to Asia, where Russian help had not been extended, where it wasn't needed, and it would do grievous harm to America and its values. A few months earlier, in August 1944, Zhou Enlai had predicted the consequences of Russian entry into the war. With the Dixie Mission having just arrived in Yenan and the Communists expressing their wish for deep cooperation and friendship with the United States, Zhou wrote a lengthy inner-party report giving his analysis of the international situation. He didn't know whether the Russians would come into the war or not at that point, but it would be highly desirable for them to do so, he wrote, though it would be better not to express this desire publicly for fear of alarming the Americans about a future Soviet-Chinese Communist alliance. The Soviet entry into the war, Zhou said, would mean nothing less than "the victory of China's new democratic revolution"—meaning the defeat of Chiang Kai-shek and the extension of Communism across the entirety of the Eurasian landmass from Warsaw to Canton—"and that is what Chiang and the Anglo-American conservatives do not want to see."

CHAPTER NINE

Hiding the Knife

John Service made his final visit to Yenan in March 1945, when he had long talks with Mao that convinced him more than ever that an opportunity for a constructive working relationship with the Chinese Communists was there for the United States to seize, if only it had the wisdom to do so. While he was there, he got the news that American troops had stormed the Japanese stronghold of Okinawa, news, he felt, that had put Mao into "exceptionally good spirits, getting out of his chair to act out dramatic embellishments of his talk, and diverging to recall amusing anecdotes." Mao expressed chagrin that the negotiations with Chiang Kai-shek mediated by Ambassador Hurley were proving "fruitless," for which he blamed Chiang Kai-shek, but he was defiantly confident that if Chiang resumed his effort to wipe out the Communists by force, he would fail. "Chiang could not whip us during the civil war when we were a hundred times weaker," he said.

But whatever happened in China, whether the negotiations succeeded or failed, whether the United States provided arms to the Communists or not, Mao assured Service that China and the United States would be natural allies. They had "strong ties of sympathy, understanding, and mutual interest," Mao said, as Service paraphrased him. They were both "essentially democratic and individualistic . . . by nature peace-loving, nonaggressive and non-imperialistic." For all of these reasons, Service cabled, continuing to summarize Mao's comments, "there cannot be any conflict, estrangement, or misunderstanding between the Chinese people and America." The Communists' goal is moderate, Mao said, encouraging what Barrett was later to call the "agrarian reformer guff." It was reduced rents, progressive taxation, and the "institution of democracy." As for the United States, Mao repeated the assurance he'd given Barrett a few months earlier, that even if the United States declined to provide his forces with "a single gun or bullet," the Communists "will continue to offer and practice cooperation in any manner possible to them. Anything they can do . . . the Communists consider an obligation and duty." But if the United States did see fit to arm the Communists, advantages would accrue to both countries. The war with Japan would come to a quicker end and the Americans would "win the undying friendship of the overwhelming majority of China's people."

These talks confirmed Service in his conviction that in its one-sided support for Chiang the United States was "letting the tail wag the dog" and losing a historic chance to build a cordial relationship with the Communists. A few months before, on an earlier visit to Yenan, Service had written, "Politically, any orientation which the Chinese Communists may once have had toward the Soviet Union seems to be a thing of the past." The United States was a far more potent prospective partner in economic and technological development than the Soviet Union, and it had no colonialist designs on Manchuria or other regions of China, like Xinjiang. "The conclusion," Service wrote in September 1944, "is that American friendship and support is more important to China than Russian." Now he and Davies felt ever more urgently that the United States needed to act on that fact. From Moscow, Davies weighed in with a memo of his own in mid-April. He warned that the KMT lacked popular support, that it had no program to attract popular support, and that it was "inefficient, venal, and stale" with little chance of prevailing against the "dynamic and disciplined" Communists. As for the Communists, Davies continued, they began "as an instrument of Moscow's policy of world revolution," but the events of the war, during which they'd gotten very little help from the Russians, have pushed them in a nationalist direction. Will they nonetheless decide to be "voluntary creatures of Russian foreign policy?" Would they be "willing to cooperate with us on terms equal to or better than those which they will extend to the Soviet Union?" We don't really know, Davies admitted. "What can be said at this juncture, however, is that if any Communist regime is susceptible to political 'capture' by the United States, it is Yenan."

In 1960, fifteen years after Davies's memo, Mao led China into a furiously angry break from its erstwhile ally and socialist brother, the Soviet

Union, accusing it of crimes of ideology and aggression, using the stilted bombast that China's Communists always use against their foes, even today. In addition to the war of words, there were armed clashes in 1969 over a disputed island in the Ussuri River (Wusulijiang in Chinese) on the border between Chinese Manchuria and Soviet Siberia. This new rivalry paved the way, after an interval of more than another decade, for the historic rapprochement between China and the United States, which began in the early 1970s.

China's anti-Soviet animosity and its balance-of-power détente with America have given great credibility to the idea that China under the Communists would always have been amenable to the "American over-tures" of which Davies spoke, and that at least non-hostile relations with the United States would have come about if only the Americans had not persisted in their blind and self-defeating support of Chiang.

Behind this perception is a historical interpretation, namely that the Chinese Communists never really trusted the Russians, never got much real aid from them, sometimes felt betrayed by them, and always yearned, as Mao repeatedly told the Dixie Mission representatives, to benefit from a normal and friendly cooperation with the United States. Mao, after all, was a "radish Communist" or a "margarine" one, not a real one, this line of thinking posits. He wanted to adapt Marxism to China's purposes, and in so doing to preserve China's independence from the USSR, which loomed gigantic and threatening on the north-ern border, practically shouting at China to engage in a strategic bal-ancing act with the distant United States. Hurley himself, in the one area of agreement between him and the China hands, believed this. The supreme authorities on the topic, Stalin and Molotov, had person-ally assured him that Mao and his followers were not real Communists.

Some historians have concluded that when Mao did, for the first decade of his rule, allow China to be a "creature of Russian foreign policy," it was because the United States had pushed him in that direc-tion. Many times during the Japanese war he had been furious at Sta-lin for the Soviet leader's unapologetic pursuit of his own interest at the expense of the Chinese Communists'. Later, Mao spoke of Sta-lin's "treason." He called him "this hypocritical foreign devil." He felt humiliated by Russia's semi-colonial exercise of power in Manchuria as well as in Xinjiang in western China, and by Stalin's haughty treatment of him. He would have wanted, this argument goes, to keep his country free of Soviet domination.

This view is supported by any number of what have become accepted facts. Mao was almost from the beginning—certainly ever since the KMT's bloody anti-Communist coup of 1927—an unorthodox revolutionary. After the massacre of Communists in Shanghai, Mao led the party to the countryside, where he believed the revolution could be based on the oppressed peasantry, an idea that would have seemed ridiculous to Marx, whose ideas about what he called "the idiocy of rural life" precluded any such Maoist possibility. Mao built up a network of rural soviets in Jiangxi province in south central China—modeled on the powerful workers' soviets, or councils, that helped pave the way for the Bolshevik revolution in Russia in 1917.

Mao's biggest rivals for power inside the CCP were for years a group of what were called the "returned students" or the "28 Bolsheviks," led by the proud and ambitious early party member Wang Ming. Wang had been sent to study in Moscow in the mid-1920s, and there he remained, except for a couple of years in China, until 1937. He missed all the action in Shanghai and in Mao's rural soviets. He was not on the Long March and therefore didn't have the prestige attached to that myth-making event. But he had tremendous stature from his association with the center of the world revolution, where he had frequent contacts with Stalin and Stalin's agents, and he was seen to represent the Comintern, the Communist International, which was founded in the wake of the Bolshevik revolution and was pledged to fight "by all available means including armed force for the overthrow of the international bourgeoisie and for the creation of an international Soviet republic as a transition stage to the complete abolition of the state."

Using the orthodox language of Marxism-Leninism, Wang criticized Mao for his "nationalist deviation," and this added to the perception of Mao as a Chinese patriot first and only secondarily as an international revolutionary. His triumph over Wang in a series of power struggles, culminating in the early 1940s, appeared to be a triumph of his independent pragmatism over Stalinist orthodoxy, a point that Mao stressed in his own writings. "Marxism apart from Chinese peculiarities . . . is merely an empty abstraction," he said. "We must discard our dogmatism and replace it with a new and vital Chinese style and manner."

Then there was the actual experience of World War II. For the entire war, Mao had gotten what Davies called "shabby treatment" from the Soviets, who formally recognized Chiang Kai-shek's government as the only legitimate government of China, never openly supported the Communists in their struggle against Chiang, never recognized them as an alternative government (as it did the Polish Communists), never even gave them much in the way of arms. In 1937 at the very beginning of the Sino-Japanese war, Stalin and Chiang signed a non-aggression pact, after which the Soviets, seeking to bolster their resistance to the common Japanese enemy, provided weaponry to the Nationalists, including what was to become the main fighter plane of the Chinese air force. Even after Yalta, the Soviets' public pledge was to continue to support the Chiang government, to the point that during the subsequent civil war, the Soviet ambassador to China, in contrast to his American colleague, accompanied the Nationalists as they retreated to the south. Even a figure like Walter Judd, the ardently pro-Chiang congressman who believed that Mao would put Russian interests ahead of China's, found that Stalin himself had been entirely "correct and circumspect" in his relations with China. Judd said he had found no evidence "that Moscow has been backing or supplying, either with materials or with guidance, the Communist government in China during the last seven years."

Judd was far away, but the Americans on the scene, particularly the members of the Dixie Mission who were in Yenan for a year and a half, saw no evidence of any strong Soviet influence or even presence at Chinese Communist headquarters. The acutely observant Service supposed there was probably "some contact between the Chinese Communists and Moscow," most likely between CCP members in the Soviet Union using a "radio at Yenan." But he believed this contact was minimal. At the time of Service's final visit to Yenan in March 1945, there had been very little travel between Yenan and Moscow for years, perhaps one or two planes a year, and those planes were thoroughly searched by agents of the central government during refueling stops in Lanzhou in western China. The last duly searched plane from Moscow had landed in Yenan the previous November. In all of Yenan, by Service's count, there were a grand total of three Russians in early 1945, one surgeon and two reporters for the Tass news agency. More important perhaps, and supporting Judd's assertion, in all the considerable contact that the Dixie Mission observers had had with the Chinese Communist armies, including months spent accompanying their guerrilla fighters, "there have been found no Russian arms or equipment."

This perception that Mao's contacts with Stalin seemed very occasional and unimportant supported the conviction of the China hands, including Stilwell, Davies, and Service, that the Chinese Communists might welcome friendly ties with the United States, in part because it would make them less dependent on the Soviet Union and therefore, once they took power, as they were inevitably going to do, less likely to be part of a monolithic anti-western Communist bloc in Asia. Under the circumstances, it made perfect sense to predict that China under Communist Party rule could be lured out of the Soviet embrace.

The preponderance of the evidence indicates, however, that these American China experts, so right about so many things, so shrewd and realistic in most of their judgments, were mistaken in this. Years later, Davies acknowledged his mistake, writing in his memoirs that it had been "unrealistic" to think there was much chance of "politically capturing" the CCP.

Davies attributed his mistake to an "underestimation of the Communists' commitment to ideology," and this is true. But another analytical fault of the China hands was to take the balance of power as the operating principle in international relations. It made sense to them that China would want to balance the awesome power of the Soviet Union with the less threatening power of the United States, and, indeed, China did do that a couple of decades later. What they underestimated was the Chinese Communists' membership in the international club of revolutionaries as the essential and ineradicable essence of their character and identity. Being straightforward men of integrity themselves, Service and Davies didn't detect the breathtaking deceit that was practiced on them by Mao and Stalin, two of the greatest masters of deception that the world has ever known. Nor did they entirely appreciate the extent to which Mao acknowledged not only Stalin's position as the leader of the worldwide proletarian revolution but also the extent to which he needed him; once the Cold War began, he would have little choice but to side with the Soviets. Logic and experience told the Americans that it would not be in China's interest to submerge itself in a bloc of states subordinate to Moscow. Logic and experience said that Mao would see Soviet domination in Eastern Europe, and he would avoid it for himself by creating a strategic balance with the United States.

But in 1945—and earlier and later too—Mao didn't see Eastern Europe the way Americans did, as satellite states deprived of their freedom and independence. He saw Soviet domination there—though he would not have called it that—as part of a grand, futuristic plan for an international revolution. By now, the idea of a proletarian world revolu-

tion seems so quaint that it's hard to believe that anybody in the United
States or in China actually believed in it. But for much of the twentieth
century, it was an idea that fired the aspirations of millions like Mao,
who saw the world divided between exploited semi-sovereign or entirely
colonized have-nots like China and the rich and powerful forces of
imperialism. Mao in this sense saw very little conflict or, as he would
have put it, "contradiction" between his interests and Soviet goals. The
scholars Alexander V. Pantsov and Steven I. Levine, whose biography
of Mao draws extensively on Pantsov's access to previously unavailable
Soviet archives on this point, conclude that as the war wound down
Stalin saw a chance in Asia "to radically alter the correlation of forces in
the world arena in favor of the USSR." And a key to that reordering was
a triumph of the Communists in China.

Mao believed in this as well, and he therefore knew that his ultimate
goal and Stalin's were the same. His eventual seizure of power in China
would, as he was famously to put it later, enable the east wind to prevail
over the west wind, or, in less metaphorical language, for the global
proletarian revolution to triumph over bourgeois capitalism, especially
as represented by the United States.

"The principal and fundamental experience the Chinese people
have gained is twofold," Mao said in a speech on June 22, 1949, just
before taking control of all of China, summing up the forty years since
the overthrow of the Manchu dynasty and the twenty-eight years since
the founding of the Chinese Communist Party. Internally, we have
learned to "arouse the masses," Mao said. "Externally," he continued,
we must "ally ourselves with the Soviet Union, with the people's democracies, and with the proletariat and the broad masses of the people in all
other countries, and form an international united front."

This is the context in which both Mao and Stalin engaged in wartime
relations with the western allies. The goal was not friendship with the
United States. It was to sustain a necessary arrangement until conditions changed. The Communists of both the Soviet and Chinese variety
understood the natural anti-Communist impulses of the United States,
and they therefore strove to neutralize those impulses. They strove to
persuade the Americans to support the CCP's wartime aims, namely by
pressuring the Kuomintang to accept a coalition government and giving the Communists arms to use in its guerrilla war against Japan. If the

United States could do those two things, then afterward, as Pantsov and Levine have written, "the CCP would be able to 'squeeze' Chiang Kai-shek and his supporters out of positions of power and next, by maneuvering among the Kuomintang left and the liberals, ultimately seize power."

Mao's moderate policy, including his amicable outreach to the United States, was in this way entirely consistent with his and with Stalin's long-term revolutionary goals. His friendly talks with the members of the Dixie Mission, his moderate, pro-democratic statements to journalists, his offer to support an American landing on Chinese soil—all of this was undertaken not just with Stalin's approval but also on his orders. These orders, moreover, were identical to the orders that Stalin gave to Communist parties elsewhere in the world—to take the kind of "progressive" stands that would attract the support of liberal intellectuals and induce western leaders to believe in their non-threatening moderation. This explains Mao's public championship of China's small democratic parties and the CCP's demand for the release of political prisoners and an end to KMT spying on Chinese citizens. This masquerade as the party of human rights and democracy in China was part of the longer-term scheme, and it was convincing.

Of course, Mao had no intention of establishing a regime of civil rights and democratic institutions once he came to power, nor did Stalin intend to keep his promise of turning Manchuria over to central government forces. In every case in the world where Communist parties took power, the mask was soon dropped and the real totalitarian face of the Stalin-nurtured regimes was revealed. Davies was right to say that the CCP had started out as an instrument of Moscow's policy of world revolution; where he was wrong was to assume that this policy had been permanently abandoned as a result of the war.

In a way, the CCP's efforts to portray itself as moderate and democratic recapitulated a famous episode from the past. During the first United Front, between 1923 and 1927, Stalin's plan, as he put it in a secret speech to party members, was for Chiang to be "squeezed like a lemon and then thrown away." Chiang's preemptive strike against the Communists in 1927 foiled that plan. Now, in 1945, the plan was operational again, and this time it was going to succeed.

The influence of the Soviet Union on China's Communists dates to the very origins of the Chinese Communist Party, when a group of leftist Chinese intellectuals, Mao among them, founded it in 1921. Comintern advisers were dispatched to China to supervise and to provide funds. They schooled the fledgling Chinese Communists in the style of discourse, the tone of propaganda, and the mode of analysis that went by the name Marxism-Leninism. They also provided it with its main source of money. The Kuomintang, which had formed only a few years earlier, was also organized along Marxist-Leninist lines and with the guidance of Soviet advisers, but when Chiang Kai-shek violently parted company with the CCP in 1927, he also parted company with Moscow. He sent its advisers packing and turned elsewhere for money and support, leaving the CCP as the only party in China to be closely supervised and funded by the Comintern.

The relationship between the Russians and the Chinese Communists from then on involved something far broader and deeper than mere advice, money, and moral support. It was an entire cultural and political transmission. It was a vocabulary, a manner of analysis known as dialectical reasoning, a set of practices, and a grand, preoccupying, thrilling political vision involving the triumph of the progressive forces of history over exploitation and reaction. Mao never departed from that vision from the time he became a charter member of the party in 1921 until his death fifty-five years later. When he made his lean-to-one-side speech in June 1949, Mao attributed his imminent success to what he regarded as the superior tools of Marxism-Leninism, the brilliance and promise of which had burst on the world with the Bolshevik revolution of 1917. "Communists the world over are wiser than the bourgeoisie," he said, celebrating the twenty-eighth anniversary of the CCP's founding. "They understand the laws governing the existence and the development of things. They understand dialectics and they can see farther."

Many of the early Communists, though not Mao himself, studied in Moscow at the Communist University of Toilers of the East, which was set up by the Comintern in 1925 to instruct revolutionaries from the colonized countries—and semi-colonized countries like China—in the theory and practice of Marxist revolution. One alumnus of this university was Liu Shaoqi, who was, until Mao cruelly jettisoned him in 1966, Mao's right-hand man, in charge of the Communist Party organization and one of the masterminds of the Rectification Campaign of 1942 to 1944. Deng Xiaoping, later China's paramount leader, attended briefly in 1926 before he moved to a sister school, half an hour's walk from the Kremlin, created also by the Comintern, in 1921, specifically to educate a corps of future Chinese revolutionaries. During his years in Europe in the early twenties, Zhou Enlai, who was on the executive committee of the Chinese Communist Party European branch, recruited Chinese youths on work-study programs in France to go to Moscow to attend these two universities. In this way and others, Moscow had the attributes of a practical training ground and a spiritual mecca for Chinese Communists as it was for other Communists, from Poland, Germany, Bulgaria, and Korea.

In 1923, the fledgling Chinese Communist Party, meeting at its Third Congress, followed the instructions of the Comintern to ally itself with the KMT by joining it as individuals, so that they would be members of both parties simultaneously. The formation of this first United Front, in other words, was an early example of Moscow's decisive guidance in the CCP's relations with the larger and more powerful Nationalist Party, guidance that continued virtually uninterrupted through the Communists' seizure of power in 1949.

The Comintern's task was to create a cadre of professional revolutionaries to be the vanguard of the proletarian cause, and it helped not just with ideological training but also in very practical ways. During the wilderness years of the CCP from the late 1920s to the mid-1930s, when its leaders were often on the run from the KMT secret police, some thirty of their children, including two of Mao's sons, were sheltered in Shanghai by what was called the International Society for Aid to Revolutionaries, which had been set up by the Comintern as part of its program to foster Communist parties abroad. When the shelter was closed down, Stalin personally arranged for the Mao boys to travel to the Soviet Union. There they were known as young "heroes" who had reached "the shores of socialism," and that's where they spent almost the entire war. Mao's daughter, known as Jiao-jiao—later Li Na—spent her entire childhood in the Soviet Union and could barely speak Chinese when she returned to the motherland after the Communist takeover. There were more than a hundred such children, the offspring of dedicated Chinese revolutionaries who studied in Moscow, or worked there for the Chinese branch of the Comintern, or who went back to "make revolution" in China itself, leaving their children behind. Among them: a son and daughter of Liu Shaoqi, a daughter of Zhu De, an offspring of Lin Biao, and many others, all of them hosted by the International Society for Aid to Revolutionaries.

We know of this from a searing memoir written by Sin-Lin, who was brought up in the Soviet Union until she was thirteen, not knowing who her parents were until she was sent back to China in 1950. The Chinese children lived in a home with the children of revolutionaries from other countries—Yugoslavia, Vietnam, Spain, Bulgaria, and many others—singing a song called "Hymn of the Interhouse Children" ("In our hearts protest burns / Like a flame of anger in the darkness") and learning to love Stalin, who, they were taught, was "the great leader of the international proletariat."

When leading Chinese Communists or their family members became seriously ill, they went to Moscow for medical treatment. Among them were two of Mao's wives, He Zizhen and Jiang Qing, and, in 1939, Zhou Enlai, after he broke a bone in his elbow falling from a horse. Membership in this society was like membership in a cult. It was all-encompassing, exclusive, all-consuming. Dozens, perhaps hundreds, of Chinese Communists in Russia were swept up in the Stalin purges of 1938 and dispatched to the Gulag. In many instances these people were informed on by other Chinese Communists; it was a foreshadowing of the savage infighting that was to take place in China itself. Sin-Lin, whose father spent seventeen years in a Siberian work camp, believes that Kang Sheng's later persecution of fellow Communists whom he had known in Moscow in the 1930s was aimed at covering up his own earlier role informing on Chinese revolutionaries in the Soviet Union. When the teenage Sin-Lin asked her mother, a dedicated revolutionary, how "the Great, Glorious, and Correct Party" of Stalin could have perpetrated such an injustice, her reply was: "What you are talking about is only individual incidents that represent zigzags in the revolution, they cannot eclipse all of socialist construction in the Soviet Unon; they can't blacken the entire international communist movement." There is no evidence that the Chinese Communists ever protested to the Soviets the disappearance of their members into the Soviet prison camp system, from which hundreds never emerged. One can only speculate on the reason for this, but most likely Mao and senior cadres like Kang Sheng did not want to acknowledge that such practices were an essential part of the movement to which they belonged.

The very language of Chinese Communism, its symbols and modes of discourse, the style of its propaganda, its wood-block prints, its notions of socialist realism, its central committees, politburos, congresses, and plenums, its newspapers and ultra-serious theoretical journals, its specialized vocabulary of internal debate and struggle, its invention of an entire lexicography of ideological labels, all of them newly minted isms, like "left adventurism," "right opportunism," "deviationism," "dogmatism," "subjectivism," "empiricism," "revisionism," as well as the "correctness" of the party line, and, later, the boilerplate of adulation that victorious revolutionaries such as Mao, the Korean Kim Il Sung, the Romanian Nicolae Ceauşescu, and the Vietnamese Ho Chi Minh used in their own cults of the godlike genius-leader—all of this was nurtured and supported by an encyclopedia of terms, concepts, beliefs, and techniques transplanted from the original Russian, the success of the Bolshevik revolution having made the Soviet Union, in the eyes of countless oppressed and colonized people, a pathbreaker toward a radiant future—"the shores of socialism," a promised land.

Again, given China's later and complete break with the Soviets and the country's ferocious attachment to its national independence, it requires a strong historical memory to resurrect the era of obedience to an outside authority. But in those decades when China's revolutionaries sought to imitate and emulate the Soviets' magnificent success, the relations between Moscow and the Chinese Communists were the relations of authority and compliance inside a church of the great cause, where a pope-like ruler issued edicts, based on a secular scripture whose truthfulness was guaranteed by a combination of the sacred and the infallibly scientific, or at least informed by the superiority of dialectical materialism over other modes of analysis.

It isn't by some weird coincidence that after the deaths of the great revolutionaries Lenin, Mao, Ho, and Kim, their bodies were embalmed and placed on view for public veneration, like the fragments of the Buddha's body or relics of the Christian saints. The origin of the practice lies in the Russian Orthodox veneration of the saints wherein it was believed that spiritual purity triumphed over the decay of the flesh; the Communist adoption of that notion was that the supreme leaders of the revolution would live eternally in the ultimate triumph of pure Communism. Nobody believed in this semi-religion—though he wouldn't have called it that—more than Mao.

One of the strongest appeals of Marxism-Leninism was the explanation it offered for the powerlessness of the internationally dispossessed, an explanation that fit perfectly with Chinese national grievances and aspirations. This explanation was advanced by Lenin's extremely influential idea of imperialism as the last stage of capitalism, an idea that was no doubt instilled into students at places like the University of Toilers of the East. In advanced capitalism, wealth became concentrated in the hands of a few monopolies; the subsequent impoverishment of the working class led these monopolies, which controlled their governments on behalf of the ruling class, to seek raw materials, cheap labor, and markets for their products wherever they could throughout the world. This explained in persuasive, easy to understand, and, to an extent, truthful—if somewhat mechanistic—terms everything the young revolutionary needed to know about China's condition going back to the Opium War and the beginning of what the Communists in China still call the Hundred Years of Humiliation. After all, what was the Opium War but the armed effort of the monopolistic and greedy British East India Company to ensure a market in China for its Indian opium? Lenin's theory explained the treaty ports, the foreign concessions, Japan's naked aggression, the decadent and privileged, servant- and concubine-rich lifestyles of the foreigners in China, who were exempt from Chinese law and whose missionaries conveyed the message that Chinese beliefs and customs were inferior to foreign beliefs and customs. Deeply embedded in the thinking of China's early revolutionaries and patriots was this conviction that imperialist exploitation and profiteering was the final bulwark of the bourgeoisie in its life-and-death struggle with the international proletariat.

In the self-contained, sealed-off world of Communist ideology, much that was viewed in the rest of the world as benign or certainly inoffensive was construed to be wickedly conspiratorial. Around the time of the CCP's founding, the major world powers, including the United States, Japan, and Britain, attended a conference in Washington whose main result was a set of agreements limiting the size of one another's navies. Seen by the treaty makers as a hard-won victory in the effort to prevent an arms race and the outbreak of another world war, these Washington treaties were castigated by the Chinese Communists as an imperialist "robbery" that "will compel 400 million Chinese people to enter into slavery under the new international trust."

An interpretation like that would, if Americans had known of it, have been difficult for them to understand. They had, in general, a benign view of themselves and an especially benign view of themselves when it came to China. Americans have always felt that their "open door" policy, first formulated at the end of the nineteenth century when other countries were forcibly extracting colonial privileges from China, was consistent with the idealistic American impulse to help remake

China as a Christian democracy. When, for example, China was forced to pay a huge indemnity to the imperialist powers after its defeat by them in the Boxer Rebellion of 1898, the United States put the funds it received into an educational trust for bright Chinese students to study in America.

But for a Chinese of the first half of the twentieth century, American intentions were not always seen in so favorable a light. In 1915, while war raged in Europe, Japan imposed its notorious twenty-one demands on China, pressing China to agree to a host of concessions, from giving Japan control of the Manchurian railways to allowing its Buddhist preachers to proselytize in China. The weak Chinese government acceded to these demands, setting off massive protests, especially by students. A few years later, in the wake of World War I, the victorious Allies wrote into the Versailles peace treaty a clause awarding Japan control of the German colony of Qingdao in Shandong province. Chinese intellectuals responded to this new insult with a four-year period of protests and self-examination known as the May Fourth Movement, which powerfully engaged the minds of intellectuals, including those who would soon found the Communist Party. For them, the spectacle of the supposedly benign United States agreeing to give hated Japan control over Chinese territory validated the suspicion that the "open door" was an American euphemism for maintaining its share of the China market.

This view of America was one of the main points of difference between the CCP and the KMT. Both parties wanted to achieve full independence for China by eliminating extraterritorial privileges in the treaty ports. Chiang Kai-shek always suspected, correctly, that British policy was not to help China become strong and independent but to keep it weak and tethered to the West, so Britain could preserve its empire, including Hong Kong and its extraterritorial compounds in Shanghai and elsewhere. But, especially after the break with the Communists in 1927, the KMT became increasingly tied to the United States even as it constituted itself, in Communist eyes, as the party of the landlords and the big capitalists. Chiang and the rest of the Kuomintang were as patriotically committed to full Chinese independence as the Communists; nonetheless, they grew closer to the United States as time went by, and many of its leading figures were educated not in the University of Toilers of the East but in American universities. Chiang himself was a convert not to Marxism-Leninism but to Methodism; his glamorous wife went to Wellesley; his brother-in-law and prime minister, T. V. Soong, was an alumnus of Harvard; his finance minister, H. H. Kung, a graduate of Oberlin College and the Yale Law School. China's government ministries were heavily populated by English-speaking graduates of American universities. Theodore H. White organized a Harvard Club in Chungking in 1940 and, he later wrote, it "included a larger proportion of the high officials of Chiang Kai-shek's government than a Harvard Club would have in John F. Kennedy's Washington." Chiang was open to missionary activity in China and to big business, and he failed before the outbreak of World War II to eliminate the extraterritorial privileges in the treaty ports—such things as immunity from prosecution in Chinese courts and foreign-run police forces—that were so injurious to Chinese pride. And so, as the KMT came to seem ever more an American acolyte, it lost its anti-imperialist credentials.

Nobody in the Chinese Communist leadership went to Harvard, Wellesley, or Yale. There were no private or public links, no sentimental old school ties, and few religious affiliations connecting senior Chinese Communists with the United States. The Communists always held anti-imperialism as a central tenet, along with their interpretation of global politics as a series of "contradictions" among the imperialists themselves or between them and the colonized world.

The anti-imperialist credo showed itself in large things and small, in the political and the personal. Illustrating the last of these, in 1937, Mao's wife, He Zizhen, became infuriated when she caught Mao in a flirtation with a comely actress known as Lily (her real name was Wu Guangwei), who was introduced to him by the leftist American journalist Agnes Smedley. One night, during a quarrel with Mao, He Zizhen turned her wrath against Smedley, accusing her of being an "imperialist"—later, when she complained to other party leaders, she called Smedley an "imperialist procuress"—while asking Mao, "Are you really a communist?"

Mao most definitely was a Communist, and while his observance of what was supposed to be superior Communist morality was inconsistent, his vision of American imperialism was unchanging, and it was one of the things that made his friendly attitude toward the United States a temporary departure, a tactical move. The classic Chinese *Thirty-Six Stratagems for Waging War and Politics* includes the ploy known as "Hide the knife behind a smile." The aim of it is to ingratiate yourself with your enemy when you need to keep him at bay, confuse him, or, to use the Marxist-Leninist terminology, exploit the "contradictions" between him and other enemies, to prevent them from combining against you. Once Mao was in power, the approved jargon changed to a kind of bombastic boilerplate about "American imperialism" and its "running dogs" that, while rhetorically ridiculous, represented his default ideological position. His belief in the Soviet Union as the fountainhead of revolutionary authority was also permanent. The war caused both Stalin and Mao to relinquish ideological goals, to hide the knife for a while, so that ideological goals could be achieved later.

Even before the Japanese war, Mao consistently demonstrated obedience to this principle. During the Xian Incident of 1936, when, as we've seen, Mao's initial impulse upon hearing of the Xian kidnapping was to put Chiang, the man he'd been calling a "traitor," on trial, with his execution the most likely result, Stalin told Mao to agree to a United Front instead. Mao obeyed, and a few months later he made a public self-criticism, admitting that he had been wrong and Stalin right.

According to the historian Michael M. Sheng, who has examined Chinese records unavailable to earlier researchers, Mao and Stalin did, as Service suspected, use a radio contact to communicate with each other during the war, and this contact was more important than Service believed. The radio was a secret, inherited from the earlier days of Comintern influence. It had fallen into disuse during Chiang's encirclement campaigns against the Communists, but it was restored at Mao's behest in 1936 and it remained in place for the entire war. In 1940, Zhou Enlai, after his sojourn in the Soviet Union for medical treatment, brought back to China a set of radio transmitting equipment and two sets of codes—for example, the phrase "remote place" meant Stalin—to make the Moscow-Yenan connection more reliable. The radio connection in Yenan was referred to as an "Agriculture Department," and put under one of Mao's most trusted lieutenants. The man who translated Stalin's messages to Mao, Shi Zhe, wrote in his memoirs decades later that Mao kept total control over the files of these messages, keeping them in his residence where nobody else had full access to them. The files were burned at Mao's orders in 1946, probably so that Stalin's close, everyday involvement in the CCP's affairs, at a time when he was supposedly being "correct and circumspect" toward China, would remain secret and any suggestion that the CCP was a Soviet proxy could be avoided.

Zhou Enlai also brought $300,000 with him from Moscow, one of numerous financial contributions that the Soviets secretly made to the CCP over the years, which both added a measure of influence and control and belied the Soviet pretense of non-interference in China's internal affairs. Even after Hitler attacked the Soviet Union and Stalin was plunged overnight into a desperate struggle for survival, the money flow to the CCP continued. Pantsov and Levine cite in particular a document unearthed from Soviet archives showing that on July 3, 1941, a bit more than two weeks after the German onslaught began, $1 million was released for assistance to the CCP central committee, and $1 million in 1941 was a great deal of money.

The pattern for the entirety of World War II and, indeed, until after the CCP's seizure of power in 1949 remained one of close consultation, cooperation, and agreement between Russia and China's Communists. For the entire length of the Sino-Japanese War, Stalin's greatest fear in the east was of a Japanese attack, a sort of renewal of the war of 1905 extended from Japan's Manchurian base into Soviet Siberia. To prevent that, Stalin wanted the strongest possible China, and the strongest possible China was one led by Chiang Kai-shek with the Communists cooperating with him. Stalin understood that the Communists were not yet capable of taking power. They had barely survived Chiang's annihilation campaigns against them in the early and mid-1930s, and their forces, now bottled up in their fortress in northern Shaanxi province, were small and badly armed compared to those of the central government. The best option under those circumstances was to support the Kuomintang and to do nothing that might anger its leader, Chiang Kai-shek, or to push him into a peace deal with Japan, which would free the Japanese to turn their attention to Russian Siberia.

And so, from the Xian Incident on, Stalin's essential orders to Mao were threefold: to support the Soviet Union, maintain the United Front, and avoid arousing American suspicions that the Communists' long-range plan was for revolutionary conquest. This involved numerous twists and turns; Mao frequently had difficulty suppressing his go-it-alone impulses, but he did consistently yield to Stalin's preferences. In 1939, to take a striking example of this, leftists the world over were shocked and dismayed when Stalin and Hitler agreed on their non-aggression pact, followed by their division of Poland. The various Communist parties had to make a quick and awkward ideological about-face, offering praise of an alliance with Hitler, who until then had been their devil incarnate. Mao was no exception. Suddenly, what was yesterday's unthinkable alliance was today's brilliant tactical stroke, one that destroyed the imperialist warmongers' goal of profiting from a German-Soviet war. The Nazi-Soviet Non-Aggression Pact, Mao told a group of New China News Agency reporters, "has shattered the intrigues by which the reactionary international bourgeoisie . . . sought to instigate a Soviet-German war." It also, Mao said, enumerating numerous advantages of the Hitler-Stalin Pact, "has broken the encirclement of the Soviet Union by the German-Italian-Japanese anti-Communist bloc . . . and safeguarded socialist construction in the Soviet Union."

In 1940, with Chinese men being used alive for bayonet practice and thousands of its women being raped by the Japanese, Franklin Roosevelt made a radio address in which he declared an American national emergency. Thinking that this was preliminary to an American entry into the war, the Kuomintang was ecstatic over this speech. The Communists, however, expected to support the German-Soviet pact, were in the odd position of having to oppose any military move against the Russian ally, Germany, or its ally, Japan. Therefore, the CCP's response was to call Roosevelt a "warmonger." Drawing on its theory of imperialism, *Liberation Daily* warned that the American ruling class was preparing to "drive the American people into the slaughterhouse of imperialist war to generate great war profits for some sixty of the richest families in America."

Mao was to change this perception the following year, impelled to do so by the German surprise attack on the Soviet Union, which led both Stalin and Mao to call for an "international anti-fascist United Front," and Roosevelt was transformed in China's propaganda from "warmonger" to "enlightened bourgeois politician."

This does not mean that the underlying vision had altered. Years later, when he was on the verge of taking power, Mao repudiated the notion that China needed help from the United States and the West. "Their capitalists want to make money and their bankers want to earn interest to extricate themselves from their own crisis—it is not a matter of helping the Chinese people," he said.

There were times when Mao's obedience to Stalin put him into conflict with others in the CCP's leadership, at a time when these other members were equals, not the obedient subordinates they later became. In 1940, Zhou Enlai and Zhu De, wanting to fight Japanese aggression, acting against Stalin's instructions, pushed the CCP into the Hundred Regiments Offensive. When the offensive produced a horrific result for the Communists, Mao, back in control, returned to a policy of limited guerrilla hit-and-run attacks; in doing so, he was restoring the standard low-risk, low-casualty, maximum-propaganda-value strategy that had been proposed by Stalin.

At least twice over the course of the anti-Japanese struggle the impetuous Mao became convinced that Chiang was gearing up for an attack against him—he remembered Chiang's murderous assault on the Communists in Shanghai in 1927—and he wanted to strike preemptively, which of course would have damaged or destroyed the United Front. On both occasions, Stalin, communicating through the secret radio connection, told Mao that he was exaggerating the risk of a KMT attack, and he asked him to stay patient and to do nothing to weaken the United Front. Mao acquiesced.

One of these instances involved the biggest military confrontation between the two parties that took place during the Japanese war, known as the New Fourth Army Incident. In early 1941, perhaps without Chiang's permission, one of his generals attacked a division of the Communist New Fourth Army (NFA), inflicting heavy losses on it over a three-day period. The two sides blamed each other for this violation of the United Front. The NFA division had agreed to a government order to withdraw from south of the Yangzi River to north of it. According to the KMT, it had disobeyed this order and was maneuvering for position. The Communists claimed that the division was simply looking for a safe place to cross the river and had been attacked before it was able to do so.

It is very likely that the Communist version of this is the true one, because at the time both Stalin and Mao felt it in their interest to maintain good relations with the KMT. After the attack, a furious Mao wanted to declare the United Front dead and to mount a full-scale offensive against the KMT, both military and political. But in radio messages to Mao, Georgi Dimitrov, the Bulgarian Communist who headed the Comintern for Stalin, ordered Mao to "rely on the people who advocate the maintenance of the united front . . . and do everything to avoid the spread of civil war." When Mao expressed some annoyance at this, Dimitrov radioed him two more times to insist on maintaining the United Front, and Mao assented.

In April 1941, Stalin delivered what must have been another shock to Mao. He signed a non-aggression pact with Japan in which he recognized the Japanese puppet state of Manchukuo in exchange for Japan's recognition of the People's Republic of Mongolia, which, though nominally independent, was controlled by the Soviet Union. This was an extraordinary development. All the while, Mao had worried that Chiang Kai-shek, his past and future mortal enemy, would make peace with Japan, and now here was Stalin himself doing exactly that! The deal, moreover, would enable Japan to put more troops into China, since it no longer had to guard against a move by the Russians. Moreover, China claimed Outer Mongolia as its own.

Still, Mao endorsed the new agreement. He did so because it was in the preeminent interest of the Soviet Union, since, as Mao argued, the threat of an Asian war between the Russians and Japan had now been averted, and Stalin had defeated the Anglo-American plot to pit the Axis against the Soviet Union. (Russia had not yet been attacked by the Nazis.) In addition, Mao said, engaging in a bit of twisted logic to explain why it was a good thing that the Soviets were recognizing Japan's conquest of three provinces of China, until this point Chiang had seen himself as crucial to the Soviet strategy of deterring a Japanese attack. He could feel he was more important to Moscow than the CCP, which might have emboldened him to surrender to Japan and attack the Communists. Now he couldn't.

Two events later in 1941 changed everything about the strategic picture, but they didn't change Mao's obedience to Stalin. The first was Hitler's great betrayal of Stalin. On June 22, Hitler mounted Operation Barbarossa, a surprise, three-front attack on the Soviet Union. Stalin, having been allied to the fascists for two years, now put out a call to Mao asking for all-out support of the antifascist struggle. Mao wrote to Zhou to ease off on his already weakened opposition to American participation in the war. "No matter whether they are imperialist powers or not, if they are antifascist, they are good."

The second event was the Japanese attack on Pearl Harbor on December 7, 1941, which brought the United States into the war as a declared combatant, pledged to use its own armed forces to defeat Japan and to expel it from China. The day after the attack, Chiang cabled Roosevelt offering "to stand with you until the Pacific and the world are free from the curse of brute force and endless perfidy."

For Mao, the American entry eliminated any remaining possibility that Japan would attack the Soviet Union, but he still nurtured his chief worry about an alliance between Chiang and the Americans, an alliance that would turn its attention to the Communists once the Japanese were disposed of. The best way to avert this, and to give Mao a chance to build up his forces for a long-drawn-out war, was to establish his own ties with the United States and to gain American recognition as a legitimate political party. Mao had already done public relations work with leftist journalists like Edgar Snow, but the purpose of that venture was as much to get attention in China, where Snow's book would and did leak through the gaps in KMT censorship, as it was to build a favorable image in the United States.

Now the goal was to win over the Americans, inviting mainstream journalists to Yenan, hosting the Dixie Mission, and helping to rescue downed American fliers, assuring the Americans of their friendly feeling, and making the gestures of friendly relations that the Communists perfected in 1944 and 1945. There were those assurances made by both Mao and Zhou that it would take decades to create true communism in China and in the meantime they admired American democracy— assurances that would prove false within a few short years of the Communists' takeover of power in 1949. There were Zhou's comments to American visitors in Chungking about the Communists' intention of respecting individual freedoms and rights and his demands that the Kuomintang do the same by releasing political prisoners and curbing its secret police. As we've seen, near the end of 1944 Mao told members of the Dixie Mission that he would welcome an American landing of troops on Chinese soil and that he would happily place his forces under American command. "There is no such thing as America not intervening in China," he told Service in March 1945. "You are here as China's greatest ally. The fact of your presence is tremendous. America's intentions have been good."

In some ways, Mao probably meant what he said, or some of it, especially when he enlisted American help in creating a coalition government and when he offered military help to an American landing on the China coast. Mao was always confident of his ability, if given a meaningful place in the central government, to use it to expand his influence and eventually to take power. By the time of the Yalta agreement, he had more than a million well-fed, highly motivated troops under his command, facing government forces that were severely depleted. If he had gotten the go-ahead to provide logistical support for an American landing on the China coast, he would have been able to extend his power to new areas south of the Yangzi River, which was a stated goal.

But his expressed willingness to put his troops under American command was pure public relations. "We shall never agree to that," Mao cabled Zhou in Chungking on January 25, 1945, and his reason harked back to Lenin's theory of imperialism. It would put the party's troops "under foreign command, turning them into a colonial army," Mao said. America was the imperialist power, the Soviet Union the revolutionary one. And that is what mattered when it came to distinguishing between permanent friends and permanent enemies.

CHAPTER TEN

The War over China Policy

At the end of February 1945, Wedemeyer and Hurley left China together, arriving in Washington a week later. Wedemeyer went about laying out plans to seize a port on the China coast in the spring. Hurley's purpose was more amorphous, more political, and more divisive. He was troubled by rumors he had heard in Chungking that Stalin and Roosevelt had reached a secret deal regarding China when they met at Yalta in February, and he wanted information on that from Roosevelt himself. He also wanted to be given total control of policy on China, and to make public what that policy was—essentially unconditional support for Chiang Kai-shek.

As we've seen, Hurley was a man prone in the final weeks of 1944 to eruptions of fury. He was convinced that his attempts to get the KMT and CCP to make a deal were failing because a few Foreign Service officers wanted them to fail, and the talks Bird and Barrett had had with Mao and others in his camp about intelligence cooperation and supporting American paratroopers in northeast China were proof of this infidelity.

One of Hurley's biographers attributes some of this irascibility to physical discomfort, the dankness and filth of Chungking, insomnia, and even toothaches, to which the ambassador was prone. Hurley needed glasses but refused to wear them, with the result that he suffered from splitting headaches. His attention span was short; he couldn't read lengthy documents. Once, at a Chungking cocktail party, with Chinese guests in attendance, he and McClure got into such an angry exchange that only the intervention of friends prevented them from coming to blows. He commanded little respect, even if most people behaved properly toward him. The Communists called him Little Whiskers. At sixty-two years of age, it's not out of the question that he was suffering from mental decline; at least, some observers believed that to be the case. "With increasing frequency [Hurley] forgot where he was, with whom he was, and even what he had just said," *Time*'s Annalee Jacoby told an interviewer.

To the consternation of the professional China experts in the embassy and on Wedemeyer's staff, Hurley began censoring their dispatches. "He said that he was sent to China to support the Nationalist government and that we should not report anything which reflected [poorly] on the quality and caliber of the Chinese administration," Arthur R. Ringwalt, the senior political officer at the embassy, recounted later. "We would write dispatches saying what we thought of the situation, and he refused to send them in."

In one instance, Hurley sat for weeks on a paper submitted by Ringwalt describing the tendency of arms given to Chiang's government to be sold to the Communists or lost in local conflicts. When Ringwalt asked the ambassador what he planned to do with the report, Hurley summoned T. V. Soong to his office and in Ringwalt's presence showed him the document. Not surprisingly, Soong declared that it was untrue. The dispatch was never sent.

All along, Hurley insisted that he was on the verge of success, that he would have achieved it already had it not been for the unauthorized meddling of people like Davies, Barrett, and Bird. The paradox is that, while he disagreed with them about everything else, Hurley's view of Mao's followers as not "real Communists" was in agreement with the China hands' view of them. "I pause to observe that in this dreary controversial chapter two fundamental facts are emerging," Hurley wrote in February, after the Chungking talks had collapsed, Zhou had returned to Yenan, and Mao was ignoring the American pleas to return to the table:

(one) the Communists are not in fact Communists, they are striving for democratic principles; and (two) the one party, one man personal Government of the Kuomintang is not in fact Fascist. It is striving for democratic principles. Both the Communists and the Kuomintang have a long way to go, but, if we know the way, if we are clear minded, tolerant and patient, we can be helpful.

In the face of Hurley's irascible wrongheadedness, the China hands fought back, their opposition ripening into an open rebellion against their boss and ambassador. In the late fall, Raymond Ludden and three other members of the Dixie Mission went on a 1,500-mile, four-month-long journey from Yenan due south about one hundred fifty miles to Fuping, most of it in supposedly Japanese-controlled territory that had been infiltrated by Communist forces. Ludden's observations exercised a powerful influence on the China hands. The men put on Chinese padded winter clothing and traveled by jeep, by mule, and on foot through rugged, mountainous terrain, sometimes coming within a mile or so of Japanese detachments. They met Communist guerrillas all along the route and were impressed by their stalwart simplicity, their dedication, and, perhaps most important, their good health and high morale. They encountered young urban Chinese who were teaching in rural villages. They saw primitive factories making everything from textiles to explosives. What they didn't see was military action of any significance, as an informal truce prevailed between the Chinese and Japanese in North China, under which the Communists and their million troops did not engage Japanese forces except in small hit-and-run attacks. At one point, the five Americans met the crew of a downed American bomber who had been brought by the Communists safely through enemy lines, a feat that required a great deal of organization along a large swath of territory as well as the cooperation of local people.

Returning to Yenan in January 1945, Ludden discovered that there was an American plane at the airstrip that was heading back to Chungking, so he jumped aboard, returned to the embassy, and described to his fellow China hands what he'd seen. When he met Hurley, Ludden naturally expected the ambassador to be at least a little curious about his expedition, but what Hurley seemed most interested in was who exactly had authorized the trip (the answer was Barrett, the commander of the Dixie Mission) and whoever that person was, who had authorized him.

Early in 1945, Ludden's findings finally arrived in Washington, where they fell straight into the heated and ongoing China debate. Ludden's firsthand observations were entirely consistent with what Davies, Service, Barrett, and Bird had been saying. He stressed the geographic breadth of the Communists' operations and the support they enjoyed from local people. "There is no valid reason to doubt but that popular support of the Communist armies and civil administrations is a reality which we must consider in future planning," he wrote. The impression that the Communists were not well-liked by the people under its rule was not, as some (namely Hurley) were maintaining, "a stage-setting for the deception of foreign visitors. . . . The simple Communist program of decent treatment, fundamental civil rights, sufficient food, and sufficient clothing for the peasant has brought about genuine unity between the Eighth Route Army and the people."

During his journey, Ludden and his team members had talked with local commanders about what they needed in the way of supplies and what they would do with them, and from his observations and their answers, Ludden estimated that if they were provided with "adequate explosives," the Communist armies "can with a maximum advance notice of 40 days cripple North China rail communications." Ludden also reiterated the opinion of Service and others that the Communists were "liberal democratic and soundly nationalistic."

To be sure, they were nationalistic, but liberal democratic? Ludden in this rosy judgment reflected either that there was an element of "stage-setting for the deception of foreign visitors," or that the China experts' eagerness to promote cooperation with the Communists made them overeager to find virtues in them that were lacking in the KMT. But Ludden was surely right that with better weapons and supplies, the Communists could have made a major contribution to the war against Japan.

For his part, in a cable of the same day, Davies, now in his new post in Moscow, elaborated on the advantages to the United States of closer ties with Yenan. Moscow, he said, must be viewing the situation in China with "sardonic satisfaction" as the Chiang regime decays, the Communists grow stronger, and the United States remains uncertain about what to do. If the United States would cooperate with Yenan, Davies averred, it would have a chance of strengthening the pragmatic, nationalistic faction inside the Chinese Communist Party, while weakening "those doctrinaires favoring reliance upon the Soviet Union."

"The profound suspicion and hostility in the United States to the tag 'Communist,' the Kremlin probably knows, prejudices the American public against the Chinese Communists," Davies wrote. "Marshal Stalin must be informed that . . . most Americans are attached to the fiction that only through Chiang Kai-shek can China in war and in peace realize its destiny." This ideological stubbornness, this "inability to engage in realpolitik," could lead us "to lose what we seek: the quickest possible defeat of Japan and a united, strong and independent China. And the Soviet Union may stand to gain . . . a satellite North China."

In a similar vein, Service and Ludden wrote to Wedemeyer, arguing,

"The intention of the Generalissimo to eliminate all political opposition, by force of arms if necessary," and his habit of paying more attention to his domestic opposition than to the fight against Japan, was the heart of the KMT's gradual loss of standing with its own people and the reason for its poor military performance. "Support of the Generalissimo is desirable in so far as there is concrete evidence that he is willing and able to marshal the full strength of China against Japan," the two American China experts wrote. "Support of the Generalissimo is but one means to an end; it is not an end in itself."

The person on the receiving end of these communications was the head of the China desk in the Bureau of Far Eastern Affairs, John Carter Vincent, a distinguished-looking forty-five-year-old Kansan who'd had half a dozen assignments in far-flung posts in China, including as minister-counselor of the embassy in Chungking, where he knew the leading China hands well — not that he always shared their opinions. Vincent, like most of the Foreign Service professionals, had a low opinion of Hurley, and he liked Davies and Service, the most ardent advocates of building ties with the Communists, but he also thought they were a bit rhapsodic in their visions of Mao and his cohort. "They overdid it," Vincent told his biographer, Gary May, speaking of Davies and Service, who were a decade or so younger than Vincent, more impatient than he was, and prone, because of their awareness of Chiang's shortcomings, to "ascribe all virtue to the Communists," as he put it in a speech in 1944, not mentioning Davies and Service by name but clearly having them in mind.

Vincent was pretty sure that Hurley's mission would fail, and though he had an aversion to the Communists, without any truly attractive options his policy recommendation was pretty close to that of the China hands. The best option for the United States and for China, he felt, was for Chiang to stay in power but for him to move quickly toward a more inclusive, democratic political system — otherwise he was likely to be overthrown, most likely by the CCP. But, Vincent understood, Chiang was unlikely to relinquish one-party rule, and therefore the United States needed to have "an alternative solution," not to find itself stuck with the failing leader of a failing government. And the alternative was more or less what Service and Davies were recommending: arming the Communists without asking Chiang's permission to do so.

These views made their way into a State Department paper on China policy that was given to Wedemeyer when he arrived in Washington but, tellingly, was kept from Hurley. The paper was an effort to bridge the divide between those favoring all-out support for Chiang and those who wanted to build relations with the Communists. The short-term objective in China, the one Wedemeyer should concentrate on, was defeating Japan, the paper said, and this was to be achieved in the political sphere by uniting all the Chinese factions, which, of course, is what Hurley was attempting to do. It would be good, the paper allowed, if the United States were able to arm all of the factions, including the Communists, but, unfortunately, that was politically impossible—unless circumstances arose under which it became possible. If the United States at some point needed to land troops on the China coast, for example, then American commanders "should be prepared to arm the Communists." Moreover, while American policy was to encourage a unified China, that "did not necessarily mean that China should be united under the Generalissimo." It was important to maintain "a degree of flexibility" in this regard.

Smart and realistic as this was, Vincent's alternative lacked concrete practicality. It didn't answer the question about the consequences to the Chinese central government of making a separate military deal with the Communists, which would have been so severe a blow to Chiang and would very likely have precipitated his overthrow. At what point would Chiang's unwillingness to give up his one-party rule justify American military cooperation with the Communists? In not addressing these questions, Vincent's paper illustrated the lack of clear direction and the absence of good options at a time when strong, clearheaded leadership was needed. With President Roosevelt in his final, frail days, nobody at the top of the American government was providing leadership on China. Instead, into the vacuum, it was the least qualified, most temperamental, dangerously injudicious man on the scene who took charge.

For his part, Chiang was perfectly aware of his dilemma, and prone to alternating bouts of gloom and fury about it. Following the Yalta agreement, he felt, as he put it in his diary, "fear and suspicion" that something had been hidden from him, and of course he was right. No fool, he dispatched his ambassador in Washington to query Roosevelt on the matter, and when Chiang learned that Roosevelt had admitted to the secret protocol to the Yalta accord, he felt that he had been "sold out."

Illustrating Chiang's sour mood, when he attended a meeting of the State Council, a powerless group that rarely convened, a party elder from Canton by the name of Tsou Lu asked about Zhou Enlai's demand that the Communists be allowed to send a representative to the San Francisco Conference, the upcoming meeting at which the future victors in the war would discuss the creation of the United Nations. The Communists had, to Chiang's annoyance, been making propaganda hay out of the Gimo's refusal to broaden China's representation at the conference, arguing that China would appear to all the world to be the unrepresentative dictatorship that it was. Chiang, an American embassy account of the State Council meeting said, "became enraged and delivered a stinging reprimand to Tsou . . . and damned the liberals generally." When the subject of the Communists came up, Chiang's "face was red with anger and his voice and hands shook. When he finished his frightened audience remained completely silent and he adjourned the meeting."

In Chungking, the China hands were increasingly feeling that China policy was in a crisis. E. J. Kahn, a writer for The New Yorker, interviewed Ludden, Davies, Service, and other China hands in the early 1970s. They told him that back then they were all living in the same house in Chungking where "there were no women around, and they spent their evenings in desultory addiction to bridge or darts or crossword puzzles, or in analyzing and reanalyzing the gloomy condition of China." They nursed the conviction that "if they didn't do something fast, everything the United States had tried to do in and for China up to then might go down the drain."

And so the China hands decided on a drastic step. They deputized Service to write an analysis that would be sent on to Washington where it would arrive at just about the same time as Wedemeyer and Hurley. George Atcheson, the diplomat in charge of the embassy during Hurley's absence, expressed some misgivings about this initiative. "They'll say we're all traitors, that when the cats were away the mice began to play," he said. So to preempt that possibility, they inserted this sentence: "The presence of General Wedemeyer in Washington as well as General Hurley should be a favorable opportunity for discussion of this matter." Atcheson then signed the paper and off it went, with an unabashed declaration in it that Hurley's reporting on the KMT-CCP negotiations had been "incomplete and non-objective," which is about as powerful a statement of dissent inside a diplomatic staff as it's possible to imagine. According to Service later, all of the political officers on the staff of the embassy agreed with this telegram. Even General Mervin E. Gross, Wedemeyer's chief of staff, who was in command during Wedemeyer's absence, had endorsed it. The United States, it said, should present Chiang with an ultimatum. Roosevelt should "inform Chiang Kai-shek in definite terms that we are required by military necessity to cooperate with and supply the Communists and other suitable groups who can aid in this war against the Japanese." Moreover, there was no need to wait until a KMT-CCP unity pact had been agreed to before giving this notification to China's president. As the historian Herbert Feis summarized the argument, the recommended policy would "secure the cooperation of all Chinese in the war; hold the Communists on our side instead of throwing them into the arms of the Soviet Union; convince the Kuomintang that its apparent plans for eventual civil war were undesirable; and advance the cause of unification within China."

For Hurley, who believed exactly the opposite, the telegram was a declaration of war. Clearly it had been timed not just to coincide with his arrival in Washington but also to undermine him as the policy debate took place. In the fashion characteristic of him, he wasn't able to see it for what it was, an urgent and even brave expression of disagreement on the part of a group of intelligent and well-informed men. It was, he charged, "an act of disloyalty." To arm the Communists would be to recognize the Communists as "armed belligerents," and this would "result in the speedy overthrow of the National Government." Hurley now felt there was nobody in the embassy or the diplomatic service he could trust. Lending substance to this conviction, on March 5 he was summoned to the Bureau of Far Eastern Affairs of the State Department for a meeting where, as he put it, he got "put on the carpet" and made to defend what he regarded as settled matters of policy. His authorized, totally sympathetic biographer quotes him describing himself at this event as facing "a full array of the pro-Communists of the State Department as my judges and questioners."

The battle lines were drawn, and the stakes were the nature of the American role in Asia. But in this first American contest between two radically opposed points of view on what to do in a poor Asian country where a weak government faced a Communist revolution, Hurley's direct access to the president was the trump card. He went to the White House, which had been given a copy of the dissenting Chungking telegram on March 2, and, as Feis records it, "the President upheld Hurley." There would be no arms or supplies given to the Communists, no separate agreement with them that was not approved in advance by the central government.

As before, Roosevelt simply had no stomach for exacting concessions from Chiang by putting a gun to his head. He may have felt, especially after the secret agreement he'd made with Stalin at Yalta, that he couldn't further humiliate the president of China by forcing him into concessions that Chiang believed would lead to his overthrow. The whole point, as Roosevelt saw it, was to bring colonialism in China to an end, and to encourage the country to emerge as a strong, independent, and friendly power. Turning Chiang Kai-shek into an obedient vassal was not the way to achieve that end.

There was a practical matter as well. The Yalta agreement, while devastating for Chinese pride, bound the United States ever closer to the Chiang government. Russia, by the terms of the secret deal, was pledged to give aid only to the KMT government, not to its ideological allies, the Communists. And now, here was a proposal that the United States effectively recognize the Communists as the de facto government of northern China and that, in defiance of the wishes of an allied government, it provide arms and aid to that de facto government! And what if Chiang were to fall from power as a result of this American help to its enemy? Then, as the historian Gary May has written, the Russians would be freed from their obligation to support only the Nationalists. "They could therefore," May concludes, "join the Chinese Communists and seize control of China."

Whatever FDR's reasoning, Hurley was now armed with a vote of confidence from the president, and he used it to press what amounted to a purge of the professional China experts in the field, the men who had been in the country for years, who spoke the language, who knew the place and its dramatis personae. John Davies, luckily for him, had already left for Moscow where he was greatly appreciated by George Kennan, the chargé at the embassy there. But John Service, who had gone to Yenan in March to report on a Communist Party congress, learned, upon his return to Chungking, that he was to disembark for Washington right away, which he did, the only passenger on a military plane making the long trip via South Asia, the Middle East, Africa, and

South America, arriving on April 12, the very day of FDR's death. Arthur Ringwalt was also reassigned. So were several others, including a third secretary, a language officer, and George Atcheson, the embassy's number two, who was replaced at Hurley's insistence by a Virginia banker, Walter S. Robertson, who knew nothing about China and, perhaps because of that, got along well with Hurley.

Hurley also imposed a ban on American diplomatic travel to Yenan, so the easy access that the China hands had had to senior Communist officials was cut off. Service also later reported that Hurley's habit of showing diplomatic dispatches to Nationalist Chinese officials had a dampening effect, because their sources might be endangered. "Some," Service said, "were called on the mat to receive a lecture, in muleskinner language, from the Ambassador." Hurley's triumph was not the main reason that the possibility of friendly relations with the Chinese Communists evaporated, but it was a contributing factor, since it confirmed to Mao and his advisers what they were disposed to believe anyway, which was that the United States was an imperialist power dominated by monopoly capitalists that was going to be their enemy inevitably.

The men whose services on China were now lost to the United States had kept up a remarkable, often brilliant flow of reporting on China for the entire war. They were interested in everything. John Stewart Service wrote fact-rich reports on cleavages within the Kuomintang military, about the propaganda on both sides of the war, on why some Chinese collaborated with the Japanese, on the effects of censorship on public opinion, on how the Communists were able to expand their bases into Japanese-occupied territory, and many other topics, even on the wall slogans and posters of both the Kuomintang and the Communists and what they showed of the nature of China's political culture and the image that the two parties strove to present of themselves and each other. Service's report in March 1945 on Chiang's rivalry with a group of commanders known as the Guangxi Clique was a deft dissection of the inner workings of Chinese politics, showing, among other things, why it was more important to China's president to weaken his potential rivals than to promote capable officers to higher positions. This thoroughly Machiavellian application of "Divide and Rule," Service wrote, "may have seemed to Chiang to be his only alternative. Being itself weak, the only hope of the Central Government, by this limited view, was in weakening—and keeping weak and disunited—all the opposition groups. 'Unity,' to Chiang obviously means domination."

Service and the other diplomatic pros made a major mistake, which was to become starry-eyed about Mao, to stress the "democratic" impulses of the CCP, to miss utterly the repression of dissent that the Communists engaged in even as they called on the KMT to respect civil rights. They were duped by the Communists. There is no avoiding that conclusion. But they were in no way pro-Communist, as Hurley and the committees of witch-hunters would later allege in their efforts to blame them for "losing" China. The term that Hurley insisted on applying to them—"disloyal"—was an ugly slander. Not until forty years later, when a new generation of China experts was able to go to China again, would the United States enjoy such a consistently high level of reporting and analysis on China as was provided by Service, Ludden, Davies, Atcheson, Rice, John Emmerson, and the others who were removed from their posts in Hurley's purge.

At the beginning of April, still in Washington, Hurley gave a widely covered press conference, watched attentively in Chungking and Yenan, announcing in no uncertain terms that there would be no aid to the Communists, because such aid would be equivalent to recognizing another Chinese government other than the one the United States was pledged to support. Hurley threw in a statement of his usual optimism, saying that the various parties in China were "drawing closer together" and that his goal of unity was achievable. But the main message was that, until this unity could be achieved, there would be no "fostering or assisting the development of armed Chinese Communists." This declaration was inconsistent with the position paper that the State Department had given Wedemeyer only weeks before, but nobody emerged to contradict the man the press referred to as Major-General Hurley.

Even before that, Hurley had pressed the president for information about Yalta and what exactly had been decided there with regard to China. At first, FDR had denied to his ambassador that there had been a secret agreement on China between him and Stalin, but on his final visit to the White House, Hurley finally got him to acknowledge the truth, and FDR showed Hurley the text of the deal with Stalin. In later accounts of this incident, Hurley says he was deeply shocked. "American diplomats," he charged, had "surrendered the territorial integrity and political independence of China . . . and [written] the blueprint for the Communist conquest."

But as his unauthorized biographer, Russell D. Buhite, has noted, he was probably feigning his outrage or at least exaggerating it. Hurley understood full well the need to induce the Soviet Union to get into the war, and he accepted the concomitant necessity of giving them something in China in return. What he wanted—or, more accurately, what he unrealistically wished for—was a deal between Moscow and Chungking that would preempt Soviet help to the CCP. Hurley seems to have taken it on himself to go to London and Moscow in an effort (sanctioned, he later said, by Roosevelt, though this is uncertain) to get British and Russian support for his China policy.

And so, once again, Hurley was off swimming naïvely in the treacherous waters of international diplomacy. He met with Churchill, who dutifully agreed to support the Chiang government and to encourage the KMT and the CCP to make a deal, and who subsequently did nothing of the kind. Then it was on to Moscow, where Hurley saw Stalin and Molotov, who assured him that they supported Chiang Kai-shek's government and his government alone and that they had no intention of throwing their weight behind the "radish" Communists of China.

It is amazing how easily Hurley, so ready to suspect the China hands of dark, hidden, and nefarious motivations, was taken in by this confection. He never seems to have suspected that Molotov and Stalin could be trying to neutralize the United States by providing false assurances about their intentions. Ironically, one of the China hands that he had battled with, John Davies, was now in Moscow, and he tried to warn his old boss that he was being sold a bill of goods—and yet it was Davies who was later accused of softness on Communism rather than Hurley. "There was ample advice to [Hurley] which he showed no desire to tap," George Kennan commented.

While the political maneuvering took place, the war in China sputtered on. Thousands were dying as Japan's China Expeditionary Army, under General Yasuji Okamura, made a last-ditch effort to knock China once and for all out of the conflict. Okamura had 820,000 men organized into twenty-five divisions, an armored brigade, eleven independent infantry brigades, a cavalry brigade, and ten independent brigades.

These troops were deployed in three formations—the North China Area Army holding the territory between the Yellow River and the Great Wall, the Sixth Area Army, which faced the Chinese and the Americans in east China, and the Thirteenth Area Army in Shanghai and the lower Yangzi Valley. Okamura himself commanded the Sixth Area Army, which, with five divisions and 228 cannon, was the elite force that kept the Americans of China theater headquarters, and especially its commander, General Albert Wedemeyer, up at night.

Okamura was the type of Japanese officer—ruthless, determined, and capable—to inspire worry. He had been in China since he commanded troops in the occupation of Shanghai in 1932, and in that role he had gained the dubious distinction of being the first such commander to order the forced prostitution of local women, given the stupendously euphonious name "comfort women," who were made available to Japanese troops in virtually all of the territories they invaded and occupied.

After the Marco Polo Bridge Incident of 1937, Okamura commanded the Japanese Eleventh Army in some of the major battles in the Yangzi River Valley. Transferred to the northern provinces in the spring of 1939, Okamura requested permission to use poison gas, arguing that it was needed to give his troops "the feeling of victory," and he subsequently commanded the largest chemical attack of the war.

In 1940, a full general and overall commander of the North China Area Army, Okamura was in charge when the Communists launched the surprise Hundred Regiments Offensive, which Japan countered with the brutal tactic known to the Chinese as the Three Alls policy— "burn all, kill all, loot all." Japanese troops under his command were responsible for the deaths of what scholars have estimated to be 2.7 million noncombatants. After that, in 1944, Okamura was the overall commander of the Ichigo offensive, the effort stretching over many months in 1944 to conquer all of east and southeast China, knocking out along the way the American 14th Air Force's bases. The photographs of him show a stern, dour, grim man in uniform, every inch the graduate of the Imperial Japanese Army Academy that he was, deeply imbued with the Japanese military values of iron discipline, the unsparing massacre of the enemy, and the glory of victory for the emperor.

As 1945 dawned, Okamura and the Japanese could congratulate themselves on some important recent successes in China—this in contrast to the war elsewhere, where devastating losses in the Pacific, in the Philippines, and in Burma, as well as the defeats earlier at Midway, Iwo Jima, and other Pacific atolls, were already spelling doom for the empire. Still, in early 1945 there seems to have been little thought of giving up. Nor did American commanders believe that the hardest fighting was behind them. In November 1944, even as the newly arrived Wedemeyer was familiarizing himself with the situation, Japan seized the portions of the Canton-Hankou-Beijing railroad line that were still in Chinese hands, thereby creating an unbroken railroad line stretching from the port of Haiphong in French Indochina all the way to Manchuria and Korea, potentially a critical supply line if a showdown battle between the United States and Japan were to take place on Chinese soil. At the same time, the 11th Army, with four glory-seeking divisions and a company of tanks, seized the American airfields of Guilin and Liuzhou, from which Chennault's 14th Air Force had harassed Japanese supply lines in China and bombed shipping at sea.

At a press conference a few weeks later, Secretary of War Henry L. Stimson announced that victory was a long way off. "For many years the Japanese have been squatting on the China coast," he said. "They have many thousands of troops there and lately have been reinforcing their grip. They have taken over an inland supply route from Canton to Hankou to Peiping, and have occupied three more airfields east of this route that were helpful to our airmen." In addition, Japan still possessed powerful home defenses against an invasion, with production capacity still strong and large reserves of oil and gas.

The losses of Guilin and Liuzhou were serious and worrisome, since not only were these the sites of large American airbases, they also commanded the roads further to the west, especially to Kweiyang and Kunming. Kunming was the terminus of the over-the-Hump airlift and the about-to-be-reopened Burma Road, the point of distribution for the American supplies without which China couldn't stay in the war.

Guilin was an old southern town with colonnaded streets and shops shaded under wide porticoes, a weather-beaten, stained, and picturesquely shabby place near an ethereally beautiful range of mountains that arose spire-like from the verdant countryside. Almost since the beginning of the Japanese war in 1937, American pilots had flown into and out of the military airport there, catching glimpses of the Li River, the early morning sunlight flashing on rice paddies plowed by water buffalo below, even as the pilots took off for bombing and strafing runs in the most lethal and modern aircraft known to men.

At night, the pilots and maintenance crews had steaks and beer in bamboo shacks near the airfield, and then in the morning they sat at briefings for that day's run. They talked about near misses and about their buddies who were shot down and never made it back. They expressed murderous fury at the Chinese desperadoes, some of them war refugees, who descended on Guilin precisely because the Americans were there, getting their hands on Lend-Lease supplies and selling them on the black market or, as was widely suspected, operating radio transmitters to let the Japanese know when the American planes took off.

There was an old hostel near the airfield, where the American airmen drank and danced with local girls and then retired with them to cubicle bedrooms built on two wings alongside the main building. Not for nothing was Guilin known as the sex capital of Free China. One popular spot was the Ledo Club, where a certain Fatima Ismail, widely suspected of selling information to the Japanese, entertained guests.

Three days after the Japanese seizure of Guilin, Wedemeyer had his first working session with Chiang and his staff, during which he presented an overall plan to stiffen China's defenses and eventually to be able to push the Japanese back. Code-named Alpha, the plan was to equip and train thirty-nine Chinese divisions and to place teams of American advisers in every one of them. Chinese troops, whose standard condition was one of malnutrition, were to be fed properly. The very foreign concept for China of medical evacuation and care for the wounded was to be introduced. Every soldier was to be adequately equipped. All of this followed the model that Stilwell had created for Chinese troops he had trained in Ramgarh, India, and who were fighting well in Burma.

Wedemeyer was uncertain whether Alpha would work, not at all confident that even with proper training and equipment, Chinese troops would have the will to fight, or, more accurately, have the leadership that would induce them to. In the early weeks and months of his China sojourn, he had been strangely inconsistent in his assessments, unwaveringly admiring of Chiang, whom he compared to Churchill, but skeptical of a Chinese military leadership that, he felt, was afflicted with a severe case of "stupidity and inefficiency," which made it "apathetic and unintelligent," "impotent and confounded," and therefore either unable or afraid to report accurately on conditions to the Generalissimo or to do much to improve them. Wedemeyer felt it should have been possible to defend Guilin. The Chinese 97th Army, which was well fed and well equipped, had held what appeared to be strong positions north of the city. Chiang had assured Wedemeyer "categorically" that if the Japanese attacked, his forces could hold the Guilin-Liuzhou area for two months—but then they retreated without a fight. "The disorganization and muddled planning of the Chinese is beyond comprehension," Wedemeyer wrote at the time. "We can throw in great numbers of troops at tremendous cost logistically, but we do not know whether the Chinese will stick and fight."

On the positive side, supplies were increasing substantially in volume, so there was more fuel and ammunition than ever before. About five thousand tons of supplies a month had moved over the Hump during most of the war; by early 1945, the American C-47s were delivering up to sixty thousand tons a month, a very big difference that the Japanese, whose supplies were diminishing, well understood. Indeed, if Wedemeyer had known what was in the minds of the Japanese high command on this point, he would have had more reason for cautious optimism. The Ichigo offensive had wound down because Okamura's supply lines were overextended and, where they weren't overextended, they were snarled by the 14th Air Force's effective attacks, which was the reason Okamura had wanted to seize the Guilin and Liuzhou airfields.

Okamura's headquarters were in the Yangzi River port of Hankou, and there he had watched with his own eyes as Chennault's B-29 bombers had hurled ordnance down on the factories and warehouses sprawled out on the riverbanks, causing spectacular blazes and creating massive congestion for ships, so that as much as one hundred thousand tons of Japanese supplies were stuck at various points on the river. On December 18 alone, seventy-seven B-29s and two hundred fighter planes had raided Hankou and its sister cities of Wuchang and Hanyang (now all part of the conglomeration Wuhan), and the Japanese, whose planes had been diverted to defend the coast against a possible American landing there, were unable to stop them. When it was over, a pall of thick, impenetrable smoke hung over the three cities.

American planes had also destroyed the bridges on the Beijing–Hankou railroad, spoiling Japan's plan to use rail transport as an alternative to the river. The Japanese countered by unloading supplies where the rail line was broken, putting them on trucks, and reloading them where the line resumed, but the American bombs had destroyed so many locomotives that this method was of limited use. The Japanese were getting perhaps one-fourth of the supplies they had planned for. They had enough food, clothing, and ammunition, but gasoline was going to run out in a few months, and Okamura foresaw the day, unless some action was taken, when the railroads south of the Yangzi would be entirely useless.

The situation had produced a lull in the fighting as the Japanese regrouped, tried to reorganize their supply lines, and decided what to do. The high command in Tokyo was in favor of relinquishing its bases in south China and concentrating instead on defending the China coast from the anticipated American landing there. The lull reflected Japan's troubles, though the interpretation of the lull on the Allies' side exposed the ambiguities of fighting in China. Rumors were flying to the effect that the Chinese government was secretly in cahoots with the Japanese, allowing them to seize the American airfields in exchange for a moratorium on the war against China itself. When Wedemeyer, diplomatic and respectful as always, brought these rumors up with the Generalissimo, Chiang was "absolutely non-committal," Wedemeyer reported at the time. "There was no indication, emotional or otherwise, that he either denied or admitted it. His spontaneous reaction was a dry cackle."

Wedemeyer gamely moved on as though the rumors didn't exist. The training of Chinese divisions and the assignment of American advisers—eventually there were more than three thousand of them—continued. Meanwhile, as spring approached, Okamura, ignoring the views of Imperial General Headquarters in Tokyo, decided on an audacious plan of his own. In January 1945, he took another American airfield, at Suichuan, northeast of Guilin. But he knew that taking the minor airfields like that one was only a temporary gain, or perhaps no gain at all, because Chennault's planes and fliers could simply relocate to another field and resume operations from there. Whereas at Guilin there had been infrastructure, warehouses, barracks, an intelligence headquarters, and equipment, at Suichuan, according to the official American account of the China theater, "all the Japanese inherited were empty runways." Taking this into account, imperial headquarters had decided to abandon the conquest of more Chinese territory and instead to guard the south China coast. This decision had been forced on the Japanese by the American recapture of the Philippines, which opened a staging area for the landing of American troops in China itself.

But Okamura thought the fear of an invasion was exaggerated. He wanted to attack Chungking and deal a lethal blow to the enemy, not merely to put a temporary check on his actions. It was a critical moment.

If the Chinese defenses crumbled as they had so often in the past, Oka-mura could still hope that he could knock China out of the war. But if the Chinese resistance was stiff, Japan would have little choice but to resort to a war of defensive attrition, withdrawing to the coasts and try-ing to stop the Allies from using China as a springboard for the invasion of the home islands.

Okamura chose the town of Zhijiang to be the first target of this des-perate new offensive. Zhijiang was an otherwise undistinguished place in western Hunan province, a rugged area with few roads where most of the goods transport took place on the backs of coolies running on foot-paths from village to village or by sampan on the region's many rivers and streams. The town itself held one of Chennault's most important airfields, which made it a rich target, but Okamura saw it in addition as a potential base for raids against Chungking itself, about three hundred miles to the northwest, or perhaps against Kunming.

Early in the spring of 1945, he massed twenty thousand Japanese troops on the plains east of Zhijiang. On April 13, under the watchful eyes of Allied air reconnaissance, these troops began a general advance. To meet this menacing force and turn it back, avoiding a direct threat to Chungking and Kunming, was now the challenge facing the joint Chi-nese and American command, a test of the new spirit of cooperation taking place even before the initial Alpha training was done.

The Chinese 51st Division of the 74th Army was a few miles north of the main road leading east and west into Zhijiang, along which the Japanese advance was expected to proceed. But the Japanese here in western Hunan were getting past the troops placed between them and Zhijiang by infiltrating in large numbers through the maze of hills and valleys. It was the same tactic they had used successfully in Burma in 1942, their men cutting quickly through the jungle, avoiding the roads and outmaneuvering the British, the Americans, and the Chinese.

The American liaison officer for the 51st was Colonel Louis V. Jones. The Chinese division commander told Jones that he was moving out of the area with two regiments in an effort to stop the infiltration, so Jones, along with a radio team, an interpreter, and forty-four coolies, trekked through the hills to follow them. The next day, he discovered that the two regiments had overshot the valley through which the Japa-nese were likely to advance. A third Chinese regiment, the 151st, which had not moved out with the other two, was left in position, and it went into action by itself against the Japanese on the night of April 17. The next day, Jones caught up with the Chinese division commander and persuaded him to redeploy his troops; in doing so, they held a six-mile front against the advancing enemy.

On the 19th, the division commander requested air support. One plane arrived the next day, four the day after, but then rain closed in, putting an end to aerial operations. The tough fighters of the Japanese 116th Division and the 133rd Infantry Regiment ground ahead, at the slow pace of a mile and a half an hour. Soon, they took the town of Shanmen, which provided a base of operations in the hills. But, as the official history puts it, despite the pressure, the Chinese 151st Regiment "held stoutly."

So did other Chinese units, all along the seventy-five-mile-long front of the Japanese attack. When a large gap appeared in the front northwest of Shanmen, a Chinese army, the 18th, moved in and prevented an enemy breakthrough. Elsewhere along the front, Chinese units were "holding well, and replying to every Japanese gain with counterattacks." Meanwhile something rare in the struggle against Japan was occurring. Zhijiang became one of a string of bases stretching all the way to Kunming, where supplies poured in. A field hospital was established to care for the wounded, and a vehicle maintenance company was set up so that damaged supply trucks could be fixed and continue to function. A network of supply points extended out from Zhijiang on both roads and navigable streams. Food, weapons—submachine guns, 60-millimeter mortars, Bren guns—ammunition, and even summer uniforms arrived at those points and then were distributed by truck or sampan to the Chinese troops, even as portable surgical hospitals were set up to the rear of the front.

The fighting continued for months in this Chinese backwater. Eventually, eight base hospitals were operating so wounded Chinese soldiers got medical attention rather than being left to die as had happened so often during this long war. Rice came in by boat from the Dongting Lake area to the northeast and was distributed by truck to the troops, so there was no need for another of the malign practices common among Chinese soldiers, stealing food from local villages or going desperately hungry. An army does indeed travel on its stomach, a basic and elementary point that often seemed lost on Chinese Nationalist armies, but not in the battle for Zhijiang.

Meanwhile, as the experience of Colonel Jones indicated, there was good cooperation between Chinese commanders and their American advisers. Stilwell's frustrations in 1942 in Burma, where his orders were ignored or countermanded by Chiang, were not repeated in western Hunan in 1945. One liaison officer, Colonel George L. Goodridge, who had arrived in February to help with the training of Chinese troops, reported, "Whenever the situation changed, the general called the liaison officer to the map and after explaining the situation, asked for his opinion. . . . In most cases the ensuing order followed along the lines of the plan suggested by the liaison officer."

On May 2, at the entrance to the Wuyang Valley, on the southern route of the Japanese advance, the Chinese Fifth Division directly faced the enemy. A decision was made, with the agreement of American advisers, to attempt an encirclement, which, the official history says, "was a complete success," with "a fair amount of Japanese equipment including artillery, some documents, and six prisoners" seized. In the days ahead, China's 121st Division moved north and succeeded in turning the Japanese left flank. Other units streamed down from the north and cut behind the Japanese concentrations, forcing the enemy to find ways to retreat.

On May 11, the 11th Division of the Chinese 18th Army captured a Japanese supply dump along with five hundred horses. Meanwhile, seeing the magnitude of the effort that would be required to avoid defeat, and aware of the orders of Imperial General Headquarters to redeploy toward the coast, Okamura decided against sending in reinforcements and ordered his forces to withdraw from the Zhijiang campaign.

Around this time, apparently sensing an opportunity, Chiang Kai-shek did what he had done so often before. He sent orders to his commanding general, He Yingqin, to seize the city of Hengyang in central Hunan province. This was exactly the kind of aggressiveness and boldness that Americans, most notably Stilwell, felt Chiang always lacked. Still, it was interference, and Wedemeyer, learning of the order, reminded the Gimo that he, Wedemeyer, couldn't very well coordinate the overall battle if Chiang was giving orders to his generals without telling him about them. The Chinese, Wedemeyer also said, weren't ready for an operation on the scale required to retake Hengyang. Chiang backed down, saying that he hadn't issued an order but only expressed an opinion. In other words, Wedemeyer had managed what the irascible Stilwell had failed to do, which was persuade China's president and commander in chief not to meddle.

By June 7, the fight to hold Zhijiang was over. The Japanese had retreated to their original positions. The battle for Zhijiang has to be counted among the successes of the Chinese. The immediate threat to Chungking and Kunming was averted. The way for further moves east toward Canton and Hong Kong by the Chinese lay open. The Japanese lost 1,500 men killed and 5,000 wounded. Chinese casualties were higher—nearly 7,000 dead and 12,000 wounded—but the Chinese had had many more troops in the fight than the Japanese. Assessing their failure, the Japanese command attributed it to the "great advance" the Chinese had made. And this came even though the battle had broken out well before the training program envisaged by Alpha was finished.

"Real progress was being made in China theater," the official history concludes. The Chinese had adopted procedures "contrary to their accepted practices" and this "reflected credit upon both their spirit of cooperation and the powers of persuasion of Wedemeyer, McClure, and their staffs." Not everything went well. The Americans in particular cited the Chinese tendency to allow surrounded Japanese units to escape, which was a time-honored practice in Chinese warfare. The *Thirty-Six Stratagems,* written at a different time and under different circumstances, aims to avoid the costs of battle by always leaving open to the enemy a path of retreat. China's Nationalists adhered to this tradition, to the irritation of their American advisers. But they had also shown that, when properly equipped and led, they could fight with the best of them.

This demonstration, moreover, came at a time when many American observers, encouraged in this view by the Communists, were in a state of what they regarded as realistic despair about Chiang's armies, believing that they were hopelessly inadequate and would always refuse to fight. Hadn't Mao told Barrett that the KMT's troops were turning and running away rather than fighting the Japanese? Here was one important instance, in a new situation, where they stood, fought, and won.

But there was something else as well, something truly sinister and sensational at the same time, and that was to haunt any sort of free discussion of China for years to come. It was an episode that came to be called the Amerasia spy case, which was to affect all of the China experts, but John Service most directly and most devastatingly. It all began in January 1945 when a small but influential journal, *Amerasia,* read by many of those professionally interested in Asia, whether in the State Department or universities, published a report innocuously titled "British Imperial Policy in Asia."

The article was read by Kenneth Wells, who worked in the South Asia department of the Office of Strategic Services, the wartime predecessor of the Central Intelligence Agency. Wells noted that some sections of the report were almost verbatim copies of parts of a report that he had written on British-American relations in Southeast Asia. Wells's report had been classified; it was secret. And Wells wanted to know how *Amerasia* had gotten it. So did the FBI, which put the editors of *Amerasia* under surveillance and, in an illegal operation, broke into the magazine's offices in an effort to discover the presumably traitorous sources of the leak.

CHAPTER ELEVEN

Mao the God, Service the Spy

While Hurley purged the Chungking embassy of its best China hands, Mao Zedong was enjoying the fruits of his own purge and Rectification Campaign of the previous two years, having himself crowned the demigod of the Chinese revolution. From then on, he was to be much more than a first among equals, more than just a charismatic and respected party leader. From now on, he was to be a genius of a sort of papal infallibility, a giant of history, a magnificent hero bringing light and hope to what would otherwise be a dark and oppressive world. A catchy and tuneful anthem, composed in 1943, put it this way (it rhymes in Mandarin Chinese):

> *The East is Red,*
> *The sun is rising,*
> *China has produced a Mao Zedong.*
> *He serves the welfare of the people,*
> *He is our great savior.*

Mao's apotheosis was a gradual thing, built on a series of victories in the internal struggles for power that had always taken place inside the Communist movement, but it reached its culmination at the Seventh National Representative Congress of the Chinese Communist Party, which opened in April 1945, and whose five hundred delegates obediently elected Mao chairman of all of the CCP's ruling bodies—the Central Committee, the Secretariat, the Politburo, and the Military Council—thus concentrating power into a single leader's hands in a way that had never been done in the history of Chinese Communism. But as important as Mao's formal posts was the nonstop adulation, the continuous and fulsome praise of Mao that was a mandatory ritual for the Communists' assembly. Those party figures who had previously held enough power and influence to rival Mao inside the top leadership confessed that they had been mistaken to oppose him in the past, and they pledged their loyalty in the future.

This secular deification blended some of China's own imperial customs with practices originating with Comrade Stalin and found useful by his most important acolyte, Mao. The previous spring, the Chinese leader had been invited to plant the first grain of millet, replicating the ritual of centuries past when the emperor symbolically plowed the first furrow. But the cult of Mao's personality was also an almost inevitable feature of twentieth-century totalitarianism, adopted by dictators of the right, like Mussolini and Hitler, and those of the left, Mao himself as well as the Vietnamese Communist Ho Chi Minh and the North Korean "genius of all mankind," Kim Il Sung. In the case of the revolutionary left, this exaltation of the leader derived from the notion of the Communist Party as the vanguard of the proletariat, with the Great Leader serving as the indispensable vanguard of the vanguard, the embodiment of history's inevitable progress toward the proletarian ideal. Of course, it also served the goal of unopposed power by the party and the delegitimation of any opposition, which is the reason China's Communists today keep Mao on a pedestal, despite their acknowledgment of his many mistakes.

The irony of Mao's apotheosis in 1945 is that it took place at the very time that the Communists were expressing outrage over the KMT's one-party dictatorship and the excessive, dictatorial concentration of power in the hands of Chiang Kai-shek. The CCP raised Mao to superhuman and superlegal status even as it made its demands in Hurley's negotiations that Chiang share power in a democratic coalition, that political prisoners be released, the Nationalists' secret police curbed, and freedom of the press restored. The party laid the groundwork for Mao's elevation to all-powerful dictator even as it made reassurances to the Americans in the Dixie Mission and to Hurley that the Communists' intentions were entirely democratic.

The Seventh Congress was held in an auditorium in Yenan that rang with chants of "Long Live Chairman Mao" (echoing the "Long Live" chants that for centuries had greeted China's emperors). The proscenium arch bore the slogan in large Chinese characters meaning "March forward under the banner of Mao Zedong." For the first time

Mao Zedong Thought—known in Chinese as *Mao Zedong sixiang*—
was written into the constitution as an official pillar of Chinese Communist ideology, given equal status with Marxism-Leninism. Liu Shaoqi,
chosen number two in the party, made one of the major addresses of the
congress, almost every paragraph of which was laden with boilerplate
phrases about the brilliance of Mao's leadership, the correctness of his
policies, and the need to study his thought. Mao had prepared carefully
for this event. About half of the party members originally chosen to be
delegates at the Seventh Congress had been purged during the Rectification Campaign that had ended a few months before and then been
replaced by new delegates screened by a party leadership to be sure they
had been cleansed of any dissatisfaction with the cult of Mao.

Just before the congress's opening, Mao had presided over a Central
Committee plenum that adopted a lengthy text called "Resolution on
Certain Historical Questions." The purpose of this document was retro-
actively to find Mao's policies of the past correct in every instance. This
supposedly scientific and scholarly substantiation of the Great Leader's
legitimacy came straight from Soviet practice. In 1938, his own apotheosis complete after the Great Purge, Stalin published his *History of
the CPSU (Bolshevik), Short Course* that stigmatized his past rivals and
declared all his own policies to have been correct. Stalin's short course
was translated into Chinese and made mandatory reading for political
indoctrination. It is not enough in a totalitarian system for the Great
Leader to eliminate all opposition and to establish his cult of infallibility; he also has to give a scientific gloss to the eradication of any intellectual foundation for opposition. Accordingly, as preparation for the
Seventh Congress of the CCP and the adoption of Mao's official history
as party doctrine, even Wang Ming, the most powerful, prestigious, and
recalcitrant of his past rivals, admitted that his past opposition to Mao
was an ideological error. In exchange for this gesture, Mao held up the
congress's opening session until Wang, who was ill, could be wheeled
on a gurney into the meeting hall.

If Mao had had his way in the matter, he would have cashiered
Wang entirely, severed him from the party, and perhaps put him in
prison, but it was at Stalin's insistence that he didn't carry out these
wishes. There is an obscure element of score-settling here, dating to the
vicious Kuomintang-Communist struggles of years before. At the end
of 1943, Mao wrote to Georgi Dimitrov, the head of the Comintern
(which was abolished in May 1943, though Stalin, often through Dimi-

trov, continued to have unofficial ways of giving instruction to Communist parties around the world), charging Wang with having "engaged in various anti-party activities." Wang had once been arrested in Shanghai, Mao said, and while he was in prison, he admitted that he was a party member, after which he was released. The implication was that Wang Ming had been turned by the KMT and was possibly a double agent. It was the sort of vague charge of disloyalty that Kang Sheng specialized in as he rooted out Mao's enemies real and imagined and subjected them to reeducation during the Rectification Campaign. Now Mao seemed to be applying it to his chief rival in the party.

But Wang had lived in Moscow for several years, and he had his own contacts there, including with Dimitrov, and for several months in 1943 both he and Mao were sending messages to the headquarters of the global revolution asking for support of their position in what was otherwise an internal Chinese Communist matter. Wang's letters to Dimitrov accused Mao of being an "anti-Leninist" and a "Trotskyite," both grave, veritably mortal accusations in the world of international Communism. Dimitrov, no doubt at Stalin's insistence, issued a Solomonic judgment in this matter, throwing his support to Mao in the Chinese power struggle, but asking Mao not to sever Wang from the party. Mao, for the sake of "unity," complied with this wish.

The episode is a further demonstration of the closeness of the relations between the two Communist parties, and the higher status of the Soviet party. Mao adhered to Moscow's wishes even in this case of a rival whom he had accused of being a traitor. In subsequent years, after the death of Stalin and the Sino-Soviet split, Mao would suffer no such moderating influence, and his attacks on former close colleagues would end in their disgrace and humiliation. These former close colleagues included the aforementioned Liu Shaoqi, who showered adulation on Mao and the Seventh Congress but who was savagely persecuted later by the young people whom Mao incited to acts of mob violence during the Cultural Revolution. Liu was publicly beaten, denounced as a "capitalist-roader," a "revisionist," and a KMT agent, and allowed to die of untreated diabetes.

Wang signed on to the compromise brokered by Moscow in 1945, abjectly admitting that policies he had previously claimed credit for were "Mao Zedong's contribution, not mine as I had earlier believed." It was all in the spirit of the moment. "Resolution on Certain Historical Questions" made Mao the hero of every major success of the Communist Party, even when, in historical fact, Mao had had nothing to do with that success or even opposed the thinking that had led to it. "Resolution," for example, gave credit to Mao for the battle of Pingxingguan of 1937, a minor and rare victory over the Japanese aggressors much celebrated in Communist lore, though it was fought at a time when Mao, in contrast to Zhou Enlai and Zhu De, opposed using Communist forces in direct engagements with the Japanese.

In one major respect, the congress must have been a confusing event for at least some of those attending it. On the one hand there was the conspicuously undemocratic concentration of power in the hands of one of the most illiberal Great Leaders of all time, a concentration that was itself the fruit of the ruthless suppression of any wayward thoughts or tendencies that others engaged in. To be sure, Mao's ascendency was due in significant measure to his extraordinary leadership and to the fact that the movement under his command had not only survived but also expanded remarkably during the Japanese war. But this ascendency was also due to Mao's extraordinary ability to outmaneuver his potential rivals for power by gathering around himself a hard core of avid supporters who saw to it that his writ was enforced. Every member of the Communist movement in Yenan knew that Mao's commanding position was sustained by terror, repression, imprisonment, reeducation, and purges, administered by Kang Sheng's secret internal security apparatus.

But in his speeches at the Seventh Congress, Mao made repeated and emphatic assurances that the Chinese Communist Party favored a democratic system and that it would never favor a Soviet-style one-party state. Those words "democracy" and "democratic" appeared and reappeared in every one of Mao's statements. "Beyond all doubt," Mao declared in his major speech, a nearly book-length text that must have taken hours to read aloud, "the urgent need is to . . . establish a provisional democratic coalition government for the purpose of instituting democratic reforms," after which "it will be necessary to convene a national assembly on a broad democratic basis and set up a formally constituted democratic government." This, in turn, "will lead the liberated people of the whole country in building an independent, free, democratic, united, prosperous and powerful new China."

Mao's concrete ideas for China's government of the future were actually vague and general enough to allow for almost any interpretation, because the "New Democracy" that he advanced in his speech— "namely a united-front democratic alliance"—would fall "under the leadership of the working class," a phrase that hints at the iron fist that was hidden by the rhetorical velvet glove. Mao anticipated this objection. "Some people suspect that the Chinese Communists are opposed to the development of individual initiative, the growth of private capital, and the protection of private property, but they are mistaken," Mao assured his listeners. It's true, he said, that "the future of incomparable brightness and splendor" is a Communist one, but, as Zhou Enlai had assured David Barrett on that plane ride to Chungking a few months previously, that was for the distant future. "So far from fearing capitalism, Communists should advocate its development in certain given conditions," Mao said at the Seventh Congress. "Domestic capitalism" is fine; what couldn't be allowed was "foreign imperialism and domestic feudalism."

Continuing to correct supposed misperceptions, including those held by foreign critics of the CCP, Mao repudiated the idea that "once in power, the Communist Party will follow Russia's example and establish the dictatorship of the proletariat and a one-party system." This is of course exactly what the Chinese Communists did after they took power in 1949, establishing a one-party system in which all dissenting opinion was banned. Within eight years of the seizure of power, the Maoists had essentially eradicated domestic capitalism, from large industries down to streetside noodle stands, and entirely eliminated private farming, one consequence of which was the world's worst famine since the one in Ukraine in the early 1930s, which occurred when Stalin abruptly collectivized Soviet agriculture. But in 1945, Mao seemed piously to repudiate the very idea of Stalinist tyranny.

In his New Democracy speech, however, while he explicitly rejected the Soviet system for China, he also uttered phrases about "the leadership of the proletariat and of the Communist Party" that gave him cover to deny any meaningful power to any party or group that he didn't control, and to brand as "counter-revolutionary" any idea that he didn't approve. Even when it came to specific proposals, a long list of which he enumerated in his speech, Mao's calls for democracy were belied by already established Communist practice. For example, he called for the "reactionary secret service" to be eliminated, meaning the Kuomintang security apparatus, but that left space for a secret service, namely Kang Sheng's, that was even more secretive and ruthless, though it was presumably *democratic* and *revolutionary*, unlike the KMT's. Mao promised that he would "revoke all reactionary laws and decrees aimed at suppressing the people's freedom of speech, press, assembly, association, political conviction, and religious belief." This Bill of Rights–like coda was qualified by that word "reactionary"—and, by definition, nothing the proletariat did was reactionary, certainly not the suppression of the democratic freedoms of the class enemy.

Understood, or perhaps not understood, at the time was the principle that all of these freedoms would be exercised "under the leadership of the proletariat and the Communist Party," which would allow no checks and balances, no independent courts, no autonomous press, no ability to create organizations or to propagate views that might limit the party's power. "Release all patriotic political prisoners," Mao demanded, not specifying how to define "patriotic" or who would define it, though what he meant was all political prisoners held by the KMT, and none that were being held or might later be detained by the Communists. The appearance of moderation at the Seventh Congress, all that lip service paid to democracy, was aimed at discrediting China's central government and winning popular support, while leaving the Communists exempt from antidemocratic suspicion.

There is a western school of Maoist apologetics that attributes Mao's later radicalism—illustrated by the Anti-Rightist Campaign of 1957, the drastic collectivization of agriculture starting that year, and the Cultural Revolution of the 1960s, when Mao's cult peaked in a kind of lunatic frenzy—to the American decision to throw its weight behind Chiang Kai-shek as China's civil war gathered speed. Or, at least, if Mao's domestic radicalism was not a direct product of American foreign policy, his venomous hostility to the United States, all those slogans like "Down with American Imperialism," his intervention in the Korean War, his support of North Vietnam, his alliance with the Soviet Union, his aid to guerrilla movements in neighboring countries—all this might not have happened if only the United States had followed the advice of the China hands rather than that of Hurley, collaborating militarily with the Communists rather than giving one-sided support to Chiang. Or, barring that, at least a friendlier America would, as Davies and Service were arguing, have enabled Mao to keep his distance from Stalin.

The sequence of events in that spring of 1945 lends some substance to this argument. Mao was a practical man as well as an ideological one, and there is no doubt he would gladly have accepted help from the

United States had it been offered then, especially if that help involved bullets and guns, just as he would have accepted a deal with the KMT that gave the Communists a place in a new government while they retained control over their own armies.

But as we've seen, a few weeks before the Seventh Congress convened, Hurley announced at his Washington press conference that all American aid would go to the central government and none to the Communists, unless Chiang Kai-shek approved of it. The Communists made no secret of their disappointment at this news. When Service saw Mao in March, Mao had assured him that he would remain friendly to the United States even if it didn't give arms to his troops. But only a few days after word reached Yenan of Hurley's press conference in Washington, the *Liberation Daily* published a furious analysis written anonymously by Mao himself. Hurley had started out as a genuinely impartial mediator, Mao wrote, recalling that scene in Yenan when he and Hurley had signed their names to a five-point proposal for a Chinese unity government, but then he had "betrayed what he said." Hurley was stating only a "personal opinion," Mao added of his press conference declaration, but it was also "the opinion of a group of people in the United States, and it is a wrong and dangerous opinion."

There is a passion in this statement by Mao that feels authentic, a genuine sense of betrayal. It's the same anger that Barrett had witnessed during his long talk with Mao in Yenan a few months earlier when Mao had warned against propping up "the rotten shell that is Chiang Kai-shek." Now he changed the metaphor. "If the United States maintains the Hurley policy," he warned in the wake of the Hurley press conference, "the American government will be trapped inside the deep, stinking pit of the Chinese reactionaries, and it will find itself facing the hostility of hundreds of millions of awakened and awakening Chinese people."

That is not yet a statement of unremitting hostility. That kind of rhetoric would come later. For now, Mao still held out the hope that American policy might not continue along the lines Hurley seemed to be setting for it. Nonetheless, his open, public denunciation of Hurley marked a shift in tone, a sign of the not-very-distant future.

Things surely would have been different in the short term had Hurley not sided publicly and privately with the KMT just at that moment, but it is unlikely they would have stayed different for very long. The Hurley press conference was genuinely upsetting to the CCP; it was a betrayal, from their point of view, of the implicit promise of American arms and aid that Hurley had made when he signed that five-point proposal with Mao in Yenan the previous November. But more important than anything an American ambassador could do or say were events on the international stage that had a larger effect on Mao's thinking and on his strategy for the rest of the war.

There were two such events unfolding even as Mao's apotheosis took place at the Seventh Congress of the CCP. One was Stalin's abrogation of the Soviet Union's Neutrality Pact with Japan, which was a clear signal to Mao, whether he knew of the Yalta accord or not, of the Russian intent to attack Japanese forces in Manchuria. The other was the end of the war in Europe, which, Mao knew, or at least could safely assume, would free up Soviet troops for that very military action.

The Soviet Union was the second most powerful country in the world, and it shared a thousand-mile border with China. It had guided and supported the Chinese Communist Party literally since its founding in 1921. If and when it came into the war in Asia, most likely by kicking the Japanese out of the puppet state of Manchukuo, it would be able to turn territory and arms over to Mao's forces, which would shift the balance of power in North China to the CCP and devastatingly weaken the KMT government. Mao knew this. For him, a good relationship with the United States would have helped him to gain arms, to enhance his prestige within China, and to expand the territory under his control, especially if there were an American landing on coastal China to which the Eighth Route Army would lend its hand. Why not, under the circumstances, cultivate American goodwill? The United States was a kind of backup, a second source of help, especially on the off chance that the expected Soviet assistance didn't materialize. Mao's courtship of America was in this sense a defensive move, a kind of preemptory diplomacy, aimed at keeping the United States neutral in China's domestic conflict while encouraging it to provide material assistance to the CCP.

By contrast, Mao's obedience to Stalin was both tactical *and* strategic. Mao had a permanent need to forestall any American intervention on the side of his once and future enemy Chiang Kai-shek. But whether the United States helped the CCP or not, Mao's primary goals were total power in China and the advance of the world revolution, and these goals ensured that his primary international allegiance was always going to be to the Soviet Union.

Mao made nine speeches at the Seventh Congress, and in all of them he reaffirmed this primary allegiance. His remarks were even more pointed in his internal speeches. In those, he stressed the idea that an alliance with the Soviet Union was indispensable to the Communist victory in China. Some skeptics among the delegates felt the Soviets had provided little in the way of material help, aside from some money, during the long years of the anti-Japanese war. Mao's argument to them was, yes, the Communist International made some mistakes with China in the past, but its contribution was much greater than the mistakes, and without its help, there would be no Chinese Communist Party. "Can we Chinese succeed without foreign support?" he asked rhetorically. "The Chinese revolution cannot succeed alone. The Chinese revolution must have the support of the proletariat of the entire world"—by which he meant the support of Moscow.

It was in one of his internal speeches that Mao delivered himself of a grandiloquent acclamation of Stalin's special historical role and the requirement of obedience to it. It was the statement of a true acolyte, not that of a man simply reacting to American policy. "Is Stalin the leader of the world revolution?" Mao asked. "Of course he is." We have to avoid saying this publicly, Mao warned, "so as to avoid the attacks of the reactionaries," but, Mao continued, let there be no mistake: "Who is our leader? It is Stalin. Is there a second person? No. . . . Our party and every member of the Chinese Communist Party are Stalin's pupils. Of Marx, Engels, Lenin, and Stalin, three are dead, and only one is alive. That is Stalin. He is our teacher."

True, Mao said, the Communist Party had to be prepared for all eventualities, including the possibility that it would have to fight in China on its own. "We have to prepare for a situation where the faraway water does not put out the nearby fire," he said at the Seventh Congress. But he assured the delegates that it wasn't going to come to that. Soviet help was on its way. "Do you believe it?" he asked. "I believe it." Then he formed his hand into a kind of blade and held it like an executioner's knife above his neck. "If it doesn't," he said, "you can chop off my head."

A chance encounter at the airport gave Patrick J. Hurley further proof, as he saw it, that the China hands weren't just wrong but treasonous. He was leaving Washington in early April on his return journey to Chungking when he ran into OSS director Wild Bill Donovan. Donovan gave

Hurley some astonishing information about John Carter Vincent, head of the State Department's China desk, whom Hurley had encountered during his unpleasant appearance a couple of weeks earlier before the Far Eastern division, the one at which he'd faced "a full array of the pro-Communists of the State Department as my judges and questioners." Donovan told him that Vincent was "overly friendly with the Reds," and moreover that there was an investigation going on about leaks of official government documents to a pro-Communist magazine called *Amerasia*. This news no doubt was all the confirmation Hurley needed that the China hands were actively undermining his and the United States government's official policy of support to Chiang Kai-shek, and they were doing so because they wanted the Communists to win.

Shortly afterward, on June 6, 1945, John Stewart Service, a close ally of Vincent and, as we've seen, one of the brightest of the State Department China hands—the person who had met with Mao in Yenan more often and on more intimate terms than any other Foreign Service officer, and the leader, with John Davies, of the group attempting to "politically capture" the Chinese Communists—was arrested by the FBI and charged with espionage.

"FBI SEIZES SIX AS SPIES, TWO IN STATE DEPARTMENT" read the alarming headline in *The New York Times.*

SECRETS STOLEN

NAVAL OFFICER AND TWO EDITORS
OF MAGAZINE HERE ARRESTED

WIDE SERIES OF THEFTS

DATA FROM ARMY, NAVY AND
OTHER FILES DECLARED USED
IN PERIODICAL AMERASIA

"After almost three months of shadowing and snooping," *Time* informed its millions of readers, "the FBI's quiet supersleuths in New York and Washington last week arrested five men and a woman on charges of conspiracy to violate the espionage laws. Promptly, the U.S. had its biggest State-secrets case of the war."

It is a noteworthy coincidence that the other big news event receiving front-page treatment on the same day was a disclosure of the Soviet intention to occupy one-third of soon-to-be-defeated Germany, an early first step in what was to become the Cold War. The war in Europe had just ended, on May 8, and already a new conflict was brewing with the Soviet Union, which was quickly becoming an ex-ally. Meanwhile, victory in Asia still seemed a long and costly way away. Three weeks after V-E Day, on June 1, President Truman told Congress that twice as many troops as were needed to defeat Germany, a total of seven million altogether, would be sent to Asia to finish off Japan. Casualties would mount. Sacrifice was still in order.

It was, in other words, not the moment for a diplomat to be accused of leaking documents to a left-wing magazine suspected of sympathizing with the Communists. Only a few weeks before, Hurley had removed Service from his post in China. After the China hands sent their dissenting telegram to the State Department in February, Hurley had declared of its author, Service, "I'll get that son of a bitch if it's the last thing I do." And now the fates had intervened. Service was spending the night in prison, accused of disloyalty to the United States when the country was still at war. Hurley must have felt vindication, while Service, as he later told a friend, was "overwhelmed with disgrace and shame." "I remember some guy in another cell, booked for car theft or rape, or whatever, asking, 'What are *you* in for?'" Service recalled. "I said, 'Conspiracy to violate the Espionage Act,' and he said, 'I don't know what that is, but it sounds like something real big!'"

As it turned out, Service was brought before a grand jury in August and the government's case against him fell apart. The grand jury vote against an indictment of Service was twenty to zero. Three of the others were indicted. In the end, nobody went to prison, and after Service was exonerated, he was welcomed back to the State Department and sent to Japan to serve on the staff of Douglas MacArthur during the occupation.

What has come to be called the Amerasia Affair was the first public episode of the bitter aftermath of the American wartime entanglement in China. It was to be followed for years by an irrational and mean-spirited hunt for saboteurs in the American midst, a hunt that profoundly affected the futures of Service, Davies, and several of the other China hands. In the immediate instance, the sensational arrests of the six alleged spies reflected the maneuvering over China policy taking place inside the American government just as the struggles over the postwar world were looming. Like all such maneuvering before and since, it involved efforts by proponents of one side or another in the debate to influence public opinion by releasing selective information to the press.

Service had been indiscreet in this matter. He'd arrived in Washington and was at loose ends while awaiting his next assignment. He had an office in the Far Eastern division, but he didn't have much to do there. His wife and two children were in California, and he was lonely, especially in the evenings. To help him pass the time, he accepted social invitations, and it was at one of these that he met reporters and editors who were interested in what this deeply informed man who had spent months in both Chungking and Yenan had to say about China.

In February, while still in China, Service had met with Joseph Alsop, FDR's distant cousin and a senior member of Chennault's staff and, like Chennault himself, ardently supportive of Chiang Kai-shek. Alsop had told him that it was "idiotic" not to see the Chinese Communists as pawns of the Soviet Union, and foolish not to understand the necessity for Chiang to focus his attention on the Communist threat, rather than on the Japanese. A few years later, Alsop, who became an influential Washington columnist, summed it up in an article in the *Saturday Evening Post*. In demanding political reform of Chiang, pressing him to make a deal with the Communists, and insisting that the central government use its troops to fight Japan rather than Yenan, the United States had fatally weakened him, and helped to bring the Communists, whose anti-American hostility had been glossed over by the China hands, to power. Alsop's argument was that it would have been better for the United States to dispose of Japan by itself and to let Chiang take care of the Communists.

Service saw things differently. He didn't believe that Chiang's weakness was due to the policies of the United States. Rather, it was his own limitations that doomed him. Like Davies, Service knew it was likely that the Communists would fall under the Soviet sway, and it was exactly to give them an option that he favored building ties with them. As for Chiang, pressing him for political reform was the only way to preserve him—assuming there was any way to preserve him at all—while to coddle him was to prop up what Mao had called a "rotten shell." It was then, and it remains now, fanciful to imagine that anything short of another full-scale war involving hundreds of thousands of American troops could have maintained the KMT in power in all of China, or even in just the southern half of the country. Service, believing that, wanted to prevent the United States from making a drastic mistake.

And he got encouragement from higher-ups, including from Lauchlin Currie, formerly FDR's administrator of Lend-Lease, and from Vincent, who urged Service to provide selective leaks to the press advancing their collective point of view and discrediting that of Hurley. Service had done this sort of thing when he was still in China, meeting with journalists and providing background information, including the views that he was sending in his reports to Washington. "I was Lauchlin Currie's designated leaker," he later told E. J. Kahn. Among his contacts was Drew Pearson, the influential columnist, whose opinions were decidedly unfavorable to Hurley, to Hurley's rage. As we've seen, Hurley had complained to the State Department about what he called a campaign to smear his reputation.

One of Service's contacts was Philip Jaffe, the editor of *Amerasia*. Jaffe was a naturalized immigrant from Ukraine who had made money in the greeting card business. He was a friend of Earl Browder, the chairman of the American Communist Party, and clearly a leftist, though there's no indication he was a Communist himself—and in any case Browder was under attack from Moscow for reasons having to do with the sectarian quarrels that often took place in the international Communist movement. *Amerasia* had a point of view similar on the subject of the Chinese revolution to that of Edgar Snow or any of the others enchanted with the Communist movement in China and disillusioned with the national government. But it was a serious magazine, not a piece of propaganda, and it was not under the control of Moscow or any other foreign power.

Jaffe was active and enterprising, and he managed to obtain copies of government documents, provided to him by several sources, one of whom was Service, who gave him copies of some of the classified reports he had written during his days in China. Jaffe had been under FBI surveillance since the end of January, when Kenneth Wills of the OSS had reported to the FBI that *Amerasia* had published almost verbatim his classified report on British policy in Southeast Asia. FBI agents were stationed outside the *Amerasia* office, which was in a building at 225 Fifth Avenue in Manhattan, and in March, seeing that the office was empty, a five-man team, which did not have a warrant, broke into the magazine's office and found what appeared to be powerful and abundant evidence of a criminal conspiracy.

They discovered that the magazine was equipped with a darkroom even though it didn't publish photographs. They found photocopies of many government documents, some of them marked "Top Secret." There were locked suitcases crammed with materials from army and navy intelligence, from the State Department, and from the OSS. From that point on, a team of seventy-five FBI agents was assigned to keep watch on Jaffe and his associates, tapping their phones, listening in on their conversations.

In such a way did Service come to be overheard by the FBI. Jaffe had cultivated him, invited him to dinner in Washington, introduced him to some of his contributors, and established common ground with him on the general subject of China and on the particular subject of Hurley. Once Service visited Jaffe in his room at the Statler Hotel in Washington, and with the FBI's tape machines turning, he talked about what he called something "very secret"—evidently the initiatives taken the previous fall by Donovan and McClure, and carried out by Bird and Barrett, to broach a plan for military cooperation with the Communists. It was the most indiscreet comment that Service made to Jaffe, but was it an act of criminal disloyalty to the United States?

The grand jury didn't think so, and neither did some of the wiser American commentators. Liberals like Pearson, Walter Winchell, and Max Lerner produced columns early on denouncing the FBI arrests as efforts to stifle the press and to suppress dissent inside the State Department. Pearson called it "America's Dreyfus case," after the Jewish captain in the French army falsely accused of espionage. Others recognized the case for what it was, simply an instance of some leaking of the sort that government officials of all persuasions had always done. Even though the case was to disappear from public attention pretty soon, the aftertaste produced by the initial, sometimes lurid coverage was long-lasting. The appeal of a good story, of espionage, hidden dangers, secret and sinister forces, was just too much to resist. The New York Journal American warned that the case of the six provided "sensational proof that Communist organizers had access to highly confidential files of vital government agencies." A headline in the New York Herald Tribune asserted, with no evidence, "WAR SECRETS LEAKS WIDESPREAD, SIX ARRESTS MAY BE ONLY A START." The Scripps-Howard chain of newspapers, whose motto was "Give light and the people will find their own way," and whose Ernie Pyle was probably the most famous war correspondent of the time, reported without any truthful evidence that Service had engineered what the paper alleged to be an American turn away from Chiang and toward the Communists. The Chinese Communists themselves, perhaps confused about the waywardness of American China policy, were paying attention. For them, the arrests represented proof of the unchangeable nature of imperialist countries. Three weeks after those sensational headlines in American newspapers, the Communists' *Liberation Daily* provided a full analysis of the event, and while the analysis was couched in Marxist-Leninist terms, it wasn't wrong. The ordeal of Service et al., the newspaper said, wasn't really about "confidential information," as the American press had it; it was about the deeper battle in the United States over China policy, which, in turn, was really about the ability of big capitalism and imperialism to endure in the postwar world. "The arrest of the six people is the emergence of the heated debate on the two roads of American policies toward China," the newspaper said, one of which "acknowledges the Chinese people's great democratic force," namely "the Eighth Route Army and the New Fourth Route Army." And then there is the other force, the one "that does not acknowledge the great power of the Chinese people but only the anti-democratic KMT government along with the reactionary elements and the murderous devil Chiang Kai-shek."

The newspaper struck some themes that would remain constants of the Communists' propaganda, even as it became shriller over the following years. The enemy was not the "American people" or "the American friends who support the Chinese people's cause." The enemy was American imperialists, "Hurley and his ilk," as the common phrase had it, because their aim was "exactly the same as that of the autocrat and traitor who drinks blood from the bodies of the Chinese people"—meaning, Chiang Kai-shek. From now on, the CCP's broadsides against the United States—with occasional periods of remission—would become both more bitter and more formulaic, with the phrase "the Hurley-Chiang double act" becoming the standard reference to the American ambassador and his support of the KMT, along with the boilerplate assurance that both Hurley and Chiang would inevitably be defeated. The Communist commentators increasingly referred to Hurley's press conference of April 2 as a watershed event, the moment when American policy shifted in favor of "the goal of victimizing the Chinese people." Hurley became the first of several Americans over the years to be held up as a Great Enemy even as the United States came more and more to be described as a "capitalist dictatorship" seeking to gain "hegemony" in China. The American ambassador became "Master Hurley," the puppeteer without whom Chiang would never have dared to attempt to uphold his dictatorship. And with this denunciation of the United States and its "imperialist bureaucrats" came countervailing praise of the Soviet Union as "a real democracy of the laborers" that is "a hundred times more democratic" than "the American democracy under its capitalist dictators."

We see here what would become a signal feature of Chinese Communist propaganda, a superheated, demonizing, radically simplifying an inescapable rhetorical extremism, a barrage of exaggerations, distortions, and lies, that was among the tools the Chinese Communists learned from the Leninist-Stalinist model. The Communists' irritation with the United States, moreover, was not confined to Mao's speeches and Yenan's propaganda machinery. It was reflected in events taking place in the embattled territory of China where the war continued and soldiers died. On May 28, 1945, a five-member American team led by Major F. L. Coolidge was parachuted behind enemy lines near the town of Fuping in Hebei province. Known as the Spaniel Mission— after the dog of one of its members—it was an OSS operation aimed at collecting information about the pro-Japanese puppet government.

The Americans knew that the Communists had succeeded in infiltrating Chinese army units that were ostensibly loyal to the collaborationist Nanjing government. In 1945, these puppet forces came under ever greater scrutiny by American intelligence, especially the secret operations, or SO, arms of SACO, the cooperative organization jointly commanded by the American naval officer Milton "Mary" Miles and his chief Chinese collaborator, Tai Li, the head of Chiang's secret police. Among SACO's subdivisions was a propaganda production unit that put out slick and clever misinformation aimed at demoralizing both Japanese soldiers in China and the puppet forces, and, in the case of the latter, at encouraging the belief that Japan was nearly defeated and that they should think about defecting before it was too late.

One poster, distributed in occupied territory, consists of a dark and melancholy image of a woman tending to a dying man. It represents itself as a warning by the puppet government about infectious diseases coming from Japan, where because of the "many unburied bodies of bombing victims" the drinking water had become polluted. The aim was indirectly to persuade Japanese soldiers in China that their relatives back home were in dire straits. Another poster, this one aimed at Chinese collaborators, shows a knife pointed at the back of a receding man. "Save your life, protect your family," the text reads. "For eight years the enemy has forced you to work for him. Now he must rush to the defense of his homeland. Is he going to leave you behind him? No. You are a danger. You know too much and you must die. . . . Already in Canton and Fuzhou these assassinations have begun. What can you do? Desert him now. Save your life."

Puppet troops faced with defeat might, the Americans believed, be susceptible to recruitment. They knew that some of the weaponry in the hands of the Communists was not, as the Communists often claimed, captured from the Japanese, but had come from bribes paid to the well-armed puppet troops. Now the Spaniel Mission was being dispatched to contact the Communists and to carry out joint intelligence operations to determine the extent to which the puppets could be turned against their Japanese masters, providing intelligence and perhaps cooperating in sabotage. It was, in short, exactly the sort of cooperation against the common enemy that the Communists had been pleading for since the middle of 1944.

Within two days, the Spaniel Mission's five members were captured by Communist guerrillas, who subjected them to intense questioning, then brought them to two senior Communist political commissars, who made the decision to detain them indefinitely. They stayed in detention, despite American protests, for four months and were released only a month after the end of the war in September. The reason given for this hostile treatment at a time when the United States and the Communists were cooperating over such things as the rescue of downed American fliers was, as the chief American scholar to examine this incident has written, that "no prior notice had been given to Yenan," and therefore the assumption in Yenan was that "the Spaniel mission must have ulterior motives to organize people against the Communists." Another historian of Sino-American relations in this period has written that the Communists, already disillusioned by the partiality Hurley and Wedemeyer were showing to the central government, feared that this effort to contact Chinese puppet government troops was part of an effort to turn them against the Communists.

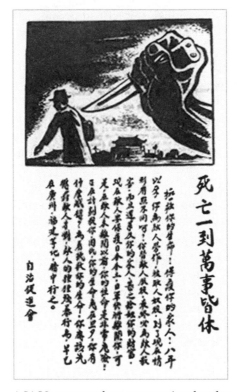

A SACO propaganda poster warning that the Japanese will murder Chinese collaborators as they withdraw. The caption reads: "When the angel of death arrives, all affairs cease."

A few months later, in August, with the men of the Spaniel Mission still detained and cut off from contact with American headquarters, General Wedemeyer vehemently protested their treatment directly to Mao, who was in Chungking for talks with Chiang. Wedemeyer argued that as China theater commander, he had the authority to operate behind enemy lines and that "it is not always feasible" to get permission in advance either from Communists or Nationalists who might be operating in the same areas. Numerous such missions had been dispatched before, Wedemeyer said, and local commanders had "recognized and accepted [the American agents] as friends and co-workers," taking them in "and treating them kindly."

Maochun Yu of the U.S. Naval Academy, the author of an account of the OSS's wartime activities in China, concludes that the Communists didn't want the Americans to discover that Yenan's propagandistic portrayal of their valiant struggle against the Japanese and the puppet regime was essentially false, and that in many areas they and the supposed Japanese enemy observed an unwritten truce, carrying on barter and the selling of arms but rarely fighting. In fact, the Spaniel Mission made exactly such an observation, reporting to American headquarters that the Communist claim of fighting an active guerrilla war against Japan "has been grossly exaggerated," and that Yenan's actual policy was "to undertake no serious campaign against the Japanese or puppets." The Communists could well have detained the Spaniel Mission and kept it incommunicado because they didn't want any foreigners in the vicinity to make such observations.

When Mao was confronted by Wedemeyer about the arrest of the Spaniel Mission members, Mao recapitulated the friendly and cordial treatment given to the Dixie Mission in Yenan, the implication being that the Communists had no policy to treat Americans badly. "I consider the Fuping incident to be very unfortunate," he said. But the warm reception of the Dixie Mission had been months earlier, before the collapse of the Hurley negotiations, before Hurley's April 2 press conference, and before the explosion of the Amerasia Affair. It is likely that Mao did not order the arrest of the Spaniel Mission, though it seems unlikely he wouldn't have been quickly informed of it, and could, had he wanted to, have ordered the quick release of the detained men. It also seems that the Eighth Route Army commander who was so suspicious of the Americans dropping into Fuping was following a general order. On June 11, 1945, Wilbur J. Peterkin, acting head of the Dixie Mission in Yenan, reported to Wedemeyer, "All communist headquarters have been instructed to arrest and disarm and hold all unauthorized Americans encountered anywhere."

There was in this sense a signal difference between the Spaniel group and the Dixie Mission members, like Raymond Ludden, who traveled in the company of Communist guerrillas behind enemy lines. The Dixie Mission was authorized, its members accompanied by what later travelers to Communist China would call "minders," official guides who chose the places to visit and the people to be met. The Spaniel Mission operated without minders, and was therefore "unauthorized." Whatever the reasons for the treatment of the Spaniel Mission, the unfriendliness and suspicion that it demonstrated foreshadowed what was to come when, after eight long years of conflict, the war against Japan suddenly came to an end. With the war against Japan won, the United States and the Communists would no longer have a common enemy, and its disappearance would strip away the incentive to cooperate, leaving behind many reasons for each to see in the other a mortal foe.

PART III

Victory and Failure

CHAPTER TWELVE

Hearts and Minds

Ma Yingchu was the sort of man whose support the Chinese government needed but lost, to the tremendous benefit of its mortal rival the Communists. He was one of those figures of influence in China who straddled both the centuries and the era. He was born in 1882, the seventh year of the Guangxu emperor, and educated during the last years of the Qing dynasty, the decadent and deeply conservative mandarin China of silk robes and imperial government, but he spent his career in the new China, a country whose educated class was engaged in a deep self-examination, seeking the reasons for its long decline and a formula that would enable it to be wealthy and powerful, as it had so often been in its past.

Ma's hometown was Shaoxing, an ancient place of Buddhist temples, literary teahouses, and wooden homes built Venice-like alongside a warren of lakes and canals. Shaoxing was, and still is, the country's capital of vintage rice wine. Ma's father was a winemaker who wanted his son to follow him into the family business, and who then disowned him when, in the newborn modern spirit, Yinchu wanted to study science, metallurgy, and economics, which he did at some of China's best schools.

He was a good-looking young man, intense, ambitious, extremely intelligent. There is a photograph taken of him when he was about twenty wearing the high-collared robe of a young scholar, his expression serious and determined as he looks at the camera through wire-rimmed spectacles. He was a very good student, and in 1907 he received a scholarship to study at Yale University, a dream come true. What tremendous benefit that could have both for him and for his country, to which he intended to return.

Ma was the beneficiary of American idealism directed toward China, its earnest wish to help it overcome the decrepitude and decay of its recent history. After the defeat of the Boxer Rebellion at the turn of the twentieth century, China, prostrate and humiliated, was forced to pay an immense indemnity to make up for the damage done and lives taken by the Boxers. The United States, alone among the recipients of this money, put its share into a scholarship fund for Chinese students. That was where the funds came from for Ma to get his BA in economics at Yale, which he did in 1911, just as the last dynasty, the Qing, was being overthrown. Then, in 1914, as the rest of the world was tumbling into the Great War, he received a PhD at Columbia University in economics and philosophy.

Equipped with new ideas and with the prestige that these degrees conferred, Ma, now a thorough man of the world, returned to a China where revolutionary ideas were gripping the minds of the country's best young people, Ma included. He experienced the disorder and violence of the warlord years but also the excitement of the reunification of much of the country under the Kuomintang and Chiang Kai-shek. Eager to participate in the country's resurgence, he helped found a new institution of higher education, the Chinese College of Commerce, in Shanghai, and he became president of the Chinese Economics Society, where he began to advocate the idea that economic growth and democracy went together, that you couldn't succeed in the first without the openness, the exchange of ideas, and the freedoms of the second.

Ma supported the Kuomintang for a time, but during the 1930s he became a critic of Chiang's authoritarian, undemocratic tendencies, and in 1940, in the midst of the Japanese war, Chiang's security services put him under house arrest and banned him from public activities. He spent the next five years under this ban, but was not forgotten by other Chinese writers and teachers, members of the small, often western-educated elite that enjoyed great prestige though no power in China, who tended to share Ma's loss of faith in the KMT and its ability to command a bright future for his country.

At the end of 1944, the ruling party, feeling the pressure both from its own intellectuals and from the United States to relax its repressive policies, released Ma from house arrest. If the government was hoping that this gesture would turn a grateful Ma into a supporter, it was grievously mistaken. He made his first public appearance at a meeting of what was called the Friday Dinner Gathering, which was held in a ballroom in Chungking. This was a regular event sponsored by progressive merchants and businessmen and attended by hundreds of people whose purpose was to meet each other and exchange views about that most preoccupying question: China's present plight and future prospects.

All the seats in the hall were occupied when the lights suddenly brightened and the evening's host walked in with Ma, dressed in a sky-blue satin robe. "Tonight, we will welcome Professor Ma Yinchu and celebrate his new-gained freedom," the host, Wu Gengmei, announced, and the audience, apparently not having been informed that Ma would be among them that night, broke into enthusiastic applause.

Ma took the floor, thanking the assembly for its welcome, and then assured it that he had made no deal with the government in exchange for his release. "I, Ma Yinchu, am still the old disobedient Ma Yinchu," he began. As a price for the termination of his detention, the authorities had banned him from giving speeches, he said, even as he plunged ahead with a speech. It was entitled, typically for Ma, "China's Industrialization Is Inseparable from Democracy," and it was a public chastisement of his audience and of people like himself for a kind of moral and practical apathy. There are people, he said, "who hide in the Great Rear Area [the unoccupied zones of China], consume farmer's rice, and deploy farmer's sons to risk their lives, who eat fish and meat, wear silk and satin, live in tall buildings, and drive cars" at a time when China urgently needed altruistic civic involvement and self-sacrifice. Ma's words were harsh and unsparing, like those of an Old Testament prophet, lambasting China's "leading citizens" for being "cruel and rapacious" and for "plundering the wealth of people at this moment of life and death" while so many other people suffered the death, poverty, and dislocation of the war. China's real heroes, Ma declared, were the peasants, the millions who "lost their arms and legs, bled or were killed by famine and pestilence, or struggled between the gullies."

There was something in this speech and even in the academic-sounding title of it that echoed of the recent past and prefigured later events in China, after the Communists had taken power. China had never been a democracy, not in its entire four thousand years of recorded history, but its modern intellectuals like Ma wanted it to be. Earlier in the century, the dominant slogan among students and intellectuals looking for ways to build a new country was "Mr. Science and Mr. Democracy." The science part of it would lift the country out of the morass of useless custom and superstition. Lu Xun (formerly transcribed as Lu Hsun), China's leading twentieth-century writer, wrote a powerful story about a sick boy whose parents used the last of their money buying the only medicine that, they were told, could cure him, a steamed bun dipped in the blood of a freshly killed child. For Lu, this grim medical hoax symbolized the country's larger imprisonment in ignorant tradition, in the desperation of the poor, in the power of family patriarchs, the subordination of women, the virtual enslavement of daughters by their mothers-in-law, who themselves were victims of one of the country's darkest and at the time still widely observed practices, footbinding. Science could cure China of these multiple afflictions. It was why Ma Yinchu had studied metallurgy.

And then there was *Minzhu Xiansheng*, Mr. Democracy, which alone could detach China from stultifying authority, enliven it with a sense of civic engagement, and awaken the unused energies of its people. Hence Ma's idea that industrialization was inseparable from democracy, that the country couldn't create a modern economy with a premodern political system. "The world has already become democratic," he said. "All countries must take the democratic path after the war ends, or they will not be able to guarantee their own survival and independence."

For "democracy," Ma does not seem to have had in mind a western-style electoral system. For him democracy was a focus on popular welfare, especially the welfare of the rural masses, and in this he clearly believed that the Communists were more in tune with national needs than the Nationalists. The Communists accepted Mr. Science, especially after the death of Mao in 1976. They called it the Four Modernizations. But they rejected Mr. Democracy, and this led, in 1978, to another dissident slogan, coined by an electrician named Wei Jingsheng who worked at the Beijing Zoo. It was "Democracy: The Fifth Modernization," and whether Wei knew it or not, the main idea of his slogan came directly from Ma Yinchu's speech at that Friday Dinner Gathering in Chungking in 1944. The irony is that for all the nasty authoritarianism of the Kuomintang in 1944 and 1945, Ma was able to continue to voice his opinions. Even though he was supposedly banned from making speeches, he did make them, at that meeting of the Friday Dinner Gathering and later at other events. As for Wei Jingsheng, living under Communist Party rule in 1979 in a country suffering no foreign assault, after a closed and secret trial, he was arrested and sent to prison for a total of eighteen years.

For the remaining months of the war in 1945, while the United States tried to figure out what its China policy should be—whether total support of Chiang Kai-shek or a balanced policy that included arms aid to the Communists—Ma was denouncing the Kuomintang but not the Communists, who were a lot closer to his peasant heroes than the KMT was. At a meeting of the Chinese Muslim Association in Chungking in March, Ma used the rather strange metaphor of a vacuum tube to lament the absence in China of a great political leader. Of course, Chiang Kai-shek was supposed to be exactly such a leader, but Ma likened him to a device that is empty inside and refuses to heed anything on the outside. "The 'Vacuum Tube' I was talking about was him— Chiang Kai-shek," Ma said, lest he be misunderstood.

Still later, in an article published in the pro-Communist *Xinhua Daily* in Chungking, there was Ma again, this time "trembling with fear" for his country as he chastised his fellow countrymen for tolerating the intolerable—the desperate poverty in the streets, the millions of hungry people, the disease, the famine, the deaths, the filth. And while this terrible suffering was taking place, the country's leaders "still want to solicit grains and recruit soldiers, driving paupers to the battlefields of ice and snow where they risk their lives for 'them.'"

Ma's brave and tough criticism seems, especially from the vantage point of decades later, to have been willfully and erroneously one-sided. There are no harsh words in his speeches or articles about Mao's Communists, though they were to prove far more repressive than the KMT. But Ma felt that Chiang had reached a point of hopelessness, while the Communists, both fresh and distant, seemed a cleaner and brighter alternative. This was a mixed and complicated matter in China as the great war in Asia came to an end and a new war loomed, between the weakened Kuomintang and the strengthened Communists. There were many in the country who feared the Communists, who criticized them for their subservience to the Soviet Union, and who were aware of their heavy-handed attempts within their own ranks to silence or intimidate truly independent writers and thinkers. Ironically, it was among left-wing writers who identified with the Communists or who belonged to the highly influential League of Left-Wing Writers, which received instructions from the party's cultural bureaucrats, that the awareness of the CCP's intolerance of dissent was most acute. During the 1930s, there were ferocious quarrels between these bureaucrats and some of China's best-known and most beloved writers, including, most conspicuously, Lu Xun, the most prominent of them all.

Still, among most intellectuals—or, in the absence of precise data on this, what seemed to have been most writers and thinkers—it was the Kuomintang that caught their fire for the simple reason that the Kuomintang was in power, and had been in power for nearly two authoritarian decades. As the war came to an end, not very many people either inside China or outside it—except for the more prescient analysts like Service and Davies—predicted that within a few short years the KMT would escape to Taiwan and the Communists take power. The central government seemed strong. It had a huge army, including thirty-nine top-flight divisions being trained and equipped by the United States, while the CCP was still perceived to be a poorly armed mass of guerrillas. The government enjoyed a total monopoly among armed Chinese forces in air and sea power, and, of course, it maintained a many-tentacled secret police organization. So when Ma and others disparaged the KMT, while remaining silent about the CCP, it was in part because they were willing to give the Communists the benefit of the doubt and in part because they saw the KMT as the government of China likely to remain in place indefinitely, while the Communists were a faraway rival merely asking at that point to be included in a coalition.

Moreover, there were bitter memories among these people of the Kuomintang's violent attacks on writers and thinkers during the years when Chiang was consolidating his power and terror reigned in the places where artistic creation and intellectual ferment were taking place, Shanghai especially. These were men largely unknown to or forgotten by Chiang's avid supporters outside of China, like Qu Qiubai and Hu Yepin, leftist writers and poets, men of eloquence and passion, who sided with the Communists in the early years and were arrested by Chiang's secret police and killed by firing squads during the 1930s. These events were not forgotten in China, especially among what might be called the cognoscenti, the writers, poets, and playwrights—Lao She, the author of the celebrated novel *Rickshaw Boy*, is a prominent example—who began to find their voices with the end of the war and who tended to give the Communists but not Chiang Kai-shek the benefit of the doubt. Lu Xun himself always despised Chiang as a dictator, and this dislike was shared by the left-leaning Shanghai intelligentsia that in 1945 was beginning to envisage a future without the Japanese occupying army. And then there were the suspicions, the sense of alienation, and the fears of the KMT felt by members of what came to be called the third force, the people like Ma Yinchu, often educated in the United States, who didn't become Communists but who watched with growing disillusionment and anger the KMT's continued recourse to the tools of repression. And, finally, there were the students, imbued, as young people generally are, with a kind of idealistic impatience, furious at the slothfulness, the corruption, the arrogance of a government that was unable to defend the country, compared to the Communists, who were believed to be waging courageous guerrilla warfare against the hated occupier.

"China is now divided into two countries: the democratic China, composed of various parties under the leadership of the Communist Party, and the Fascist dictatorship of the Kuomintang," read a letter from students at Fudan University, handed over to the American vice president, Henry Wallace, when he was on an official visit to Chiang in the summer of 1944. "The former is positively carrying on the war and protecting the people, while the latter sits back and oppresses the people."

And so, when the war ended, it was difficult to find independent-minded people ready to proclaim Chiang's heroism or brilliance. No doubt, millions of Chinese still lionized Chiang, still saw him as the symbol of the wartime refusal to surrender, as the man on the white horse brandishing that sword of patriotic defiance. But the public defection of the immensely prestigious Ma Yinchu, of many of the country's other famous writers and scholars, and of thousands of restive students suggested a weakness at the core, and it was a weakness that the only other armed force in the country knew how to use for its advantage.

All over China, the sudden surrender of Japan announced itself in different ways, but the reaction was the same: joy followed by a sober realization that for China almost nothing had been settled by the victory and that, at worst, another war loomed. At a prison camp for American and Allied soldiers in Manchuria, a Japanese lieutenant announced at the morning roll call, "By order of the emperor, the war is amicably terminated." The word "amicably" brought raucous, bitter laughter from the soldiers. Most Americans and most Asians had thought the war would go on for a lot longer, but it was shortened by the dropping of atomic bombs on Hiroshima and Nagasaki on August 6 and 9, 1945, and the simultaneous entry into the war of the Soviet Union, which, in accordance with the promise Stalin made to Roosevelt at Yalta, invaded Manchuria on the day after the Hiroshima bomb.

"Yenan boiled over," Shi Zhe, Mao's Russian translator, remembered, as news of the end of the war reached the Communists' headquarters:

> There were red flags all over, in the center [of Yenan] and the surrounding mountains, drums beating, fireworks exploding, and people throwing their hats into the air. The farmers gave away apples and pears, and people who didn't know each other hugged and danced. That night the mountains and fields were seas of fire and floods of joy. Eight years of hard fighting against the Japanese finally ended with success. The carnival went on for three days.

The unexpectedness of the end intensified the euphoria that engulfed China, though the giddy mood was tempered by the agonies of the war's dreadful aftermath. "In mid to late August, people around the country were showered in happiness and rebirth and people in the occupied zone celebrated until sunrise," recalled Chu Anping, a young writer for a new magazine called *Keguan,* or *Objectivity,* one of the many new journals that sprang into existence when the end of the war led the government to relax its strict censorship rules. On the evening of August 10, there were fireworks displays all over China. The head of a government office in Chungking spent ten thousand Chinese yuan on fireworks. "Most of the people, especially government employees, students, merchants, and other so-called people of the upper class threw themselves into a swirl of revelry," wrote Lu Ling, an essayist and playwright, remembering the short-lived euphoria that came with the enemy's surrender. College students sang lines from "La Marseillaise." Drums were set up on the streets; the din of hardwood clappers and cymbals, used in Sichuan opera, filled the crowded streets.

Within hours, American planes appeared in China's skies to drop parachute packs of food and medicine into prisoner-of-war camps. In Shanghai, Theodore White rode down Bubbling Well Road from the airport and found it jammed with Chinese "cheering, waving little American and Nationalist flags." At the waterfront, where the peddlers usually sold dried fish, they were offering silk-screened portraits of Chiang Kai-shek, one small sign that the Gimo was still regarded as the man who had seen China through its ordeal. The White Russian owner of a cabaret offered free drinks to any American in uniform, as well as his "choice of any woman in the house, any race, any color, any size—and he had them all."

This was more than the end of a war. There was a sense of a new era dawning and the ending of an old one that had begun with the Opium War in the mid-nineteenth century and included China's defeat by Japan in 1895—the era of Chinese humiliation. In his memoirs, the writer Xia Yan, a senior editor for the *Xinhua Daily* and a founder, with Lu Xun, of the League of Left-Wing Writers, listed the elements of national shame related specifically to Japan: there was the loss of Taiwan in the first Sino-Japanese war; the Twenty-One Demands of 1915, when China acceded to Japan's sphere of influence in the northeast; the Mukden Incident of 1931, when Japan seized Manchuria; the bombing and occupation of Shanghai that year; the Marco Polo Bridge Incident six years later, when Japan signaled its intent to conquer all of China. "This near hundred years of humiliating history had finally come to an end," Xia wrote. "The entire *Xinhua Daily* staff went crazy. Actually all of Chungking, all of China went crazy."

Chiang Kai-shek learned that the struggle for national survival was over while having dinner with some senior officials and the ambassador of Mexico in Chungking. He and his companions heard cheering and firecrackers from the nearby United States military headquarters. They investigated and learned that Japan had given up. A few days later, Chiang made a radio speech to the Chinese people jubilant over the great victory and, in a show of magnanimity, instructed his people not to exact vengeance against the many hundreds of thousands of Japanese troops and civilians in China. He sent his chief of staff, He Yingqin, to Nanjing to accept the formal document of surrender from General Okamura, and the day after that, Chinese troops entered Nanjing, the first time in seven years that any Chinese authority except the puppet government had set foot in what had been the national capital. "I am very optimistic," Chiang told *Time* in an interview, part of a rhapsodic cover story on China at war's end that declared the country had never before "been so close to an era of peace and progress." And at the top of it all, the magazine declared, "moved the alert, taut, indefatigable Generalissimo, the first architect of victory and now the first hope of peace."

China, however, was materially devastated, deeply divided, and backward, and the rhapsody of victory was soon replaced by a sober and anxious assessment of the problems that lay ahead. The tremendous progress it had made in the ten years of relatively stable Kuomintang government between 1927 and 1937 had been wiped out, except in Manchuria, which was soon to be systematically stripped of most of its industry by the Russians. Most of the railways were out of operation. Shipping was crippled. The roads were terrible, the bridges and tunnels wrecked, farms were saddled with shortages of everything they needed, from draft animals to fertilizer. All over China, millions of refugees, on the move from their places of wartime refuge to their homes, were without resources or work and faced with a roaring inflation that was making whatever money they had nearly worthless. Already by late 1945 the wheelbarrow had become the common mode of conveyance for money, because so much of it was needed. In November in Shanghai, a rickshaw race was held for public amusement. Chinese, White Russian, and American women sat in the rickshaws, which were decorated with crepe paper and banners and pulled by Chinese coolies. The winning coolie got seven million Chinese dollars, which was equivalent to twenty-two American dollars, and when he put it in his rickshaw to take away, it took up the same space as the passenger he'd just discharged.

Chiang himself actually had a firmer grip on reality than Henry Luce and the other editors of *Time* writing about him in New York. "Everybody takes this as a day of glory," he wrote in his diary. "I alone feel great shame and sorrow."

He doesn't explain why he felt that way, but the devastation of his country must have weighed heavily on Chiang's mind, the ruination of the great plans he'd had for China when he'd established his government in Nanjing eighteen years earlier. Had it not been for the Japanese invasion, Chiang Kai-shek would almost surely have been president of a unified country with the Communist revolt quelled, national sovereignty fully restored, and the most populous country on the planet on its way to being a significant world power. Instead, he had to worry that rather than enjoy rewards from his stubborn eight-year refusal to surrender to Japan, he would face an even greater challenge to his rule. Stalin and Mao, as he put it in his diary, could "plunge China into chaos and anarchy."

Chiang was not alone in this worry. The end-of-war euphoria was quickly replaced by the fear that a new civil war would soon follow. Aside from that, for intellectual leaders like Ma Yinchu there was the more general anguish about the country's miserable condition. "I was excited for a while," the left-wing poet and essayist Hu Feng wrote later, remembering the carnival atmosphere in Kunming, the firecrackers exploding, the crowds massing in the streets, the American jeeps flooding into the downtown areas, "but I cooled down pretty quickly." Hu had studied in Japan in the 1930s and was a prominent member of the League of Left-Wing Writers after returning to China, a friend of Lu Xun, a critic of the Communist apparatchiks who tried to impose an ideological orthodoxy on the dissenting culture, an opponent of censorship. "Japan, China's nemesis for ten years has fallen, but how can China stand on its own in the future? . . . The victory can cloud people's minds, but, sadly, my mind isn't susceptible to being clouded."

"Within these few weeks," Chu Anping, the commentator at *Keguan*, wrote, referring to the few weeks in September and October after the end of the war, "the lands that were once occupied for seven or eight years have been occupied for a second time," this time by "indescribably unethical and incompetent national officials." The country was in terrible condition on every civilian front, he wrote. "Our finances in the recuperated areas are in tatters, and in the great rear areas they are chaotic. Industry is bankrupt. There are closed shops everywhere. . . . Transportation is a tangle and in the past three months, even the shipping on the Yangzi River hasn't recovered its normal state. At first there was a lot of regulation; now there are a lot of black markets."

Most ominously, Chu wrote, the civil war that both the KMT and the CCP promised they wanted to avoid was already occurring, and the *laobaixing*, the ordinary people, who yearn for peace, "can't do anything but sigh." The KMT was corrupt and exhausted, devoid of "vital young people," while the CCP, as he put it, demonstrated "excessive support of the values of another country," namely Russia.

For months following V-J Day, literally millions of people were on the loose, trying to get home from the places they'd fled to during the war. At what had been a small stop on the Lunghai Railroad, the major east–west line that had been bombed and strafed repeatedly during the war, an immense crowd of refugees had gathered with no place to go. It rained heavily for days, and so people turned the teahouses, drinking places, restaurants, and other shops along a small market street into dormitories. Two locomotives exploded in the station, causing hundreds of casualties. People lucky enough to get on trains found that the trains' roofs were full of holes. "The waiting area has become a little river," a visiting journalist, Dong Luoyu, reported, "and people urinated and more than urinated around the station so the stench is terrible." What China needs, he wrote, is "revolutionary change, a new spirit, but what we see offers no promise."

Dong moved east along the railroad line, finding that the walls of villages had been destroyed, grass was growing everywhere, "and all we could see were abandoned grass shacks and barely a human trace." This was a consequence of the flood and famine of 1943, when the government had broken the Yellow River dikes trying to stop the Japanese advance. "The trees along the roads near the village were all stripped of bark because the people had eaten it," Dong wrote. "Victory has arrived, but a month later there's no substantial return of people or any rebuilding." It's only when he got all the way to the coast and the former German colony of Qingdao, where detachments of American marines had landed, that he found anything hopeful. "The market is full of laughter and chatting. American friends are always so youthful and energetic."

The places that suffered the least were those that had been seized by Japan early in the war and thus avoided being the scenes of battle. In big cities like Qingdao, Beijing, and Shanghai, all scenes of decadent collaborationism during the war, there was less wholesale wreckage than in areas like Changsha and Guilin—but life nonetheless underwent a kaleidoscope of changes. Goods hoarded for the entire war suddenly appeared on the market, like shiny American cars, all of them from 1941, the last year before Pearl Harbor. "Shanghai was bulging," the American scholar Owen Lattimore wrote, with such items as American electrical appliances that had been almost impossible to get in the United States itself, but had been hoarded in Shanghai by merchants who, in exchange for their cooperation with the Japanese occupier, had been able to seal their warehouses, which were now reopened. But even in Shanghai, then as now China's richest city, the proliferation of goods didn't make up for all the things that were absent. For many the city seemed not newly opulent but bare, stripped down, because before they left, the Japanese had taken away everything from the light fixtures to the spigots. "It was a raw, unheated city," according to one historian. "This place called Shanghai is very, very cold," an American colonel, John Hart Caughey, wrote in a letter home, because "all the radiators are gone." The Japanese, he said, "seemed to think that if they got all the scrap metal up into the vicinity of Manchuria that it would make for a Great East Asia Corporation and so they moved everything out." Caughey, looking from his window in the Metropole Hotel (where hot water was provided three times a week), noted people "who walk along in a daze and poorly dressed. You know to look at them that they are about to freeze to death and no one pays the least bit of attention." At the same time, the age-old Chinese custom of "squeeze," a kind of normative corruption, took on new forms. A brisk extortion business emerged as Chinese who had remained behind in Shanghai or Beijing were made to pay fines or risk being accused of collaboration, whether they had collaborated or not. Officials sent by the KMT to recover factories that had been taken over by the Japanese during the war sold them off and pocketed the money.

An observant young Chinese journalist named Mei Huangzao wrote a series of articles on Shanghai for the *Da Gong Bao* describing what he called the postwar chaos and the inability of the government to regulate it. He reported a widespread, disillusioned remark heard on the streets: "The Shanghai that is out of the darkness isn't as good as the Shanghai that was in the dark." There were crowds everywhere competing for a paucity of services. "When the trolley arrives at the station, people jostle for position like soldiers advancing in a war."

"There are a lot of robberies," Mei wrote:

Three or five people form armed gangs and invade people's houses. Incidents like that can always be seen in the newspaper. The officials won't tolerate this. Right next to Jingansi Road, the world famous race track, has become the execution ground. . . . This reporter arrived in Shanghai on November 22, and, according to my friends, the day before a group of criminals was executed. After a couple of days, another group was executed. In the first group there was a former company commander in the army, a Mr. Song, and his crime was to have led a group of people with weapons to steal gold bars from people's houses.

The robberies were a consequence of unemployment. Poor, desperate men unwilling to "face the risk of the race track worked the crowded trolleys," since picking pockets didn't lead to execution. These petty criminals, Mei reported, were hauled to a police station and beaten if they got caught, and then they "resume their business and sharpen their skills. Such a spirit of daring should be attributed to their empty stomachs." There were other problems. Hyperinflation was one of them, and the Shanghainese who had spent the war in the city blamed the free-spending habits of the returnees who had gone to Chungking during the war and who were now "buying up whatever they wanted" with the paper currency that was being printed by the government. There was impatience over the handling of what were called "traitors," the people who had worked for the puppet government in Nanjing and who, according to public regulations, were supposed to be sent to courts for trial. But they were "just hanging around and nothing was being done with them," Mei reported. Again, there is a sense here of inefficiency, malfeasance, and incompetence on the part of the authorities. "The reunion of the government and the people after eight years should be like the reunion of a father and a son after a long separation, but why does the government put on this mask of harshness and indifference as if they're thousands of miles away?" Mei asked.

CHAPTER THIRTEEN

Everything Stalin Wanted

The Soviet invasion of Manchuria began one minute after midnight on August 9, 1945, when eleven armies and more than one million men shouting "Death to the samurai!" swept into the Japanese puppet state of Manchukuo along a two-thousand-mile front. The tattered and depleted Japanese were no match for the battle-hardened Soviets, who were equipped with 27,000 artillery pieces, 5,500 tanks and self-propelled guns, and 3,700 aircraft. The Japanese, though they knew an invasion would come eventually, were taken by surprise, their intelligence having missed the massive Soviet buildup, which was itself in large part a product of American deliveries of supplies by some seventy Liberty ships landing in Vladivostok. Most of the elite Kwantung Army, the Japanese force that had conquered Manchuria fourteen years earlier and occupied it during most of the war, had been moved to defend against American attacks in the Pacific. Within a few days, the Soviets were in full occupation of Manchuria and parts of North China.

The Soviet invasion, the last major land battle of World War II, was one of the largest and easiest military successes of the war. Coming three days after the atomic bomb attack on Hiroshima, and only hours before the atomic bomb exploded over Nagasaki, it was surely unnecessary to secure the surrender of Japan, though it may have played a role in Japan's decision to give up the fight. The Soviet troops behaved with astonishing brutality, even by the standards of World War II. Bands of Russian soldiers looted and raped in various places in Manchuria and northern Korea, the victims mostly civilian Japanese who had lived in Manchukuo after it became part of the Japanese empire. Not surprisingly after fourteen years of humiliating occupation, it was not only Russians who exacted reprisals. The Soviets allowed "the non-Japanese, one and all, three days of open looting," an American intelligence group, known as Team Cardinal, reported from Mukden. Chinese mobs, armed with ordnance from the fourteen thousand Japanese civilians who were trying to flee the carnage, attacked or burned down Japanese buildings. Casualties, Team Cardinal estimated, ran into the hundreds.

Many civilians committed suicide, encouraged to do so by Japanese army officers who believed that was a better option for them than to suffer Russian or Chinese reprisals. Years later, a popular Chinese television series told the story of a young Japanese girl who, finding to her horror that her entire village had destroyed itself, took refuge with a Chinese family, where she became the concubine of a Chinese man. When the American Cardinal intelligence team asked about the atrocities committed in Mukden, the Russian high command explained that the first troops into the city comprised soldiers whose homes and families had been destroyed by the Germans. These "revenge troops" were used as a shock force, a Russian two-star general reported, and "'not being normal in their minds,' were bent on looting, killing and rape."

The chief beneficiary of the Russian invasion was that great master of ruthless, amoral realpolitik, Joseph Stalin, for whom it was part of a larger scheme to expand Soviet power and influence in East Asia, or, as George Kennan put it in a cabled enumeration of Russia's postwar goals, to seek "domination of the provinces of China in Central Asia contiguous to the Soviet frontier." Stalin had assured Roosevelt at Yalta that he'd invade Manchuria within three months of the end of the war in Europe, and he fulfilled that promise, to the day. He also vowed to leave Manchuria within three months of the Soviet invasion. As we'll see, this was a promise he did not fulfill.

The invasion was the major element in a policy of masked aggression that was as audacious as it was successful. Another part of it was to lull the United States and the central government of China into a state of complacency about Soviet intentions. Stalin's greatest fear, especially in the wake of the awesome demonstrated power of the atomic bomb and the exclusive American possession of it, was that the United States would become alarmed over Soviet expansion in the East and would do something about it, most likely by giving Chiang massive support or even sending American troops to North China. So Stalin's scheme in 1945 was to accomplish that expansion of influence without making the Americans nervous. The always perceptive Davies wrote in a memo at the time, "The Kremlin will be careful in performing its political surgery in Asia to cause during the next two or three years as little shock and pain as possible to the United States." Moscow would pursue what he called a policy of "anesthetization," and in this the Soviet leader had no better or unwitting a helpmate than Hurley.

The American ambassador, having gotten rid of the best of the China hands, had met with Stalin and Molotov in Moscow on his way back to Chungking from Washington in April, and they had told him what he wanted to hear, namely that they would support his effort to reach a negotiated settlement between the KMT and the CCP. As Kennan pointed out, Stalin was safe in making this promise, because he knew that Mao would agree to nothing requiring him to give up his own army, and that Chiang would agree to nothing that allowed Mao to keep it. In this respect, supporting American policy in China meant absolutely nothing in practice.

But Hurley, a man ever ready to find nefarious hidden motives in the analyses and actions of the professional China hands, believed that Stalin's assurances meant everything. Only a few days after Hurley's meetings with Stalin, Harriman, who had been in the room, warned that Hurley had been too optimistic. An aide who summarized Harriman's analysis of the situation for Washington's benefit said that "Marshal Stalin would not cooperate indefinitely with Chiang Kai-shek and that if and when Russia enters the conflict in the Far East, he would make full use of and support the Chinese Communists even to the extent of setting up a puppet government in Manchuria and possibly North China."

Hurley paid no attention, nor does he appear to have registered the display of Soviet intentions elsewhere. Even before he left for Moscow in early April, the Russians had already imposed a compliant Communist government in Romania, and they had expressed their intention of moving Poland's borders to the west into what had been Germany, exchanging that for a broad swath of territory in the east that would go to Ukraine—this without the sort of consultation with Britain or the United States that had been promised at Yalta. It was becoming clear also that Stalin intended to put a pro Soviet group into power in Poland, which prompted Roosevelt to complain directly to him that his actions were putting at risk "our program of international cooperation." Nor does Hurley seem to have noticed the commentary in the Soviet press, which, according to Everett Drumright in the division of Chinese Affairs at the State Department, was aimed at "discrediting the Chungking government—with which it maintains diplomatic relations—and of praising the Chinese Communists and enhancing their prestige."

The question Hurley didn't want to face was why Stalin would take a different approach to China than he had to Poland or Romania. Stalin's forces were on the verge of occupying several Chinese provinces contiguous to the provinces where the CCP had established networks behind enemy lines. As Davies had warned, it was wishful thinking to believe that the Soviets would, if they had a choice in the matter, turn those territories over to a government its controlled press was denouncing as "reactionary" rather than to the Communists, whom the same press was describing as "democratic."

To be fair, most American officials who saw through Stalin's posturing, like Davies and Kennan, believed the dire situation made a KMT-CCP deal in China all the more imperative. It was the only way to lock Mao into an arrangement by which he recognized the authority of the existing Chinese government, and in this they supported Hurley's effort. Except for the China hands whom Hurley had purged, there was almost nobody who appreciated the fact that such a deal was extremely unlikely. But Hurley was convinced that Stalin and Molotov were ready to abandon the Chinese Communists for the sake of good state-to-state relations with Chungking, which gave Stalin the semi-colonial privileges in Manchuria that Roosevelt had promised him at Yalta. In Hurley's view, Stalin would make a deal with the KMT because Stalin knew what Hurley knew, which is that, contrary to the alarmist predictions of the China hands, the Communists were much too weak to take power. In July, Hurley wrote to the State Department about what he termed a triple "exaggeration" of Communist strength. Their military strength, the amount of territory under their control, and the degree of popular support they enjoyed were all overstated, he argued, giving no evidence for these incorrect conclusions. Once Stalin had signed an agreement with Chiang, he further believed, Mao would understand how isolated he was and would quickly come to terms. "Without the support of the Soviet [Union], the CCP will eventually participate as a political party in the National Government," Hurley wrote.

The Truman administration believed this also—or, if some senior members of the administration didn't quite believe it, they still felt that a deal between the central government and the Chinese Communists provided the best hope of a good future, and one way to get that deal would be for the Soviets explicitly and unambiguously to recognize the

Chiang government as the only legitimate government of China. But the Americans had already agreed at Yalta to give the Russians certain privileges in China. This embarrassing fact had been kept a secret from Chiang, the leader it would most affect, but now the prospect of the end of the war meant the secret couldn't be kept any longer. In July, Truman met with T. V. Soong in Washington and outlined the terms that Roosevelt had agreed to at Yalta.

This was, of course, extremely bad news for Chiang. It was a national disgrace, a sellout, an abandonment of the solemnly avowed promise to restore full sovereignty to China. But despite all the tiptoeing and whispering about Yalta, Chiang and Soong most likely already knew about it anyway, and they also understood they had no choice but to accept it—mainly because if they didn't accept it, the Russians might do more to support the Communists, who would. More fundamentally, Chiang understood that he couldn't stay in power in all of China without Soviet consent. So he dispatched Soong to Moscow with instructions to essentially agree to all of the Yalta provisions. He abandoned China's historical claims to Outer Mongolia, which Stalin wanted to turn into a puppet state. Stalin, for whom anti-imperialism was a pillar of the faith, admitted that these concessions on China's part would be equivalent to a new, unequal treaty of the sort that China signed with the western powers in the nineteenth century, but he justified his demands—for example, control over the ports in Dalian and Port Arthur and of the Manchurian railways—as necessities not just for Soviet security but for China's as well. Japan, he told Soong, will be back as a major power in another couple of decades, and China and the Soviet Union needed a treaty to deter its ambitions. "One should keep Japan vulnerable from all sides . . . then she will keep quiet," he said. "[The] whole plan of our relations with China is based on this."

There was no ideology in this argument, no yearning to sponsor global revolution, and this must have been somewhat reassuring to Chiang. Moreover, Stalin assured him that the Soviets would turn over all of the territory they had seized in Manchuria to him and only to him when the Russian troops left, which, he promised, would happen within three months. Chiang, more realistic than Hurley, knew the risk of making a deal with Stalin, trading away chunks of Chinese sovereignty in exchange for promises that he knew perfectly well Stalin might break. At the final negotiating sessions between Stalin and Soong in Moscow, Stalin exploited Chiang's greatest fear when he hinted that if the Chinese didn't sign an agreement on his terms and sign it right away, the result might be massive Soviet aid to the Communists. Even with the new agreement, Moscow might well help the Communists by turning Manchuria over to them rather than to the central government, so Chiang was in the awkward position of yielding to avoid a consequence that might be imposed on him anyway. It was a gamble, but he felt that the deal with Stalin gave him his best chance of keeping the Russians neutral in the looming Chinese internal struggle.

On August 14, the day that Emperor Hirohito announced Japan's unconditional surrender, the new Sino-Soviet Treaty of Friendship and

One truckload of the 1.5 million Soviet troops who invaded Manchuria in the waning days of the war, being greeted by Chinese civilians in the city of Mukden, September 28, 1945.

Alliance was signed. It gave Stalin everything he wanted—control of Dalian, a naval base at Port Arthur, management of the Manchurian railways, and recognition of the independent status of Outer Mongolia; in exchange he promised exclusive recognition of Chiang's government, the transfer of Manchuria to Chiang's forces, and no help to the CCP, all promises he could violate with impunity if he chose to do so.

If Chiang was nervous about this, Hurley was joyful and unsuspecting, because for him "Russia has pledged her entire material and moral support to the Chungking movement, thus depriving the hostile Communist regime of Yenan of what might have been its strongest foreign ally." Hurley was not the only one infected by this optimism. "This kicked the props out from under the Chinese Communists," *Time* declared, "who without hope of future help from their Soviet comrades . . . might well be forced to surrender their separate army and administration and take their place as one of several political minorities in a united China." *The New York Times* reported a bit more cautiously but along the same lines, concluding that the deal with Moscow had "minimized, at least for the time being, the danger of a disastrous civil war in China."

The proof, as Hurley and others saw it, was that after refusing for weeks to resume the talks with Chiang, Mao in late August accepted an invitation from Chiang to go to Chungking for a sort of Chinese summit. Negotiations would resume, Hurley believed, because the Communists were weak, isolated, and without other options.

Years later, speaking of Stalin's demand that he go to Chungking to resume the talks under Hurley's auspices, Mao would talk bitterly of Stalin's "treachery"; he would call Stalin a "hypocritical foreign devil." He would also say that he had been "compelled to go because Stalin insisted," and this seems to have been true. Unlike the Soviet leader, Mao veered toward what Lenin had called left-adventurism, the impulse to take radical action, specifically attempting to seize full power before the situation was ripe for it. The Japanese war had enabled him to expand his armies into a large and powerful force by Chinese standards and to control the population in some eighteen "liberated areas," mostly in rural districts in the north, but some in the east and south as well. Now Mao felt ready to try to capture some of the country's major cities.

The very day after the huge Soviet armies crossed into Manchuria, Mao sent a telegram to the New Fourth Army, his main force in the east, ordering it to "concentrate main forces to occupy major cities and key strategic points." The Communists sent emissaries to Japanese commanders in Shanghai, who were waiting for a chance to surrender formally and then to be repatriated, and to some members of the Chinese puppet regime, hoping to enlist their cooperation in an insurrection there. The Kuomintang secret police noted this maneuvering and succeeded in assassinating two top officials of the puppet regime. Mao, undeterred and contrary to the advice of the senior underground Communist official in Shanghai, ordered the New Fourth Army, which held a ring of territory about ten miles from the city, to infiltrate three thousand troops into Shanghai to foment a pro-Communist uprising.

It was a bold plan, reminiscent in its way of the Communists' attempt to seize Shanghai in 1926 and 1927, when, under orthodox Soviet tutelage, they put their effort into organizing among the city's factory workers. Now, in the days after the Japanese surrender, the Communist "Red workers" seized control of more than ten factories, where they faced off with the pro-KMT "Yellow workers." The city's students were eager to go on strike. But on August 15, General MacArthur, the commander of American forces in Asia, issued Order Number One, which instructed the Japanese units in China to surrender only to the Nationalist authorities. Mao would have no authority to send his troops into Shanghai to take control there. At the same time, Chiang sent a message to General Okamura, authorizing him to use force to resist any attempt by the Communists to disarm him; the strongly anti-Communist Okamura would surely have resisted a CCP takeover in Shanghai. But it was the ever prudent Stalin who stopped Mao from his foolish plan, which, in Stalin's view, would have provoked an immediate civil war for which neither he nor the CCP was ready. On August 21, he sent two telegrams to Yenan telling Mao to desist, and, as always in such situations, Mao did.

Stalin also ordered Mao to go to Chungking, and Mao did that too, though, contrary to what Hurley believed, not out of a sense of weakness or abandonment by the Soviet Union. We've seen his confident speeches at the seventh CCP congress about Soviet help coming, even if that help couldn't be overt for the moment. Stalin's endorsement of the Sino-Soviet treaty raised some worries in Mao's mind, but fundamentally he was willing to see it as a tactical move, a piece of necessary deception.

At worst, Mao was frustrated by Stalin's caution. According to his Russian interpreter, Shi Zhe, he was "very distressed and even angry" about the order to go to Chungking, but he also understood its source in the Soviet leader's eagerness not to provoke the nuclear-armed Americans into active opposition to Soviet and Chinese Communist aims in China. A year later Mao argued in an interview with the left-wing journalist Anna Louise Strong that, unlike Stalin, he had never been worried about an atomic bomb attack on China, confident as he was in the ability of the ideologically awakened masses to defeat even a technologically superior foe. It was then, in 1946, that Mao began using the term "paper tiger" to refer to American strength, a term he would continue to use for decades.

But that was later. At the time of the Sino-Soviet treaty in 1945, Mao had plenty of reasons to feel things were going his way. For one thing, Stalin, as he usually did when he embarked on a policy that was not to Mao's liking, provided a back-channel assurance to the CCP that his move was in their long-term interest. Even as Stalin was cabling Mao with instructions to go to Chungking, he was telling Mao's official number two in the Chinese Communist movement, Liu Shaoqi, who was in Moscow with another senior Communist, Gao Gang, that the talks between Chiang and Mao were just a tactic. Meanwhile, he told them, as two scholars have written of this episode, that "the talks would buy time for the Chinese Communists to regroup and mobilize their armies for the coming battles."

In any case, for Mao the event of historic significance was not the Sino-Soviet Treaty of Friendship and Alliance but the Soviet invasion of Manchuria. Four days after the Soviet troops crossed the border into Chinese territory, he was writing, accurately, that the "political implication" of that move was "beyond any measurement"; it was more important than "the two bombs"—the ones dropped on Hiroshima and Nagasaki. If the atomic bombs were so powerful, Mao asked, why did the United States ask the Russians to come into the war against Japan? In fact, he continued, establishing a "fact" of Chinese historiography that has endured ever since, the belief held by many that the war was ended by the atomic bomb was false. It was a product of "bourgeois influence" coming "from bourgeois education, from bourgeois press and news agencies." The truth, as Mao saw it, was that the entry of the Soviet Red Army into the war led Japan to finally give up.

Mao felt that, if all went well, the massive entry of the Soviet army into the eastern front would have the same result as its entry into Poland, where Stalin had engineered a Communist takeover using methods that would be replicated, more or less, in China. John Davies agreed. "If the Red Army enters North China," he wrote, "it should not be surprising if those sympathetic to the U.S. were liquidated and American aid and cooperation effectively obstructed or eliminated." Wherever the Red Army has gone, he noted, "Russian political domination has followed." In Poland, Stalin had agreed at Yalta for the eventual holding of free elections; in the meantime, a provisional coalition government representing all major Polish political factions would be established. One such faction was the non-Communist government-in-exile, which, though based in London, contributed tens of thousands of troops to Allied military operations in Western Europe. The other main faction was the pro-Soviet Polish Committee of National Liberation, which Stalin had set up in Lublin, the first city in eastern Poland that Russian troops seized from the retreating Germans. As Soviet troops moved across the country, pushing the retreating Germans ahead of them, the Lublin group was allowed to take over the administration of the country and the non-Communist members of the coalition were pushed aside, ignored, or imprisoned. In March 1945, under the pretext of holding a meeting on Poland's political arrangements, the Soviets lured sixteen non-Communist Poles to Lublin, where they were arrested, brought to Moscow for trial, and sent to prison in Siberia. Stalin's clever and ruthless strategy resulted in the replacement of the Nazi dictatorship by a Polish puppet state subservient to Moscow that lasted for the next four and a half decades.

Poland was not China, one big difference being that Chiang Kaishek stayed in China for the whole war and never headed a government-in-exile. In addition, unlike Poland, China had never been an invasion route to Russia. Still, there were eerie similarities between the situations. The Chinese Communists were like the Lublin group, confident that Stalin would find ways for it to extend the areas it controlled. Chiang was akin to the non-Communist Poles, ostensibly recognized by the Russians but undermined by them at the same time. In Poland, Stalin captured territory, and turned it over to his Polish proxies; now he had 1.5 million troops in Manchuria, and the question was, would he find ways, despite his recognition of Chiang's government and his promise to turn the land he controlled over to China's central government, to give real power to the Communists?

Years later, after Stalin's death and the opening of the Sino-Soviet split, Mao was to denounce just about every aspect of Soviet policy, but in 1945, he approved of everything Stalin did, completely and without reservation, including the outcome in Poland. To him, the non-Communist Polish government-in-exile was the "reactionary" representative of "Old Poland," the Poland of landlords and capitalists, while the pro-Moscow Lublin group responded to the "unanimous demand of the Polish people"; it marked "an upsurge of the new democratic movement in liberated Eastern Europe."

That word "liberated" is noteworthy. In the West, the imposition of puppet regimes in Eastern Europe without elections or any other procedure for popular consent was properly seen as an act of political domination, but for Mao it was a thrilling step toward revolutionary fulfillment. His own eventual rise to power in China would be another such step, and he fully expected the Soviets to support him in making it.

On August 27, Hurley, bringing with him two cases of Scotch, flew in an American plane from Chungking to Yenan, and the next day he escorted Mao on the Communist leader's first-ever airplane ride to the temporary capital of his sworn enemy. Observers on the scene at the Yenan airport said that Mao looked nervous, like a man "going to his own execution," *Time* reported. Just before he boarded Hurley's plane, he did something that he had never done before and that he would never do again, which was to kiss his wife, Jiang Qing, in public. Mao was worried that he would be kidnapped in Chungking or perhaps even murdered, so perhaps the gesture was meant as a sort of good-bye, just in case. But Hurley had guaranteed his safety, as had Stalin, and so he was off, the bandit in the hills going to meet the sheriff who had been trying unsuccessfully to kill or capture him for years. Before they took off, Hurley leaned out of the door of the plane and produced what one Chinese Communist on the scene described as a "weird, loud scream as if a predator has gotten its prey"—the Choctaw war whoop.

The press was on the scene at the airport in Chungking when the party arrived. Someone asked Mao what he thought of the airplane and he replied, "Very efficient." While Hurley didn't let loose another Choctaw whoop, he shouted out what sounded to some observers on the scene like "Olive oil! Olive oil!" as he and Mao drove off in the embassy's black Cadillac. There was a welcoming banquet that night at which Chiang raised a glass of rice wine and said he hoped "we can have the cordial atmosphere of 1924." The reference was to the short-lived period of harmony of the first United Front when Mao was an organizer for the Kuomintang and Zhou Enlai was Chiang's political commissar at the Whampoa Military Academy. There was a mood of optimism in the air. American journalists had reported on the shift in Communist propaganda since the Sino-Soviet treaty was signed—the CCP's newspapers were calling Chiang "president" rather than the leader of the "reactionary clique." The Central News Agency, the official source of

Zhou Enlai and Mao Zedong, accompanied by American ambassador Patrick J. Hurley, arriving in Chungking in August 1945 for talks with the Nationalists.

information of the national government, for its part cited "well-informed observers" to the effect that a "comprehensive settlement" between the two parties was "inevitable."

Both leaders played the roles assigned to them, Chiang the perfect host, Mao the respectful guest, referring to Chiang as "President Chiang Kai-shek" and pledging his support. At a banquet early on in his stay, he raised a glass of mao-tai and proclaimed "ten thousand years to President Chiang." It was the toast normally given to China's emperors, and it would be the slogan joyfully shouted to Mao once he had become the ruler of all of mainland China.

Chiang and Mao held nine private meetings. They walked side by side in Chiang's private garden in Chungking. The two men wore similar clothing, the high-collared tunic popularized years earlier by Sun Yat-sen; Chiang's was crisp and sleek, Mao's had a more homespun quality to it. Contrary to the usual pattern in China, there were no leaks on their talks until, after five weeks or so, *Ta Gong Bao* published a scoop announcing that they had been successful. The very next day, Mao, "smiling and confident," according to the *Time* reporter present, held a press conference at which he said, "I am confident of the outcome of the negotiations. . . . The Chinese Communist Party will persist in a policy of avoiding civil war." The Soviets also fanned the embers of hope, Radio Moscow broadcasting joyfully at the end of September that the two sides in China had agreed that "a complete central unified government will be created for the whole of China." The broadcast concluded, "Unity in China has been established." Meanwhile, in a gesture that the Hurleys of the world greeted with great satisfaction, the

Soviet commander in Manchuria, Rodion Malinovsky, was reported to have refused to allow the Communists' Eighth Route Army to occupy the cities of northeast China. Theodore White reported in *Time*, in an article headlined "Bright with Hope," that the Soviet Union had given the "back of its hand" to the Chinese Communists in Manchuria, surely a sign that Stalin was living up to his treaty commitments to Chiang.

Encouraging this confidently optimistic mood, Chiang and the Kuomintang announced a series of measures that seemed to fulfill the three demands that Zhou Enlai had made earlier in the year and that at the time, because they were new demands, were deemed a serious obstacle to a settlement. The government pledged to release political prisoners, to end censorship and ensure the rights of free speech and assembly, and to curb the activities of the secret police. All political parties would be legalized as well. The central issue in the talks was the degree of separate control the CCP would be allowed in the provinces where it already had base areas. The Communist delegation, led by Zhou Enlai, wanted forty-eight divisions and five provinces in the north to be controlled by the CCP. Chiang rejected that as a de facto division of the country, but, abandoning his insistence on what he called "one country, one army," he did consent to the Communists' keeping command of twelve divisions, which would have been something over one hundred thousand men.

On September 18, after four weeks of talks, Mao seized the occasion of a cordial tea party to announce, "We must stop [the] civil war and all parties must unite under the leadership of Chairman Chiang to build modern China." On his last night in Chungking, Chiang went to Mao's headquarters and the two men talked until late in the evening. Chiang later asked himself in his diary whether his appeal for peace had "touched the Chairman's heart." The next morning was the anniversary of the fall of the Qing dynasty in 1911. In all China's big cities, huge numbers of people came into the streets to celebrate the country's national day, the first since the defeat of Japan. Chiang and Mao had breakfast together while their aides drafted a vague agreement. The two sides promised to establish a political democracy, to convene a national political consultative conference that would establish the rules for elections to a new national assembly, and to unite their armed forces under Chiang's command.

Hurley took some pride in urging the two sides to keep the conversation going but offering no "details" about a solution, making no specific proposals; he has been justly criticized for this by later historians. A specific American plan is exactly what was needed, a plan that would have recognized the balance of forces in China as they were, followed by maximum, relentless American pressure on both sides to accept reality, something along the lines of Zhou's forty-eight divisions in control of eight northern provinces, while the rest of China remained in the hands of Chiang and the KMT. This would have been a de facto division of the country, though ideally elections for a constituent assembly would have followed, the beginnings of democracy, perhaps avoiding civil war.

It was not to happen, of course, and it does not seem likely, even if Hurley had managed to press the two sides for a clearer, detailed division of power and territory, that it could have happened. Chiang is likely to have been too fearful that a coalition government would lead to his ejection from power. And as for Mao, as soon as he got back to Yenan, he assured his closest colleagues that the deal that was struck in Chungking was "only words on paper" that were "not equivalent to reality." His visit to Chungking had served its purpose. He mollified the Americans, whom he was anxious to keep on the sidelines. He conveyed the image of a reasonable man seeking peace.

But what he was really illustrating was a strategy summed up in a four-word phrase attributed to Zhou Enlai: *da da tan tan*, or "fight fight talk talk." The purpose of negotiations in his eyes was not to reach a compromise agreement, but to buy time, to deter aggressive action by your enemy even as you exploit opportunities to enhance your power as well as your reputation as a peacemaker. Then, when conditions are ripe, you abandon negotiations, blaming your adversary for their breakdown, and go all out for military victory. The real battle in China was not going to be fought around a conference table in Chungking. It would be waged in the cities and countryside of Manchuria, where the Soviets were now in control. What counted was what in a later conflict in another place came to be called "facts on the ground," and there Mao set out aggressively to ensure that the facts favored him.

CHAPTER FOURTEEN

Facts on the Ground

On August 16, one day after the formal Japanese surrender, a note from Communist headquarters in Yenan arrived at the embassies of the United States, Great Britain, and the Soviet Union in Chungking. It started out by listing the wartime achievements of the Chinese Communists. The Communist armies, it said, had recovered "vast lost areas abandoned by the Kuomintang Government, with more than 100 million people." This army now consisted of one million regular troops and 2,200,000 members of local militias in nineteen "liberated areas." The note made the precise numerical assertion that 69 percent of the Japanese troops invading China (not including Manchuria) and 95 percent of the troops of the pro-Japanese Chinese puppet government "were opposed and encircled by our forces" during the recently concluded war, all of this while the Kuomintang "adopted a policy of watching with folded arms and waiting for victory."

These achievements, the note continued, getting to its main point, had earned for the Communists the authority "to accept the surrender of the Japanese and puppet armies surrounded by them, to take over their arms, material and resources." It was signed by Zhu De, who identified himself as commander in chief, anti-Japanese Forces in the Liberated Areas. "Our troops," a Yenan radio broadcast of the same time said, making this same argument in less diplomatic terms, "have the right to enter and occupy any city, town or communication center occupied by the enemy or the puppets . . . . Those who oppose or obstruct such actions will be treated as traitors."

Zhu De's message signaled a new stage in the relationship between the Chinese Communist movement and the United States. Ostensibly about a single issue, the taking of the Japanese surrender, it had enor-

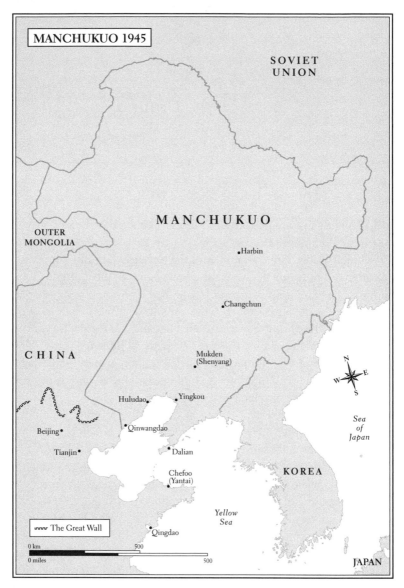

MANCHUKUO 1945

SOVIET UNION

MANCHUKUO

OUTER MONGOLIA

•Harbin

•Changchun

CHINA

Mukden (Shenyang)

Huludao•   •Yingkou

Beijing•   •Qinwangdao

Tianjin•   •Dalian

Chefoo (Yantai)

Sea of Japan

KOREA

ᨅᨃ The Great Wall

Yellow Sea

•Qingdao

0 km   500

0 miles   500

JAPAN

mous implications because the party that took the surrender of the Japanese troops got their weapons and the territory they controlled, both of which translated into strength in the looming civil conflict in China.

The subtext of Zhu's message made clear the Communists' view of themselves, which they had now chosen to broadcast. They were not simply an armed party, as Hurley liked to call them. They were a legitimate alternative government of China, *the* government of about one-quarter of the country's total population, even if the countries to which they made this claim, including the Soviet Union, were treaty-bound to support only the central government, still temporarily ensconced in Chungking, as the sole government of China. The Communists had earned their authority by fighting harder and more bravely than the recognized government, which had, in the Communist view, abdicated, fled, or stood by as thousands of villages fell to the hated invader.

Zhu De's note threw down a challenge to the outside powers, especially the United States, because it was saying that anyone whose presence in China impeded the Communists in their effort to expand their power would be deemed an enemy. Moreover, the Communists were doing a lot more than sending diplomatic notes to foreign emissaries, more than stating theoretical rights to participate in the Japanese surrender. In the hours after the Japanese surrender, and even before, they were on the move, sending their lightly armed, heavily indoctrinated guerrillas into areas that were going to be contested by them and the central government, getting their boots on the ground, as the common later phrase for introducing ground forces into an area would have it. The Nationalists, for their part, were trying to do the same thing, though the Communists had a clear geographical advantage. In other words, the news of Hirohito's surrender was still ringing in the ears of a joyful China while the country's next brutal conflict was starting.

Quick decisions had to be made by a United States most of whose soldiers, diplomats, and spies were caught entirely by surprise by the atom bomb and the war's quick ending. First, how to respond to Zhu De's demand? One option, of course, was to acknowledge the facts as Zhu saw them and to remain neutral in the postwar struggle for territory. This was essentially what the professional China hands, John Davies and the others, had recommended in the fall and winter of 1944. They accepted that such a policy would quickly lead to the division of China into two zones, a Communist one north of the Yellow River, including Manchuria, and a KMT zone south of it. Such a course, Davies and his like-minded colleagues believed, would also keep the United States from backing the eventual loser in the civil war. It might also, in their view, enable the Chinese Communists to avoid falling into the Soviet orbit. As Davies put it in a memo of June 1945: "It is debatable whether Moscow could have counted on Yenan's unquestioning obedience had the American government last autumn and winter (while the Soviet Union was still unprepared to act in Asia) accepted the fact of a divided China and realistically and vigorously sought to develop the nationalistic tendencies of Communist China."

Hurley, of course, didn't agree. Shown Zhu De's letter, he fired off a cable to Washington warning that the cost of acceding to Zhu's demand would be an immediate civil war in China, because the Communists would quickly abandon the talks with Chiang and the two sides would have no choice but to fight. Hurley continued to believe in the assurances he'd gotten from Stalin and Molotov in Moscow in April, to the effect that the Soviets supported American policy in China and did not deem the Chinese Communists to be real Communists. He was convinced that the Soviets had sold out the Chinese Communists, who, weak and isolated, had no choice but to make a deal with the KMT, which he would use his good offices to bring about. He put his trust in the Sino-Soviet Treaty of Friendship and Cooperation, to which Soong and Stalin had affixed their signatures the day before Zhu's letter arrived in Chungking. The whole point of that treaty, as Hurley understood it, was for China to give away some of its sovereignty in Manchuria in exchange for a Soviet pledge, as the treaty clearly specified, "to render to China moral support and aid in military supplies and other material resources, such support and aid to be entirely given to the National Government as the central government of China." That document, Hurley assured Washington, "has demonstrated conclusively that the Soviet Government supports the National Government of China, and also that the two governments are in agreement regarding Manchuria"—meaning that the Soviets would expedite the transfer of the three northeastern provinces to central government control in speedy fashion.

A reply was dutifully sent to Zhu. It rejected the right he claimed to take the Japanese surrender, reminded him of the famous agreements, and, in the spirit of goodwill, asked him and the Communists for their cooperation. The Americans had refused to arm the Communists during the war; now they were excluding the Communists from the division of spoils.

While Hurley was talking abstract principle and practicing wishful thinking, Zhu was stating reality. The Communists effectively controlled large sections of North China, the fruit of their wartime efforts to create "liberated areas" behind enemy lines. They had set up parallel governments in them and created peasant organizations. They also had those million or so men under arms, plus even larger militia organizations, and many of these troops were installed in areas ostensibly controlled by the Japanese and the Chinese puppet regime—as those American fliers found out when they were led to safety by the *Balus*, the Eighth Route Army men.

In some respects Zhu did exaggerate—as in those precise percentages of Japanese and puppet troops "surrounded," and in his contention that the Communists had been fighting while the KMT folded its arms. The Communists were extremely successful in propagating the notion that they had struggled bitterly, bravely, and continuously against the invader, but their million-man army had engaged in only small-scale hit-and-run attacks and not a single major military operation since the Hundred Regiments Offensive of 1940. Like the KMT, they had preserved their forces for the postwar showdown with the rival party. "The Eighth Route Army," Vladimirov, the TASS correspondent, noted contemptuously, limits itself "to sluggish defensive fighting of local importance. Whenever fighting starts on the enemy's initiative, the Eighth Route Army rolls back to the mountains avoiding clashes." After a fellow TASS correspondent visited one of the liberated areas behind enemy lines, he reported back to Vladimirov: "Like everywhere in the Special Area, meetings are the only form of work carried on in the army units. In the summer this is supplemented to some extent with the laying in of farm produce."

But the Communists were in place in strategic areas, especially Shaanxi, Hebei, and Shandong provinces, at a time when American intelligence estimated the central government's military presence in those places to be negligible. This was a crucial fact. For a time, the only force available to prevent the Communists from taking over in those areas was the very Japanese army that was supposed to surrender. That is why Chiang sent out his near-desperate directive to Japan to surrender only to the central government and, meanwhile, to keep the peace in the areas they occupied. The Japanese did this, becoming allies of the government they had been trying to annihilate for eight years. For weeks, the Japanese fought off Communist attempts to disarm them, and they patrolled the all-important rail lines of North China. While this use of the Japanese divisions was a necessary expedient, it was also a sign of weakness on the part of the central government, an indication of its lack of preparedness to take control of the territory the international agreements assigned to it.

The facts on the ground included an almost absurd anomaly: that the group authorized to take the Japanese surrender had no capacity to do so, while the group that had the capacity was denied the authority. This problem could presumably be overcome by moving government troops into position. But there was no overcoming what was the most portentous fact on the ground in the weeks and months after the end of the war in the Pacific: the presence of those 1.5 million seasoned Soviet troops in Manchuria, which bordered the areas where the Chinese Communists were strongest. It is difficult to overstate the importance of this fact, though Hurley seems almost completely to have ignored it.

The Soviet occupation of the vast territory of Manchuria marked a turning point in Asia. It made impossible the arrangement that the United States desired in postwar Asia by which China, the largest country and potentially the wealthiest and the most powerful, would be united under a central government that would be both democratic and friendly to the United States. The Russian troops had taken up their positions on Chinese territory just as the alliance of convenience of World War II was breaking up and the world was entering the Cold War stage, in which Washington and Moscow would confront each other throughout the world in an existential contest for global power.

Even before the end of the war in Asia, the Soviet goal of dominating Eastern Europe was becoming crystal clear to the Truman administration, which made some fleeting and belated efforts to forestall a similar effort in Asia. In July, during the conference at Potsdam among Stalin, Truman, and Clement Attlee (who replaced Churchill as British prime minster during the meeting), the American secretary of state, James Byrnes, was moving away from the idea that a Soviet invasion of Manchuria would be necessary for a quick end to the war against Japan. Byrnes, a close aide recalled, wanted to "outmaneuver Stalin on China." The atomic bomb was a secret, but an ultimatum was issued to Japan at Potsdam to surrender or face annihilation, and Byrnes hoped that an early Japanese surrender would preempt the agreement made at Yalta by which the Soviets would send their divisions into China.

Japan ignored the ultimatum, however, and in any case Byrnes was overruled by Truman, the only president since Teddy Roosevelt who had actually been in combat during a war and whose priority, like Roosevelt's at Yalta half a year earlier, was to save the lives of American soldiers. "I've gotten what I came for—Stalin goes to war August 15 with no strings on it," he wrote to his wife from Potsdam on July 18. "I'll say that we'll end the war a year sooner now, and think of the kids who won't be killed!"

And now the Soviets were in Manchuria, their armies commanded by a tough Bolshevik veteran, Rodion Malinovsky, a man about whom John Melby, the Soviet expert at the American embassy in Chungking, commented, "there was not a drop of gentleness or mercy." And once the Soviets were installed in Manchuria, all the other arguments and possibilities of past years and months—and especially whether a smarter policy by the United States might earlier have encouraged Chinese Communist independence of Moscow—faded into insignificance. With the end of the war, the situation was drastically and irretrievably different, and the biggest difference was that the Chinese Communists now sensed that victory for them was in view. The Soviet invasion meant that the Communists were dominant in North China and there was virtually nothing that could be done, short of a massive effort by the United States on a scale of the recently concluded war, to dislodge them.

This was the underlying reason American relations with the Chinese Communists steadily soured with the end of the war even as American emissaries tried to broker a peace agreement between them and the Nationalists. Something opposite to Hurley's hope and expectation occurred. So far from feeling abandoned by the Sino-Soviet treaty, the Chinese Communists felt emboldened by the Soviet occupation of China's three northeastern provinces. Rather than needing the United States more than ever, the Chinese Communists needed it less. They didn't want open conflict with the United States, but they were ready now aggressively to confront it if and when they found the Americans acting against their interests. A few months before, Mao had told John Service, "There is no such thing as America not intervening in China. You are here, as China's greatest ally. The fact of your presence is tremendous." Now, Mao understood that American intervention would inevitably help his opponents in his struggle with them for control of China, and therefore the Communists just as inevitably had to see the United States as an obstacle to its aims.

On August 12, three days after the Nagasaki bomb but three days before Hirohito's surrender announcement, Zhu De was already ordering four armed groups to move to Manchuria and to cooperate with the Russian troops already there. A few days later, on the eve of his trip to Chungking, Mao dispatched nine regiments to the northeast and told Communist cadres who had come from Manchuria years before to return home. Then, while Mao strolled with Chiang Kai-shek in the presidential garden in Chungking, recognizing his authority, he continued to maneuver to expand the CCP's power into Manchuria, the eventual goal of which was to oust Chiang from power. Getting hold of Japanese arms was, as always, the key immediate goal for the poorly armed Communists. In January, Zhu De had asked for $20 million in American money to buy arms from puppet troops. Now it was the Soviet Union that would be the main supplier, even though for the Soviet Union to provide arms to the CCP was a blatant violation of the Sino-Soviet treaty. Very quickly, the Soviets took 925 airplanes, 360 tanks, 2,600 cannon, and 8,900 machine guns from the Japanese along with huge quantities of smaller weapons. How much of this weaponry ended up in Communist hands is not clear, though much of it clearly did.

Despite this provision of captured arms, it would have been hard for the Chinese Communists to know exactly what help they would get from the Soviets, or how Moscow would balance its wish to help them with its obligation under the Sino-Soviet treaty not to help them at all. But the Communists understood that ultimately they and the Soviets were on the same team and shared the same purpose. "They are Red Army; we are Red Army too," Liu Shaoqi, number two in the Communist hierarchy and now back in Chungking during Mao's absence, assured his colleagues. "They are Communists; so are we."

On the day after Mao's arrival in Chungking for his talks with Chiang, the CCP in Yenan published an order governing the Eighth Route Army troops it had sent to Manchuria. The Chinese forces should refer to themselves not as the Eighth Route Army but as the Northeast Volunteer Army. They should keep a low profile, stick to minor roads, enter only villages and cities where there were no Red Army units, and avoid publishing newspaper accounts of their movements. Striking in these orders is Yenan's confidence that they were going to get help from the Russians, even if that help had to be kept secret. "The Soviet Union doesn't interfere with Chinese internal politics," the order declared. "It takes an indulgent attitude toward our activity in the Northeast as long as we don't cause diplomatic difficulties." The Chinese historian Yang Kuisong, a researcher at the Chinese Academy of Social Sciences, puts the matter this way: "The Soviets not only gave secret help to establish the revolutionary center in Dongbei [the Northeast] but also provided weapons and ammunition that was enough to arm a hundred thousand guerrilla soldiers, enabling them to completely defeat the KMT in much less time than was expected."

Certainly, relations between the ragged Chinese Communist soldiers and the Red Army veterans quickly warmed up after the Soviets kept CCP troops out of Mukden. In their first meetings with the Eighth Route Army, Yang has written, the Soviets took them to be bandits, so poorly armed and clothed were they, which prompted Yenan to order its units to pay attention to how they dressed. But this early caution soon gave way to close and cordial contact.

On September 9, while he was negotiating with Hurley and Chiang, Mao received a report from Zeng Kelin, the commander of the Eighth Route Army detachments that had gone to Manchuria, describing the cordial welcome he received from the commander of the Russian troops outside the port of Shanhaiguan, where Zeng had arrived ten days earlier. The two of them held what a Chinese historian has called "a grand city-entering celebration," after which the Soviets allowed Zeng, his troops, and his civilian cadres to go on to the port of Jinzhou and then to Mukden itself, taking over the territories on the route. This was around the time that Theodore White was reporting that the Soviets had given "the back of their hand" to the Eighth Route Army, but according to Zeng, he was guest of honor at a festive banquet held for him at the Dahe Hotel in Mukden. "They affectionately called us 'comrades,'" Zeng later wrote of his Soviet hosts.

They gave high praise to the contribution our army had made in the victorious War of Resistance, but, because of the relations between the Soviet Government and the Nationalist Government, they asked us not to engage in activities under the name of *Balujun* [Eighth Route Army], so, after careful study, we decided to rename our troops the Autonomous Army of the People of the Northeast. . . . One after the other, we took over the Shenyang Arsenal, warehouses, military clothing factories, water and electricity companies, post offices, banks, and radio stations. We also utilized the radio station to report the important news that our army had advanced into Dongbei, vigorously promoted the policies of our party, repeatedly played *Sanda jilu, Baxiang zhui* ["Three Main Rules of Discipline" and "Eight Points for Attention"] and other revolutionary songs. We also sent troops to other cities and towns.

In the middle of September, Malinovsky, who had set up headquarters in Changchun, the main city of Jilin province northeast of Mukden, sent an emissary to Yenan to sort things out with the Chinese Communists. This was a big event in Yenan. The Communists told the members of the Dixie Mission to stay away from the airfield, which the next morning was ringed with Communist security troops armed with rifles and fixed bayonets. At noon, the Soviet emissary's plane arrived from Mukden. It disgorged a small group of uniformed Soviet military personnel who were quickly escorted to the CCP's headquarters. Malinovsky's emissary made a public statement to the effect that CCP troops would have to withdraw from Manchuria. The members of the Dixie Mission would presumably get wind of that statement, and that was probably its purpose, though the head of the mission, Colonel Ivan D. Yeaton, says nothing about it in his memoirs. In any case, the Soviet emissary's public speech was followed that night by a private meeting with the Communist leaders during which he spelled out what would be the real Soviet policy. Large Manchurian cities like Mukden, Changchun, and Harbin would be turned over to the central government, and the CCP would have to withdraw from those cities, but the Soviet Red Army would support Communist troops elsewhere, as long as these troops were in the guise of local armed forces.

The Communists were delighted with this arrangement. It was the opportunity they had been hoping for. It meant in practice that, while they would be kept out of a few big cities, they would be free to send their forces anywhere else. Mao had announced, after he'd given up his adventurist plans to seize Shanghai and other big cities, that Communist strategy would be to occupy the countryside and mobilize the people there. This would not result in the overthrow of Chiang for the time being, but, as he put it, "We want to bore our way in and give Chiang Kai-shek's face a good washing, but we don't want to cut off his head."

After their session with the Soviet colonel, the Politburo members held a late-night meeting. They proposed a program summed up in the slogan "expand to the north and defend toward the south," which in practice meant dispatching twenty-five thousand cadres and two hundred thousand troops to the north. Mao signaled his approval from Chungking, and within months the number of Chinese Communist troops in the northeast had reached four hundred thousand, under the command of Lin Biao. Among the subterfuges used by the Soviets, always eager to keep up the appearance of adherence to the Sino-Soviet treaty, was formally to prohibit armed Eighth Routers from passing through their lines, but to permit them to go as civilians. These "civilians" would then be given Japanese weapons, which were superior to the ones they were not allowed to bring into Manchuria with them.

"There is a possibility that they armed the people," a Communist spokesman in Chungking admitted to American journalists, meaning the civilian "volunteers" who had been allowed to cross the Soviet lines. "They may have gotten some arms from the Japanese." In such a way were Communist soldiers able to take up positions behind the Manchurian ports of Huludao and Yingkou. Many of these troops marched overland across Inner Mongolia from the Communist base areas in the northwest, but there were also tens of thousands of Eighth Routers in the eastern province of Shandong, and these needed to be sent by boat to Manchuria.

In this connection, while Mao was still in Chungking, Lu Yi, a CCP army leader, told him that Chinese Communist troops had arrived in Dalian from Chefoo, which was taken over by the Eighth Route Army on August 23. There, Lu said, the Chinese were in contact with the Soviets, who told them that they would not interfere with their activities in villages and that they would be able to organize unarmed mass organizations in the large cities.

The United States also swung into action. The OSS, which, like everybody else, was surprised by the sudden end of the war, switched its mission from gathering intelligence about the Japanese occupiers to gathering intelligence about the postwar situation. "Although we have been caught with our pants down, we will do our best to pull them up in time," Colonel Richard Heppner, the OSS chief in China, wrote to Wild Bill Donovan, who was on his way back to the United States after a trip to China only a few days earlier. Since the war ended in Europe, OSS had expanded its operations in China and now had nearly two thousand agents in the country. By August 12, the same day that Zhu

De's note arrived at the American embassy in Chungking, Heppner had assembled several teams to be dropped into territories all over China. The Magpie Team went to Beijing; the Duck Team to Shandong; Sparrow to Shanghai; Flamingo to Hainan Island; and Cardinal to Mukden, the largest city in Manchuria. Other teams went elsewhere in Asia—Quail to Hanoi, Raven to Vientiane, Eagle to Korea.

The teams arrived in place within the next week. In Beijing, Magpie quickly discovered a large POW camp. So did Duck, in the central Shandong city of Weixian. Cardinal parachuted to a place on the outskirts of Mukden on August 16, sent there urgently to arrive before the Soviets did and to collect intelligence on them once they were there. When the Soviets did arrive, the Americans immediately sensed a sort of petty harassment and unfriendliness directed toward them by the Soviet military that foreshadowed the two countries' future conflict of interest in Manchuria. Cardinal quickly learned of a nearby POW camp housing 1,321 Americans and several hundred others. The team's efforts to get there and liberate it were stalled by the Soviets. "Russians very non-cooperative," a member of the Cardinal Team, Major R. H. Helm, wrote in a letter to Heppner on August 25. "They delayed us until they could send a detachment to our camp to 'liberate' them and accept the credit. Took four days to arrange for us to go to camp. Not the consideration and cooperation we would give a similar group if the situation were reversed."

Once the OSS team did get to the camp, it began sending back reports on what it learned from the newly liberated GIs, especially about the deaths of thousands of American troops at the hands of the Japanese. Lieutenant Ray Harrelson, of Crossville, Alabama, the pilot of an observation plane who was captured on April 2, 1942, in the Philippines, said that of 398 pilots who boarded a Japanese ship in Manila for transport to Manchuria, 13 survived the journey. Cardinal estimated that of 1,600 POWs evacuated from the Philippines on a forty-five-day trip via Taiwan and Japan, 1,300 died of malnutrition and lack of medical treatment.

The repatriation of these prisoners was the ostensible reason for Cardinal's presence in Mukden, but it quickly established covert operations there, keeping an eye on the Russians and the Chinese both and reporting on their activities. This included the arrival, "suddenly and unannounced," of the first contingents of Chinese Communist troops on September 7. Former Chinese collaborators, also caught by the sudden end of the war, desperately tried to conceal their identities by creating a police department and so-called peace preservation committees to maintain order in Mukden, sewing KMT insignia onto their old puppet uniforms. Cardinal observed the Eighth Routers ferreting out these people and arresting them. The Communists quickly removed or defaced the KMT flags that had been posted on buildings all over the city. Red flags proliferated, some people waving them, the OSS team concluded, "for protection against Eighth Army persecution." Among the popular street slogans were "Down with Chiang Kai-shek" and "Manchuria for the Communists."

Meanwhile, American tensions with the Russians did not abate. On August 29, the Americans reported that the Russians had informed them that there was insufficient gas to refuel American planes so that "all planes coming to Mukden must have sufficient gasoline for return trip . . . . Do not plan on Russian cooperation in any respect." There were robberies of Americans at tommy-gun point. There was "a stabbing of a B-24 tire, drunken abuse of 'Americanskis,' flagrant insults to American flags, etc." Captain Robert Hilsman Jr. and three other Americans were robbed of their watches, sidearms, and money by a Russian private who also, according to Hilsman, "insulted President Truman and Americans in a vile manner." The Americans went to the Russian headquarters, where they were able to recover their sidearms and one watch. "The Russian General assured us the private would be punished; however, the next day the private was put on guard at the intersection outside our hotel, from which point of vantage he sneered and chuckled at us each time we passed. I believe this was a planned insult."

"Americans are very unpopular in Mukden with the Russians," Cardinal reported on September 13, "probably because the Russians do not desire American observation of their actions which are as follows: prior to their departure date of November 1, they are proceeding with a policy of scientific looting. Every bit of machinery is being removed and all stocks of merchandise from stores and warehouses. Mukden will be an empty city when they get through."

Eventually, the Soviets, no fools about the intelligence-gathering purposes of Cardinal, ordered the team out of Mukden. By mid-October it was gone, but not before it clearly perceived what was at stake. "The Communist Chinese Eighth Route Army . . . has categorically stated that it intends to occupy this section of Manchuria," read the team's report. "This raises the question: can the Central Government move into the Mukden area without a fight?"

Chiang was well aware of the Communists' quick move to expand their forces wherever they could, and his response was to ask Wedemeyer for help transporting government troops by air and ship to the north and east. The Americans agreed to do this, and in their doing so the lines of the present and future conflict in China were drawn. The Soviet Union was giving clandestine help to the Communists; the United States was giving open help to the central government, though under somewhat false pretenses. The ostensible reason for the airlift was to enable the government to receive the surrender of Japanese troops, which was an important task. There were still more than a million of them in North China, many doing temporary guard duty, and taking their weapons, replacing them with government troops, and sending them home was the big unfinished item of World War II.

Therefore, in response to Chiang's request, the Joint Chiefs in Washington instructed Wedemeyer to help China repatriate the Japanese and to recover some of its lost territory, though at the same time, American forces, the order made clear, were "to avoid participation in any fratricidal conflict in China." To army officers in China, this requirement seemed both naïve and impossible to carry out. As Wedemeyer pointed out in a series of increasingly irritated and pointed cables, moving government troops into areas where the Communists were already present was participation in China's fratricidal conflict. Certainly the Communists treated it as such. After August 15, denunciations of the American action became a staple of Yenan's newspapers and radio broadcasts, commonly described as "support for Chinese reactionaries in their efforts to promote civil war."

The Americans also decided that it would be necessary to send American marines to China, specifically fifty thousand members of the Third Amphibious Corps (IIIAC), a task force that had fought some of the bloodiest battles of the Pacific war and that when the war ended had been training in Guam to participate in the expected invasion of Japan. These men would ensure against disorder and help with the immense task of repatriating Japanese soldiers and civilians.

After Zhu's letter to the embassy in Chungking, the Communists made one more effort to dissuade the United States from helping the national

Army general Rodion Malinovsky, the commander of Soviet forces in Manchuria, September 1944. He had "not a drop of gentleness or mercy," said one American diplomat.

government in North China. In the third week of September, Brigadier General William A. Worton, chief of staff to the IIIAC commander, flew from Guam to China to make preparations for the arrival of the marines at the end of the month. Worton had twelve years of experience in Asia before the outbreak of the war, most of it in North China. He spoke the language and knew the country. He flew to Shanghai, where he met Hurley, then went on to Tianjin to talk with the Japanese, who were exceedingly cooperative, about the marines' takeover of the local garrisons. Then he went to Beijing to arrange for the billeting there of the expected marine detachments.

At the end of his Beijing visit, Worton received a message that "people opposed to Chiang Kai-shek," as he put it in a later interview, wanted to meet him. That night, Zhou Enlai turned up at the American's headquarters and wasted no time in issuing a blunt warning: The Communists "would fight to prevent the Marines from moving into Peiping." What Worton called a "stormy" hour-long meeting ensued, during which Worton was equally blunt, telling Zhou that the marines would be coming to Beijing, using both the roads and the rail lines, and that these marines would be "quite capable of driving straight on through any force that the Communists mustered in its path." A few months before, Mao had been practically pleading with the United States to land troops on the China coast. Now, with the war over, the situation had drastically changed and American forces were no longer welcome.

But welcome or not, in the middle of the morning of September 30, six weeks after the Japanese surrender and while Mao, Chiang, and Hurley were locked into their talks in Chungking, a convoy of nearly twenty-five thousand men belonging to the IIIAC appeared at the mouth of the Hai River, the opening to the port of Danggu, which served the big northern Chinese city of Tianjin. For most local people it was a welcome sight. A flotilla of Chinese sampans emerged from the estuary, and the marines lined their landing craft railings, exchanging mutually unintelligible greetings with the Chinese boatmen and buying cheap trinkets as souvenirs.

At 10:30 that morning, the commanding officer of the First Division of the Seventh Marines, Brigadier General Louis R. Jones, led a procession of landing craft over the sandbar at the mouth of the Hai and upriver to the port to arrange for the troops to disembark. Crowds of Chinese stood on the entire fifteen-mile-long route from the estuary to the port as Jones's boats went by. The next day, the marine Seventh Division went by railroad to Tianjin, where the crowds of people, many of them waving paper American flags, were so thick that the marine trucks had to force their way through them on the way to their billets in the former International Settlement.

Within days, the marines had spread out, a battalion sailing north to the port of Qinwangdao just south of the Manchurian border, where they found some troops of the now-defunct puppet regime exchanging fire with Communist guerrillas. Qinwangdao was not only the historical coastal gateway to Manchuria but also the terminus for the freight cars of coal from the mines of inland Hebei province. When the American commander, Lieutenant Colonel John J. Gormley, replaced the puppet troops with a perimeter defense of marines, the Communists ceased firing as a signal of their willingness to cooperate.

This was to be a short-lived truce. Within a month, the Communists began an ongoing campaign of sniping, harassment, polite negotiation, and not-so-polite intimidation in an effort to prevent the Americans from enabling the central government to build up its forces.

Simultaneous with the marine landings, Wedemeyer began the airlift of Nationalist troops from their bases, mostly in southwest China, to the eastern and northern parts of the country. It was a massive operation. Writing to Dwight Eisenhower, who was now chief of staff, having replaced the venerable George Marshall, Wedemeyer called it nothing less than "the largest troop movement by air in the world's history." For two months, China buzzed and rumbled with the sound of giant two-engine C-47 transport planes. Most of them flew over the Hump from India, picked up their cargo of troops, flew them to their new posts, and then returned over the Himalayas to India. These planes brought 35,000 men from Liuzhou to Shanghai, a distance of 900 miles; they flew 40,000 Chinese veterans of the Burma campaign the 800 miles from Zhijiang to Nanjing; thousands of other troops were dropped into Beijing and the vicinity.

Meanwhile, the marines took over Qingdao, the former German colony, a "fragment of Westphalia." General Jones commanded a Beijing Group, which took up residence in the old Legation Quarter, the district of stately foreign embassies, apartments, clubs, churches, and hotels that had been put under siege by the Boxers decades before. Among the marines' duties was to guard the train lines between Tianjin and Beijing and between Tianjin and Qinwangdao, and to protect the Chinese work gangs maintaining the tracks. An aircraft wing was set up at the beginning of October at a former French arsenal near the airfield east of Tianjin. Other air squadrons took up positions at airfields near Qingdao and Beijing. Chinese peasants living in the hundreds of mud-brick villages near rail lines got used to the drone of American planes on reconnaissance missions over China's beleaguered transportation network.

All of this activity was undertaken as the public back home demanded and expected American troops to be coming home from the war rather than setting up new, very faraway deployments. The demobilization of one of the greatest war machines in history was so fast and so pell-mell that Truman called it a "disintegration." Had he tried to halt it, his biographer David McCullough has concluded, "he might have been impeached, so overwhelming was the country's desire for a return of its young men and women now that the war was won, the enemy crushed." This public mood imposed a sharp limitation on the ability of the United States to make a big commitment in China. The China hands were nervous about the marine deployment for a related but different reason: it involved exactly the kind of intervention in Chinese affairs that it was official American policy to avoid. John Carter Vincent, the head of the China desk at State, asked Dean Acheson, the undersecretary of state, what the Americans would do if the Communists attempted a takeover of one of the ports controlled by the marines. The United States would either have to fight them off, or "stand aside" and allow them to take over, Vincent pointed out, and neither option was an attractive one. "Unless there are over-riding military reasons for carrying out these dispositions of American Marines," he wrote, "the plan should be abandoned in favor of occupation by Chinese troops."

The question that Vincent was raising was the key one: Should the

United States intervene in China or not? It was a question that was
raised and examined numerous times as 1945 rolled into 1946, even as
the United States *was* intervening, however modestly, while staying officially neutral in the Chinese domestic quarrel that was becoming more
intense by the day. The policy was both ambiguous and contradictory
because the goals were irreconcilable, one being to help the Nationalist
government move its troops and extend its authority, and the other to
refuse to be drawn into Chiang's intensifying conflict with the Communists. In order to keep the Americans out of China's domestic quarrel,
Vincent wanted Chinese troops to perform the tasks Americans had
been sent to perform.

But how were those Chinese troops to get into position if not in
American planes? And what if they were unable to maintain order?
What if they couldn't prevent the Communists and their Russian
patrons from taking over all the ports in northeast China? Should the
United States simply stand aside and allow that to happen? If not, how
could it avoid taking sides? If it did take sides, how much could it do
given the public clamor for peace?

Wedemeyer did think of these problems. He thought that Hurley's
optimism regarding the Soviets was naïve. He believed their long-range
plan was to foster a Chinese Communist takeover of the entire country,

American marines arriving in Tianjin, September 1945, among the 50,000
American troops who landed in North China after the end of the war.

and this led him to a conclusion opposite to Vincent's. Wedemeyer argued vociferously that a "strong" occupation of key port areas by the United States was essential. He believed the situation in China was potentially explosive. There were anywhere from four to six million Japanese nationals in the country, including a million soldiers still in possession of their weapons, who needed to go home. There were millions of Chinese refugees trying to make their way to their prewar homes. There were desperate economic needs that had to be met right away. Coal had to be moved from the mines near Tangshan to the ports by train—Wedemeyer called guarding them a "military necessity"—or there would be no power to fuel the power plants and factories of places like Shanghai during the coming winter, and if the economy collapsed, Wedemeyer warned, there would be massive starvation.

The Communists, already engaged with the Nationalists in a fierce race to occupy territory, were the ones attacking the rail lines. Acheson agreed with Wedemeyer that the marines were indispensable, writing that "the ports in question were those in the neighborhood of which trouble was most likely to start . . . and that therefore the presence of American troops would strengthen the position of the National Government, help to prevent any disorders from starting, and was desired by the Generalissimo." That hardly sounded like staying aloof in China's war.

In September, President Truman weighed in with a masterpiece of diplomatic ambivalence. The United States, he said, responding to Chiang's request for help, would provide airplanes, naval vessels, and support for Chinese land forces. He said this help could be given without bringing the United States in on one side in China's looming internal battle, a prime example of America's wishful thinking. In his policy declaration on China, Truman invoked American democratic ideals, specifying that American aid could not be "diverted" for use in civil war against the CCP or "to support undemocratic institutions"—a nice-sounding requirement that ignored the inconvenient fact that the government of Chiang Kai-shek was an undemocratic institution. From that point on, American emissaries repeatedly warned Chiang that the United States did not want civil war in China, and if it broke out, the aid would stop.

The Communists, not surprisingly, took the American position as an unfriendly one. Throughout the fall of 1945, as the American airlift proceeded and the marines carried out their activities, the contacts between Americans and Communist Chinese fell into a pattern of tension and small-scale confrontation. On August 15, Captain John Birch became the first American to be killed by Communist forces in Asia, the first of many thousands to come.

Birch, whose name was adopted years later by a subsequent far-right political movement, was, as noted earlier, an army officer working for the OSS. He had been commended by Stilwell, was admired by Davies, and declared by the War Department to be "one of the outstanding intelligence officers in our organization." Paul Frillman, another OSS officer, met him in his little headquarters outside Changsha and found him "a lean, hearty, enthusiastic young man of about twenty-five, an attractive character." He had been in China for two years before Pearl Harbor, when the United States was neutral in the Sino-Japanese war, and he had seen enough atrocities to become "implacably anti-Japanese." He was "most conscientious and knowledgeable in his work," Frillman later wrote. He was from Macon, Georgia, a man of deep religious faith who, as Frillman put it, thought "it was God's war and our side was all good, the Japanese all bad."

Birch was working specifically for AGFRTS, the agency collecting information for Chennault's 14th Air Force, for which Birch had set up a dozen or so listening posts behind enemy lines. When the Japanese surrendered, Birch was ordered to go to Shandong province to scout airfields that could be used by the 14th Air Force for the return of American prisoners of war being held in Japanese camps in that area. From the Communists' point of view, his mission was a complicated and largely undesirable one. Shandong was an area where the Communists had tried hard to establish a presence behind enemy lines. It was strategically important not for its size and centrality but because its two main seaports, Qingdao in the south and Chefoo, now Yentai, in the north, commanded the approaches to much of the China coastline, especially Manchuria. In early 1945, the Communists had proposed that the Americans use a port in northern Jiangsu province, just south of Shandong, in exchange for the $20 million that Zhu De requested as a sort of slush fund to help him get arms from puppet troops.

Conditions in Shandong during the war illustrated the unspoken truce in place between the Communists and the Japanese, neither of which was interested in depleting its forces in what was essentially a vast military stalemate. The Communists had also managed some under-cover cooperation from the puppet regime whose main enemy was the central government. It was useful for both the puppet government and the Japanese that the Communists be able to tie down a sizable portion of the Nationalists' army. A key figure in this clandestine mutuality of interest in Shandong was a former Nationalist commander named Hao Pengju, who had gone over to the puppet regime and become a garrison commander in east China.

This was the very person whom Birch was instructed to contact for help as he reconnoitered potential air bases, and the Communists didn't like it. They had close contacts with many commanders in Hao Pengju's four divisions. When the war ended, Chiang Kai-shek ordered Hao to await incorporation into the central government army. The Communists wanted to persuade him to go over to them, and they didn't want any American interference with that plan. When the Birch party of four Americans, seven Chinese, and two Koreans arrived in Shandong via northern Jiangsu, they were stopped by Communist troops. An angry parley ensued. Birch was not there to interfere in the emerging KMT-CCP contest for power in east China. He wanted only to survey airfields, and he angrily demanded that the Communists allow him to continue on his mission.

The Communist troops allowed him and his party to proceed, then stopped him a second time, and a third time, on August 25, at a place called Huangkou Station. Birch's deputy, a KMT officer named Tung Chin-sheng, tried to persuade the Communists that the Americans were friends and that detaining and disarming them would cause "a serious misunderstanding between Communist China and America." Birch refused to allow his party to be disarmed. He demanded to see the Communist commander. He behaved in an angry, even imperious manner that has led some historians to conclude that he provoked his own death.

At one point, while the entire group was looking for the local Communist commander, Birch grabbed a CCP orderly by the collar, shook him, and asked, "Are you bandits?" The commander, the same soldier who initially had ordered their arrest, now ordered his men to disarm Birch and his men. According to Lieutenant Tung, who was wounded in the incident but survived to testify to American investigators later, Birch was shot in the thigh, carried to a cinder pile near the train station, and bayoneted to death. "The body was found wrapped in a straw mat," Lieutenant W. J. Miller, a surviving member of the mission, later reported to Wedemeyer. "The hands and feet were bound. There was a large wound in the left thigh, a large hole in the right shoulder, and the whole of the face had been mutilated beyond recognition."

Birch's killing took place at a time when the Communists were becoming strikingly more aggressive against anybody whom they perceived to be standing in their way. The four American soldiers in the Spaniel team were still under arrest. A few weeks later, another American OSS team was captured and held by the Communists in Shaanxi province. And there were very soon to be other incidents centering in Shandong in which Communist opposition to any American presence would be expressed vociferously at the point of a gun.

Manchuria is some six hundred thousand square miles in area, bigger than France, Germany, and Poland combined. It is rich in the resources needed for a modern industrial economy, which is the reason the Russians and the Japanese went to war over it in 1905 and why Japan took it over in 1931. It contains nearly 10 percent of the entire population of China. It has excellent year-round ports on the Yellow Sea and on the large bay known as the Bohai—Dalian, Port Arthur, Yingkou, Huludao, and others. In the south, Manchuria is menacingly close to key points in North China, especially to Beijing, which is only about a hundred miles from its southernmost province, Liaoning, fifty or so miles from the Great Wall. Most important strategically, it had a thousand-mile border with the Soviet Union and an additional border with Soviet-dominated Mongolia, so whatever party held the area could easily be supplied with Russian arms and have a vast hinterland to serve as an impregnable refuge.

Manchuria had at least twice before served as a base for the conquest, or the attempted conquest, of all of China, most recently in 1937 when the Japanese sent their divisions southward from their puppet state of Manchukuo. Three and a half centuries earlier, when the central Chinese government was weak, a Manchu chieftain, Nurhaci, rebelled against the last Ming dynasty emperor, sending his troops through the mountain passes between Manchuria and inner China. Just like the Japanese later, they clambered over the Great Wall, which had never been a very effective barrier against determined invaders, and poured out onto the vast North China Plain and its thousands of undefended villages, which is what Mao was going to do later in some of the largest battles ever fought. To control Manchuria is not to control China, but it provides an enormous advantage for any insurgent force.

Mao was well aware of that. His image, especially in the West, is of the peasant guerrilla who used the countryside to surround the cities but didn't need the cities to win. But already at the Seventh Congress of the Chinese Communist Party in the late spring of 1945 Mao was saying that the CCP needed industry, a communications system, a way of generating wealth, in order to counterbalance the government's control of the industrial region near Shanghai. "Once we occupy the Northeast," a confident Mao told a concluding session of the Seventh Congress, "we can lay a solid foundation for the Chinese revolution even if we lose all the existing base areas."

The foundation was being established with Stalin's help in those weeks and months after the Japanese surrender, but the Communists' movements were largely surreptitious and Stalin's help a secret so that both sides could preserve the fiction that they were peace parties striving to avoid a Chinese civil war. Stalin continued to give assurances that he would live up to the agreements he'd signed on China, assurances that were foolishly believed by Hurley and others. Months of American confusion and uncertainty would pass before it became clear that Stalin's policy was to pay lip service to his agreements with Chiang while helping the Chinese Communists as much as he could, short of provoking a vigorous American response.

With that strategy, Stalin was bound to come out a winner. If the Communists gained control of North China, he would have helped them do it, and he would have gained what he assumed would be a friendly and even subservient regime on his border. That would be the best outcome from his point of view. Stalin, however, knew that the Communists might lose. If the national government prevailed, Stalin would claim to be innocent of intervention in China's internal affairs, keeping the gains he had made at Yalta, stationing Soviet warships at Port Arthur, and maintaining friendly relations with a government that depended on his goodwill. In both cases, Stalin would succeed in replacing Japan as the paramount power in northeast Asia, reversing the effects of the Russian defeat in the war of 1905 and the Japanese occupation of Manchuria, and maintaining a safe buffer zone between Soviet Siberia and the rest of Asia.

If he got that from China's national government, Stalin would have no reason to risk the animosity of the nuclear-armed Americans in order to have even more. So he did his best to minimize that risk, pursuing a policy of such extraordinary flexibility that at times it seemed self-contradictory. He would urge the Chinese Communists to act aggressively, and when they did, he would curb them and demand that they make concessions to the national government. Later, when the situation allowed it, he would again urge a more aggressive policy. Stalin managed this masterfully. He never lost his influence among the Chinese Communists, even during those times when his caution provoked fits of frustrated anger on the part of Mao, and at the same time, he maintained correct, even cordial relations with the national government, until the forces he helped set in motion forced that government into exile.

Assured of Soviet non-interference, the Communists devised an aggressive strategy to deal with the new American military presence. The very day the marines landed in China, an editorial in *Liberation Daily* said, accurately: "No matter what the intention of the Americans is, their landing will in fact interfere in China's internal affairs, and inevitably assist the KMT to oppose the CCP and 100 million people in the liberated areas." A few days later, the paper warned that the Americans should not advance into "places that have already been liberated and where there are no Japanese troops." Communist policy was to be polite to the Americans and even to welcome them "if they respect our interests." But if they tried to force their way into Communist-held areas, "we should formally inform them of our objection [and] be prepared militarily for resistance."

The first test of the CCP's guidelines came near Beijing, where Zhou had warned General Worton there would be resistance. On October 5, a marine reconnaissance patrol on the route from Tianjin to Beijing discovered thirty-six scattered roadblocks that made it impossible for truck-sized vehicles to get through. The Communists wanted to impede deliveries of supplies from the port to the former imperial capital, where the marines had already set up their encampments and where Nationalist soldiers were arriving by air. The next day, when marine engineers, guarded by a rifle platoon, went to clear the road, some forty to fifty Communist troops opened fire on them from behind the surrounding trees and foliage. Three marines were wounded and the whole platoon withdrew. The next day, a rifle company and a tank platoon arrived on the scene, protected by planes based on a carrier off the coast, and they cleared the road without further incident.

That same day, the marine commander, Major General Keller E.

Rockey, presided over the surrender of all the Japanese forces in the area of Tianjin, about fifty thousand officers and men. The ceremony took place with due pomp—a marine band, a color guard, the flags of the United States and the Republic of China flying—in front of the French Municipal Building, the city's most imposing European-style structure, now converted into the IIIAC headquarters. Tens of thousands of Chinese jammed the roped-off area where the surrender took place, or peered down from rooftops. A group of six Japanese officers walked past the marine guard to the surrender table where they symbolically laid down their swords before Rockey. Afterward, as they were escorted to waiting cars, the Chinese hissed and booed.

The next day, Rockey, accompanied by a naval commander, Rear Admiral Daniel E. Barbey, boarded the command ship *Catoctin* and headed along the north Shandong coast to carry out the task of occupying the port of Chefoo. The Americans knew that the Communists had seized control of Chefoo from the Japanese in the days after the end of the war. Chefoo held tremendous strategic importance because whoever held it could use it to ferry troops to Manchuria via the port of Dalian, just 150 miles across the Gulf of Zhili, and Manchuria was where the opening battle for control of China was looming.

A few days before, on September 27, knowing that the Americans planned to send troops to the port, Ye Jianying, chief of staff of the Communist armed forces, sent a message to Wedemeyer telling him that since there were no Japanese in the vicinity, the deployment of American troops in that area would be taken by the Communists as interference in China's internal affairs. Despite that, the *Catoctin*, escorted by the cruiser *Louisville* and its detachment of marines, arrived at Chefoo on the morning of October 7. Barbey, a specialist in amphibious warfare from Oregon who had commanded marines in battles in New Guinea, the Philippines, and Borneo, dispatched an American colonel to ask the Communists to leave, but the Communist official who met the American colonel politely refused to do so. He repeated what Wedemeyer had already heard from Ye. All was in good order thanks to "Chinese troops supported by the people of the province who have fought the enemy many years with many sacrifices." At the same time, Ye sent a second warning to Wedemeyer's headquarters: If American troops landed, there might be trouble, and it would be the fault of the United States.

On board the *Catoctin*, Barbey confirmed to Wedemeyer that

indeed there were no Japanese forces in the area, which meant that any landing by the marines would not represent the liberation of a Japanese-held city but "an interference in the internal affairs of China" and that would be "bitterly resented by the Communists." At Barbey's urging, the American high command decided to forgo the Chefoo landing. The Communists had won a victory whose significance was not lost on at least one of the American reporters on the scene. The United States, Tillman Durdin wrote in *The New York Times*, had already given the Kuomintang government—"now in a relationship bordering on civil war"—a great deal of help by transporting government troops to the north and by directly taking over Tianjin, Beijing, and Qinwangdao. "The decision regarding Chefoo draws a line beyond which the United States will not go at present in supporting Generalissimo Chiang Kai-shek in relation to rival factions in China."

How things had changed. Only a few months earlier, while the war against Japan was still going on, American officers and members of the CCP Politburo were going together to the Saturday night dances in Yenan. In the fields and villages of occupied China, Eighth Route Army soldiers, the friendly *Balus*, were risking their lives, and sometimes sacrificing them, to rescue downed American airmen. Now the Communist policy was to make it just unsafe enough for the Americans, short of actual open warfare, that they would decide to leave.

And, as the firefight on the Tianjin–Beijing road and the killing of John Birch demonstrated, it was unsafe, even if the danger didn't seem all that serious to American military leaders. At a meeting with Secretary of State James Byrnes and the secretary of the navy, James F. Forrestal, the new secretary of war, Robert P. Patterson, dismissed these incidents with the Chinese Communists as of the "comic opera" variety, asserting that the marines could walk from one end of China to the other without "serious hindrance."

This was no doubt true. No force in China, except for the Soviets themselves, matched the marines in firepower or tactical know-how. Still, the China duty was tense and hard. The marines heard from the Japanese awaiting repatriation about the constant sniping, the ambushes, the mines, the sabotage of tracks and signal equipment that they had experienced from Eighth Route Army guerrillas as they patrolled the roads and rail lines of North China. That duty had fallen to the Americans, who rode the dusty coal trains and patrolled the earth-packed roadways in jeeps and trucks. Whatever a bureaucrat in a suit and tie might say ten thousand miles away, the marines faced a tricky indigenous group of armed partisans who wanted them to leave. *From the Great Wall to Mukden*, a Marine Corps history, states that "every mile of track, every bridge, and every switch was the potential target of Communist attacks." During their entire deployment in China, the marines suffered twelve killed and forty-two wounded in eighteen armed clashes and several small-scale Communist attacks.

On October 11, a marine reconnaissance company landed on the docks of Qingdao, the big port across the Shandong peninsula from Chefoo. The Eighth Route Army was in control of much of the nearby interior and a great deal of the coast. The central government was absent. The marines took over the port and secured the airfield ten miles outside the city. Within two days of the initial landing, a letter arrived for the division commander, Major General Lemuel C. Shepherd Jr., later commandant of the Marine Corps. It was from the Communist commander in Shandong, and it proposed cooperation in "destroying the remaining Japanese military forces and the rest of the traitor army," meaning the army of the Chinese puppet regime. He said that the Communists were getting ready to enter Qingdao and that he expected no resistance from the marines, who he hoped would stay out of the "open conflict" looming with government troops.

Shepherd wrote back that he wasn't there to destroy anybody, that it was not desirable for the Communists to enter Qingdao, and that "the Sixth Marines will in no way assist any Chinese group in conflict against another." Shortly thereafter, Shepherd stood side by side with the commander of the central government troops as the Japanese garrison, ten thousand strong, formally presented its surrender at the Qingdao racecourse, built during the days when Qingdao was a German colony.

After that exchange of letters between Shepherd and the local CCP commander, there were frequent clashes among the various armed groups, the puppet remnants, the Japanese who did guard duty while awaiting repatriation, and the Communists. Despite the buildup of government forces, Qingdao, as the marine history puts it, remained "an island in a Communist Sea." Only the marines kept the Communists from taking the biggest port in China between Shanghai and Tianjin, a fact that, certainly in the eyes of the Communists, meant that, contrary to Shepherd's assurance, the Americans were assisting one side against the other in China's civil war.

The tension also led to armed incidents farther north. In the middle of November, DeWitt Peck, a four-star general from Bakersfield, California, who commanded the First Marine Division, was on a train near Guye, a village on the main line between the coalfields of Tangshan and the port of Qinwangdao—the freight line whose protection General Wedemeyer had called a military necessity. Suddenly, Peck and the troops he was accompanying, a group of marine guards, were attacked by Communist forces based in a village five hundred yards north of the track. A squadron of marine planes was called in and made mock strafing runs on the Communist-held village—not wanting to risk civilian casualties—and the attacking Communists slipped away. When a rescue company from the Seventh Marines arrived on the scene the next day, they discovered that during the night the Communists had ripped up four hundred yards of track. Several Chinese railroad workers were killed by mines planted on the roadbed.

Peck took a plane to Qinwangdao, where he conferred directly with the Nationalist commander for the whole northeast, General Tu Li-ming. The two agreed that central government troops would be deployed to clear the railroad line of Communist guerrillas and that in order to release the troops for this duty, the marines would take over guard duty for all the bridges over one hundred meters long for the entire 135-mile distance between Tangshan and Qinwangdao. From the marines' point of view, the arrangement kept them from a direct role in fratricidal war; from the CCP's perspective, the marines were helping the central government take back territory that the Communists, by dint of bravery and sacrifice, had taken under their control behind the Japanese lines.

These small skirmishes do not figure prominently in American military history. Yet they were the first such confrontations between American forces and a new kind of enemy, one that was going to become familiar over the succeeding decades in Vietnam and, still later, in Iraq and Afghanistan, in the kind of confrontation that gave rise to the term "asymmetric warfare." Hostile guerrillas materializing from anonymous villages, firing and then melting away when American fighter planes appeared in the skies, became a pattern for the later American wars in Asia. In the background to these skirmishes fought on the railroad line in China's Hebei province was the looming Cold War. They were small proxy fights between the United States and the Soviet Union whose contest for spheres of influence and power had already begun.

As part of the Sino-Soviet agreement, a negotiating committee, set up ostensibly to supervise the transfer of control from the Soviet Union to China, was already in place in the city of Changchun in south central Manchuria, which was where Marshal Malinovsky had his headquarters. Malinovsky, the hard, seasoned, highly decorated, utterly reliable Communist officer, the man in whom there was "not a drop of gentleness," was from an impoverished family in Ukraine. He had escaped a nasty childhood by joining the pre-Soviet Russian army when he was fifteen years old, and he had been fighting ever since, participating in just about every Russian and Soviet armed conflict occurring during his lifetime. He was wounded twice during World War I. He fought on the Soviet side in the civil war that followed the revolution of 1917. He was a volunteer during the Spanish Civil War, and when he returned home he was awarded the Order of Lenin in recognition of his bravery. After the German attack in 1941, he became one of the heroes of the bloody, do-or-die defense of Stalingrad where, for the first time in World War II, the tide turned in favor of the Russians, and he got the Order of Suvorov for outstanding generalship, the highest decoration in the Soviet army.

Later, Malinovsky was the victor in the battles for Budapest, Brno, and Bratislava as the Russian armies ground down German divisions in the march to Berlin. At the end of the war in Europe, he was transferred to Asia, and he commanded the Soviet rout of the Japanese in Manchuria. Years later, he was minister of defense of the Soviet Union; in 1960 he was pictured on the cover of *Time* magazine under the headline "Russia's New Hard Line." He was "hulking" and "impassive," the magazine said; he was "a true son of the socialist motherland," according to the Soviet leader Nikita Khrushchev. He was short and heavy-set with a kind of bulldog determination imprinted on his unsmiling face, not a man to be intimidated or to be afflicted by the sentiment known in the Communist lexicon as bourgeois humanitarianism. He was also, as the Chinese delegation soon discovered, a master of a kind of bureaucratic obstructionism, of the fake excuse.

The Chinese team, led by General Hsiung Shih-hui, arrived in Changchun on August 12. They soon had occasion to count the many ways by which the Russians could hinder them in achieving their purpose, which was to replace the Soviets with soldiers and officials of the central government. There were petty obstructions. The Chinese learned, for example, that the Soviets had ordered a suspension in the Bank of China's activities in Manchuria, so the negotiating team had difficulty paying its expenses. At one point, complaining of some press coverage of Soviet domestic politics, the Russians actually searched the KMT offices in Changchun, summoned the entire staff for interrogation, accused them of distributing propaganda without first getting permission from the Soviet high command, held them overnight, and then ordered them to cease all their activities, including the sending of teams to investigate conditions in various places in Manchuria. For weeks, the Soviets complained about what they called "anti-Soviet activities" in Manchuria, and they held the KMT's representatives responsible. The Soviets even refused to allow the Chinese to send representatives to Jehol, the region just west of Manchuria, to buy leather for uniforms, saying that the route to Jehol was "disorderly."

One member of the team, an American-educated economist named Chang Kia-ngau, noted on arriving at the Changchun airport that it was "filled with Soviet officers and soldiers," and that there were very few Chinese around. "Then we found that we cannot use the national currency," he wrote in his diary. "On the same day I received a report saying the Soviet Army was plundering industrial equipment"—power generators, furnaces, broadcasting equipment, automobiles, even office furniture. When the Chinese asked when they could install their own administrations in various places, Malinovsky replied that he needed to get instructions from his superiors. When asked if he could provide transportation for the Chinese delegates, Malinovsky said there were no vehicles, ships, or planes available, though, he added, "this issue can be negotiated between the two governments on the basis of the Sino-Soviet treaty." Would the Soviets allow the Chinese to take over the printing bureau of the former puppet regime? Malinowsky needed to seek instructions from his superiors on that too.

Not surprisingly, the initial meetings with the Soviet commander led Chang to the impression that "the Soviets have no intention of actively supporting the transportation of our troops into the northeast," though Soviet obstructionism was always veiled behind a phony offer of some other way to help. Malinovsky urged the Chinese to use the railroads to move their men into position, but the Chinese knew, and surely Malinovsky knew, that Communist troops in Shanhaiguan had cut the railroad lines between Manchuria and China proper.

As October wore on, the fullness of Soviet control of Manchuria became clearer and clearer, the obstructionism less petty. An aide to Malinovky identified by Chang as Major General Pavlovsky, formally notified the Chinese that they considered all the former Japanese industrial equipment in Manchuria to be war booty that belonged to the Soviet Union. The Chinese protested. The Soviets compromised, saying that Japanese state-owned industry would be war booty. Private Japanese property, of which there was much less, could go to China. The Soviets had 1.5 million troops on the ground. There was nothing China could do to resist.

It's easy to imagine the disadvantage of the Chinese in what was supposed to be collaboration but was really a dictation of terms. Here was Malinovsky, representing the triumphant army of the second most powerful country on earth, facing off against the representative of a weak, devastated, and divided country armed with nothing much more than the declared friendship of a faraway superpower. On the most urgent matter of the ostensible return of Manchuria to Chinese government control, General Hsiung informed Malinovsky that China intended to transport troops from Hong Kong on American vessels and land them at the port of Dalian. Malinovsky's reply was that the Sino-Soviet treaty had declared Dalian to be an open city devoted only to commercial purposes, and therefore it would be a violation of the treaty to allow Chinese troops to land there. In other words the Soviets, having, in that very treaty, recognized China's central government as the country's sole legitimate authority, to which they were obliged to give moral and material support, were now telling that same government that it was barred from dispatching its own armed forces to portions of its own territory.

Astonished at the bluntness and audacity of Soviet obstructionism, Chang Kia-ngau wrote to Chiang Kai-shek warning him that the Soviet intention was to create a "special regime" in the north wherein the northeast provinces of China would be "completely surrounded." "I'm afraid even the Manchurian coastline is in danger of being blockaded," Chang said, and when that happened, "the northeast is bound to become a sitting duck for the Soviet Union."

Malinovky, always ready with some reasonable alternative solution, assured the Chinese and their American escorts that, while Dalian, which was Manchuria's biggest and best deep-water port, was closed to them, they could land troops farther north at the smaller ports of Huludao and Yingkou, and the Americans, not wanting a fight, agreed to that. But when the small armada of American ships arrived at Huludao, they found that Chinese Communist troops were in control of the port and were vowing to fight if the government forces tried to land there.

It was an extraordinary scene. As at Chefoo earlier, Rear Admiral Daniel E. Barbey was in command of the American ships, charged with helping the government retake control of its territory. Barbey had ample forces with him to deal with the Communists if it came to a fight, but he had been instructed to avoid conflict. Given the circumstances, he told the Chinese Nationalists to negotiate the matter with the Russians. General Hsiung duly brought up the landing at Huludao with Malinovsky, pointing out that the Soviet commander had assured him of a safe disembarkation there. Malinovsky had given a window between November 5 and 10 for the landing. The American task force arrived on the 7th. Malinovsky replied that the Communist troops had not come through territory under Soviet control but from the south, so what could he do? The ever-eager-to-help Malinovsky suggested that Hsiung talk things over with the Eighth Route Army, which Hsiung naturally said he could not do, knowing that the Communists were not going to politely give up Huludao and allow government troops to land there just because he asked them to. When Hsiung inquired of Malinovsky what the Russians would do if there was a clash between the Communists and the government troops, the Soviet commander's reply was that he would desist from interfering in China's internal affairs.

The task force, still under Barbey, proceeded to Yingkou, the last alternative Manchurian port where the government troops could be landed. There, the Communist-appointed mayor of the town was on the dock shouting to the Americans at the railings of their ships that the Communists would resist any effort by the government to land its forces. Barbey, following orders not to interfere in China's internal affairs, ordered the ships back to sea. The landing of the government forces would take place well to the south at the port of Qinwangdao, and, indeed, after sailing the Bohai for days with no result, the American task force deposited its consignment of troops there in mid-November.

By now, Chiang Kai-shek's son, Chiang Ching-kuo, who spoke fluent Russian, had joined the Chinese negotiating team at Changchun.

On November 4, the younger Chiang went to see Malinovsky and complained to him that Communist troops had prevented the expected landing of government forces at Yingkou. Malinovsky's reply was that Soviet troops were few in number in Yingkou, so resistance to the Communist troop movements was impossible. "It is very clear," Chang Kia-ngau noted in his diary, "that the Soviets deliberately are allowing Eighth Route Army men into Huludao and Yingkou to obstruct the efforts of government troops to land there."

Chang Kia-ngau was beginning to understand the reasons for Soviet obstructionism: the friendly wartime relations between the United States and the Soviet Union were turning sour in the postwar period. Many times, speaking in a "stern" tone, Malinovsky protested to the Chinese that the Americans had sent a warship to Dalian. Chang understood that the Russians wanted to exclude any and all American forces from Manchuria, and this put China in a bind. In the background to this were American actions to exclude the Soviets from playing a role in the occupation of Japan, which Moscow was demanding as a reward for the five days its troops had participated in the war. Soviet propaganda trumpeted the theory already advanced by Mao that it had been the Russian invasion of Manchuria, rather than the succession of American victories in the Pacific and the use of the atomic bomb, that had turned the tide in the Asian war. This was the justification advanced by the Russians as they systematically stripped Manchuria of Japanese-built industry. Possession of the Japanese-built factories was just compensation for the losses the Soviets had suffered in the war. The message was clear: If the United States insisted on monopolizing postwar Japan, the Soviets would do the same in northeast Asia.

And so the charade continued. Malinovsky's next helpful suggestion was for the central government to airlift troops into the cities of Mukden and Changchun, and dilatory negotiations proceeded in November on the execution of this plan. But by this time, Chiang Kai-shek was growing pessimistic about the whole Manchurian matter, uncertain that he could prevail if he forced the issue and worried that any steps toward civil war would incur the anger of the population. This was easy to understand. China's revitalized press was full of ardent expressions of hope for civil war to be avoided. At the end of October, ten liberal professors in Kunming, still the location of several of the universities displaced during the war, sent an open letter to Mao and Chiang urging the end of China's "one-party dictatorship" and the convocation of a political council composed of representatives of all parties and factions. Noting the growth of this sentiment, the American embassy cautioned that "these professors are distressed at what they described as the 'new American policy toward China.' They're at a loss to understand the 'all-out support' given to the Central Government by the U.S., which they believe merely increases the determination of Gen Chiang Kai-shek not to establish a genuine coalition government in China and not to surrender any real power now held by the KMT."

The Communists, cleverly aligning themselves with this growing trend in public opinion, were making the same complaint about the KMT's one-party dictatorship and the same demand for a coalition government. In fact, Chiang Kai-shek had announced plans to hold a political consultative conference in Chungking in November, a gathering of all the political factions in China that would decide on the means for later elections to a national assembly. Chiang seemed in this to be responding to the clamor among the intelligentsia and to pressure from the United States to move toward democracy, and, indeed, he had taken some steps in that direction. In the spring, even as the CCP was holding its ceremonial glorification of Mao at its Seventh Congress, Chiang presided over the Sixth Kuomintang Conference, the first since 1938. Among its resolutions was one calling for a general national conference for later in the year that would make arrangements for a multiparty election for a new national assembly. Chiang also ended the system of stationing political commissars with every major army unit, a move, urged on him by his American advisers, that aimed at moving away from party control of the armed forces—a move that the Communists have not made to this day. When the war ended, Chiang also took steps toward political reform, notably ending press censorship and releasing political prisoners. Was this pure window-dressing, as the Communists and many later historians have assumed? The Chinese government under Chiang was still a one-party dictatorship, but public criticism was taking place and being tolerated; there was ferment in the air. The announcement of a political consultative conference was an element of this ferment, and at the end of the talks in Chungking, Mao agreed to it in principle, though, as we will see, the Communists never really gave it much of a chance in practice.

Mao's own sincerity is deeply questionable. In Yenan after his negotiation with Chiang ended, Mao oversaw the CCP's propaganda, which advertised the CCP as the party of peace, and he continued to move his troops as fast as possible into Manchuria. The Eighth Route Army had blocked all the ports except for Qinwangdao. In mid-November, Lin Biao occupied Changchun, one of the cities that the Soviets had designated as an airlift destination for government forces. The Soviets, always eager, they said, not to interfere in China's internal affairs, did nothing to stop this from happening. Chiang Kai-shek was reduced to hoping that if he could maintain good relations with the Russians, proving to them that he would cause them no trouble in Manchuria, they could still be persuaded not to help the Communists. And so the plans for an airlift were dropped.

CHAPTER FIFTEEN

What to Do?

In Washington during October and November the mood turned gloomy as reports of Communist advances and national government troubles flowed in from the American diplomatic posts in China. In early October, the message from the American consulate in Xian was that the Communists were becoming "increasingly active" north of the Yellow River. The vision that took hold of the minds of American policymakers was of an inexorable infiltration of Communist forces into North China. The new chargé d'affaires in Chungking, Walter Robertson, who had arrived after Hurley's purge of the embassy, told Secretary of State James F. Byrnes that the Communists already controlled most of the triangle of territory formed by Kalgan, Beijing, and Tatung, a strategic, heavily populated area—Kalgan the gateway to Mongolia, Tatung on one of the Great Wall passes into Manchuria, Beijing not only a big city but, as the former imperial capital, a place of great symbolic significance. The Communists were, moreover, showing "extreme antipathy toward the United States," Robertson said, and they were growing ever closer to the Soviet Union, which was seizing former Japanese arms depots and "handing over much of the booty to the Communists," despite their treaty commitment to aid only China's central government.

Robertson's experience in government before his arrival in China had been as director of Lend-Lease in Australia. Later, after the Korean War, he would become assistant secretary of state for Asia, and in that position he was known as a diehard supporter of Chiang Kai-shek. But during his time as chargé in China, he was very unlike Hurley. He was polite, reasonable, "not an extremist," as one colleague later put it; "the soul of courtesy," said another. There is no question that later he hated the Communists and liked the KMT, but his reporting in 1945 on the machinations of Mao and the Soviets seems undogmatic and factual. Unlike Hurley, Robertson wrote reports that largely corresponded with those of others, both military personnel and civilians in the field. There was some good news in October. Robertson reported that the marines helped the central government take the surrender of the Japanese garrison in Beijing, which had the effect, Robertson said, of "reducing [the] Communist menace which has been growing steadily since [the] war ended." But as the weeks went by, most of the news from China was alarming. Robertson passed along weekly reports from the American military attaché, which amounted to a steady chronicle of Communist advances and Soviet trickery. At the beginning of November, the attaché reported that the New Fourth Army was retreating from the central provinces of Kiangsu and Chekiang and that this would "augment [the] strength of Communist forces in [the] North." The next week the attaché announced the gloomy news that "the threat of large-scale civil war in China seems to be growing." The Communists were attacking railroads and vowing to continue doing so unless the KMT ceased its troop movements. Meanwhile, the optimism of October about an imminent breakthrough in the KMT-CCP negotiations was fading. "It appears at present almost hopeless that any permanently satisfactory solution can be reached," Robertson said.

Faced with a deteriorating situation, Chiang pressed General Wedemeyer for American ships to transport two more Chinese armies to the north, via Tianjin. Wedemeyer turned him down, replying that the United States had already transported enough troops for the government to handle the Japanese surrender, and he was not authorized to do anything more. "Dissident elements," Wedemeyer cabled to Marshall, meaning the Communists, "and not Japanese are the cause of the present serious trouble and therefore the movement of additional troops is not within the scope of our mission." In addition, Wedemeyer said, he wanted to withdraw the marines by the middle of November, and moving more troops north, where Chiang already had five armies, would mean prolonging the marines' deployment in China.

A few days later, Wedemeyer again reported to Marshall that he was under "heavy pressure" from Chiang to move Chinese troops to Manchuria, but, Wedemeyer said, unconvincingly given Moscow's behavior, "The policy has always been that this was a China-Soviet matter." By the middle of November the military attaché's reports were ever more alarming and pessimistic. "Impasse seems to have reached a critical stage . . . as no progress was made toward a solution." The "conflict was increasing on all fronts [such that] large areas of China [are] already in a state of civil war." The Communists were attacking Taiyuan, there was "fierce fighting" at the Hebei-Shaanxi border, and the Eighth Route Army was continuing to destroy rail lines in the northeast in its effort to prevent a move there by the government's armies. Around the same time, the consul in Tianjin informed Washington that ordinary rail service in North China was "practically non-existent," as the Communists were "looting trains, planting mines, removing rails, burning sleepers, and destroying roadbeds on a big scale." The attaché's report for November 18 concluded that the civil war in north and central China had "reached a new high." The week after that, he wrote, despite some government success in pushing the Communists out of Shanhaiguan, the coastal gateway between Hebei province and Manchuria, the Communists were moving into areas vacated by the withdrawing Russians, and they now seemed "well-entrenched" with an estimated one hundred thousand troops in place. The final hope of the American diplomats in China was that Chiang's scheduling of the People's Consultative Conference for the beginning of December, when the Communists said they would attend, might at least lead to a hiatus in the fighting. But then the Communists announced that they wouldn't attend the conference after all, and it was canceled. The cancellation, the attaché said, was "the darkest aspect of a gloomy week."

Wedemeyer was the go-to guy in China, much more so than Robertson or anybody else, the man that Marshall, the Joint Chiefs, and the secretary of war turned to for advice, and Wedemeyer was in a state of pessimistic agitation. Months before in Washington, he had, like Hurley, dismissed the Communist danger, saying it could be disposed of with relative ease. Now he was worried both about the central government's weakness and about the unreality of American policy. The State Department position on the matter was that, yes, American help to the central government would, as it was commonly put, result in "collateral aid or prestige" to Chiang, but that didn't amount to interference in China's affairs. Wedemeyer, in a lengthy cable to Marshall on November 23, the same day that Chiang reiterated his "urgent appeal" for more American help, saw the sophistry of this argument. He didn't question the need for the marines to be in China. To withdraw them, he wrote, would hand the Communists "a complete victory for their invidious propaganda campaign and acts of intimidation." But support of the national government "will definitely involve American forces in fratricidal warfare. There can be no mistake about this. . . . We need to be clear of this consequence if it is U.S. policy to help with unification of China and Manchuria under National Government."

Wedemeyer's reports from China provided very little cause for optimism. Chiang, he told Marshall, was "completely unprepared for occupation of Manchuria against Communist opposition." Even his recovery of North China between the Yangzi River and the Great Wall was uncertain. "The area is vast, communication limited, and loyalties of population doubtful," Wedemeyer told Marshall. "Communist guerrillas and saboteurs can and probably will . . . harass and restrict movements of Central Government forces."

Wedemeyer was entirely realistic about the Soviet Union, saying it maintained an "outward show of cooperation with Chiang's representatives" but it "definitely appears to be creating favorable conditions for the acquisition by the Chinese Communists of key areas in North China and Manchuria." In Wedemeyer's view, Chiang's problem was not mainly military. He liked Chiang. He found him "sincere" and "selfless" but surrounded by "unscrupulous men who are interested primarily in their self-aggrandizement." The Chinese politician, Wedemeyer said, sounding like a member of the dissenting Chinese intelligentsia, "operates with the object of enriching himself through chicanery and machination," and the Gimo is "bewildered and impotent" in the face of this corrosive problem.

The best way out, Wedemeyer now advised Marshall, seeming to forget his concern with giving the Communists a great "victory," would be to get out altogether, and thus "remove any chance of involvement in the internal affairs of China." Perhaps, Wedemeyer offered, a protectorate over Manchuria exercised by the newly created United Nations would be the solution, while the central government concentrated on getting back control of North China, though even that, Wedemeyer predicted, would take months or perhaps years of hard effort. Either way, Wedemeyer made clear, the United States faced a basic choice: either withdraw or become deeply involved in China's unremitting civil strife with all the risks attendant on that involvement, including the possibility of a direct confrontation with the Soviet Union.

For the first time in its relations with Asia, the United States faced what was to become a familiar dilemma. It felt that to refuse help to a friendly government was unacceptable, but so were the potential costs of providing that help. As in later, similar situations, every suggestion gave rise to its own countersuggestion. Send in more marines? The head of the Asia desk at the State Department, John Carter Vincent, worried that that might give the Soviets an excuse not to withdraw from Manchuria, which it was now promising to do by the beginning of December. (In the end, the Russians didn't pull their troops out until April 1946.) Withdraw the marines and withdraw from China? One of the chief goals of the United States in the war in Asia was to bring about a friendly, united, independent China. It had made a tremendous investment in lives and money in pursuit of this objective. To withdraw now would be to throw all that away.

The most eloquent appeal to stay the course might have been expected at this point from the American ambassador to China, Hurley. Instead it was left to one of the Foreign Service officers on the China desk (most of whom Hurley believed to be plotting against him), Everett Drumright, another Oklahoman and a hardworking professional diplomat who'd been consul in Xian during much of the war but was now back at State as the chief of the division of Chinese affairs. During the war, he'd been deemed by his colleagues to be more politically conservative than most of the China hands. That had not stopped him in the past from joining the professionals' consensus, which was that the United States should pressure Chiang to undertake political reforms, that it shouldn't bind itself to him no matter what, and that it should cooperate with the Communists in case of military necessity.

Now things were different. Chiang's survival was threatened not by the Japanese but by the Communists and their Soviet supporters, and this, Drumright felt, was intolerable. He wrote a paper that reverberates with a kind of moral outrage, a deep anxiety that a lack of American resolve might now cede half of China to a Communist dictatorship and that such a result would not just be inimical to the interests and values of the United States, it would be shameful as well. The Chinese Communists, Drumright wrote, were making a "supreme effort to assert control over North China" and a "strong bid to seize control of Manchuria, and they are being "aided and abetted by the Soviet Union" in these attempts, by such means as its prohibition on the landing of government troops at Dalian on the flimsy pretext that it was a free port.

How the United States faced these blatant treaty violations, Drumright wrote, "[would] have a momentous bearing on the future of China, of the Far East, and of the world." Chinese Communist control of North China and Manchuria would mean "foreign intervention" in Chinese affairs, namely Soviet intervention, and the possible consequences of this, Drumright averred, would be nothing short of a "third world war."

The danger was that the endgame in the Asia Pacific would be the replacement of one unacceptable outcome, a China controlled by Japan, with another, "a Soviet-dominated China," which would mean that "the war of resistance against Japan has been fought in vain." Preventing a permanently divided China, or perhaps the whole country controlled by an unfriendly dictatorship beholden to the Soviet Union, was the paramount interest of the United States, ahead of such other interests as political reform or avoiding "fratricidal warfare." The United States had the option of simply withdrawing, but if it did that, or if it offered only "half-hearted assistance to China," it will "destroy what we seek to achieve." The United States needed, Drumright concluded, to "move resolutely and effectively to assist the national government of China to effect restoration of the recovered area of China, including Manchuria."

It was an eloquent statement, and it anticipated such future statements about being resolute and effective in other countries in Asia, ready, as John F. Kennedy said in 1961, to "pay any price, bear any burden, meet any hardship, support any friend, oppose any foe, in order to assure the success and the survival of liberty." Vincent, Drumright's boss, passed his statement on to Byrnes, but there were arguments being made on the other side, notably by Vincent himself.

Drumright's analysis was grounded in a sense of the practical American interest. It would be bad for America if a threatening, messianic dictatorship like the Soviet Union were to dominate China. The underlying issue, however, was what kind of world Americans wanted to live in. The American conviction, going back to the Revolution, was that progress toward liberal democracy is the supreme American interest, because it is good in itself, a beacon to oppressed peoples, and because the most peaceful and secure world would be one in which democracy predominated. Drumright's memo rang of the stirring idealism of Kennedy's later inaugural address. It had that Wilsonian streak so appealing to Americans of standing for the good in world affairs, and in light of what happened in China later—millions dead of starvation, the demonic madness of the Cultural Revolution, the suppression of basic freedoms, and all the rest—Drumright's call for a preventive stand gains retrospective appeal. The choice, however, in China was not at all clear at the time. The Nationalists under Chiang were deeply flawed; it was the Communists who were posing as the champions of democracy and civil rights, and not only in China, but also in the United States and Western Europe, which is one reason so many people who labeled themselves progressive were drawn to them. If China under the KMT had been a true democracy, the issue would have been far clearer. But can there be any doubt from the standpoint of a later time that the KMT would have been a better alternative for China?

Vincent felt that a great deal was missing from Drumright's manifesto, especially a close examination of its cost and its likelihood of success. It's all well and good to wax eloquent about the struggle for freedom, but policymakers need to assess whether grand idealistic goals can be achieved. As John Davies put this later:

> Drumright's stance . . . was typical of much policy thinking in the American government then and later. The power realities of a situation, even when understood, tended to be subordinated to what "ought to be done," what should be done because of precedents, commitments, moral compulsions, sentiment, and that great catchall, "national security." The factor of cost of a policy was thus often slighted.

Vincent, in partial reaction to Drumright, made the fundamental point that desired action is not always effective action. He laid down three options on China: one, withdraw; two, continue the existing policy; or three, enlarge the mission. While he didn't say so directly, he seemed to favor the first of these, because, as he put it, there was at best a "small likelihood that Chiang Kai-shek, even with our assistance, can by military methods bring about stability in North China and Manchuria of a lasting character," and there was no point in expending American lives, resources, and reputation on what was already a lost cause.

The next day, Byrnes read Vincent's memo aloud at a meeting with Robert Patterson and James Forrestal, respectively the secretary of war and the secretary of the navy. Patterson in particular was in favor of ignoring it, and ignoring Wedemeyer as well. Patterson, as Davies described him, was a "gung-ho" type. He was the one who'd dismissed the Communist attacks on the marines as "comic-opera" affairs. He was convinced that the reports of Communist strength were "exaggerated." He said at this meeting with Forrestal that he'd just spoken to Henry Luce, who had published a strong, pro-Chiang editorial in *Life*, one in which he'd argued basically that the United States had a moral obligation to give the Gimo its full backing, and Luce had gotten what he called a good response to it.

Forrestal was not thinking so much of the obstacles to American aims on the ground in Asia; he was thinking of the mood on the home front, the wish for American soldiers to be brought home and not sent on a costly mission on behalf of a government that was itself corrupt and undemocratic. Demonstrators brandishing placards saying "Bring the Troops Home" were on the march. Editorials across the country were demanding the same thing. Luce's reply was "We have to recognize the interdependence between China's fate and our own."

Drumright had said to ignore such niceties as the heavy-handed policies of the Chinese Nationalists, but the public didn't ignore them. It was actually deeply divided about them. Here is where the slow deterioration of Chiang's reputation and the more romantic view of the Communists came into play. "It is somewhat confusing that this Chinese agrarian reform movement is called 'Communism,'" Edgar Snow, the most famous proponent of Mao the democrat, wrote in May in the *Saturday Evening Post*. "Communism in China is a watered-down thing." In a new book called *The Solution in Asia*, the China expert Owen Lattimore, who had once been a political adviser to Chiang, wrote, "The political structure under the Communists is more nearly democratic than under the Kuomintang." Chiang, he continued, was a "coalition figure" who "need not fear losing his authority in a Government in which party differences with the Communists could be reconciled by democratic processes."

These were the attitudes that Luce was determined to fight, and part of the battle was to refurbish the reputation of his tarnished Chinese hero. In September, he had put Chiang on the cover of *Time*. The week before, Churchill had been on the cover. Luce's unspoken message was that these were the two great victors in the war and the two great men of the future in Europe and Asia. The cover on Chiang showed him looking handsome in a simple uniform with no decorations, staring ahead with large, destiny-filled eyes, his demeanor firm but softened by a trace of a wise smile. "At 57, Chiang Kai-shek stood at one of the pinnacles of his own and his nation's history," the accompanying article rhapsodized. "As the war ended, the great fact was clear: the Generalissimo had justified those who had long held that his government was firmly embedded in popular support, and that given peace, it could establish an effective administration in China."

This article was meant to justify Luce's portrayal of Chiang as a wise and beloved figure. But his determination to do this put *Time*'s editor at odds with his own star reporter in China. Theodore White had refused to write the worshipful cover story on Chiang that Luce wanted. White complained in a cable to *Time*'s headquarters in New York that the story Luce wanted would be full of the "customary panegyrics" and that it would "legitimize China's somber tyrant yet once again."

Directed at Luce, those were fighting words, the result of which was White's recall home and his dismissal from *Time*. Disagreement over China had ruined what had been a father-son relationship between the indomitable Luce and the brilliant, scrappy White, who had once put a sign outside his office in Chungking saying that any similarity between what he wrote and what appeared in the magazine was purely coincidental. White had opposed even the American airlift of central government troops, arguing with American military officers in China that they would be surrounded by Communist guerrillas and that their dispatch would involve the United States in an Asian civil war, which would, in turn, push the CCP into the arms of the Russians.

China evoked family quarrels. Every person saw in China a different beast. True, we're "disillusioned about China because of its constant civil wars," Luce wrote in *Life*. We ask ourselves, "Is there now a going concern called China with which . . . America can and should deal?" Luce's answer to his own question was a resounding yes. "Most Americans grossly underestimate the significance in China of this simple fact: that the legal government of China maintained itself on Chinese soil (not in exile) as the only government over at least half the land of China, and held the allegiance of the great majority in the other half."

The policymakers were not in disagreement with Luce's argument. The day before their meeting with Byrnes, November 26, Patterson and Forrestal wrote a memo in which they parted company with Wedemeyer's pessimism regarding the national government's chances of getting North China and Manchuria under its control. Patterson and Forrestal weren't willing to give up yet. There was no detailed examination of Wedemeyer's conclusion. The secretary of state and the secretary of war brought no technical military expertise to bear on the relative strengths of the government on one side and the Soviet-supported Communists on the other. There was no talk of domestic Chinese disillusionment with Chiang, or of the possibility that, in the Chinese tradition, the mandate of heaven was passing from one imperial figure to another. They didn't discuss just what it would take in the way of troops and supplies to ensure that Chiang prevailed in his contest with the Communists. Forrestal and Patterson simply didn't like the idea that the United States might, as the later expression had it, "cut and run" where a long-standing ally was concerned. It "appears undesirable . . . to retreat from any of the stated objectives without the most careful consideration," they wrote to Byrnes. If America changed its policy of support for Chiang Kai-shek, the two cabinet members wrote, "we will appear to world opinion to have deserted an ally."

That very day, Wedemeyer sent off another cable to Marshall, reiterating his "considered opinion" that Chiang would be unable to gain control of North China and Manchuria without "further U.S. and/or allied assistance" and, in the case of Manchuria, without "the wholehearted cooperation of the Soviet Russians." In his talks with Chiang, Wedemeyer said, the Chinese leader had agreed to "temporarily forgo reoccupation of Manchuria" and to concentrate on North China instead. But even that, Wedemeyer said, might be too much for him. The lines were too long and "Communist depredations" too damaging. Wedemeyer was not saying that the United States should "cut and run," but merely making it clear that if the United States opted to help the central government, that help was going to have to be substantial and sustained over a long period of time. "Also," Wedemeyer warned, "it's impossible for me to carry out orders to help Central Government forces and to carry out [the] order to avoid participation in fratricidal warfare."

Byrnes started the meeting of the next day by reading aloud the Patterson-Forrestal letter. After that, Forrestal expressed his opposition to "yanking the marines out of North China now." He offered a solution to the likely opposition by the public to any long military commitment in China: America should talk to the Russians and "get the UN into the picture," he said. But what, Byrnes asked, would the United States actually ask the Russians to do? Stay in Manchuria beyond the date they had promised to withdraw, December 2, which was less than a week later?

Forrestal: "No, but we can ask them to support the Chiang Kai-shek government."

Byrnes: Well, the Russians are already treaty-bound to support only the national government, so it's "difficult to know just how we should approach the Soviet government on the subject."

Byrnes repeated what he had been told by the Chinese ambassador to Washington: that the Soviets had promised not to permit any armed Communists to enter Manchuria.

While Byrnes saw the pointlessness of asking the Soviets to do what they insisted they were doing already, though Byrnes knew they weren't, he had little new to offer to solve the crisis in China. Instead, he went back to the same formula that previous American officials had proposed in their relations with Chiang. "Taking everything into account," he said, "perhaps the wise course would be to try to force the Chinese Government and the Chinese Communists to get together on a compromise basis, perhaps telling Generalissimo Chiang Kai-shek that we will stop the aid to his government unless he goes along with this." He recommended that Ambassador Hurley be sent back to China right away to give this message to the Chinese leader again. It was decided that the marines would stay on in China for the time being; exactly how long nobody seemed to know. Meanwhile, the United States would press ever harder for the Communists and the Nationalists to come to an agreement and stop their fighting.

This was how the United States found itself more deeply involved in China's civil war, neglecting Drumright's warning against doing it "half-heartedly" and Wedemeyer's warning that it would require a big and long commitment or it wouldn't work. The policy emerged as a sort of in-between measure, since the two main alternatives, of abandoning an ally and coming in heavily with substantial American forces, were both impossible. Byrnes's "wise course" does not even examine what the United States should do if the KMT and the CCP refused to go along with it. All of this illustrated the tendency of a democracy, when in a period of befuddlement, to do a little here and a little there, to try to satisfy opposing constituencies without making any clear or burdensome commitments, and at the same time, to nurture the hope, however forlorn, that the whole problem might go away if the two sides to the conflict would settle their differences through an American-mediated negotiation.

Forrestal, though he seems to have said nothing at the meeting with Byrnes, noted the almost casual way in which the decision was made to delay the marines' departure from China and to press for a negotiated settlement of the CCP-KMT conflict. It showed, he noted in his diary, "the symptoms of that 'on-the-one-hand—on-the-other-hand' disease which was to blight so many documents on Chinese policy in the ensuing years."

This time Hurley refused to cooperate. On the 26th, the day before the Forrestal-Patterson meeting, he'd told Byrnes that he didn't want to go back to China. He was thinking of resigning, he said. Byrnes persuaded him to stay on. His country needed him, Byrnes said. Chiang insisted he be ambassador. On November 27, the very day of the Byrnes-Forrestal-Patterson meeting, Hurley visited at the White House with Truman, who told him the situation in China was looking grave and that he needed to get back right away, preferably by leaving the next day.

Truman, thinking that Hurley had agreed, then went to a lunch with his cabinet. During the meal, he got an unexpected message: Hurley had issued a statement to the press that he was resigning after all. Without the courtesy of letting the president or the secretary of state know of this decision in advance, Hurley, headstrong and erratic to the end, had allowed his accumulated fury to overcome his better judgment.

In a letter given to the press, Hurley addressed what he regarded as the root of America's China problem: not Soviet machinations, or Communist aggressiveness, or the popular disillusionment with Chiang, but, he said, the professional American diplomats who, despite his efforts to relieve them of their posts, remained in positions of power and responsibility. At a press conference and in his written statement Hurley named no names, mentioning only "the professional foreign service men [who] sided with the Chinese Communist armed party and the imperialist bloc of nations whose policy it was to keep China divided against herself," but of course he meant the China experts in Chungking and Washington who had questioned his judgment: John Service, who after being exonerated in the Amerasia case had been reassigned to Tokyo as an adviser to MacArthur, accompanied there by John Emmerson and George Atcheson, the latter the formal author of the letter to the State Department of a few months earlier that had called Hurley's reporting on China "incomplete and non-objective;" John Davies, a particular bête noire of Hurley, who was now a valued aide to George Kennan in Moscow; and John Carter Vincent, head of the East Asia desk at State, where, Hurley complained in his letter, he was one of "my superiors."

This was sensational news, the big story of the moment. *The New York Times* reprinted Hurley's statement in full, describing it in a separate page-one article as a "blistering denunciation of the administration of foreign policy by professional career diplomats." In an editorial, the *Times* solemnly advised the Truman administration to look into the charges and "give some assurance to the country . . . that policy adopted at the top is actually followed faithfully down the line." And Hurley wasn't done.

At the American embassy in Chungking, the news created "an uproar, with all barriers down and all tongues wagging with what they have wanted to say for a long time," John Melby, the Soviet specialist, noted in his diary. Hurley's accusations had now exposed "the internal controversy over what we should do here and the deep bitterness between opposing points of view." The Nationalists were dismayed, but the Communists were delighted. Radio Yenan, which had been denouncing Hurley as the chief representative of "American imperialist elements," said, "China's civil war instigators in Chungking regret his resignation, [but the] Chinese people regard it as a victory for American people."

A few days later, Hurley, speaking at the National Press Club in Washington, did name names—Atcheson's and Service's in particular, as the men who had worked so hard to subvert American policy and turn China over to the Communists. Then he was off to the Senate where in two days of testimony he again accused Atcheson and Service of conspiring to bring about Chiang's fall. "Pat Hurley came out with a roar, both fists swinging," *Time* recounted of this appearance. "His white mustache bristled, his black-ribboned pince-nez wobbled on his nose. He pounded away on his main theme." In reply, James Byrnes, the secretary of state, was forced formally to investigate these grave charges to determine if they were unwarranted, thereby unintentionally adding to their visibility. American Foreign Service officers had reported their views and analyses in the way they were supposed to—nothing disloyal about that, he said. But Hurley's sensational accusations had for the first time put the charge of disloyalty and double-dealing on China into the public arena, and it was to remain there in its poisonous and prosecutorial way for decades.

Truman, mightily annoyed at Hurley's abrupt departure, needed another ambassador right away, and he knew who he wanted. That night, he called George Marshall, who had just arrived at his home in Leesburg, Virginia, looking forward to a restful retirement after his busy career as a soldier and chief of staff. Marshall's wife was halfway up the stairs to have a brief rest before their first dinner at home when the phone rang. "General, I want you to go to China for me," Truman said. Marshall, who wanted to wait until after dinner to break the news to his wife, said, "Yes, Mr. President," and hung up. An hour later the radio news announced Marshall's new appointment. "I couldn't bear to tell you until you had had your rest," Marshall told his wife. What is not clear is whether Marshall himself understood the full import of that very brief conversation with Truman, that he would not only be ambassador to China but that the task of reconciling the two armed parties of China and bringing a halt to the nascent civil war would now fall on his shoulders.

Meanwhile, the situation had turned modestly for the better. In mid-November, tired of Soviet trickery and intent on calling international attention to it, Chiang ordered the negotiating team to leave Changchun. The initial reaction of the Soviets was to step up harassment. A member of the Communist-controlled police force was killed, and immediately posters appeared all over the city blaming the KMT and demanding the expulsion of the government delegation, ignoring the fact that the delegation had been ordered to leave by the country's president. The headquarters were "haunted by the sound of the wind and the cry of the cranes," Chang Kia-ngau, the economist on the Chinese government team, wrote in his diary, sounding like a Tang dynasty poet. The water supply and telephone service were cut off. "The feeling is that a great catastrophe is about to occur."

That day, one hundred sixty members of the KMT delegation left Changchun by airplane for Beijing, and almost immediately the Soviet tone changed. Until then, Stalin's main tactical instruction to the CCP was that it could "act" in Manchuria by moving its own troops and blocking those of the government, but it could not "speak out"; it could not openly declare its intention of taking over Manchuria. All along Stalin had maintained the show of normal, exclusive relations with Chiang, keeping his embassy in Chungking and having no official contact with Yenan. Stalin's communications with Mao took place informally and in secret through his representatives in Yenan and via the radio transmitter that had been provided by the Comintern years before.

Two days after the withdrawal of the KMT team from Changchun, Stalin sent a note to Chiang saying that he would "eradicate all mob action" in Manchuria, and proposing that the Soviet Red Army postpone its departure in order to help in this endeavor. A few days later, the Russians told Chiang that they would guarantee the landing of government troops in the major cities of Manchuria, Mukden and Changchun. Meanwhile, Stalin told the Communists to get their own troops out of those cities and not to fight government forces in those areas — even as the Soviets stepped up their supplies of arms to the Communists from the arsenals in Dalian and North Korea.

In Changchun, a Soviet officer called in local newspaper reporters and told them that opposition to the national government was to be banned. Almost from one minute to the next, the posters criticizing the KMT disappeared and were replaced by others supporting it and praising international cooperation. Malinovsky vowed to prohibit Communist activities in areas where the central government established its authority. He banned the issuing of banknotes by the Communist army, and he expressed the hope that the KMT delegation would return to Changchun.

The Russians were following their usual flexible policy, helping the Communists while avoiding anything to provoke stepped-up American involvement, and Mao, though impatient and annoyed at this caution, understood this. On November 20, Yenan sent new instructions to its bureau in Manchuria, informing it that instead of trying to occupy Manchuria's big cities, the Communists' main force should take "middle and small cities and minor railways as the focal points, and backed against the Soviet Union, Korea, Outer Mongolia, and Jehol, create powerful base areas." Naturally, many of the Communist rank and file, the thousands who had migrated to the "liberated areas" during the war, were unhappy with this policy. They were told to "look at the whole situation," and engage *Mei-Chiang*, a newly minted pejorative shorthand for the supposed alliance between America and Chiang Kai-shek. The contest between the KMT and the Chinese revolutionaries was a mirror of the looming, larger global struggle between Russia and America, between the "New Democracy" and the capitalist reactionaries, but as a tactical matter, to avoid American interference, the Soviet Union had to "separate itself in appearance from the CCP." The Chinese Communists had, likewise, to "pretend that the CCP has no connection with the Soviet Union," even as it should "try to neutralize the United States."

There were other improvements in the situation. Government troops, helped by the United States, made progress in Manchuria by forcing the Eighth Route Army to retreat from the area around Qinwangdao. Student demonstrations took place in some big cities, and for a change, rather than target the central government, they protested the Communists' closeness to the Russians. On December 16, 1945, Chiang visited Beijing. It was the first time the recognized leader of China had been to the city since the full-scale war broke out in 1937; for that entire length of time, China's glorious former imperial capital had been in the hands of the Japanese invaders. One hundred thousand students were on hand to greet the Gimo at Tiananmen Square before the entrance to China's grandest imperial relic, the Forbidden City, and they gave him what Chiang's biographer Jay Taylor has called "a thunderous greeting." Thousands of people rushed forward to touch him or simply to stare. A huge portrait of him, showing him in his stern, authoritarian persona rather than in his avuncular scholar's pose, was put up over the *wumen*, or Meridian Gate.

From Beijing, Chiang flew to Nanjing, his own former capital, to take up full-time residence in the military academy compound there, where he thanked "Our Heavenly Father" for "glorious victory" and surveyed the throngs of citizens lined up along his route to cheer him.

On the main strategic question, namely the role of the Soviet Union, Chiang no doubt understood the Communists' two-sided policy, but he was nonetheless happy with the Soviets' apparent change in attitude. His Russian-speaking son, who had carried out negotiations with Malinovsky in Changchun, told him in early December that the Soviets had "agreed to almost all the Government's proposals, including abolishment of all non-government armed forces."

Is it possible that the leaders of China's central government believed this, especially when the Russians were simultaneously adding to the

Communists' arsenal? Chiang had always hoped that by appearing strong and demonstrating that the CCP had no chance of overthrowing him he could induce Moscow to keep its distance from Mao. Consequently, Chiang decided not to protest the wholesale removal of billions of dollars' worth of former Japanese industrial plants from Manchuria. He made no effort to reduce the neocolonialist advantages the Soviets had gotten in Dalian and Port Arthur and on the Manchurian railways. He hoped that he could satisfy Moscow, persuade the Russians that their interest lay in supporting him rather than Mao. It was a reasonable calculation at the time, but as events would soon show, it was entirely wrong.

The American diplomatic reporting on the situation in China became notably more optimistic. The military attaché's report in early December noted that a government plane had been dispatched to Yenan to bring Zhou Enlai to Chungking for more talks on convening the elusive Political Consultative Conference and that the editorials in the Communist press "indicate a more positive attitude toward discussion of compromise measures." The Communist opposition has been "weakened," the attaché concluded, and now it seemed "unlikely that the Chinese Communists can hold long against well-equipped and trained Central Government forces now being moved in."

By early December, seven government armies were embarked on a large-scale three-pronged move to take over the north. One column was moving to capture Kalgan, which was north of Beijing and controlled the main overland route to Manchuria. A second column was advancing along the Beijing–Gubeigou Railway to capture the passes in the region of the Great Wall. A third prong, consisting of troops that the Communist press had earlier declared to be wiped out, was thirty miles from Mukden, where a major battle was shaping up. These government troops were the best in the national army.

By the middle of December, American intelligence believed that the Communists would decline to defend Mukden. The attaché's report said that the Communists were facing "more serious threats to their domination," as the government's forces moved closer to Kalgan and into Jehol province. The government's Eighth Army meanwhile had landed, with American help, in Qingdao and was moving to chase the Communists from the ports they controlled in Shandong, most importantly Chefoo, where they had earlier prevented the marines from landing.

By the third week in December, Zhou was back in Chungking and the convening of the PCC seemed "certain." The tide was turning in favor of the government, and the timing was perfect because the new ambassador to China was about to arrive at his post and the United States to embark on another concerted effort to broker a deal between the Communists and the government that would lead to a unified and democratic China. And George C. Marshall, a figure of impeccable manners, reputation, and credentials, the architect of military victory on two continents, a man whose stature and reputation dwarfed those of the mercurial Hurley, was sure that while American diplomatic efforts in China had failed in the past, this time they were bound to succeed.

CHAPTER SIXTEEN

Marshall Comes Close

E verybody is waiting for Marshall and too much is being expected of him," John Melby told his diary two days before the arrival of Truman's distinguished new emissary and the man who was going to avert a Chinese civil war, if anybody could.

> Everybody scurries around here doing not much of anything . . . and all scared to death over the impending arrival of the great man himself. . . . It begins to have the earmarks of an anti-climax, and I have a growing feeling that the whole thing was dreamed up under pressure and panic. Many here now regret it, but don't know what can be done, except to go through with it. Most are agreed that it cannot help but impair the great reputation.

Melby doesn't say why many were regretting the formation of the Marshall mission, but most likely the regret came from a worry over the United States expending its resources and putting its prestige at stake in a highly visible pursuit of the impossible. There was a divide between the Americans inside China with their realistic sense of the bitter irreconcilability of the two sides in the conflict and the Americans back home in the United States with their abiding faith in political compromise and institutionalized nonviolent struggle for power, both of which were entirely absent from China's tradition. But perhaps overriding it all was the commanding figure of Marshall himself, his stature, his record so entirely unmarked by failure. "He is a modest man and completely without vanity," one of his senior aides wrote home after his first glimpse of Marshall. He was the kind of man who refused to accept any awards or decorations during the war, feeling that to do so while soldiers were dying in the field would be unseemly. "I have seen a great many soldiers in my lifetime," Henry Stimson, the secretary of war, told Marshall at a ceremony marking his retirement as chief of staff, "and you, sir, are the finest soldier I have ever known."

Melby, who first met Marshall in Chungking at the end of December, found that he made "a good and direct impression," though he wasn't as tall as he'd imagined. Marshall, who had organized the armies, the logistics, and the commands that defeated the Axis, was famous for never interfering with the men he named to lead troops in the field or attempting to manage battlefield decisions from afar. As Melby got to know him, he had "the growing impression of a man who is a really great soldier and a great man in the sense of being truly humble and unimpressed with himself," but he also didn't quite appreciate that the task of diplomatic mediation in China was going to be more frustrating, more littered with unanticipated obstacles, than even winning a global war. Marshall, Melby observed, was a man "whose outlook and experience have the limitations of a professional soldier."

Everybody was waiting for Marshall. Chinese and American honor guards were on hand when his plane landed in Shanghai on December 20, 1945. Albert Wedemeyer, the American military commander in China, escorted him in a black Buick sedan to the Cathay Hotel, the grand, tarnished edifice on the city's famous Bund where sixteen years earlier Noël Coward had written his play *Private Lives*. The Cathay, built by Victor Sassoon, the Iraqi Jew who was the great real estate magnate of the International Settlement, was the showplace of the foreign-run part of Shanghai, overlooking the broad Huangpu River, which was crowded with junks, sampans, steamships, and, now, American naval vessels. Marshall was in the city during what amounted to an American military occupation: the marines were making their presence felt. They played football and baseball at the city's famed racecourse and caroused at night, exploring what *Time* delicately called "the licentious pleasures of the cities," Shanghai and others.

Some of Marshall's entourage went out to view this American occupation. On their way back to their ships late at night, some of the marines engaged in the pastime of pedicab racing. Coolies were hired. The servicemen took their places in the passenger seats. The race began down broad Nanjing Road or Bubbling Well Road or one of Shanghai's other main streets, which wasn't so bad, one member of Marshall's party reported, "except that they try in some way or other to spur the coolie on and that usually takes the form of hitting him on the back with a belt."

By the time of Marshall's arrival in China, the euphoria evoked by Japan's defeat had been replaced by a sour, contentious, and pessimistic mood. The reality that after eight years of Japanese occupation the country was already engulfed in a civil war was setting in. Intense fighting between central government forces and the Communists was taking place in numerous areas stretching from Shaanxi province in the west to Shandong in the east. And there was more than just the division between Communists and Nationalists spoiling the thrill of the victory over Japan. There were also deep arguments among the non-Communists as well, especially among the KMT and the several democratic parties representing businessmen, intellectuals, and students that emerged as wartime restrictions on political activity came to an end. In many quarters, Chiang Kai-shek was still revered as the hero who had led the nation through the years of resistance. He was the best-known man in China, his picture everywhere, his speeches duly reported in the pro-KMT press, and he had a glamorous wife who slept in the White House when she visited Washington. But a powerful disillusion about the ruling party was also setting in, and there was a feeling among many that the postwar American presence in China, exemplified by those marines hitting Chinese pedicab drivers with their belts, was a neoimperialist imposition.

In late November, student demonstrations erupted in Kunming, where several universities were still in the places of their wartime exile. Kunming had been the headquarters of Chennault's Flying Tigers during the war and under the political control of Lung Yun, the warlord of Yunnan province. It had therefore always been a freer place than most of unoccupied China, less burdened by the KMT's wartime restrictions. It was also a rare center of successful resistance and counterattack against the Japanese, as Chinese forces, with indispensable support from Chennault's fighter planes, drove the Japanese from the Salween Gorge back to Burma. In one notable battle, Lung Yun had helped to turn near defeat into victory, taking command after a Chinese general was shot dead and rallying Chinese troops to prevent what would otherwise have been a disastrous enemy crossing of the Salween. But with the war over, Chiang sent his own army to Kunming, where after several days of bloody confrontations, they took over the city, sending Lung to a meaningless job in Chungking.

Now in total control of the city, the KMT troops, enforcing the Gimo's writ, had prevented a meeting from being held in the central hall of Yunnan University, leading to an open-air assembly that was addressed by members of the faculty. The meeting was broken up by troops firing over the heads of the crowd but not before students had expressed their demands, one of which was the withdrawal of American troops from China. The demonstrations mostly targeted the KMT government, its perpetuation of one-party rule, its corruption, the terror-inducing operations of its secret police. Student demonstrations had a particular meaning in China, a historical portentousness that went back to the clamorous protests against Japan's Fifteen Demands of 1915 and the years of ferment known as the May Fourth Movement that preceded World War I. There were reports that during the demonstrations in Kunming, students had been killed or wounded in police raids as the government tried to impose order, but the demonstrations continued well into 1946, providing a kind of dissenting background noise to the Marshall negotiation, a sign of the central government's diminishing popularity.

"The murder and brutality going on there are shocking," Melby noted in his diary, referring to the events in Kunming in early December—though Melby was not in Kunming and is unclear and unspecific about the murders taking place there. "A lot of Kuomintang people are genuinely horrified, but it still goes on."

If the situation in China was uncertain and ambiguous, the policy of the United States was also fraught with vagueness and inconsistency. Before his departure for China, Marshall attended a Sunday morning meeting with Secretary of State James Byrnes and his advisers, including Dean Acheson, who was the number two in the State Department, and John Carter Vincent. In China, Wedemeyer was reporting Chiang Kai-shek's continuing demands for American help in transporting more troops to North China and to Manchuria, where, clearly, they would be used to stop Communist expansion. Because it was contrary to American policy to become involved in China's "fratricidal strife," the question naturally emerged: Should the United States agree to this request? If it did, Chiang's incentive to form a coalition government would be reduced, so a delay in responding seemed appropriate. But Marshall wanted to know what American policy would be if it was Chiang rather than the Communists who obstructed the desired settlement.

There were deep disagreements on this question. Vincent argued forcefully and strenuously against further aid to Chiang if he was the obstacle to Marshall's mission. More arms to Chiang would lead to a civil war, and the Communists were likely to win it. If that were to happen, Vincent believed that the consequences would not be disastrous for the United States. He did not think, given China's immensity and the power of its yearning for independence, that it would become a satellite of the Soviet Union. And if it did—so what? China was such a wreck of a country, so badly in need of basic rebuilding and reconstruction, that all its energies would be taken up by its pressing domestic needs. Therefore, if Chiang refused a political settlement, the United States should refuse to move his troops even if that meant the Communists would take control of the areas vacated by the departing Japanese. China would be divided, and while that would be bad, it would not be calamitous, and, anyway, in the end it was the Chinese themselves and not the Americans who would determine their fate. Vincent's was an articulation of a deeper view of foreign relations, one that recognized the limits on America's power to shape the world to its specifications and the necessity to accept less than perfect outcomes.

Vincent's argument had no traction. The looming Cold War doomed it. Byrnes spelled it out in that Sunday morning meeting with Marshall and the president. If the United States failed to help Chiang, Byrnes argued, the Soviets would delay their promised withdrawal from Manchuria, from which they would help the Chinese Communists consolidate the territories they held in North China, including Hebei, Shaanxi, and Shandong. Eventually the several hundred thousand Japanese still in North China would be forced to surrender to the Communists. The Soviets would dominate China in much the same way they were already coming to dominate Eastern Europe, installing submissive Communist dictatorships in place of the collaborationist governments that had been set up during the Nazi occupation.

Marshall entirely agreed and helped to make the case to Truman. In order to give both sides in China an incentive to come to terms with each other, he said, the question of whether or not to give more aid to Chiang should be given no clear answer. There should be an element of intentional ambiguity in American policy. But if Chiang "failed to make reasonable concessions," Marshall said, summarizing the position he took at the meeting, "there would follow the tragic consequences of a divided China and of a probable Russian reassumption of power in

Manchuria, the combined effect of this resulting in the defeat or loss of our major purpose of the war in the Pacific." That was the idea that swept away all opposition, that after all that sacrifice, after Pearl Harbor and the Bataan death march, Iwo Jima, Saipan, the Coral Sea, the airlift over the Himalayas, and the atomic bomb, after more than one hundred thousand American military deaths in the Pacific theater and another quarter million wounded, after more than twenty-one thousand American servicemen had suffered the horror of internment in Japanese prisoner-of-war camps, the end result would be even worse than a China under the thumb of Japan—it would be a China under Stalin's thumb instead. Truman was convinced. Byrnes was on board. Marshall was formally instructed, as one historian has summarized, "to try to induce both sides to make reasonable concessions toward a truce. . . . If the Communists refused to do so, he was authorized to transport government troops into the region. But if the Generalissimo refused to do so . . . he was not to be abandoned."

In other words, no matter what Chiang did, the United States would provide ships and planes to move his troops into battle, though he wasn't to know this until the moment arrived. Marshall's goal would be to bring about a peaceful political settlement in China so the transport of more government troops would be unnecessary. But there was no denying that the fallback American position was to continue to give help to Chiang if all else failed, and this help would constitute involvement in China's "fratricidal conflict" on the side of the KMT.

Success for the Marshall mission was essential, and perhaps for that reason, but also by reason of personality, Marshall refused to give credence to any of the pessimistic forecasts that preceded his visit. His chief of staff, Colonel Henry A. Byroade, who accompanied him to China, had told him in Washington that he had a two percent chance of success. Isaac Newell, who had been commander of American forces in China when the youthful Marshall had served a tour of duty there in the 1920s, wrote to him, "You have . . . been given a problem almost as difficult as the one you have just solved."

Similar cautionary opinions greeted Marshall when he arrived just before Christmas in Shanghai. Within minutes of his installation at the Cathay Hotel he summoned Wedemeyer to his suite. "I told General Marshall," Wedemeyer later recalled, "that he would never be able to effect a working arrangement between the Communists and the Nationalists, since the Nationalists, who still had most of the power, were determined not to relinquish one iota of it, while the Communists for their part were equally determined to seize all power, with the aid of the Soviet Union."

Marshall's stern reply to this realistic prognosis: "I am going to accomplish my mission and you are going to help me."

Marshall was sixty-five years old when the war ended. He came from an old Virginia family—among his ancestors was John Marshall, the first chief justice of the United States. He went to the Virginia Military Institute, served as a company commander in the war to defeat the guerrilla insurrection against American colonial rule in the Philippines, and, in World War I, became a protégé of John J. Pershing, the commander of the American Expeditionary Forces to Europe. For three years after the war, Marshall commanded the 15th Infantry Regiment, a storied unit that had been deployed to China since the Boxer Rebellion at the turn of the century. It was during that time that he met Joseph Stilwell, who was a 15th Infantry battalion commander, and the two men remained close and mutually supportive ever after. On the day that Germany invaded Poland in 1939, President Roosevelt named Marshall chief of staff of the army, a post he held for the next six years, until just before his mediation mission to China in 1945.

Chiang Kai-shek was nervous about Marshall's friendship with Stilwell, the Chinese leader's American bête noire, but the subject was discreetly avoided when the two men met for the first time in Nanjing on the second day of Marshall's China sojourn. Marshall reassured the Gimo that Truman's policy included "eliminating autonomous armies in China, such as those of the Chinese Communists," and this was clearly what Chiang wanted to hear. Marshall's goal, and Truman's, he said, was to achieve "a solution of China's internal problems by peaceful means," which didn't arouse opposition from Chiang but which wasn't entirely his goal either. Chiang's goal was to stop the Communists from threatening his rule by whatever means he had at his disposal, and if the use of military force was his best option, he was prepared to adopt it. Chiang told Marshall, as Marshall paraphrased it, that there was "a definite connection between Soviet Russia and the Chinese Communists," and the latter relied upon the former, which had given the Chinese Communists arms and equipment in Manchuria and had been "unfriendly and uncooperative" at Dalian, Huludao, and Yingkou. The

Soviet aim, Chiang affirmed, was "to establish a puppet regime in Manchuria under the Chinese Communists. He said that the Soviet military commander in Manchuria had purposely delayed the withdrawal of Soviet troops from Manchuria as a means of aiding the Communists." Marshall, in his American way and in the way of a negotiator whose success depends on a willingness to persuade others to compromise, chose at this early stage to chalk up the KMT-CCP conflict to mutual misunderstanding, or, as he put it, to a "barrier of fear, distrust and suspicions between the rival parties." He seemed to think that Chiang exaggerated the importance of the CCP's connection to Moscow, that it was more a tactical necessity than the reflection of a deep ideological commitment. Actually, Chiang was closer to reality in his view of the Communists than Marshall was. The conflict in China was not due to a failure to communicate. It was due to the existence of two parties that sought unrivaled power and represented incompatible social and political visions.

The day after their meeting in Nanjing, Marshall and Chiang flew together to Chungking, which, though no longer the country's capital, was the place where many government offices and embassies remained, where Zhou Enlai was installed in the Communists' ramshackle headquarters, and where Marshall's negotiation would take place, at least to start. "All shades and grades of brass turned up at the airport for the arrival of the American and Chinese Generalissimos," Melby reported. The police tried to get the Communists to leave, forcing the Americans to intervene to stop them from doing so, Melby recalled, and that was one reason the mood was "anything but joyous."

Chungking was into its grim winter season. It was foggy, rainy, and cold. Dark clouds boiled up from the rivers below. The day before, Melby had made his way down the alley, lined with peddler stalls and slick with mud, to Communist headquarters to do advance work for Marshall's visit. The day after the American party's arrival in Chungking, the new emissary met with Zhou Enlai, who, according to Marshall, "emphasized their desire for a cessation of hostilities and for the establishment of a coalition government." Zhou had come to the airport the day before, where he told Marshall of his admiration for Lincoln's idea of government of, by, and for the people, and Washington's spirit of national independence—a not so subtle reassurance that the Communists intended to be similarly independent and not subservient to the Soviet Union. Marshall understood the catch to Zhou's assurance of cooperation, which was that the Communists had never before shown a willingness to enter a coalition with the Nationalists if they had to give up control of their own armed forces and if Chiang insisted, as the phrase had it, on one country, one army.

The Chinese Communists had decided to welcome Marshall's mission, and this, for the time being, was consistent with their overall strategy. Early in December, Mao had sent a directive to cadres in the field to use the winter not to fight but to build up their forces in Manchuria for a later showdown with the KMT. He did this in part because Stalin, always wary of the possibility of an American military intervention, wanted him to. In January, just a few weeks into the Marshall mission, Stalin advised the Chinese Communists never to underestimate American strength and therefore to be careful not to provoke the United States into a major intervention in China on Chiang's side. At a foreign ministers' meeting in Moscow in December, Stalin, as Byrnes put it, had "pledged his support to the National Government and his intention to comply with that obligation." Stalin had denied aiding the Chinese Communists in Manchuria. He'd dismissed them as weak, inconsequential, and Byrnes, perhaps out of wishful thinking, fell easy prey to these deceptive assurances. "My estimate," Byrnes concluded, was that Stalin "will not intentionally do anything to destroy our efforts for unified China."

To be sure, the Soviets, as George Kennan in Moscow wrote to Byrnes early in January, would not make any overt effort to wreck Marshall's mission. The USSR in Kennan's view was "an expansionist force," propelled in this "by revolutionary tradition, by nationalist ambition, and by kinetic nature." Moscow, Kennan added, would not want a neutral China, "because to Kremlin minds, 'He that is not with me is against me.'" Kennan also warned about Stalin's chronic deceitfulness. The Soviet system, with its theoretical division between the government and the Communist Party, allowed the party to pursue policies that were "piously foresworn" by the government—just as Stalin had done with Byrnes in saying that the Soviet government had given no help to the Communists; what the Communist Party of the Soviet Union did was another matter. Revolutionary tradition, as Kennan called it, would lead the Kremlin to want the Chinese Communists to succeed in China, but if they were too weak, a submissive Kuomintang-controlled China would be an acceptable outcome also. The Soviets would thus maintain a confusing both-sides-of-the-fence policy in order to have a compliant Chinese regime.

This was Mao's estimate also. He knew that Stalin would help the CCP, and that he was helping it establish its strength in Manchuria, but that at least for the time being, in obedience to the Sino-Soviet treaty, the Soviets would continue to make a show of supporting the national government in its program of reestablishing control in Manchuria. Even if Mao wanted to defy the Soviet leader's cautionary advice, the military balance didn't allow it. By the end of 1945 the Nationalist government had deployed some of its best American-trained and -equipped troops—its so-called Alpha forces—between Huludao and Mukden, and they were advancing on Communist strongholds in Chengde, Jehol, and Kalgan. "The position of the Communists [is] deteriorating as [the] Central Government moves toward Jehol and masses troops in Henan and Jiangsu," the American military attaché reported on January 5. The Communists were experiencing "supply difficulties, heavy casualties, extremely cold weather, and lack of sufficient artillery."

Under the circumstances, the Marshall mission was an opportunity for the Communists to go on the political offensive. The burden would be on Chiang to allow them a share of national power because, the Communists knew, that was what the Americans would demand. It was also what Chinese public opinion wanted. The Communists knew Marshall would want them to give up their separate army, but they would temporize on that demand, play for time, and meanwhile increase their strength by recruiting new conscripts. At the same time, like the Kuomintang, the Communists would fight when it was in their interest to do so, even as their peerless emissary Zhou Enlai faithfully participated in the Marshall mission. It was, in other words, the perfect moment for fighting and talking simultaneously.

No sooner had he gotten settled into a house in Chungking than Marshall opened a series of intensive talks with the KMT and CCP representatives. Chiang's man at these conferences was Chang Chun, an army general who had known the Gimo since both were teenagers. Zhou represented the Communists. The three men held several lengthy sessions in conditions of intense urgency. Both sides, it seemed, wanted to put a halt to the civil war that had broken out in several regions of China, and Marshall proved to be the perfect mediator—patient, businesslike, attentive to detail, and able to appear fair to both sides.

The question that divided the two Chinese sides wasn't whether to agree to a ceasefire. Both wanted to stop fighting, at least for a while, especially in the areas where the other party had the advantage. The difficult question was what troop movements would be allowed after the fighting stopped, so that neither side would be able to use the cessation of hostilities to gain an advantage for future hostilities. In general, it was agreed that there should be very few troop movements. The units that were engaged in the fighting should keep to their positions until there could be a later agreement by which all Chinese armed forces would be integrated into a single national army—an idea that both sides also accepted in principle.

The central government would accept no deal that did not allow it to take over the northeastern provinces of Manchuria that made up the former Japanese puppet state of Manchukuo, and they therefore needed to move troops there, with American help. That was what they were allowed to do as the legitimate government of China. Even the Soviet Union was pledged by the terms of the Sino-Soviet treaty to help the central government, and only the central government, to do that. But the former Manchukuo is exactly where the Communists were strong, having infiltrated troops there and taken possession of Japanese stores of arms. But showing a remarkable eagerness for compromise, the Communists accepted what the negotiators called an "exception" to the non-movement of troops in Manchuria after the ceasefire. The government would be allowed to send its forces toward Manchuria and move them inside Manchuria so as to reestablish Chinese sovereignty as the Soviets withdrew. The Chinese Communists would be required to keep their troops where they were.

Even with that agreement, attained after several marathon sessions over several days, things almost fell apart. There was a disagreement about two towns, Zhifeng, in what is now central Liaoning province, and Duolun, about 125 miles west. Both were in what was then known as Jehol province north and northeast of Beijing; since then it has been divided between Liaoning and Inner Mongolia. The Nationalists claimed they had an agreement with the Soviets to take over both towns, which were rail junctions, after the Soviets withdrew. Zhou insisted that the Soviets had already left both places and that both had been occupied by the Eighth Route Army. Nationalist troops were heading toward them, he said, which made a clash almost inevitable, and since there was eventually going to be a consolidation of military forces, there was no reason for the government to be "hastening to take over these places at the present time by force." We've agreed to the exception for Manchuria, Zhou said, as the argument continued the next day, January 9, "but we can't agree to this one."

It came down to the wire. The next day was to be the first meeting of the long-delayed and long-anticipated Political Consultative Conference (PCC). There would be thirty-eight delegates there representing all the parties—eight delegates for the KMT, seven for the Communists, nine for the Democratic League, five for the Youth Party, and nine for non-party individuals. Suddenly this group, which had been proposed years before but had never met, was to be given the task of determining the shape of China's political future. But the PCC was unlikely to succeed if civil war was still raging. "It would be a tragedy," Marshall said, calling an end to the January 9 meeting because to continue it would have been pointless, "to have this conference fail at the last moment."

That night, as he later reported it to Truman, Marshall went to see Chiang at home. When he met Chang and Zhou the next morning, he told them there had been a breakthrough. The Gimo, he said, had "generously agreed to the issuance of the order for the cessation of hostilities without reference to Zhifeng and Duolun." Problem solved. The three announced the ceasefire agreement literally minutes before the opening session of the PCC.

Marshall was pleased. The Chinese parties had proven to be far more accommodating than all those pessimists predicting failure could have expected. On January 13, Chiang and Mao sent orders to their troops to stop fighting and to stay in place, both recognizing the "exception" for central government troops in Manchuria. Chiang then made a speech to the PCC that gladdened the hearts of the Americans. For years, the United States had urged him to make political reforms, loosen his control, and legalize rival parties and allow them real participation in the government. The Americans had railed against the central government for its repressiveness, its press censorship, the free hand it gave to Tai Li and his secret police to intimidate, torture, and imprison those with dissenting views. "I've tried to tell Chiang Kai-shek to liberalize, and that suppression will send intellectuals, small businessmen and students to affiliate themselves with the opposition," Wedemeyer told Marshall.

Now Chiang was formally proclaiming that he would do what the Americans wanted of him. This was an important moment, a major gesture. For the first time in China's history, liberal democratic ideals were being advanced as state policy. Chiang promised that within ten days all civil liberties in China would be assured, press censorship ended, political parties made lawful, and, within a mere seven days, every political prisoner released—except for pro-Japanese traitors. At the same time, with the inauguration of the People's Consultative Conference on January 10, China was taking another unprecedented step. Never before in the country's history had an assembly of freely competing political parties been convened, nor, as things turned out, would such an assembly ever be convened in the future.

The PCC has been little noticed in the intervening years because its life was very short and it had no lasting effect, but for the moment it had real power and real prestige. It was to create a framework for a coalition government, including the multiparty makeup of a new State Council, the rough equivalent of a cabinet, in which the Kuomintang would have just half the seats. Later, a National Assembly would be convened to draw up a new constitution, and the expectation was that the document would be modeled on the American example, with a system of checks and balances and limits placed on executive power. The PCC, in short, was to create a plan by which the KMT would give up its monopoly on power, a very big change for a country that had been ruled by all-powerful emperors for thousands of years.

It is worth noting that this is the formula that the United States promoted universally in the world in those years, a system of freely competing political parties bolstered by a free press and the rule of law, which meant in practice curbs on the power of the police. No such proposals would have come from the Soviet Union, which dismissed the idea of freely competing political parties. No doubt it was in part because of the promised democratic nature of the PCC's announced program that it was greeted with euphoria in China, with Marshall being given a great deal of the credit. Where Hurley had failed, he had succeeded, or so it seemed.

Both sides in China expressed their gratitude, the Communists in particular. On January 12, two days after the ceasefire announcement and the opening of the PCC, the *Liberation Daily* proclaimed, "The rejoicing with which the Chinese people have received the KMT-CCP cease-fire order is not less than that which greeted the Jap surrender announcement. . . . It marks the beginning of a phase of peaceful development, peaceful reform, and peaceful reconstruction unique in the modern history of China." Zhou now assured Marshall that the Communists were ready to "cooperate with the purposes of the US government." Socialism is our goal, Zhou said, repeating what he'd told David Barrett on the plane ride more than a year earlier. The Chinese Communists were really Communists, he said, but China is decades away from the possibility of socialism, and, in the meantime, "the democracy to be initiated in China should follow the American pattern. . . . We mean to acquire U.S. democracy and science . . . free enterprise and the development of individuality."

Zhou made a quick trip to Yenan to get approval from the CCP Central Committee for the Chungking decisions, and on his return to Chungking, Zhou hand-delivered a letter that Mao had written to Marshall. "The door to democracy is now pushed open, regardless of how narrow the opening still is," the Chairman wrote. Zhou said he wanted to convey an anecdote to Marshall that would reveal the Communists' attitude. There were rumors in Yenan that Mao would soon visit Moscow, Zhou said. Mao laughed at that. He said that he wasn't planning on taking a furlough even though it would be good for his health if he did. Anyway, if he went anyplace, Mao said, he'd rather that it be to the United States where he was sure he'd have a great deal to learn.

Within hours of the signing of the agreement, the Executive Headquarters, which would oversee the ceasefire, was set up in Beijing, with, Marshall reported to Truman, 125 officers and 350 men equipped with radios, planes, jeeps, and trucks, all of which had to be flown in on American transport planes. "The distances are great," Marshall said, outlining the logistical difficulties of the truce inspection effort, "the area tremendous, and the communications miserable, or completely lacking." Walter Robertson, the former chargé in Chungking, was dispatched to Beijing to be the American high commissioner. Colonel Byroade, the thirty-two-year-old West Point graduate from Indiana who had been with the Marshall mission from its inception, would be chief of staff. "We literally had a team in there the next day," Byroade recalled later. The Americans flew the Nationalist and the Communist teams to Beijing, where they were put up in separate hotels. The headquarters itself was installed in the Beijing Union Medical College, which had been founded by American missionaries in 1906 and was mostly paid for by

Zhou Enlai signs the ceasefire agreement of January 23, 1946, as the Nationalist negotiator, Chang Chun, and George C. Marshall, President Truman's special envoy to China, look on.

the Rockefeller Foundation. The college, with its twenty stately brick
buildings, had been largely abandoned during the Japanese occupation.

Almost immediately, both sides were complaining about truce violations by the other side. Zhou, talking to Marshall in Chungking on
January 14, the day after the ceasefire proclamations, complained that
government forces were marching on Zhifeng despite Chiang's vow to
leave the status of that city for later talks. Marshall replied that he'd had
a personal assurance from Chiang that the government would abide by
the ceasefire agreement and that Chiang would be in an "impossible
situation" if he failed to do that. Most likely, Marshall said, the ongoing
hostilities were "minor actions on a low level and could be straightened
out by the Executive Headquarters."

Marshall cabled Byroade, who met in Beijing with Ye Jianying, a
Long March veteran who was the Communist commissioner. There
were a couple of tense days. The commissioners agreed to drop leaflets
on the area the next day announcing the ceasefire. Byroade sent an
American plane to Zhifeng to see if a truce team could land at the airport, which was reported badly damaged, but the plane failed to return

and there had been no contact with the pilot, Lieutenant Estele I. Sims. The next day, another plane was sent, and that plane was able to make radio contact with Sims, who reported that he had been detained by the Russians and his plane interned because he did not have proper identification and no written orders describing his mission. It was the price of doing things so quickly without any past experience to serve as a guide.

Byroade wanted to send a truce team to Zhifeng immediately, but Ye resisted, saying the Communist members of the team had not arrived yet. On January 16, an American plane was sent to Kalgan, which was in Communist hands, to transport the CCP truce team members to Beijing, where both the American and the government staff were waiting, but when the plane returned with fourteen Communists aboard, they turned out to be not truce team members but one general and thirteen bodyguards for Ye. The Communists, to the Americans' irritation, also brought a cargo of propaganda brochures to be distributed to the population in Beijing. "It is obvious that General Ye does not want teams sent either to Zhifeng or Kalgan," Robertson and Byroade reported to Marshall on the 17th, and they speculated that this was because the Communists were strong in both places. "All delays so far have been due to General Ye's failure to furnish representatives."

But within days, the mechanism was up and running. Daily "trusums," truce summaries, were being sent out by Byroade, who told Marshall, "Both sides are greatly exaggerating their claims of violations." On January 21, two American journalists were able to get to Zhifeng, riding on the truce team plane. It was the first time American reporters had gotten into any place in Manchuria since the Soviet invasion five months before. Henry A. Lieberman of *The New York Times* gave a favorable description of the "weathered mud huts of a sprawling pastoral city," occupied by friendly Russian soldiers in sheepskin coats, wool-trimmed hats, and felt boots. He quoted the Soviet commander saying he couldn't wait to go home. Around the same time, Zhou in Chungking told interviewers that the fighting was dying down.

The mood was good. Madame Chiang showed up in Changchun, the Soviet occupation headquarters, bearing thirty thousand boxes of candy to give to Soviet troops as an expression of gratitude for their part in the defeat of Japan. "The fighting did stop," Byroade said years later. "Goods and medicine started moving. A lot of sieges were lifted." The three-man truce-monitoring teams were getting into the field. American newspapers quoted an official of the Executive Headquarters saying, "There is no longer any doubt that both parties want peace and will do everything within their power to attain it."

"Affairs are progressing rather favorably," Marshall wrote to Truman on February 4, summarizing the developments of the previous few weeks.

Early in March, Marshall took a three-thousand-mile trip through northern China to see the country's disputed terrain for himself, the terrain now being roamed by three-man truce-monitoring teams, each of them headed by an American military officer. The high point of the trip was Yenan, where other American officials—including Service, Davies, Hurley, and Barrett—had preceded him, and where there was a face-to-face meeting with Mao. "Thousands stormed the field to get a glimpse of the five star ambassador whom the Communists regard as the leading personality in the present China peace," Radio Yenan reported. "I was frank to an extreme," Marshall wrote to Truman about his meeting with Mao, meaning that the Communists could have real American cooperation, including arms and training for their armed forces, but only if the Communists were sincere about following a peaceful path. Mao, Marshall said, "showed no resentment and gave me every assurance of cooperation."

Wherever Marshall went in Communist-controlled territory, he reported, his reception "was enthusiastic and in cities tumultuous." And no wonder. Here was a great hero of the victory over Japan traveling to the remote headquarters that had been considered a bandit lair only a few months before. The greatest living American, as Truman had put it, was giving formal recognition to Yenan as a kind of capital, a seat of power that had to be taken into account. His visit to Yenan was an affirmation of the Communists' new stature. They were participating in the PCC; they were full members of the Executive Headquarters and of the truce-monitoring teams that were spreading out on American airplanes all over China's vast northeast. The American officers on these teams, Marshall noted to Truman, "have performed an amazing task," which was "to dominate a region larger than Pennsylvania and bring factions who have been at war for 18 years to a peaceful understanding."

In February, after more marathon sessions of the Marshall mission, the two Chinese sides agreed to reduce the size of their armies, with the balance of forces heavily in favor of the national government. In all, there would be ninety KMT divisions (a full division was almost fourteen thousand officers and men) to only eighteen for the Communists.

Starting in about eighteen months, the forces of the two sides would be combined into a single command. Both sides would give up their political commissars, so the armies would for the first time be nonpolitical, under the control of a government rather than a political party. Most remarkable perhaps—all of these provisions seemed remarkable—the Communists agreed to reduce their forces in Manchuria to a single army, compared to the thirty they had there at the time of the Marshall talks. Six armies would be allowed to the Nationalists.

This was all too good to be true. The Communists appeared to have done what they had always maintained would be suicidal for them to do: allow government troops to move into areas where they were strong and give up control of their own armed forces. In fact, the evidence is strong that they never intended to do these things. On February 12, while the Marshall talks were heading into the home stretch, Mao told a meeting of the Politburo that "the United States and Chiang Kai-shek intend to eliminate us by way of nationwide military unification," a comment indicating that Mao still saw military unification as surrender. "We want unification, but we do not want to be eliminated," he continued. "In principle, we have to advocate national military unification; but, how we shall go about it should be decided according to the concrete circumstances of the time."

The statement was vague, but Mao appears to have wanted to reassure his colleagues in the Politburo that the military talks were mainly for show. Like his "scrap of paper" comment after his meetings with Chiang in the fall of 1945, he felt the actual agreement meant very little, because implementing it would be up to him. In Changchun, Chang Kia-ngau, Chiang's representative in the economic talks taking place with the Soviets, was looking at the announced details of the ceasefire and the military integration agreements, and his reaction was prophetically skeptical. "The National Government evidently presumes that because the Northeast is an 'exception,' it can send troops to recover our sovereignty," he wrote in his diary. But what the central government didn't seem to know was that "owing to secret support from the Soviets, for a long time Chinese Communist armed forces there have grown in strength day by day." Moreover, Chang observed, the Chinese Communists could easily get aid given Manchuria's long border with Soviet Russia; the government's lines were long and depended on a single rail line and two small ports. "I shudder," Chang wrote, "as I view and ponder the future."

But that was a rare dark thought and a private thought at that. For the moment, the mood was buoyant. On February 9, three days before he told the Politburo that the military agreement was, in effect, another scrap of paper, Mao was singing a different tune to an American reporter. "Generally speaking," he said, "China has stepped into a stage of democracy. Marshall's effort to bring an end to the civil war, to facilitate peace, unity, and democracy is undeniably outstanding."

In March, Marshall went to Washington to report to Truman, who greeted him like the hero he was. The Chinese leaders "are succeeding in terminating the hostilities of the past twenty years," Marshall said at a press conference. The two Chinese sides, he said, "are now engaged in the business of demobilizing vast military forces and integrating and unifying the remaining forces into a Central Army."

Marshall's sincerity is not to be disputed. He was an honest man and a straight-talker, not given to glossing over difficulties. Mao was justly famous for his statement that power comes out of the barrel of a gun — his pithy argument for the Communist Party to have its own army and never to trust only in peaceful political struggle. But Marshall evidently really believed that the Communists would give up their independent military if they could be assured of a truly democratic system. "It was very remarkable," he declared in his press conference, "how quickly we could straighten out what seemingly were impossible conditions and which had their tragic effect on the Chinese people."

CHAPTER SEVENTEEN

From Hope to Antagonism

In March, while George Marshall was in the United States, things began to fall apart in China. He got back to Chungking in April and within a few weeks his reports to Truman were stripped of their earlier optimism. "The outlook is not promising," he told the president in a letter of April 6. "I have found a complete break between the government and the Communists on the Manchurian question with hostilities increasing in intensity and threatening to spread south into China proper."

The Nationalists had embarked on an effort to defeat the Communists by sending their armies into Manchuria, and despite some initial success, in Marshall's very expert opinion they were now in "a seriously weak and dangerous military position of which the Communists were fully aware and seized the advantage accordingly." Marshall remembered the decision made at that White House meeting in December to continue to support Chiang even if his actions caused the peace talks to break down, but that did not lessen his dismay over the failure of the ceasefire to hold. Equally demoralizing, as the Communists got stronger they became more hostile to the United States. An American intelligence analysis in July concluded that between Marshall's arrival at the end of 1945 and the outbreak of new hostilities in the spring, the CCP's attitude toward the United States changed from "one of restrained hope to open antagonism." Barring an increasingly unlikely "compromise arrangement," Marshall said, there will be "utter chaos in North China to which the fighting will inevitably spread."

What went wrong?

Initially Marshall believed that the fault lay with the central government and the faction that he called "the irreconcilables," a group of generals who didn't want to lose their privileged positions, and the group inside the KMT known as the CC clique, named after the brothers Chen Li-fu and Chen Kuo-fu, whom Chiang had known since before the revolution of 1911. Many of Chiang's most important allies—his chief of staff, Ho Ying-chin, and Tai Li, his secret police chief—had been students at the Whampoa Military Academy in the early 1920s when Chiang was the school commandant. But Chen Li-fu and Chen Kuo-fu came from an even earlier time in Chiang's life, when, shortly before the revolution of 1911, he returned to China from a military academy in Japan and joined the revolutionary forces that were striving to overthrow the Qing dynasty. The local revolutionary leader and military governor of Shanghai, Chen Chi-mei, became a patron of Chiang. The Chen brothers were Chen Chi-mei's teenage nephews, who rose in the KMT's ranks under Chiang's tutelage until, years later, they became the powerful and undisputed leaders of the party's vehemently anti-Communist right wing.

Marshall believed that Chiang himself was both incorruptible and committed to the political liberalization that was being set into motion by the PCC, but that he was unable to control the far-right factions inside the KMT that were determined to sabotage it. There was plenty of evidence to substantiate this view. While the PCC was taking place, the Democratic League organized large meetings, with up to two thousand people attending, to discuss the events of the day, showing an admirable democratic fermentation taking place. But the meetings were disrupted by what an American diplomat reporting to Washington on these events called "organized hoodlums," put up to the job by the Chen brothers—or at least that is what was suspected, though no proof was offered. There were ugly scenes, anonymous thugs pushing their way into peaceful discussions where they beat up prominent liberals. In late January, the Democratic League announced it would boycott future sessions of the PCC after the secret police searched the home of one of its delegates, though as things turned out, it didn't follow through on that threat.

In the annals of illiberal gangsterism, these incidents were relatively minor, but they left their mark. The historical record indicates two assassinations taking place during those months, which was two too many, though not a number corresponding to a generalized reign of terror. Not even the Communist press, always ready to publicize right-wing malfeasance, reported new political arrests in that spring of 1946 as the PCC did its work.

Still, the antidemocratic actions of right-wing enforcers came at a delicate time when many political actors of the moment were looking for signs of sincerity on Chiang's part. Many people remembered the white terror of the 1920s and 1930s, enforced by Tai Li's Blue Shirts, when many opponents of Chiang's regime were executed or jailed. The fact that much more systematic antiliberal brutality took place in other countries did not enhance the KMT's reputation for trustworthiness at a time when trust was most needed. The incidents gave an opportunity to anti-KMT propagandists to portray the central government as "fascist," a word that the Communist press began to use frequently.

In late December, John K. Fairbank, who had been the head of the Office of War Information, was warning the State Department that "the most striking change" of the previous two years was the "final desertion of the Generalissimo" by the very American-educated Chinese whom the United States should most want to cultivate. "Liberals say they see no hope in his regime," Fairbank said, and so the attempts to intimidate these same people in February and March could only have intensified that feeling.

Perhaps more telling, as weeks went by after Chiang's speech at the PCC, the promised release of political prisoners didn't occur, or, at least, many opponents of the regime claimed that it didn't occur. Radio Yenan complained bitterly and repeatedly about this. In January, the pro-Communist writer Guo Morou was beaten by police. In Chungking, anti-Soviet rallies were organized, American diplomats believed, by the CC clique and the offices of the pro-Communist *New China Daily* and the Democratic League's *Democratic Daily* were ransacked. These acts of hooliganism prompted furious propaganda attacks by the Communists. "There are growing signs of violence," Melby noted in his diary.

> Every night since the start of the PCC there have been big mass meetings to discuss the issues publicly. And at each one, groups of Tai Li police have heckled and thrown stones a little more than at the preceding one. The subject of political prisoners is getting particularly hot. Last Monday, the government promised to release them all in seven days, but there are repeated stories

that many are being killed. Malaria, of which there is plenty
here, is given as the cause of death.

"Marshall," Melby noted, "was becoming a very angry man—and perhaps a little discouraged" by these actions of the irreconcilables.

The repression and right-wing hooliganism that took place in these
early months of 1946 have been cited as milestones in the decline of
Chiang's domestic standing. But not all of these events, and certainly
not the biggest of them, the anti-Soviet demonstrations taking place
in cities across China, were hooliganism. These appear, on the contrary, to have been patriotic reactions to Soviet behavior in Manchuria.
The Soviets had promised to evacuate China's northeast on February 1,
but they did not do so. On February 11, on the one-year anniversary of
the Yalta talks, the world's newspapers revealed the details of the secret
agreement between Stalin and Roosevelt by which the Soviets had
obtained special neocolonialist privileges in Manchuria. This was no
doubt galling to many Chinese who had come to believe that the era
when foreign countries robbed China of its sovereign pride was over.
Thirty-one years earlier, in 1915, furious, patriotically aroused Chinese
students had held massive demonstrations to protest the list of twenty-
one demands that Japan had made on the country. Those demands
included things like control of the South Manchurian Railroad and
extended leases on the ports of Dalian and Port Arthur—virtually
identical to the privileges given the Soviets at Yalta. The Twenty-One
Demands included a phrase establishing Japan's "predominant position" in Manchuria; at Yalta, the Soviets' "preeminent interests" were
assured. It is not surprising, especially given this comparison, that the
non-Communist Chinese reaction was strong and unfavorable.

"Now that China has paid the price," an editorial in the independent *Ta Kung Pao* declared, referring to the price China was expected
to pay in Manchuria, "we hope that she will not be required to pay
any more." *The New York Times* reported from Chungking that every
newspaper in the city, except for the Communist *New China Daily*,
"including many which sympathized with the Communists in the past,
have joined not only in sharp criticism of Russian policy but also in a
campaign to compel the Chinese government to draw back the curtain
behind which events in Manchuria have been hidden." On February
22, ten thousand students in Chungking took to the streets in a mass
demonstration. There were simultaneous demonstrations in Hankou,

Beijing, Chengdu, Nanjing, and Qingdao. Perhaps, as some suspected, it was the CC clique that called them to action, but there is no more reason to doubt the sincerity of the marchers than there is to doubt the patriotism of the demonstrators of 1915. The students in Chungking carried slogans like "The USSR = Germany + Japan," and "Stalin = Hitler + Hirohito." In Shanghai students massed in front of the Soviet consulate shouting "Get out of Manchuria." At least one demonstrator carried a large portrait of Stalin with the Chinese character for "snake" drawn across it. It was during these demonstrations that the offices of the *New China Daily* and *Democracy Daily* were ransacked.

The Communists blamed the KMT secret police for the attacks on the newspapers and on liberal intellectuals, but *Liberation Daily* and Radio Yenan showed no sympathy for the student demands that the Soviets get out of Manchuria or that they desist from stripping the region of its industries and power plants. While the students were marching, the *New China Daily* denied that the Communists had gotten any help from the Soviets, claiming that Communist "underground fighters" had been active in Manchuria for fourteen years. Chang Kiangau in Changchun wrote in his diary of a visit he made to Kangde Palace, the edifice where the Japanese had installed the last emperor of China, Henry Pu-yi, as the puppet emperor of Manchukuo—Kangde being the reign name he was given. The palace had been raided by the Soviet Red Army and stripped by the Russian soldiers of just about everything, even its lightbulbs. The library, Chang wrote, was "littered with crates for books and paintings. . . . The looters had taken away scrolls and paintings and calligraphy" after tearing off the cylindrical pieces of wood fixed to the bottom of Chinese scrolls so they can be properly weighted for hanging.

Around the same time as Chang's visit to the former emperor's home, a Chinese technocrat named Chang Hsing-fu, the deputy head of the Bureau of Industry and Mines of the central government, made a trip to the coal mines near the city of Fushun. His purpose was to reestablish Chinese ownership of the mines, and he traveled in the company of a Soviet counterpart, along with seven Chinese engineers and a contingent of railway police to take control. When the party arrived, the Soviets disarmed the railway police. They told Chang Hsing-fu that his delegation would not be allowed to take over the mines and that they should leave Fushun immediately. The Chinese accordingly boarded a train to return to Changchun. A platoon of Soviet guards rode in a different car. When the train reached the station at Li-shih-chai, twenty-five kilometers from Fushun, Eighth Route Army soldiers boarded it, dragged off Chang and the seven engineers accompanying him, stripped them of their clothing, and bayoneted them to death.

When word of these murders reached the Chinese government, the Chinese vice chief of staff complained to the Soviet general in charge of the Changchun area, Lieutenant General Yefim Trotsenko, who replied that the incident was the fault of the Chinese side because it had failed to notify the Soviet army general headquarters of Chang Hsing-fu's impending trip. The Chinese officer, evidently astonished at this parry of his complaint, noted that Chang had been traveling in the company of a Soviet official and that the platoon of Soviet guards riding the train at the time of the attack did nothing to prevent it. General Trotsenko's reply was not recorded, but Chang Kia-ngai was certain of the meaning of the incident. It demonstrated that the Soviets would not allow China to restore sovereignty over the Fushun mines before "the question of economic cooperation has been settled." And by "economic cooperation," Chang meant China's acquiescence in the Soviet demand that virtually all large-scale industries in Manchuria be run jointly by the Soviets and the Chinese. The thuggery taking place in Chungking on behalf of the KMT was more than matched by the collaborative thuggery of the Chinese Communists and their Russian sponsors, but it seems to have been less noted.

It is perhaps not surprising that the Chinese Communists declined to protest the Soviets' presence in Manchuria, their economic demands, the further, unexplained delay in the withdrawal of their troops, or even the theft of paintings and calligraphy from the Kangde Palace. Mao did not want to offend Stalin. Instead, the Communists focused their ire on Chiang, on the KMT right wing, and eventually on the American "imperialists" for their aid to the central government—never mind that the United States had given up its extraterritorial rights in China in 1943 and that, along with the British recapture of Hong Kong, the most conspicuous "imperialist" behavior in China was that of the Soviet Union.

But, as we know, Mao was operating in a larger context. February 1946 may have been the high point of the Marshall mediation in China, but it was also the time when the Cold War was taking shape and the conflict between the Soviets and the West was explicitly recognized. On

February 11, Churchill made his famous speech in Fulton, Missouri, identifying the "iron curtain" that had descended in Europe. Stalin, replying, made his own speech in which he declared that war between the Soviet Union and the West was "inevitable." Later that same month, George Kennan, still at the American embassy in Moscow, sent his famous "long telegram" to the State Department laying the foundations for what was to become the containment policy.

In March, Moscow let the CCP's leaders know that it was going to withdraw from several of Manchuria's big cities, telling them that, in accordance with the Sino-Soviet treaty, they would have to turn these places over to government forces, but that the Chinese Communists should get ready for action. And so the Eighth Route Army advanced into southern Manchuria, taking a number of small and medium-sized towns there.

It was at this same time that American diplomats in China began noticing a change in the attitude of the Communists. In a long memo to Marshall, Raymond Ludden, who had traveled in Communist territories as a member of the Dixie Mission in 1944 and reported on their local popularity, said that the CCP was cleaving ever closer to the Soviet line. Their newspapers, for example, had been repeating the Soviet official position that it had been the Russians who were mainly responsible for the World War II victories in both Europe and Asia, while the American and British contributions were no longer even mentioned. The CCP, he continued, had begun to use the word "fascist" in its propaganda, "fascist in a completely Russian sense—that is, anyone who is in opposition to Russian, and now likewise Chinese Communist wishes." Ludden wondered whether these verbal gestures were signs that the Chinese Communists were no longer primarily "nationalist reformers" but had become "a satellite force of Russian expansion in Asia."

Ludden was too close to the changing situation for his suspicions to harden into established fact, but subsequent historians, notably Michael M. Sheng, have found that by March 20 a new CCP strategy had emerged. It was to seek to divide Manchuria into north and south zones, with the city of Changchun as the dividing point. "Our party's policy is to use all our strength to control Changchun, Harbin, and the whole Changchun Railway," Mao said. "No matter how much sacrifice that may take [we must] prevent Chiang's troops from occupying these two cities and the railway."

Meanwhile, Zhou Enlai continued to complain bitterly to Lieutenant General Alvan C. Gillem, who was in charge of the mediation mission while Marshall was in Washington, of American help to the central government. On March 30, he warned that if "the U.S. Forces Headquarters shall continue to move Government troops into Manchuria, we would deem such action as a change of U.S. Policy toward China, and a lack of faith on the part of the Government to implement a real truce in Manchuria." Zhou made this threat despite the indisputable fact that the ceasefire agreement with which he was intimately familiar specifically allowed the central government to move troops "toward and into Manchuria" and that these troops would be transported by the United States. By infiltrating their own forces into southern Manchuria, it was the CCP that was violating the accord.

On March 18, Mao cabled Zhou to express his current view of Chiang. "All that has happened lately proves that Chiang's anti-Soviet, anti-CCP, and anti-democratic nature will not change," Mao wrote. Two days later, Mao was writing to Zhou again, informing him that the Communist Party would no longer take part in the National Assembly, which was to draft China's new constitution. China's revolution, he had decided, had to be won on the battlefield.

Mao may have been sincere in his expression of disappointment, but he seems to have been reacting far more to the intensification of the Cold War than to Chiang's antidemocratic actions. On March 20, reporting on the fast-moving political developments in China, the counselor of the American embassy in Chungking, Robert Smyth, told Byrnes that "the Gimo has displayed . . . a laudable spirit of cooperation and willingness to compromise." Chiang, Smyth continued, "wants to implement [the] PCC program and there is no effective challenge to his authority." Meanwhile, Smyth said, "the Communists would appear by current violent diatribes against KMT to be preparing for such a contingency by an early disclaimer of responsibility therefor."

This does not mean that there was no chance the KMT hard-liners could have derailed the movement toward a more democratic China or that they didn't want to do so. The constitution was to be drafted by a national assembly that was scheduled to meet in May, and the KMT wanted to dominate that assembly. But a political process had begun in China that had popular support and that had already deprived the KMT of the kind of untrammeled power it had exercised during the war. Mao's expressed views, mirrored by the intensifying propaganda campaign being mounted by Yenan, are hard to explain other than as a product of his impatience to have power for himself. The propaganda referred in distressed terms to secret police intimidation, the imprisonment of dissidents, the suppression of student protests, and the harassment of journalists, but Mao's future actions as the godlike leader of China were to show very little concern for those things, or for civil liberties in general. Mao in the early months of 1946 had the option of persisting with the blueprint drawn by the Marshall mission—to elect a national assembly, write a new constitution, and eventually to compete for power in elections. That was the intention he signaled to Marshall when he told him that "the democracy to be initiated in China should follow the American pattern."

But there is no indication that Mao meant what he said. His ambition wasn't for China to be democratic; it was to be China's Stalin, to seize total power, which he had already done inside the CCP. He had voiced enthusiasm about Marshall's mediation and the PCC because he needed to buy time and to avoid blame for civil war, not because he wanted China's press to be free or non-Communist political prisoners to be released.

Early in April, the *Liberation Daily*, which, up to that point, had refrained from personal criticism of Chiang, published a vituperative attack on him, which was duly reprinted by the *New China Daily* in Chungking. It accused the Chinese leader of fomenting civil war while having failed to implement all four of the pledges he had made to the PCC—allow civil liberties, legalize all political parties, hold local elections, and release political prisoners.

The central government's press office presented a persuasive, even impassioned, rejoinder to the Communists' attack, making the case that all four of the pledges were being implemented.

What of the machinations of the irreconcilables? A more rigid, myopically self-serving, cynical, and corrupt political faction would be difficult to find in the historical record. If Mao was driven by the unquenchable urge to seize power, the irreconcilables were motivated by a terror of losing it. The worst moment came in July 1946 when two prominent members of the Democratic League, Li Gung-pu and Wen I-duo, were assassinated by members of the Kunming garrison, which, probably aroused by the recent student demonstrations, had put out a general order that members of the league, who tended to support the Communists inside the PCC, should be killed. There is no proof that Chiang approved of these assassinations, and, indeed, as Jay Taylor has argued, he had little reason to want them to take place, given the public relations cost of such acts of repression. The new American ambassador to China, John Leighton Stuart, reported to Washington, citing attacks by what he called the "Gestapo," that "ruthless terrorism prevails in Kunming." Following the killings, several league members, including the anthropologist Fei Xiaotung, who was perhaps the most internationally famous Chinese intellectual, took refuge for a time in the American consulate. Stuart in a meeting with Chiang complained about the assassinations and warned him that intellectuals in general were becoming disaffected. Chiang promised to do something about it.

There were no reports of assassinations of dissenting intellectuals in Kunming or elsewhere after that, so perhaps Chiang did give instructions for that kind of repression to cease. Prominent intellectuals like Fei and Chu Anping, whom we saw earlier commenting on the mood at the end of the war, carried out their activities, as did Ma Yinchu and other prominent figures who made no secret of their disillusionment with the KMT. The right wing of the KMT, guided by the Chen brothers, may have been pressing for a constitution that, had it been adopted, would have given near-dictatorial powers to the president, but they did not succeed in this endeavor, which didn't appear, at least to the Americans, to have Chiang's support. Meanwhile, despite the activities of Chiang's secret police, the Communist *New China Daily* continued to appear in Chungking, reprinting the vituperative anti-Chiang editorials of the *Liberation Daily*. Zhou Enlai and the other Communist delegates were closely watched by the KMT security police, but they lived otherwise undisturbed down their narrow alley.

Still, the Communist propaganda machinery, not surprisingly, did its best to use incidents like the Kunming assassinations to attack Chiang and the KMT. In this sense there was a tremendous irony to the actions of the irreconcilables. Their importance lay not in their ability to derail the reform program, even though that is what they wanted to do. It was to provide the CCP, a revolutionary movement as secretive, ruthless, and undemocratic as any of the revolutionary movements of the twentieth century, an occasion to present itself as a vigorous champion of political openness, the free press, and civil rights.

Marshall kept working through the winter and spring of 1946 to restore the ceasefire and to establish a working democratic government. He had literally hundreds of meetings, the transcriptions of which, all dutifully preserved in the State Department archives, run into many hundreds of pages. But the talks represented a kind of make-believe world, a cocoon closed off from the reality of the country outside. The transcripts of the meetings make for dreary, wearisome, repetitive reading, full of mutual accusations, insincere declarations of peaceful intent, and Marshall's concrete, detailed, practical proposals for ending the fighting, all of them increasingly irrelevant. The parties pored over the minute details of proposed agreements as if these agreements would come into force with actual effect. They never did.

The possibility of a deal between the KMT and the CCP wasn't destroyed by the CC clique or any other party but by the resumption of the civil war. The KMT and the CCP blamed each other. Neither wanted to be seen as the party that wrecked the chance for peace, and both were at fault for doing so. "There has always been a wealth of accusations on both sides regarding the wrongdoing and evil purpose of the other side," Marshall told Zhou Enlai. There was "a complete contrast in views," he continued. His purpose wasn't to adjudicate primary fault versus secondary fault. That would have been impossible. He simply wanted to get both sides past the stage of mutual blame toward a renewal of the agreements already made, but both sides were too prone to attack when the circumstances were favorable.

Marshall's effort would continue until 1947, but it came to an effective end on March 7, 1946, when, without any notification to the Chinese central government, some forty trainloads of Soviet troops rolled out of Mukden along with a caravan of tanks, trucks, and big guns, as well as the giant portrait of Stalin that had decorated the Red Army headquarters since the previous August. The Soviet withdrawal precipitated a scramble for territory that didn't really end until the civil war itself ended in the Communist victory four years later.

At the time of the Soviet withdrawal, some one hundred thousand Communist troops, according to American estimates, were in the vicinity of Mukden, but the Nationalists, whose best troops had moved up the rail line from Qinwangdao, were ahead of them, driving Communist detachments out of the suburbs and pouring into the city itself. The KMT commander, Lieutenant General Chao Kung-wu, proclaimed "a decisive victory" over the Communists, who, he claimed, had been pushed back to more than ten miles from the city.

There was reason for this exultation. The entry of the Nationalists' 52nd Army into Mukden marked the first time troops of the central Chinese government had been in Manchuria's largest city since the Japanese invasion of 1931. In addition, the American-trained and -supplied government armies had performed well, driving the Communists back so effectively that Chiang was emboldened to think that if he acted firmly he could destroy Mao's army by force, contrary to the urgent entreaties of Marshall, who warned him that his forces would become overextended and dispersed, and who in the world knew more about orders of battle and the importance of supplies and logistics than George C. Marshall?

Chiang held Mukden, but things went badly for him elsewhere. In April, while Marshall was still getting accolades in Washington for his job well done, the Soviets pulled out of Changchun, their Manchurian headquarters, giving the Communists advance notice of their departure and telling them, as before, to be ready for action. The central government had a force of some seven thousand troops in the city. The day after the Russian withdrawal—Nationalist propaganda claimed a half hour after it—twenty thousand Communist troops attacked. *The New York Times*'s Henry A. Lieberman, along with a half-dozen other American journalists, was present, and he reported savage street-to-street fighting and heavy casualties. The Communists' Eighth Route Army detachments, going as usual by the pseudonym Democratic Unity Army, were a "disciplined, trained, organized, well-officered fighting machine," Lieberman said, and they had an impressive arsenal of Japanese artillery, machine guns, and rifles. Lieberman noted that the Communists denied having gotten those weapons from the Russians. A large body of the attacking troops had arrived in Manchuria six months earlier, having sailed there on junks from the Manchurian port of Chefoo, where the Communists had prevented the Americans from landing government troops the previous fall.

The decisive action took place at the central government's headquarters inside a five-story bank building in the middle of Changchun. There, about one thousand five hundred KMT troops put up, in Lieberman's words, an "Alamo-like defense" against superior forces that directed withering fire at the building and turned it into an "inferno." When the government troops finally tried to escape, they got bottled up at the bank's revolving door and hundreds of them were gunned down in the plaza in front of the building.

The seizure of Changchun was the Communists' biggest military success against the government so far, and it left Marshall's mediation, the January 10 ceasefire, the PCC resolutions, and the planned armed forces reorganization all in tatters. "Marshall's Efforts Fail" was the page-one headline in *The New York Times* on April 30. The Communists justified their renewed offensive on the grounds that the government had violated the truce, and it had, especially in moving troops toward Zhifeng in Jehol province. Radio Yenan, *Liberation Daily*, and the *New China Daily* in Chungking put out a steady stream of accusations along these lines, not only for truce violations but for the right wing's efforts to sabotage the political settlement. Zhou Enlai repeated these accusations during his long sessions with Marshall, which continued despite the renewed fighting, vigorously protesting among other things the American help to the government in transporting troops to Manchuria. Still, the Communist attack on Changchun was a blatant violation of the truce. The most respected independent newspaper in China, *Da Gung Bao*, which frequently criticized the central government, called it "shameful."

The seizure of Changchun came just as Marshall was returning to China from his stay in Washington, so it would logically have been the first item on his agenda as he resumed his meetings with Zhou Enlai and the government representative, but strangely, in his first session with Zhou, on April 23, he said nothing about it. He issued not a single word of remonstrance over the Communists' aggressive action, though later he identified the capture of Changchun as a decisive element in the collapse of the agreements he had so painstakingly negotiated. With Zhou he simply plunged ahead with a proposal for a new ceasefire. By contrast, when he met later that same day with the government representative, General Hsu Yung-chang, who was filling in for Zhang Chun, Marshall scarcely concealed his irritation at the Nationalists, saying that they had now inadvertently "educated the Communists with a new sense of power." He listed a host of government failures, from not submitting reports on troop movements to searching the homes of Communists in Beijing, though most important in Marshall's mind was the government's attack on Zhifeng. "The Communists," Marshall told Hsu, "are now in a position where they can present excessive demands on the Government," meaning, it would seem, that their seizure of Changchun, which could have been avoided by a smarter government policy, had given them military advantages they didn't have before.

A few days later, Marshall wrote a lengthy report to Truman in which he assessed blame more evenhandedly. The Communists are "jubilant" over their seizure of Changchun, he wrote, and "no doubt their generals are dominating the negotiations of their representatives." Emboldened by their success, he said, the Communists had begun a propaganda campaign against the American transport of government troops to Manchuria. Zhou, he said, "urges me to withdraw shipping support to force the Generalissimo's hand," but the Gimo himself was being told by his advisers and by his generals to adopt "a policy of force which they are not capable of carrying out even with our logistical support and presence of Marines in North China ports of Tsingtao, Tientsin and up the railroad towards the Port of Chinwangtao." In other words, Marshall concluded, "The outlook is not promising and the only alternative to a compromise arrangement is, in my opinion, utter chaos in North China to which the fighting will inevitably spread."

Indeed, the outlook was not promising, though there were to be several major twists and turns on Chiang's road to defeat and the Communists' to victory. Following the advice of his generals, Chiang did take the initiative after the fall of Changchun. His crack First Army moved up the railroad from Mukden to Szepingkai and retook Changchun on May 24, then headed farther north toward Harbin, the big city in northern Manchuria that was in Communist hands. Early in June, after persistent entreaties by Marshall, who was rejecting new requests by Chiang to transport still more Nationalist troops into the battle, Chiang agreed to a new ceasefire, which lasted for a crucial three weeks.

It will always be a matter of speculation whether in agreeing to a truce at just the moment when his forces seemed to have taken the initiative Chiang lost the best chance he ever had to defeat the Communists once and for all on the battlefield. Marshall didn't think so, and the weight of the argument seems to be on his side. The Communists were outgunned by the American-equipped government armies, but time nonetheless favored them if it came to a long campaign, as it always had in the past. The Communists enjoyed their long border with the Soviet Union through which Stalin could have provided Mao both with refuge if necessary and with a supply of arms. The government's forces, as Marshall put it, were overextended and dispersed, their supply lines endlessly long and subject to harassment by the Communist guerrillas in Shaanxi and Hebei provinces. Moreover, as the government attacked in Manchuria, the Communists were able to press for more gains south of the wall, notably in Shandong, where their troops were on the outskirts of Qingdao.

Chiang had seemed to have the Communists in his hands so many times. He forced them into the Long March after his "bandit extermination" campaigns in Jiangxi province in the early 1930s. Then, in 1936, he seemed to be on the verge of wiping out the ragged remnants of the Long March, but he was stopped by the Japanese invasion and the demand of the Chinese nation that he ally himself with his mortal domestic foe in order to defend the country against the non-Chinese one. And now, once again, victory over Mao would elude him.

The United States would help him to a considerable extent with both money and arms, but that help was never unlimited. Following the temporary loss of Changchun in April, Chiang asked the United States to transport two more Chinese armies to the Manchurian battlefield. Marshall refused, explaining to Truman that the Americans had already transported 228,000 government troops and that to move more "would be tantamount to supporting under the existing circumstances, a civil war." Marshall didn't want, as he put it, "to leave [the Chinese government] in the lurch," but he also didn't want to encourage Chiang in an all-out effort to conquer Manchuria, which he believed to be a losing proposition. At the same time, Marshall detailed his plans to reduce the marine detachments in several northern ports and Beijing from a total of 55,000 men to 28,000 by the summer, even though the marines were needed to provide transportation and safety to the Executive Headquarters in Beijing and to the truce-monitoring teams it continued to send to numerous places in North China. Marshall also had talks with Zhou Enlai about the American training of Communist troops, which was supposed to take place once the military reorganization plan went into effect.

In short, Marshall persisted in an effort to maintain some degree of evenhandedness in the Chinese civil war, a kind of biased neutrality by which the United States fulfilled its obligations to China's central government without writing what Chiang's American critics termed a blank check. The talks went on, but mainly as a device with which the Chinese sides strove to appear to be the parties of peace even as war once again engulfed their country. Blame can be put on both sides, but it was the Communist attack on Changchun that made the civil war in China unstoppable. It is a matter of speculation whether Chiang would have been amenable to a political settlement even if that attack had not taken place; but once it did, he no longer had any reason to believe that anything other than force would resolve China's divisions.

Meanwhile, Communist propaganda can be used to trace the decision by the Communists to drop the pretense of friendly intentions toward the United States and to identify America as China's enemy number one.

This came very rapidly. In February 1946 Radio Yenan was broadcasting heartwarming accounts of Sino-American cooperation, as in a report from Weixian in Shandong province about a memorial service for an American airman who had died the previous May when his plane was shot down by Japanese antiaircraft fire. The radio painted a touching picture of wreaths decorating the site of the memorial and of messages sent "by various circles of the liberated areas." The magistrate of Weixian conducted the service, the radio reported, "and made [a] speech hoping that Chinese-American friendship will last forever."

In early March, just before Marshall's visit to Yenan, the *Liberation Daily* praised his "brilliant achievements," saying that his "warm welcome by the Chinese people lies in the fact that the direction of his efforts accords with the basic interests of the Chinese people and the basic interests of the American people and world peace." Then, of course, there were Mao's well-publicized words of appreciation, his vow "wholeheartedly to abide by all the agreements," his references to "the leadership of Generalissimo Chiang Kai-shek," and to "American friends."

Four weeks later came the renewal of verbal attacks on the United States, and with them the renewal of a tone of grievance and obfuscation that was to be a feature of Communist propaganda thereafter — "renewal" because in many respects these new attacks mirrored the Communists' strenuous objections to the arrival of the marines in North China the previous fall. On April 4, 1946, the CCP newspapers carried angry reports that American warplanes had strafed Communist positions in Szepingkai, an important railroad junction south of Changchun. One of these planes was shot down, and, the Communist press reported, an American pilot was found in the wreckage, which proved that "American planes and officers have openly participated in the unscrupulous acts of KMT troops." Marshall ordered an investigation of these charges and found that no American airplanes had been in the vicinity of Szepingkai, ever. When Zhou Enlai was presented with this finding, the Communist press printed a retraction, admitting that the dead pilot was a Chinese wearing an American uniform, and his features had been mangled so badly that his identity was mistaken. Still, the Communists' initial accusation that the United States was taking part in military action against the Communists was telling, and, in any case, the critical drumbeat continued. The Communist press published repeated reports on intellectuals affiliated with China's various democratic parties calling on the United States to stop transporting government troops and opposing proposed American loans to the Chinese government, on the grounds that they would "bring disaster to the Chinese people." In May, the Yenan broadcasts included a different argument: that American aid to the government was undermining Marshall's role as an impartial mediator, which may in its way have been true, but American aid to the government was allowed in the agreements that Mao had vowed "wholeheartedly" to follow. With fighting picking up, Radio Yenan argued, "it is an undeniable fact that American aid is one of the important factors aggravating the Manchurian civil war today." The radio made no mention of Soviet aid to the Communists or the possibility that such aid made Mao less likely to come to a political agreement with the KMT.

Radio Yenan, June 5:

> American forces also organized air and naval forces for these Chinese civil war instigators. They supplied them with a vast number of planes, war vessels, bazookas, artillery, tanks, gasoline and all the necessary war materials . . . it is only too obvious that without such vast aid, the Chinese reactionary clique would never have been able to carry on large-scale civil war. . . . Such military intervention by the US is not devoid of imperialistic designs. The day may even dawn when the [Kuomintang reactionaries] might find America demanding military bases and political and economic rights from China, thereby degrading China as a protectorate or colony of America.

Never mind that the advantages the imperialist Americans would hypothetically demand were precisely the same as the advantages that the Soviets had actually seized for themselves, without Chinese Communist objections, in Manchuria.

Also in June, Marshall, who had been exempt from Communist criticism, came under personal attack, a trend that resulted later in the use
of the boilerplate expression "the Truman-Marshall clique" to refer to
the supposed reactionary faction within the United States that wanted
to establish imperialist rule in China. Marshall, the press reported,
could have stopped the government from moving new troops into the
battle for Manchuria, but he didn't. In fact, as we've seen, Marshall had
rejected Chiang's request for more government troops to be moved to
Manchuria, and he was ordering a reduction in the size of the marine
deployment.

On June 7, in *Liberation Daily*: "Never in the past hundred years of
the history of China has imperialistic intervention in Chinese internal
affairs, and the naked suppression of the Chinese movement to attain
freedom and democracy, reached its present scale."

That statement is striking in its degree of hyperbole. In a century
that included the Opium War, the Anglo-French Expedition of the mid-
nineteenth century, the turn-of-the-century suppression of the Boxer
Rebellion, the resulting indemnity imposed on China, then the seizure
of Taiwan and Manchuria by Japan, followed by the full-scale Japanese
invasion of 1937, it was ridiculous to present American military assistance to the internationally recognized government of China as the
worst-ever imperialist intervention in Chinese affairs. Most important
from the American point of view at the time, the intensifying tone of
anger illustrated the Communists' turn to an unremitting anti-American
hostility that the United States could do little to change. In August, the
propaganda blamed Marshall one more time for failing to stop what
Radio Yenan called "the aggravation of China's civil war," when, as Marshall pointed out, the Communists were making their contribution to
that aggravation, including their seizure of Changchun in March and
an offensive they mounted in Shandong in June. When toward the end
of the year Marshall began suggesting to Truman that there was no longer any reason for his mediation effort to continue, he cited the "vicious
Communist propaganda of misrepresentation and bitter attacks" as a
principal reason.

Marshall understood that these expressions of aggrieved animosity,
"full of inaccurate statements" as they were, marked the definitive end
of Communist good faith in the effort to avert a civil war. For reasons
of public relations, they would keep talking, but they would also keep

fighting. They knew that the civil war they pretended not to want was already under way and was going to be fought to a finish. Their public animosity toward the United States and their portrayal of the central government as the "lackey" of an imperialist foreign power were integral parts of the strategy by which they intended to achieve victory.

On July 29 at a place called Anping, on the road between Tianjin and Beijing, an incident took place that fully exposed the Communist strategy. There, Communist forces ambushed a convoy carrying supplies for the Executive Headquarters, the group that continued in its heroically futile way to monitor compliance with KMT-CCP agreements, as well as for the United Nations Relief and Recovery Administration (UNRRA), which had begun its humanitarian mission in China. Like all such convoys, this one was guarded by a platoon of American marines, and when shots rang out from behind the trees and farmhouses along the side of the Beijing–Tianjin road, three of them were killed and twelve were wounded. According to Marshall's later account of this incident, the Communists "privately admitted" that their forces had carried out the assault, but in public, they furiously blamed the central government, accusing it of killing the marines in order to frame the Communists and further their insidious plan to engulf the country in civil war.

When Marshall informed Zhou Enlai of the attack, Zhou's response was to ask for an investigation, and Marshall agreed, though from a reading of the American military's reports, he felt there was no question about what had occurred. The Communists had resumed sniping at American troops in an effort to induce them to withdraw. When the investigation began, Marshall said, the Communist member of the team obstructed it with procedural demands, angry speeches lasting hours, refusals to allow witnesses to testify, then further procedural demands when the old ones had been satisfied, and, when all else failed, simply not showing up at scheduled meetings.

"It was a repetition of the familiar Communist pattern of seizing upon some incident, justifiably or otherwise, and embroidering thereon without regard to truth and accuracy to form the basis for an almost hysterical campaign of vituperation," Marshall concluded wearily.

The Anping incident was a rather small one in the long history of warfare and slaughter in East Asia, but it was telling nonetheless. The

Communists had mounted an attack and then used it in a propaganda campaign, utterly unhinged from the truth, whose purpose was to portray the United States as an imperialist enemy. This was to be the pattern for the next twenty-six years, during which tens of thousands of Chinese and American young men were killed in wars that needn't have taken place.

The Tragedy of the Chinese Revolution

When the police came in the middle of the night, Mei Zhi and her husband, China's most famous literary critic, Hu Feng, couldn't bear to tell their three children they were about to be arrested. They said instead that guests had arrived; they put their two boys and a girl to bed and kissed them good night. Then they were taken away.

Mei, a writer of essays, poems, and children's stories, was released from prison six years later, and even then she was given a "rightist hat," as the Chinese expression had it, meaning that she was infected with thoughts associated with the capitalist class, and she was forced to undergo political reeducation to have it removed. Hu Feng, a founding member of the League of Left-Wing Writers in Shanghai in the early 1930s and a leader of the anti-Japanese patriotic movement, was buried in the Chinese prison system for almost all of the next twenty-five years, during which he refused to confess to his "crimes," on the grounds, he said later, that he hadn't committed any. Hu's offense was to have written and circulated a long, instantly notorious essay in which he criticized China's new rulers for imposing restrictions on art and culture. This offense led Mao Zedong to declare him the leader of a "counterrevolutionary clique," and Mao had decreed that "counterrevolutionaries are trash; they are vermin." In 1979, three years after Mao's death, Hu was released from prison, and three years after that, he was officially exonerated. But he had been destroyed physically and mentally. He sank into a tortured madness and died in 1985.

Hu was one of several of the prominent Chinese scholars, writers, and academics whom we have referenced in these pages, examples of Chinese intellectuals whose public disillusionment with Chiang and the KMT helped to turn the tide of public opinion against them and in favor of the lesser-known Communists. They were of different persuasions. Some, like Hu, were convinced Marxists; others were western-educated liberals. All of them, like other intellectuals the world over, fell under the sway of Communism, with its satisfying certainties and its claim to embody the progressive yearnings of all humankind, except the capitalist/imperialist enemy. In China, as elsewhere, from Cuba to Czechoslovakia, the appeal was enhanced by the corruption, nastiness, and ineffectiveness of the central government. Without much knowledge of the workings of Communism in practice, many Chinese intellectuals enthusiastically welcomed Mao and his armies when they came to power in 1949.

It was risky to do what they did. To belong to a pro-Communist organization, like the League of Left-Wing Writers, or simply to criticize Chiang and the KMT was to risk imprisonment and torture. Nonetheless, except for a few among them who did suffer grievously and, in some cases, mortally for their beliefs, most of the anti-KMT dissidents were able to keep their jobs and to do their work, publishing stories, poems, and essays, teaching, and, as we've seen in the case of Ma Yinchu, expressing their views in public meetings.

The Chinese literary critic Hu Feng and his wife, Mei Zhi. Hu was a prominent Marxist critic of the Chinese Nationalists during the war and among the first victims of a Maoist purge after the Communists took power.

Then, after the Communist Party took power in mainland China in 1949, virtually all of these men and women who had looked to Mao for China's new beginning were savagely persecuted, punished for demonstrating the very independence of mind that had led them to favor the Communists years before. In some instances, like those of Mei Zhi and Hu Feng, their lives were utterly destroyed. Others endured long periods of criticism and public humiliation but were eventually able to restore some semblance of normal life. Their treatment illustrated one of the chief features of Mao's twenty-seven years of rule: the compulsion of the man known as the Great Helmsman to track down and eradicate enemies within. In a grim imitation of Joseph Stalin, Mao and his loyal lieutenants, most important of them Kang Sheng, now head of the powerful Public Security Bureau, purged former comrades-in-arms, determined now to have been counter-revolutionaries all along. For more ordinary people, writers, poets, professors, people who had studied in the United States, people to whom the imprecise sobriquet "bourgeois" could be applied, they elaborated a system of ideological purification, complete with its own sprawling gulag and its own methods of physical and psychological torture and intimidation. The methods used during the Rectification Campaign of 1942–44, which was already Stalinism with a Chinese flavor, were reemployed in the new persecutions: total isolation, the separation of the prisoner from family and friends and from any source of emotional support or legal help, and the mobilization of all the tools of the totalitarian state—the press, the propaganda apparatus, the howling mobs—to persecute the defenseless ideological victim.

Needless to say, Hu Feng had no lawyer. No journalist in China independently investigated the case against him. There were no open hearings, no habeas corpus petitions, during which the government had to justify his detention. For the first ten years of his imprisonment, Mei Zhi was not allowed to know where her husband was being held or even whether he was alive, until, in an act intended to show the "leniency" of the party, she was allowed to visit him and to send him small gifts of food and clothing. "You should trust the party," an official at the Ministry of Public Security told Mei Zhi, adding of her husband, "we are all committed to reforming him."

The punishment of dissent, or of fabricated dissent, was harsher and psychologically more insidious under the Communists than it had been under the KMT, and the scope of individual freedom far smaller. In July 1946, as we've seen, several members of the Democratic League, fearful of the right-wing thugs who had assassinated two of the league's members, took refuge for a time at the American consulate in Kunming. Among them was Fei Xiaotong, China's pioneering anthropologist and champion of the peasantry, widely known both inside China and abroad. A graduate of Yenching (later Peking) University, he had studied with Bronislaw Malinowski, the pioneering anthropologist, at the London School of Economics, and, like many of his colleagues, he was a member of the Democratic League, which generally allied itself with the Communists. He was, with good reason, fearful of the KMT's secret police and hired thugs, but he was never imprisoned or persecuted during the reign of Chiang Kai-shek. During the war, he lived at one of the universities in exile in Kunming and carried out research in villages in Yunnan province. He was able to spend a year in the United States. He wrote many articles in Chinese publications and enjoyed considerable fame.

In the years right after 1949, Mao generally pursued the moderate policy toward non-Communist intellectuals that he had adopted during the war years and during the long struggle for power. Many of the intellectuals who had criticized the KMT were given important positions in the new society. Fei was named vice president of the National Institute for Minorities and a member of the prestigious, if powerless, National People's Congress.

In 1956, in order to flush out opponents, Mao, in what came to be known as the Hundred Flowers Campaign, encouraged China's intellectuals to speak their mind, and Fei offered some critical ideas. As a result, he was forced to stand before howling crowds and to admit his "crimes against the people." Later, during the vast purge known as the Cultural Revolution of the mid- to late 1960s, he was beaten and forced to clean toilets by the youthful Maoist enforcers called Red Guards. Unlike many other such victims of Maoist cruelty, Fei survived and later taught at Peking University, but he said that he had lost what would have been his twenty-three most productive and useful years.

Others suffered similarly. Ma Yinchu, the American-educated economist who, in 1944, had likened Chiang to a "vacuum tube," became the president of Peking University. Chu Anping, whose writings in *Keguan*, or *Objectivity*, made him a prominent figure in the days after the Japanese surrender, became the editor of the *Guangming Daily*, a newspaper read largely by intellectuals. Ma fell from grace when he proposed a population control program for China at a time when Mao believed that population control was a plot by the imperialist powers to keep the Third World weak. Under another kind of leader than Mao, Ma's suggestion that China curb its birth rate would have been treated as what it was, an idea to be debated. Under Mao, it was deemed instead to be a kind of thought crime, an implicit collusion with the enemies of China.

Ma was ridiculed in person at an assembly of students and faculty at Peking University by Kang Sheng, and for several years he was singled out for the kind of rhetorically bloated attack that only a Communist propaganda machine can muster, illustrating the daily "minute of hate" that Orwell described in the novel *Nineteen Eighty-Four*, during which all people stand to shake their fists and shout epithets at the great enemy. Ma was dismissed from public life, accused of a nonsensical list of political crimes, and made into a sort of non-person as long as Mao was alive; after Mao's death, like Fei, he was rehabilitated and he was able to resume his scholarly life.

At least Ma avoided actual incarceration. Many others didn't. In 1957, Mao initiated the first mass purge since the Yenan Rectification Campaign. Hundreds of thousands of people were accused of being "rightists," including numerous western-educated people who had returned to the country from abroad to help build the "new China." Many of them were sent to labor camps to "remold" their thoughts. Many died there. In 1958, Chu Anping was branded an "anti-party, anti-socialist bourgeois rightist." He was made to clean the streets — it became a standard practice of Maoism to force people to do hard manual labor as a way of getting them to adopt a "proletarian world view." He was imprisoned, and when he was released, he disappeared, probably a suicide, though this is not known for sure.

The writer Wang Ruowang, imprisoned for three years by the KMT in the 1930s, then imprisoned under Mao for four years in the 1960s, testified in *The Hunger Years*, his autobiographical novel (banned in China), to a difference between the two regimes. Chiang's secret police's use of torture, unjustified as it was, was aimed at extracting information about the activities of members of the Communist Party. Under the Communists, torture was also commonly used, except that it was aimed at extracting confessions to crimes that had never been committed, or to thoughts that should not have been illegal. "The basis of the interrogation," Wang wrote, "was nothing more than the order from above that so-and-so should be overthrown."

Mei Huanzao was the young newspaper reporter for *Da Gong Bao* who wrote the description of Shanghai in the months after the end of the war that I cited earlier. After the "liberation" of 1949, *Da Gong Bao* moved its office to Beijing, and Mei was invited by the editor of another paper, *Wen Hui Bao*, to stay in Shanghai and work there. The editor in question was Xu Zhucheng, another prominent non-aligned intellectual who had welcomed the Communists. Xu, like practically every member of this category in China, was declared a rightist in the purge of 1957, and sent away for the usual rounds of psychological torment and self-criticism. A new editor, appointed by the party's propaganda department, took over the leadership of Wen Hui Bao.

One day, the new editor asked Mei Huanzao his opinion of the political campaign. The editor seemed to be giving Mei an opportunity to engage in a ritual of Maoist rule, which was known as *biaotai*, to take a public stand, during which the person in question was expected to proclaim a prefabricated encomium to Mao, to praise the Communist Party and support its suppression of the "counterrevolutionaries'" plot to overthrow China's socialist system. But Mei instead expressed his distress at Xu's plight. He was immediately surrounded by a hostile group, the enforcers of Maoist writ who populated every institution in the country—the schools, the newspapers, the neighborhoods—who asked him to explain what he meant. Somehow, Mei was able to excuse himself. He may have said he needed to visit the lavatory. He went straight up the stairs to the rooftop of the Wen Hui Bao building and jumped to his death.

Forty-one years after the arrest of Hu Feng, China was a vastly freer country. And yet, in 2006, another literary critic, essayist, and advocate of free expression, a professor at the Beijing Normal University named Liu Xiaobo, was arrested by China's Public Security Bureau and, after a closed trial of a few hours' duration, was sentenced to eleven years in prison for the crime of "subverting state power." The persecution of Liu (who was awarded the Nobel Peace Prize in 2010) marked a new turn toward repression that has continued unabated. In August 2013, a party circular banned discussion in China of seven allegedly subversive subjects, among them what it called "western constitutional democracy" and the Communist Party's "past mistakes."

China has changed for the better since the days of Chairman Mao, but the practices of its senior leaders remain fundamentally incompatible with the values that Americans regard as inalienable.

Two months before Mao proclaimed the establishment of the People's Republic of China on October 1, 1949, the United States Department of State issued a 1,054-page collection of documents whose purpose was to defend the American government against the accusation that it was responsible for what was now clear, that China would be "lost" to the Communists. The formal title of this famous volume was *United States Relations with China with Specific Reference to the Period 1944–1949*, but it has been universally known as the *White Paper on China*. A preface written by Dean Acheson, when he was secretary of state in January 1949, made the case: China had not fallen into the Communist camp because of any failure by the United States; it had been "lost" by the government of Chiang Kai-shek, which had become "demoralized and unpopular," beyond saving, despite what the *White Paper* showed to have been a massive American effort over the years to prevent it.

Contrary to the Truman administration's hopes and expectations, however, the *White Paper* did not settle the argument. Most important, it failed to deter a revival of the false and ugly charge, initiated by Patrick J. Hurley as he resigned the ambassadorship of China in late 1945, that a group of pro-Communist China experts in the State Department had sabotaged American China policy and undermined China's legitimate, pro-American government. This was the key domestic American feature of Mao's triumph in China, the shameful hunt, engineered by the right-wing demagogues who emerged out of the shock of Chiang's defeat, to attribute that defeat to the treasonous behavior of a few plotters inside the government.

Not all of the Americans who served in China during the war suffered from accusations of blame, but many of them did. Albert C. Wedemeyer, who had performed competently and even wisely as commander of the China theater, joined those recklessly heaping blame on the China professionals in the Foreign Service for having sabotaged American interests. Wedemeyer's accusations were strangely belated. During his time in China, including those fateful months of late 1945 and early 1946 when the race between the Nationalists and the Communists to control Manchuria was taking place, he wrote many dispatches to Washington, but in none of them did he take the position that the State Department's China hands were guilty of disloyalty. He made these accusations later; he was awarded the Presidential Medal of Freedom by President Reagan in 1985.

Patrick Hurley went home to Oklahoma after his sudden resignation as ambassador and ran three times for the U.S. Senate, without success. Until his death in 1963, he insisted to anyone who would listen that the China hands had been disloyal and had brought about disaster. But the main task of accusation fell to Senator Joseph McCarthy, Republican of Wisconsin, who built a career by blaming the supposed Communists in the State Department for the loss of China, and for other damage to the United States.

Even a figure as highly respected as George C. Marshall, and, one would think, above any possibility of suspicion, fell into McCarthy's sights. Marshall persisted in his futile effort to mediate the KMT-CCP conflict in China until, finally, he left the country in 1947, replacing James Byrnes as secretary of state. It was then that he forged the plan of massive economic help to Europe that came to be called the Marshall Plan. In 1951, McCarthy published a book blaming Marshall for the Communist takeover in China, accusing him, in a statement that has been notorious ever since for its nonsensical hyperbole, of membership in "a conspiracy so immense and an infamy so black as to dwarf any previous venture in the history of man."

Marshall emerged largely unscathed from the McCarthy storm. In 1953, he was awarded the Nobel Peace Prize. But the lower-ranking China experts were not so lucky. Most of them were able to resume their careers at the end of the war, but eventually the "loss" of China doomed virtually all of them.

John Paton Davies served in the Soviet Union, Germany, and Peru. In 1948, he was awarded the Medal of Freedom for his bravery and leadership after the plane carrying him and a group of others crashed in Burma in 1943. But in 1954, the State Department's Loyalty Security Board decreed, with no persuasive evidence, that he lacked "judgment, discretion, and liability." He was fired from the State Department and his security clearance taken away. He became a successful furniture manufacturer in Lima, Peru, and died in 1999.

John Stewart Service, after serving as an aide to General Douglas MacArthur in the occupation of Japan, was similarly dismissed in 1952. He was reinstated by the Supreme Court in 1957, but, dogged by the accusations against him in the Amerasia Affair, he was going no place as a diplomat. He resigned and worked as a librarian and editor at the University of California's Center for Chinese Studies in Berkeley, California.

John Carter Vincent was posted for a few years to Switzerland, then to Morocco, but he too was attacked during the McCarthy witchhunts, accused on patently flimsy hearsay evidence of being a Communist. He was forced to step down from the State Department in 1952. John K. Fairbank was also accused of disloyalty by the McCarthyites, and went through an extremely stressful and trying period when he and other China experts, Owen Lattimore among the best-known of them, were investigated by Congress. But unlike the State Department officers, Fairbank was protected by his position as a professor of history at Harvard, where he nurtured a knowledge of China among generations of scholars, journalists, and diplomats, including the author of this book.

There is no doubt that, whoever lost it, China's emergence as a Communist country closely allied to the Soviet Union and aiding revolutionary movements elsewhere in Asia was a tremendous defeat for the United States. Mao himself practically gloated over the American loss. In a famous speech made in August 1949, only days after the release of the *White Paper,* Mao used Acheson's own words to lampoon the American position. Acheson, he noted, admitted that Chiang Kai-shek couldn't be saved because his government was "demoralized and unpopular." Why then, Mao asked, if the Americans understood that the Chinese people no longer wanted him, did the United States provide aid to the KMT? The only possible answer, Mao declared, was that the United States was an imperialist country among whose goals was "to turn China into a U.S. colony." Chiang Kai-shek and a war "to slaughter the Chinese people" were the implements used to achieve this goal. But America had failed, Mao said, because "the Chinese people have awakened, and the armed forces and the organized strength of the people under the leadership of the Chinese Communist Party have become more powerful than ever before." Mao also emphasized what he called "the towering presence of the Soviet Union, this unprecedentedly powerful bulwark of peace bestriding Europe and Asia," which, he said, deterred the Americans from "direct, large-scale attacks on China."

Mao's speech, triumphant as it was, can be interpreted in two ways. One is to see it as a statement that Communist China and imperialist America must be enemies by their very antagonistic natures. The other way is to take it as a disguised wish for the United States to have made a wiser choice in China, to have declined to support the KMT in the civil war, since, if it had, normal or at least non-antagonistic relations would have been possible. But as it was, in making its choice to be hostile to the Communists, the Americans left Mao with no choice but, as he put it in another 1949 speech, to "lean to one side," the Soviet side, and this is what led to the twenty-five years of mutual distrust and animosity.

Could it have been different? Writers, politicians, and scholars have given heated, mutually conflicting answers to this difficult question for more than half a century. On one side of the debate has been the argument that the United States could, had it acted more firmly and more presciently, have saved Chiang Kai-shek from the Communist onslaught, and China would slowly have evolved in a pro-western, democratic direction. Had the Americans provided more help to the KMT; had they been clearer about the strategic goals in China; had they not burdened the Chinese government with demands that it halt the fight against the Communists during the Japanese occupation; had it flown more Nationalist divisions to Manchuria during Chiang's initial and almost successful offensive in early 1946; had Stilwell and the China hands not besmirched the reputation of Chiang while being smitten by Mao and the Communists—then the Communist victory could have been prevented.

There were a few people making that argument during the Japanese war, most prominently perhaps Joseph Alsop, the well-connected cousin of FDR who became an influential newspaper columnist after the war. Alsop, as we've seen, told everybody who would listen to him that it was "idiotic" not to have seen that the Communists would be pawns of the Soviet Union and that to oppose Chiang's wish to concentrate on the future struggle with the Communists was a cataclysmic mistake. Alsop believed that the United States should be ready to move large numbers of its own troops to China after the war to ensure that the KMT was able to establish its control.

Alsop also believed that the American people, once enlightened as to the strategic stakes involved, would support a war against the Communists in China. The mass clamor for American troops to be brought home once the war was over, however, indicates that Alsop was wrong about that. Very likely, had the United States followed his recommendation, it would have found itself in something like what it experienced two decades later in Vietnam—a commitment to a costly and debilitating struggle on the Asian mainland that it couldn't win. The Communists were too entrenched, too strong, and too solidly backed by the Soviet Union, which would have been perfectly happy to see Americans bleeding and dying in China as the Cold War was being waged around the world. And, as Acheson correctly put it, there was nothing that the United States could have done to overcome the deficiencies of the KMT government. The Chinese people made their choice. It may have been the wrong choice, but it wasn't an American prerogative to make that choice for them.

The opposite option would have been for the United States to have given no support to the KMT, and thereby not to incur the wrath of Mao. That was the argument of the China hands, and it was a better argument than Alsop's. Unfortunately, figures like Davies and Service, smart and dedicated public servants as they were, were naïvely dazzled by the Communists in 1944 and 1945, when they had frequent contacts with Mao and his cohort in Yenan. Their preference for Mao did not change the direction of American policy. Despite the disillusionment with the KMT and the heroic portrayals of the Communists that appeared in books and articles, the United States intervened in China's "fratricidal strife" on Chiang's side, not the Communists'.

Could the years of antagonism have been avoided, as Mao seemed, ambiguously, to suggest in that speech of August 1949, had the United States jettisoned Chiang earlier and remained neutral in China's domestic struggle? Over the years, a strong current of opinion has answered "yes" to that question. Especially in the wake of the Vietnam War, many scholars, journalists, foreign policy pundits, and ordinary people have believed that the United States made a historic mistake by opposing the forces of Asian revolution and siding instead with right-wing dictatorships, beginning with Chiang's, and that this fundamental error is what made revolutionary parties across the world—whether the Communists of China or Vietnam or, later, the Islamists of Iran—take America as an enemy. In this view, Sino-American antagonism was a product of misguided American decisions, which themselves reflected the failure to listen to the wiser voices within the American debate.

This argument may be valid when applied to other parts of the world, but it is not persuasive in the case of China. For one thing, a strict hands-off policy in China was as politically impossible as a massive military intervention. Democracies are prone to a kind of middle ground in matters that generate strong differences of opinion. A massive intervention would have been opposed by millions of Americans because the tremendous effort involved in saving a distant, not-very-democratic regime would not have seemed remotely justified to them.

Those same millions would have been convinced, however, that it would have been shameful, too narrowly self-interested, and unworthy of a superpower to leave a long-standing ally entirely to its own devices as it faced a dread challenge. The atmosphere of the impending Cold

War, the well-grounded conviction that a messianic, profoundly illiberal, and menacing force was on the rise, fostered the American belief that something had to be done for Chiang, even given his imperfections. By late 1945, it was clear that Stalin, in blatant violation of his treaty obligations to China's central government, was turning Manchuria over to Mao, and it would have violated the American sense of fairness to have stood by and done nothing to help. In retrospect, it is easy to see that what was done was not going to be enough, and that Chiang would lose mainland China. But that was far from clear at the time. When the decisions to help Chiang were made in Washington, he seemed to have sufficient resources to carry on a successful fight, certainly in China south of the Great Wall, if not in Manchuria.

The dominant force shaping China and China's future relations was not the American choice; it was the nature and actions of the Soviet Union and of Mao. The turning point of those years was not some decision made in Washington, D.C., or a press conference by Patrick Hurley, or the dispatch of the marines to Beijing, Tianjin, and Shanghai. It was the Soviet Union's invasion of China's northeast provinces in August 1945. Once that occurred, there was no further chance that Mao and the Communists would settle for a political deal with the KMT, despite the concerted efforts of American mediators to bring that about. Once Stalin had more than a million soldiers occupying Manchuria, the Chinese civil war became inevitable, because Mao understood that the central government no longer had the capability to eliminate him militarily. The irony, of course, is that the president of the United States, meeting with Stalin at Yalta, implored the Soviets to send their troops to Manchuria and that the Soviet invasion was facilitated by American Lend-Lease supplies. But as Averill Harriman and George Kennan understood at the time, Stalin was going to send his eleven armies, headed by the implacable Rodion Malinovsky, whether the United States asked him to or not. China may, in this sense, have been "lost" by Chiang Kai-shek; but mainly it was won by Stalin and his loyal acolyte, Mao.

It was not American support for Chiang that determined the future of the Sino-American relationship; it was Mao's ideological closeness to Stalin and his need for Soviet help. Mao needed the support and goodwill of the powerful and nearby Russians far more than he needed that of the ambivalent and faraway Americans. The Cold War had begun. Soviet-American animosity was an established fact, and even if he had wanted to, Mao could not have ignored Stalin's demand that he "lean to one side." Neutrality was not permitted in the universe that Stalin dominated.

But Mao didn't want to take a middle position. Mao was not a Tallyrand seeking a balance of power. He was a visionary and a revolutionary deeply imbued with the global culture of radical and violent transformation that emanated like a shock wave from the Bolshevik Revolution. The character, the beliefs, and the ambitions of Mao and the movement he led were what guided Chinese history, not some decision made in Washington. Another man might have been different. A less ideological figure and, certainly, a more democratic one, would have worked for an early rapprochement with the richest and most powerful nation on earth. He might have strived, like newly independent India did at the time, to benefit from relations with both the world's superpowers. He might, like Nelson Mandela many years later, have opted for a healing reconciliation among former enemies. But Stalinism offered Mao the path to the absolute power that he craved, and class struggle had always been his creed. Mao favored violence and not what he called "benevolence," by which he meant a foolish weakness of will. "To sit on the fence is impossible," Mao said in the summer of 1949, as the KMT was reeling and he was readying himself to take power. "In the world, without exception, one either leans to the side of imperialism or to the side of socialism."

It would have been psychologically impossible for Mao to emerge as non-aligned in the Cold War. The man who left in his wake the corpses, literal and figurative, of most of his closest revolutionary comrades, for whom the betrayal of friends was a key ingredient of his total power, who for a decade during the Cultural Revolution maintained friendly relations with only one other country in the world, tiny and, at the time, ultra-Stalinist Albania—this man was not likely to have remained for long on good terms with the United States, even if the Americans had assiduously courted his favor in 1945, even if they had sought, after 1949, to build normal relations with China's new government. A revolutionary China under Mao was destined to single out the United States as an enemy and to do so for a long interval, until China had exhausted itself in its revolutionary fervor and it faced a greater and closer rival and threat to its independence.

Acknowledgments

My thanks, as always, to my editor, Jon Segal, for his loyal support, his excellent judgment, his constructive needling, and his friendship; and, of course to Sonny Mehta and the others in the professional team at Knopf who helped to bring about this book, with a special mention to Meghan Houser. And, of course, my gratitude to Kathy Robbins, my stalwart agent, and to her helpers in the Robbins Office, whose kindness, understanding, and encouragement were, as they've always been, indispensable.

Others helped in many ways. I'm grateful to two friends from my days in graduate school, Andrew J. Nathan and Steven I. Levine, both now among the best and most informed experts on Chinese history and politics, for the many important suggestions, criticisms, and corrections they've made as the manuscript was in progress, though needless to say, if there are mistakes of fact or judgment in this book, they are mine. My thanks also to Wenyi Zhou, my amazingly smart, gifted, and resourceful researcher at Columbia University; her work was remarkable, as was her calm tolerance of my many urgent questions. My thanks also to Alice Su for her very valuable help with Chinese sources at an early stage of the research; to Jay Barksdale at the New York Public Library and Chengzhi Wang of the Columbia University East Asian Library; to Nancy Hearst, Kati Marton, David Margolick, Edward Jay Epstein, Michael M. Sheng, Max Hastings, Ben Gerson, Doug and Nancy Spelman, and Catherine Talese, all of whom helped to keep this project on track.

And, of course, to Zhongmei and Elias, the twin centers of my existence, who put up with my absences, my long hours locked away in my upstairs study in Brooklyn, and my curious obsession with events of seventy years ago.

Notes

INTRODUCTION

5 When one of the American ships: *New York Times,* Dec. 14 and 17, 2013.

5 "just because it wasn't": *Global Times,* Dec. 21, 2013.

CHAPTER ONE: A Rare Victory

13 "We got a hell of a beating": Donovan Webster, *The Burma Road: The Epic Story of the China-Burma-India Theater in World War II* (New York: Farrar, Straus and Giroux, 2003), p. 45.

13 "succeed—or else": Charles F. Romanus and Riley Sunderland, *The United States Army in World War II: Stilwell's Command Problems* (Washington, DC: Office of the Chief of Military History, Department of the Army, 1956), p. 34.

13 He ferried his seventy-two thousand: Ibid., pp. 340–49.

14 "sickeningly wasteful": Ibid., p. 346.

14 "a long, hot day of mountain climbing": Theodore H. White, *In Search of History: A Personal Adventure* (New York: Harper and Row, 1978), p. 222.

16 "shabby cover of an emaciated body": Charles F. Romanus and Riley Sutherland, *United States Army in World War II: Time Runs Out in CBI* (Washington, D.C.: Office of the Chief of Military History, Department of the Army, 1959), p. 370.

16 "an area the Japanese wanted to hold": Ibid., p. 135.

17 "a smashing climax": *New York Times,* Jan. 4, 1945.

17 "a powerful tonic": *New York Times,* Jan. 24, 1945.

18 like eating a porcupine: Webster, p. 60.

18 "is making the Ledo-Burma Road": *New York Times,* Feb. 9, 1945.

19 "It is believed": Romanus and Sutherland, *Time Runs Out in CBI,* p. 332.

21 invited to sleep at the White House: William Jones, "Correspondence Sheds Light on FDR Post-War Vision," *Executive Intelligence Review,* July 6, 2007.

21 "if I give him everything I can": Cornelius Ryan, *The Last Battle: The Classic Battle for Berlin* (New York: Simon & Schuster, 1966), p. 162.

21 "We would serve with all our hearts": David D. Barrett, *Dixie Mission: The United States Army Observer Group in Yenan, 1944* (Berkeley: Center for Chinese Studies, University of California, 1970), p. 73.

CHAPTER TWO: The Generalissimo and the Americans

23 "cook up a workable scheme": Jay Taylor, *The Generalissimo: Chiang Kai-shek and the Struggle for Modern China* (Cambridge, MA: Harvard University Press, 2009), pp. 257–58.

24 "I believe it would work": Ibid., p. 258; Frank Dorn, *Walkout: With Stilwell in Burma* (New York: T. Y. Crowell, 1971), pp. 77–79.

24 "why Chiang's troops aren't": Taylor, pp. 247–48.

25 Stilwell told Eifler that he'd changed: Ibid., p. 258.

28 "a masterpiece": Ibid., p. 125. Taylor cites Zhang Guotao, *Rise of the Chinese Communist Party* (Lawrence: University Press of Kansas, 1972), pp. 478–79, and Yang Kuisong, *Xianshibian xintao* [A New Study of the Xian Incident].

28 "the last five minutes": Taylor, p. 126.

30 "the Red Army's first sign": Ibid., p. 134.

30 "a national hero": Ibid., p. 135.

30 "a splendid and noble personality": F. F. Liu, *A Military History of Modern China, 1934–1949* (Westport, CT: Greenwood Press, 1981), p. 99.

31 "genuine patriot": Owen Lattimore, *China Memoir: Chiang Kai-shek and the War Against Japan* (Tokyo: University of Tokyo Press, 1990), p. 149.

31 "due to the genius of one man": Han Suyin, *Destination Chungking* (Boston: Little, Brown, 1942), p. 17.

31 "he is there": Ibid., p. 131.

32 "she had managed to survive": Albert C. Wedemeyer, *Wedemeyer Reports!* (New York: Henry Holt, 1958), p. 279.

32 "the bloodiest battle": Ibid.

33 "followed France's example": Ibid., p. 280.

33 more gallant and resolute: Ibid.

33 "China could hope for victory": Ibid.

34 "bent his head": Taylor, p. 136.

35 "undependable scoundrel": Barbara W. Tuchman, *Stilwell and the American Experience in China, 1911–1945* (New York: Grove Press, 1970), p. 371.

35 "great believers in make-believe": Ibid., pp. 250–51.

36 "Where is the gallant resistance?": Ibid. , p. 320.

36 "a one-party government": Ibid., p. 378.

36 "The Chinese strategy": United States Department of State, *Foreign Relations of the United States* (hereinafter *FRUS*), 1944, vol. 6, pp. 6–7.

36 "We should pull up the plug": Wedemeyer, p. 205.

37 "the first time since the war began": Taylor, p. 243.

37 In his memoir of his wartime service: Oliver Caldwell, *A Secret War: Americans in China, 1944–45* (Carbondale: Southern Illinois University Press, 1972), pp. 8–9.

39 "The Peanut says": Taylor, p. 226.

39 "He can have no intention": Tuchman, p. 153.

39 "He can't make up his mind": Ibid., p. 273.

39 "fatally compromised": Ibid., p. 274.

39 "Resisting the Japanese": Lattimore, p. 190.

39 "failure to recognize": Alan K. Lathrop, "The Employment of Chinese Nationalist Troops in the First Burma Campaign," *Journal of Southeast Asian Studies* 12, no. 2 (Sept. 1981): 405.

40 "inferiority of striking power": Tuchman, p. 214.

40 he had been rated number one: Ibid., p. 225.

40 an extraordinary communications snafu: Lathrop, p. 410.

41 "I have to tell CKS": Tuchman, p. 279.

41 "It is expecting a great deal": Taylor, p. 201.

43 "When Burma was crashing": Tuchman, p. 284.

43 "has abandoned my 100,000 soldiers": Taylor, p. 205.

43 "the retreat would have been orderly": Ibid., p. 208.

44 "We have taken Mytkyina": Taylor, p. 207.

44 "Lean back, brother": Don Lohbeck, *Patrick J. Hurley* (Washington, DC: Henry Regnery, 1956), p. 308.

45 Chiang found Hurley "different": Taylor, p. 285.

45 rejected the request: Ibid., p. 286.

45 "crazy little bastard": Ibid.

45 "been delayed, ignored": Ibid.

46 "you have won this ball game": Ibid., p. 287.

46 "I now understand": Ibid., pp. 287–88.

46 "compulsive and stormy sobbing": Ibid., p. 289.

46 "the most severe humiliation": Ibid.

46 "Rejoice with me": Ibid., p. 291.

46 "patronizing attitude": Ibid., p. 289.

47 "is a professional, works hard": Ibid., pp. 291–92.

47 "My heart is broken," Ibid., p. 292.

47 "Stilwell's every act": FRUS, 1944, p. 170; Taylor, p. 294.

47 Stilwell invited the correspondents: Peter Rand, *China Hands: The Adventures and Ordeals of the American Journalists Who Joined Forces with the Great Chinese Revolution* (New York: Simon & Schuster, 1995), p. 246.

47 "STILWELL BREAK": *New York Times*, Oct. 31, 1944.

48 "The record of General Stilwell": Lohbeck, p. 305.

48 "small, graceful, fine-boned man": Wedemeyer, p. 277.

49 "how many people": Ibid.

49 "He seemed shy": Ibid., p. 278.

49 "we would have no difficulties": Ibid.

49 "I have now concluded": Romanus and Sutherland, *Time Runs Out*, p. 52.

49 "underlay most of China's military problems": Ibid., p. 65.

50 "Conditions are really bad": FRUS, 1945, vol. 7, p. 7.

CHAPTER THREE: The Devastated Country

53 Early in 1932: Peter Harmsen, *Shanghai 1937: Stalingrad on the Yangtze* (Philadelphia: Casemate, 2013), p. 20.

55 "We Sympathize": Michael Schaller, *The U.S. Crusade in China, 1938–1945* (New York; Columbia University Press, 1979), p. 42.

55 one hundred billion dollars: Arthur Waldron, "China's New Remembering: The Case of Zhang Zhizhong," *Modern Asian Studies* 30, no. 4 (Oct. 1996): 948.

56 "When no outside pressure": Graham Peck, *Two Kinds of Time: Life in Provincial China During the Crucial Years 1940–1941* (Boston: Houghton Mifflin, Sentry Edition, 1967), p. 298.

56 "boom towns": Ibid., p. 298.

56 "sheltered well over a hundred thousand": Ibid., p. 241.

57 "After each lengthening raid": Ibid., pp. 244–45.

57 "the road to the west": Ibid., p. 252.

58 "piled with the families": Ibid., p. 256.

59 "The difficulty of survival": Ibid., p. 27.

59 "Public spirit, generosity": John K. Fairbank, introduction to Peck, p. 3.

59 "You have seen misery": John F. Melby, *Mandate of Heaven: Records of a Civil War, China, 1945–1949* (Toronto: University of Toronto Press, 1968), p. 21.

60 "Everything went on in the streets": Ruth Altman Greene, *Hsiang-ya Journal* (Hamden, CT: Archon Press, 1977), p. 6.

61 It was a quiet, privileged campus: Edward Gulick, *Teaching in Wartime China: A Photo Memoir, 1937–1939* (Amherst: University of Massachusetts Press, 1995), pp. 72–73.

61 "as foreign eccentrics": Ibid., p. 74.

62 "we all live like lords": Nora B. Stirling, *Pearl Buck: A Woman in Conflict* (Piscataway, NJ: New Century Publishing, 1983), p. 57.

62 Joseph Stilwell, at the time: Greene, p. 111.

62 "the arsenal behind the hospital": Ibid.

63 Chiang came to Changsha: Diane Lary, *The Chinese People at War: Human Suffering and Social Transformation, 1937–1945* (Cambridge: Cambridge University Press, 2010), p. 63.

63 "With the running off": Greene, p. 112.

63 "going like a bonfire": Ibid., p. 113.

63 "the fires blazed": Ibid., p. 114.

64 The fire was a consequence: *New York Times*, Nov. 21, 1938.

64 Soong Mei-ling: Greene, p. 114.

64 More than 21,000 buildings: Lary, pp. 63–64.

64 "I stood at Pa Ko T'in": Gulick, pp. 238–39.

65 "Changsha, and various industrial points": Greene, p. 115.

66 "counterbalanced by the filth": Tuchman, p. 144.

66 "No worse luck": Martha Gellhorn, *The Face of War* (New York: Atlantic Monthly Press, 1988), p. 77.

67 "smoky, with gray walls": Cecil Beaton, *Chinese Diary & Album* (Hong Kong: Oxford University Press, 1991), p. 12.

67 half the people of the country: Theodore H. White and Annalee Jacoby, *Thunder Out of China* (New York: William Sloan Associates, 1946), p. xiii.

67 life expectancy in China: Nancy E. Riley, "China's Population: New Trends and Challenges," *Population Bulletin* 59, no. 2 (June 2004): 6.

67 "Over a large area of China": Richard Tawney, *Land and Labor in China* (New York: Farrar, Straus, and Giroux, 1972), p. 73.

68 "the barking of ill-fed dogs": John K. Fairbank, "The New China and the American Connection," *Foreign Affairs* 51, no. 1 (Oct. 1972).

68 "The magnitude of the rural misery": Stephen R. MacKinnon, Diana Lary, and Ezra F. Vogel, eds., *China at War: Regions of China, 1937–1945* (Palo Alto, CA: Stanford University Press, 2007), p. 178.

68 "There were corpses on the road": White and Jacoby, p. 169.

68 "We stood at the head": Ibid., p. 170.

69 "a tomb of a city": Peck, p. 30.

69 Chiang ordered that the dikes: MacKinnon, p. 178.

69 "grandiloquent patriotism": Lary, p. 64.

70 "A Chinese soldier": Gellhorn, pp. 99–100.

70 " 'almost no Chinese war prisoners' ": *New York Times*, Sept. 25, 1937.

71 "Tens of thousands of homeless": Frederic Wakeman Jr., *The Shanghai Badlands: Wartime Terrorism and Urban Crime, 1937–1941* (Cambridge: Cambridge University Press, 1996), p. 7.

71 "the epicenter of devastation": Harmsen, p. 246.

71 "the entire town and the villages": Ibid., p. 245.

71 "What an awful scene of desolation": Diana Lary and Stephen R. Mac-Kinnon, eds., *Scars of War: The Impact of Warfare on Modern China* (Vancouver: UBC Press, 2001), p. 57.

72 The estimates of Chinese military casualties: Harmsen, p. 247.

72 "in a political sense": White and Jacoby, p. 52.

72 As a result of the desecration: Lary, p. 50.

73 "Then they herded 670 men": Lary, p. 98.

73 the population of twenty thousand: MacKinnon, p. 103.

73 "packed solid with Chinese": Gellhorn, pp. 85–86.

74 One historian of the period: Hans J. van de Ven, *War and Nationalism in China, 1925–1945* (London: Routledge Curzon, 2003), p. 233.

74 a treasonous sort of modus vivendi: Ibid., p. 243.

75 By 1940, the Japanese: Edward Dreyer, *China at War, 1901–1949* (London: Longman, 1995), p. 258.

75 the Japanese flew 5,000 sorties: Van de Ven, p. 246.

76 "incomparably more destructive": Herbert P. Bix, *Hirohito and the Making of Modern Japan* (New York: HarperCollins, 1990), p. 367.

76 "There was nothing they would not do": Harmsen, pp. 246–47.
76 "During the resistance": Wakeman, p. 271.
76 a Chinese policeman named Tse: Emily Hahn, "Black and White," *The New Yorker*, May 5, 1945, pp. 21–23.
77 "frequented by movie starlets": Wakeman, p. 273.
77 Ding used just one machine: Ibid.
77 electricity use was restricted: Ibid.
78 Torture of opponents: Ibid.
78 "fur-hat soldiers": Ibid., p. 275.
78 one "comfort woman" for every forty soldiers: Max Hastings, *Inferno: The World at War, 1939–1945* (New York: Alfred A. Knopf, 2011), p. 416.
78 "They raped many women": Yang Chengyi, ed., *Fenghuo mengyue zhong di jipin: Zhejiang kangri zhanzheng kousu fangtan* [Memories in the Blaze of Wartime: Oral Interviews on the Japanese Occupation in Zhejiang] (Beijing: Beijing Library Publishing, 2007), pp. 10–11.
79 "My mother would rub black dirt": Ibid., p. 76.
80 "malnutrition, lack of hygiene": FRUS, 1944, pp. 191–92.
80 "Famine, flood, and drought": Romanus and Sutherland, *Time Runs Out*, p. 66.
80 "hostility and opposition": FRUS, 1944, p. 211.
80 Innumerable Chinese women were left: Lary, p. 9.
80 "A sea of people": Danke Li, *Echoes of Chungking: Women in Wartime China* (Urbana: University of Illinois Press, 2010), p. 56.
81 seven thousand coolies: *Time*, Dec. 26, 1938.
81 "A long ribbon of ox carts": Lary and MacKinnon, p. 105.
81 "Some young men": Jack Belden, *Still Time to Die* (New York: Harper & Brothers, 1944), p. 84.
82 "I felt so sad": Li, p. 57.
82 "He subsists on poor quality rice": Beaton, p. 63.
83 "Living like peasants": Ibid.
83 "China was indeed at the end": Wedemeyer, p. 278.
83 $145 million in Lend-Lease supplies: Taylor, p. 194.
83 "something had to be done": Wedemeyer, p. 278.
83 "Humans in the slum": Li, p. 87.
84 "We dug a hole,": Ibid., p. 58.
84 "she died in my arms": Ibid., p. 60.
85 "I watched every disaster": Ba Jin, *Guilin di shou-nan* [Hard Times in Guilin], available online at www.xiexingcun.com.

CHAPTER FOUR: Mao, Zhou, and the Americans

87 "in which were dug caves": John Paton Davies, *China Hand: An Autobiography* (Philadelphia: University of Pennsylvania Press, 2012), p. 217.
87 Disaster almost struck: Barrett, p. 14.
88 Among these agents: Cromley's and Stelle's backgrounds are discussed

in Maochun Yu, *OSS in China: Prelude to Cold War* (New Haven, CT: Yale University Press, 1996), p. 163.

88 Another recruit, Brooke Dolan: Brooke Dolan II, *Road to the Edge of the World* (Philadelphia: Proceedings of the Academy of Natural Sciences, 1937).

88 "With the Chinese Communists": Davies, p. 214.

89 "a French national": *FRUS*, 1944, p. 489.

89 "obvious untruths": Ibid., p. 400.

89 "to prolong China's war of resistance": Ibid., pp. 401–405.

90 "the mouthing of homilies": Ibid., p. 406.

90 "to quote the Generalissimo": Harrison Forman, *Report from Red China* (New York: Henry Holt, 1945), p. 1.

90 "young and naïve": Taylor, p. 265.

90 Chiang also nurtured a certain hope: Warren Tozer, "The Foreign Correspondents' Visit to Yenan in 1944: A Reassessment," *Pacific Historical Review* 14, no. 2 (May 1972).

91 "guarantee full freedom of movement": *FRUS*, 1944, p. 408.

91 "we consider your plane a hero": Barrett, p. 30.

91 "the most exciting event": Harry Harding and Yuan Ming, *Sino-American Relations, 1945–1955: A Joint Reassessment of a Critical Decade* (Wilmington, DE: R Books, 1989), p. 21.

91 But in Yenan they impressed: Carolle J. Carter, *Mission to Yanan: American Liaison with the Chinese Communists, 1944–1947* (Lexington: University Press of Kentucky, 1997), p. 37.

92 "a magnificent symbol": Forman, p. 46.

92 Service reported to the State Department: *FRUS*, 1944, pp. 517–20.

93 "ideal of democracy": Davies, pp. 215–16.

94 "we have aligned ourselves": Ibid., p. 160.

94 "steps committing us": Ibid., p. 183.

94 "One of our major mistakes": Ibid., p. 196.

96 "The lines of future conflict": Ibid., p. 139.

96 "The Communists are in China": Ibid., p. 225.

96 "I hoped that my show of interest": Ibid., p. 221.

97 "I obviously underestimated": Ibid., p. 224.

97 "As I see it now": Barrett, p. 46.

97 "belief in a creed": Davies, p. 224.

98 "China is in a mess": *FRUS*, 1944, pp. 38–39.

98 "general gloom": Ibid., pp. 100–101.

98 "handle Stalin better": Fraser J. Harbutt, *Yalta 1945: Europe and America at the Crossroads* (Cambridge: Cambridge University Press, 2010), p. 55.

99 "American public opinion": *FRUS*, 1944, p. 39.

99 "China is unquestionably losing": *New York Times*, July 20, 1943.

100 "If the book has been correctly interpreted": *New York Times*, Jan. 9, 1938.

100 *Red Star over China* was and still is: Alexander V. Pantsov and Stephen I. Levine, *Mao: The Real Story* (New York: Simon & Schuster, 2007) pp. 1–2.

101 By 1935, Snow was living: Rand, pp. 148–51.

101 Yui was a well-placed man: Ibid., pp. 155–56.

102 "a world scoop": Ibid., p. 157.

102 "To change this situation": Ibid., pp. 157–58.

102 "a romantic adventurer": Ibid., p. 159.

103 "like a generalissimo": Ibid., p. 166.

103 "Ten thousand years!": Ibid., p. 167.

103 Zhou Enlai was not just covering: Ibid., p. 165.

104 They called themselves the last-ditchers: Davies, *China Hand*, pp. 25–30.

104 "air raids, troop movements": Ibid., p. 25.

105 "close collaboration": Stephen R. MacKinnon, *Wuhan, 1938: War, Refugees, and the Making of Modern China* (Berkeley: University of California Press, 2008), p. 104.

105 More than a few other young Americans: Steven R. MacKinnon and Oris Friesen, *China Reporting: An Oral History of American Journalism in the 1930s and 1940s* (Berkeley: University of California Press, 1987), pp. 37–47.

105 "a thrilling description": Nathanial Peffer, "The China at War and the China Behind the Lines," *The New York Times Book Review*, Dec. 24, 1939.

106 "land ownership under reasonable conditions": Taylor, p. 192.

106 "were not allied to Moscow": *FRUS*, 1945, vol. 7, p. 2.

106 "a force to be reckoned with": Ibid., p. 8.

106 "is hated more every day": Ibid., p. 12.

107 In May 1942, Zhou gave a letter: Michael Sheng, *Battling Western Imperialism: Mao, Stalin, and the United States* (Princeton, NJ: Princeton University Press, 1997), p. 76.

107 "Zhou Enlai had an amazing mind": Theodore H. White, *In Search of History: A Personal Adventure* (New York: Harper & Row, 1978), p. 117.

108 "a man as brilliant and ruthless": Ibid., p. 118.

109 "with the same coarse blue cloth": Ibid., p. 120.

110 "no one could have seemed": Ibid.

110 "was the most beautiful Chinese woman": Ibid., p. 121.

110 who loved reading Chinese Robin Hood fiction: John K. Fairbank, *Chinabound: A Fifty-Year Memoir* (New York: Harper & Row, 1982), p. 268.

111 "On the tiny screen": Qiao Songdu, *Qiaoguanhua yu Gong Peng: we di fuqin muqin* [Qiao Guanhua and Gong Peng: My Father and Mother], trans. Wenyi Zhou and Richard Bernstein (Beijing: Zhonghua Shu Ju, 2008), p. 23.

111 their meager wardrobe was stolen: Fairbank, *Chinabound*, p. 272.

111 In Chungking, Gong achieved: Ibid., p. 268.

112 "a taming effect on everybody": Ibid., p. 273.

112 "a tall-stemmed flower": Eric Severeid, *Not So Wild a Dream* (New York: Alfred A. Knopf, 1947), pp. 327–38; Rand, p. 237.

112 "The CCP in Chungking": Fairbank, *Chinabound*, p. 270.

112 "the voice of dissidence": Ibid., p. 268.

112 "What she put forward": Ibid., p. 267.

113 "If only I could be for a little while": Severeid, p. 329.

113 "silent conspiracy": Ibid., p. 328.

114 Service volunteered to donate: E. J. Kahn Jr., *The China Hands: America's Foreign Service Officers and What Befell Them* (New York: Viking Press, 1972), p. 107.

114 another journalist, Barbara Stevens: Rand, p. 276.

114 "She was not only young": Qiao, p. 70.

114 she snubbed the old friends: Rand, p. 310.

115 When the Canadian journalist: William Stevenson, *Past to Present: A Reporter's Story of War, Spies, People, and Politics* (Guilford, CT: Lyons Press, 2012), p. 240.

115 "in seclusion at the Beau-Rivage": Godfrey Blunden, "The Two Faces of Chou En-lai," *Life*, June 28, 1954.

115 "Zhou overwhelmed you": Quoted in Freda Utley, *The China Story* (Washington, DC: Regnery, 1951), p. 143.

115 "It was so utterly hopeless": Ibid.

115 "The police state features": Israel Epstein, *My China Eye: Memoirs of a Jew and a Journalist* (San Francisco: Long River Press, 2005), p. 174.

116 deserter from the Eighth Route Army: Ibid., p. 175.

116 "We learned later": Forman, p. 4.

116 a dissenter's proclamation: Ibid., pp. 5–7.

116 "another world": Epstein, p. 179.

117 "Every once-barren hilltop": Ibid., p. 180.

117 "and who had ever heard": Ibid., p. 183.

117 "loyalty dance": For photographs of this and other rituals of obeisance to Mao, see Liu Heung Shing, ed., *China: Portrait of a Country* (Cologne: Taschen, 2009), pp. 178–83.

118 "Everything is open": *New York Herald Tribune*, June 23, 1944, cited in Tozer.

118 "The men and women pioneers": *Christian Science Monitor*, June 23, 1944, cited in Tozer.

118 "much more American than Russian": Taylor, p. 220.

118 "so-called Communists": *FRUS*, 1944, p. 103.

118 "margarine Communists": Dieter Heinzig, *The Soviet Union and Communist China, 1945–1950: The Arduous Road to the Alliance* (Armonk, NY: M.E. Sharpe, 2004), p. 22.

119 regular hunting expeditions: Carter, p. 42.

119 On Saturday nights: Barrett, pp. 50–51.

119 "Far-seeing Mao Zedong": Forman, pp. 88–89.

120　"is no unapproachable oracle": Ibid., p. 177.

120　"We are not striving": Ibid., p. 178.

120　"we believe in and practice democracy": Ibid., p. 179.

120　"tremendous character": Davies, *China Hand*, p. 218.

120　"a first rate soldier": Barrett, p. 33.

121　Davies draws a verbal portrait: Davies, *China Hand*, pp. 18–219.

121　"dominated the room": Henry Kissinger, *White House Years* (New York: Little, Brown, 1979), p. 1058.

121　His conclusion was: Davies, *China Hand*, p. 222.

122　Varoff's mission had been to hit: "Report of Capt. Varoff Crew Rescue," Mar. 22, 1945, 40th Bomb Group Association, available online at www.40thbombgroup.org. For news coverage of rescue, see *New York Times*, Jan. 17, 1945.

123　"All he knew": Barrett, p. 37.

124　"our bitter enemies now": Ibid.

CHAPTER FIVE: The Dark Side

125　Michael Lindsay: Yu, p. 166.

125　To gain access to Yenan at all: Gao Hua, *Hong taiyang she tsenyang shengqi de: Yenan zhengfeng yundong de lai long qumai* [How Did the Red Sun Rise: A History of the Yenan Rectification Movement] (Hong Kong: Chinese University Press, 2000), p. 234–36

126　"how bloodthirsty and evil": Dai Qing, *Wang Shiwei and "Wild Lilies": Rectification and Purges in the Chinese Communist Party, 1942–1944* (Armonk, NY: M. E. Sharpe, 1994), p. 4.

127　"their own reputation": Ibid., p. 91.

127　"I will dare": Ibid., p. 18.

128　"the foot-bindings of a slattern": Philip Short, *Mao: A Life* (New York: Henry Holt, 1999), p. 381.

128　"fiendishly clever": Ibid., p. 384.

128　big-character poster or wall newspaper: Ibid., p. 385.

129　who encouraged the paper: Dai Qing, p. 50.

129　"pure and noble image": Ibid., p. 5

129　"the youth of Yenan": Ibid.

129　"not an egalitarian": Ibid., p. 20.

130　"It was not enough": Short, p. 386.

130　"The first step": Ibid.

131　"Party meetings are fixed": Vladimirov, p. 26.

132　"genius leader": Gao Hua, p. 227.

132　"Kang always wore Russian jackets": Shi Zhe, *Feng yu Gu: She Zhe hui-yi-lu* [Peaks and Valleys: The Memoirs of Shi Zhe] (Beijing: Hungxi Publishing, 1992), p. 229.

133　"a shrill and hissing voice": Pyotr Vladimirov, *The Vladimirov Diaries, Yenan, China, 1942–1945* (New York: Doubleday, 1975), p. 10.

133　"the ugliest nightmare": Dai Qing, p. xvi.

134 With tears streaming down his face: Gao Hua, pp. 483–84.
134 "Once you confessed": Shi Zhe, pp. 200–202.
135 "counter-revolutionary shit-hole": Short, p. 389.
135 A mob of other writers obediently: Dai Qing, pp. 31–32.
135 accused Wu Han: Jonathan D. Spence, *The Gate of Heavenly Peace: The Chinese and Their Revolution, 1895–1980* (New York: The Viking Press, 1981), p. 345; Short, pp. 527–29.
136 "the close friend and ally": Lynne Joiner, *Honorable Survivor: Mao's China, McCarthy's America, and the Persecution of John S. Service* (Annapolis, MD: Naval Institute Press, 2009), p. 330.
136 "Korea and Vietnam": Ibid., p. 331.

CHAPTER SIX: The Wrong Man

141 "I shall never forget": Barrett, p. 57.
141 "a prolonged howl": Davies, p. 226.
142 "everything but Shay's Rebellion": *Time*, Jan. 1, 1945.
142 "disappeared in a cloud of dust": Barrett, p. 57.
142 "He tried to corral both sides": Herbert Feis, *The China Tangle: The American Effort in China from Pearl Harbor to the Marshall Mission* (Princeton, NJ: Princeton University Press, 1953), p. 214.
143 "If imperial Japan had not": Quoted in Waldron, "China's New Remembering": 972.
143 "the saltiness of the General's remarks": Barrett, p. 57.
144 "If I haven't been given American policy": Arthur R. Ringwalt, "Oral History Interview with Arthur R. Ringwalt," Truman Memorial Library, online at www.trumanlibrary.org/oralhist/ringwalt.htm.
145 "the United States is the greatest hope": Quoted in Kahn, p. 136.
146 "Hurley arrived at Yenan": Davies, *China Hand*, p. 227.
146 bitter and highly publicized dispute: Barrett, p. 57.
146 Hurley was born in 1883: Lohbeck, passim. Russell D. Buhite, *Patrick J. Hurley and American Foreign Policy* (Ithaca, NY: Cornell University Press, 1973), passim.
148 "Patrick Hurley is one": Lohbeck, p. 49.
148 "He was a realist": Ibid., p. 148.
148 "You know, Mr. President": Ibid., p. 153.
148 "a little piracy": Ibid.
148 "We were out-shipped": Ibid.
149 "It was obvious to me": *FRUS*, 1944, p. 201.
149 "We do not wish to be alarmists": Ibid., p. 199.
150 "is extremely grave": Ibid. p. 159.
150 "we are rolling the enemy back": Ibid., pp. 157–58.
151 "at least an additional year": *FRUS*, 1944, p. 287.
151 "true unification": Ibid., p. 159.
152 "no longer able to fight": Barrett, p. 60.
153 "Chiang's men were starved": Ibid.

153 "I had myself seen": Ibid.
153 "what I have said about Chiang": Ibid., p. 61.
153 Well, it's a foot in the door: Mao-Hurley dialogue is from Barrett, pp. 60–62.
154 "to promote progress and democracy": Ibid., p. 63.
155 "a love feast": Barrett, p. 63.
155 "I cannot guarantee": Ibid., p. 64.
155 "bill of goods": Davies, *China Hand*, pp. 228–29.
156 "We consider the Soviet Union": Barrett, p. 65.
157 American simplicity versus Chinese complexity: Tang Tsou, *America's Failure in China, 1941–1950* (Chicago: University of Chicago Press, 1968), p. 91.
157 network of personal relations: Ibid., p. 112.
159 AGFRTS: Yu, p. 156. Davies, *China Hands*, p. 287.
160 "Your honor, General Donovan": Yu, p. 144.
160 "face was not only handsome": Fairbank, *Chinabound*, p. 215.
160 "freed of all official relationship": Yu, p. 138.
161 "special measures": Ibid., p. 99.
161 "a tight little kingdom": National Archives and Records Administration, College Park, Maryland (hereafter NARA), RG 38, Office of the Chief of Naval Operations, Records of the U.S. Naval Group, Box 39b.
161 "This Special Party Branch": Yu, p. 44.
162 "unsavory": Davies, *China Hand*, p. 288.
162–63 "assassination by poison": Yu, p. 102.
163 "is mainly preoccupied": NARA, RG 38, Box 39.
163 "If the American public": Quoted in Davies, p. 289.
163 "Hundreds of Tai Li's victims": NARA, RG 38, Box 39b.
163 Blue Shirts carried out: Taylor, pp. 104–105.
164 Zhang Deneng, shot: Ibid., p. 273.
164 large numbers of executions: Ibid., p. 105.
164 "numerous adverse reports": NARA, RG 38, Box 39.
164 "As head of the National Police": Ibid.
166 "One outstanding weakness": Yu, p. 199.
166 "crook": Davies, p. 229.
166 "ultimatum basis": Tsou, p. 93.
167 "The Generalissimo finds it necessary": Romanus and Sunderland, *Stilwell's Mission*, p. 270.
167 "the concept of a loyal opposition": Davies, p. 228.
167 "By December": Kahn, pp. 145–46.
168 "We are having some success": *FRUS*, 1944, vol. 6, p. 748.
169 a remarkable confrontation: Mao's conversation with Barrett is from Barrett, pp. 70–75.
170 four new conditions: Feis, p. 219.
171 "It was a routine trip": Davies, p. 235.
172 "The Chinese Communists were going to win": Ringwalt, oral history.

172 "the age-old ploy": Davies, *China Hand*, p. 235.
172 "an old fool": Ibid., p. 236.
172 "Hello" and "Good-bye": Kahn, pp. 122–23.
172 "at routine staff meetings": Ibid.
173 "principal occupation": Melby, p. 23.
173 "a vacillating compromise": Davies, *China Hand*, p. 238.
174 "And you do the same": Ibid.
174 "Hurley flushed": Davies, p. 239.
174 an extraordinary ensuing scene: Wedemeyer, p. 319.

CHAPTER SEVEN: The Rage of an Envoy

175 "wants to dispatch to America": Barbara Tuchman, "If Mao Had Come to Washington," *Foreign Affairs* 51 (Oct. 1972).
179 "to create a large new strip": *FRUS*, 1945, vol. 7, p. 168.
179 "certain officers": Ibid., p. 176.
179 "I did not know": Ibid.
180 "a little confused": John Paton Davies, *Dragon by the Tail: American, British, Japanese, and Russian Encounters with China and One Another* (New York: W. W. Norton, 1972), p. 385.
180 The Communists had guerrillas: Yu, p. 166.
180 to be assigned: Ibid., p. 167.
180 Ye suggested that the Communists: Davies, *Dragon by the Tail*, p. 361.
181 "offered all the cooperation": Ibid, p. 362.
181 "underestimated the influence": Ibid.
181 "deviated so far to the right": Ibid.
181 "I did not inquire": Ibid., p. 363.
182 they drew up an ambitious plan: Memo from Willis Bird to chief of staff, subject: Yenan trip, 24 Jan. 1945, RG 38, Entry 148, Box 7, Folder 103, "Dixie." Cited in Yu, p. 187.
183 "It was most embarrassing": Wedemeyer, p. 313.
183 "unauthorized loose discussions": Yu, p. 93.
183 Wedemeyer held a press conference: *New York Times*, Feb. 15, 1945.

CHAPTER EIGHT: A Moral Compromise

185 no way for Mao to have known: Sheng, pp. 93, 211.
186 "in order to get take full advantage": Ibid., p. 93.
186 "Do not be afraid": Zhou Enlai, *Zhou Enlai nianpu* [Chronological Record of Zhou Enlai] (Beijing: Peoples' Publishing Co., 1991), pp. 600–603.
187 mass rally of twenty thousand: *New York Times*, Nov. 17, 1944.
188 "their own selfish interests": *FRUS*, 1945, vol. 5, pp. 817–20.
188 "We must clearly realize": Walter Isaacson and Evan Thomas, *The Wise Men: Six Friends and the World They Made* (New York: Simon & Schuster, 1986), p. 249.
188 "cause further trouble": *FRUS*, 1945, vol. 5, p. 843.

190   "sphere of influence": S. M. Plokhy, *Yalta: The Price of Peace* (New York: Viking, 2010), p. 131.

190   This required that Roosevelt travel: Rudy Abrahamson, *Spanning the Century: The Life of W. Averill Harriman, 1891–1986* (New York: William Morrow, 1992), p. 370.

191   "free, independent, and powerful Poland": Plokhy, pp. 166–67.

191–92   "to restore their sovereignty": James Reardon-Anderson, *Yenan and the Great Power: The Origins of Chinese Communist Foreign Policy* (New York: Columbia University Press, 1980), p. 74.

192   "the shabbiest sort": Isaacson and Thomas, p. 246.

192   "dictating terms to the Japanese": Davies, *China Hand*, p. 248.

193   urged Roosevelt to get the Russians: Ibid., p. 250.

193   "By the time of the Yalta Conference": Tsou, p. 71.

194   First, he wanted to restore: Plokhy, pp. 223–24.

194   Roosevelt in a difficult position: Ibid., pp. 224–25.

195   Harriman didn't like it: Abrahamson, p. 390.

195   "The prescription for this": Davies, *China Hand*, p. 247.

195   "happiness, prosperity or stability": John Lewis Gaddis, *George F. Kennan: An American Life* (New York: Penguin Press, 2011), p. 188.

196   "leapfrog over my top-hatted head": Abrahamson, p. 345.

196   "Russia promises": *Life*, Sept. 10, 1945.

196   "masterful and effective": Gaddis, p. 189.

197   Zhou wrote a lengthy inner-party report: Sheng, p. 82.

CHAPTER NINE: Hiding the Knife

198   "Chiang could not whip us": Lynne Joiner, *Honorable Survivor: Mao's China, McCarthy's America, and the Persecution of John S. Service* (Annapolis, MD: Naval Institute Press, 2009), pp. 130–31.

198   "strong ties of sympathy": Joseph W. Esherick, ed., *Lost Chance in China: The World War II Dispatches of John S. Service* (New York: Random House, 1974), pp. 372–73.

199   "a single gun or bullet": Ibid., p. 383.

199   "Politically, any orientation": Ibid., p. 308.

199   Davies weighed in with a memo: *FRUS*, 1945, vol. 7, pp. 337–38.

200   "this hypocritical foreign devil": Pantsov and Levine, p. 346.

201   "Marxism apart from Chinese peculiarities": Ibid., p. 326.

202   "correct and circumspect": *Time*, June 18, 1945.

202   he had found no evidence: Esherick, pp. 350–53.

203   "unrealistic": Davies, *China Hand*, p. 232.

204   "to radically alter the correlation": Pantsov and Levine, p. 343.

204   "ally ourselves with the Soviet Union": Mao Zedong, "On the People's Democratic Dictatorship," *Selected Works of Mao Zedong*, vol. 4 (Beijing: Foreign Languages Press), online edition, www.marxists.org/reference/archive/mao/selected-works/volume-4/mswv4_65.htm.

205   "the CCP would be able": Pantsov and Levine, p. 343.

205 "squeezed like a lemon": Robert Carson North, *Moscow and Chinese Communists* (Stanford, CA: Standford University Press, 1963), p. 96.

206 "Communists the world over": Mao, "On the People's Democratic Dictatorship."

207 sheltered in Shanghai: Pantsov and Levine, p. 250.

207 offspring of dedicated Chinese revolutionaries: Sin-Lin, *Shattered Families, Broken Dreams: Little-Known Episodes from the History of the Persecution of Chinese Revolutionaries in Stalin's Gulag,* trans. Steven I. Levine (Portland, ME: Merwin Asia, 2012), pp. 86–89.

208 "In our hearts protest burns": Ibid., p. 91.

208 "What you are talking about": Ibid., p. 118.

209 "the shores of socialism": Pantsov and Levine, p. 329.

210 "the new international trust": Sheng, p. 58.

212 organized a Harvard Club: White, *In Search,* p. 73.

212 "imperialist procuress": Pantsov and Levine, p. 310.

213 a public self-criticism: Sheng, p. 31.

213 a radio contact to communicate: Sheng, pp. 22–23.

214 numerous financial contributions: Pantsov and Levine, p. 334.

215 "shattered the intrigues": Mao, "Interview With New China Daily correspondents on the New International Situation," Sept. 1, 1939, in *Collected Works,* vol. 2, online at https://www.marxists.org/reference/archive/mao/selected-works/volume-2/mswv2_17.html.

215 "slaughterhouse of imperialist war": Ibid., p. 70.

215 "enlightened bourgeois politician": Ibid., p. 72.

215 "Their capitalists": Mao, "On the People's Democratic Dictatorship."

216 "rely on the people": Sheng, p. 49.

217 Mao endorsed the new agreement: Ibid., p. 71.

217 "if they are antifascist": Ibid., p. 73.

217 "to stand with you": Taylor, p. 188.

218 "There is no such thing": Lyman P. Van Slyke, ed. *The Chinese Communist Movement: A Report of the United States War Department, July 1945* (Palo Alto, CA: Stanford University Press, 1968), p. 220.

219 "We shall never agree to that": Sheng, p. 90.

CHAPTER TEN: The War over China Policy

220 One of Hurley's biographers: Buhite, p. 191.

220 Little Whiskers: *FRUS,* 1945, vol. 7, p. 115.

221 "We would write dispatches": Ringwalt, oral history.

221 The dispatch was never sent: Ibid.

221 "I pause to observe": Feis, p. 222.

222 what Hurley seemed most interested in: Kahn, p. 149.

222 "There is no valid reason": *FRUS,* 1945, vol. 7, p. 201.

223 "liberal democratic": Ibid., p. 158.

223 "this inability to engage": Ibid., p. 157.

224 "one means to an end": Ibid., p. 218.

224 "They overdid it": Gary May, *China Scapegoat: The Diplomatic Ordeal of John Carter Vincent* (Washington, DC: New Republic Books, 1979), p. 120.
224 "ascribe all virtue": Ibid.
224 The best option for the United States: Ibid., p. 124.
225 "a degree of flexibility": Romanus and Sutherland, *Time Runs Out*, p. 337.
225 "fear and suspicion": Taylor, p. 302.
225 "sold out": Ibid.
226 "a stinging reprimand to Tsou": *FRUS*, 1945, vol. 7, pp. 239–40.
226 "if they didn't do something": Kahn, p. 152.
226 "They'll say we're all traitors": Ibid.
227 all of the political officers: Feis, p. 268.
227 "inform Chiang Kai-shek": *FRUS*, 1945, vol. 7, pp. 87–92.
227 "secure the cooperation of all Chinese": Feis, p. 271.
227 "a full array": Lohbeck, p. 381.
228 "the President upheld Hurley": Feis, p. 272.
228 "seize control of China": May, p. 126.
230 a widely covered press conference: *New York Times*, Apr. 3, 1945.
230 "American diplomats": Buhite, p. 203.
231 a deal between Moscow and Chungking: Ibid., pp. 203–205.
231 "There was ample advice": Kahn, p. 158.
231 Okamura had 820,000 men: Romanus and Sutherland, *Time Runs Out*, p. 49.
232 "the feeling of victory": Bix, p. 362.
232 2.7 million noncombatants: Ibid., p. 366.
233 "For many years": *New York Times*, Feb. 9, 1945.
233 At night, the pilots and maintenance crews: Severeid, pp. 337–38.
234 "apathetic and unintelligent": Romanus and Sutherland, *Time Runs Out*, pp. 53–54.
235 "We can throw in": Ibid., p. 62.
235 Okamura's supply lines were overextended: Ibid., pp. 174–75.
236 "a dry cackle": Ibid., p. 176.
236 "empty runways": Ibid., p. 179.
238 "held stoutly": Ibid., p. 282.
238 "holding well": Ibid.
239 "Whenever the situation changed": Ibid., p. 285.
239 "complete success": Ibid., pp. 285–86.
239 Chiang backed down: Ibid., p. 287.
240 "real progress": Ibid., p. 290.

CHAPTER ELEVEN: Mao the God, Service the Spy

242 Mao's apotheosis was a gradual thing: Pantsov and Levine, p. 342.
243 to plant the first grain of millet: Short, p. 393.
244 About half of the party members: Chang and Halliday, p. 269.

244 Stalin's short course was translated: Short, p. 393.
244 admitted that his past opposition: Ibid., p. 395.
245 "various anti-party activities": Panstov and Levine, p. 338.
245 a Solomonic judgment: Ibid.
245 "Mao Zedong's contribution": Ibid., p. 339.
246 gave credit to Mao for the battle of Pinxingguan: Sheng, p. 44. Chang and Halliday, p. 269.
246 "Beyond all doubt": Mao, "On Coalition Government," *Selected Works*, vol. 3.
249 "the deep, stinking pit": *Liberation Daily*, July 11, 1945.
251 "Can we Chinese succeed?": Yang Kuisong, *Mao Zedong yu Mosike di Ennen-yuanyuan* [The Love-Hate Relationship Between Mao Zedong and Moscow] (Nanchang: Jiangxi Renmin Chuban [Jiangxi People's Publishing Co.], 1999), pp. 519–20.
251 "Who is our leader?": Chang and Halliday, p. 282.
251 "the faraway water": Yang Kuisong, *Zhonggong yu Mosike di Guanxi* [Relations Between the Chinese Communists and Moscow] (Nanchang: Jiangxi Renmin Chuban She [Jiangxi People's Publishing Co.], 1997), pp. 519–20.
252 "overly friendly with the Reds": May, p. 169. Harvey Klehr and Ronald Radosh, *The Amerasia Spy Case: Prelude to McCarthyism* (Chapel Hill: University of North Carolina Press, 1996), p. 54.
252 "the FBI's quiet supersleuths": *Time*, June 18, 1945.
253 President Truman told Congress: *New York Times*, June 2, 1945.
253 "I'll get that son of a bitch": Klehr and Radosh, p. 26.
253 "something real big": Kahn, p. 169.
254 Alsop had told him: Klehr and Radosh, p. 20.
255 "designated leaker": Ibid., p. 62.
255 found what appeared to be: Ibid., p. 31.
256 "very secret": Kahn, p. 168.
256 columns early on denouncing the FBI arrests: Klehr and Radosh, p. 100.
256 "sensational proof": Ibid., p. 98.
256 The Scripps-Howard chain: Kahn, p. 170.
257 "The arrest of the six people": *Liberation Daily*, June 25, 1945.
258 "a hundred times more democratic": Ibid., July 11 and July 20, 1945.
258 "many unburied bodies": NARA, RG 226, Box 148, Folder 9.
259 "For eight years": Ibid.
259 had come from bribes: Yu, pp. 220–21.
259 the Spaniel Mission was being dispatched: Ibid.
259 "no prior notice": Ibid.
260 "treating them kindly": Ibid., p. 223. NARA, minutes of Wedemeyer meeting with Mao, Aug. 30, 1945.
261 "grossly exaggerated": Yu, p. 222.
261 "I consider the Fuping incident": NARA, Minutes.
261 "All communist headquarters": Yu, pp. 222–23.

CHAPTER TWELVE: Hearts and Minds

266 Friday Dinner Gathering: Yang Jianye, *Ma Yingchu* (Shijiazhuang: Huashan Wenyi Shuban She [Huashan Arts and Literature Publishing House], 1997), p. 87; Deng Jiarong, *Ma Yinchu Zhuang* [The Biography of Ma Yinchu] (Shanghai: Wenyi Chuban She [Arts and Literature Publishing House], 1986), p. 98.

267 "cruel and rapacious": Peng Hua, *A Biography of Ma Yinchu* (Beijing: Dangdai Zhongguo Chuban She [Contemporary China Publishing House], 2008), p. 52.

268 "The world has already become": Ma Yinchu, *Complete Works*, vol. 12 (Hangzhou: Zhejiang Renmin Chuban She [Zhejiang People's Publishing House], 1999), p. 263.

269 "The 'Vacuum Tube'": Peng, pp. 52–53.

269 "trembling with fear": *Supplement to the Collected Works of Ma Yinchu* (Shanghai: Sanlian Shudian Press, 2007), p. 328.

270 there were ferocious quarrels: Jonathan Spence, *The Gate of Heavenly Peace: The Chinese and Their Revolution, 1859–1980* (New York: Viking Press, 1981), pp. 256–60.

270 like Qu Qiubai and Hu Yepin: Ibid., pp. 207–36.

271 "China is now divided": *FRUS*, 1944, p. 472.

272 "Yenan boiled over": Shi Zhe, *Feng yu Gu: Shi Zhe hui-yi-lu* [Peaks and Valleys: The Memoirs of Shi Zhe] (Beijing: Hungxi Publishing Co, 1992), p. 17.

272 "In mid to late August": Chu Anping, *Keguan* [Objectivity], Nov. 11, 1945 in *Chu Anping Wenyi* [Collected Essays of Chu Anping] (Shanghai: Dongfang Chuban Zhungxin [Eastern Publishing Center], 1998), pp. 3–8.

272 "Most of the people": Lu Ling, *Qiu Ai* [Night of the Chinese Victory] (Haiyan Bookstore, 1946), pp. 194–202.

272 At the waterfront: White, *In Search*, pp. 235–36.

273 "all of China went crazy": Xia Yan, *Xia Yan Zejuan* [Autobiography of Xia Yan] (Nanjing: Jiangsu Wenyi Chuban She [Jiangsu Literature and Arts Publishing House], 1996), p. 172.

273 "I am very optimistic": *Time*, Sept. 3, 1945.

274 a rickshaw race: John Hart Caughey, *The Marshall Mission to China, 1945–1947* (Lanham, MD: Rowman & Littlefield, 2011), p. 53.

274 "I alone feel great shame": Taylor, p. 320.

274 "plunge China into chaos": Ibid.

275 "I was excited for a while": Hu Feng, *Hu Feng Zizhuan* [Autobiography of Hu Feng] (Nanjing: Jiangsu Wenyi Shuban She [Jiangsu Literature and Arts Publishing House], 1993), pp. 343–44.

275 "occupied for a second time": *Keguan*, Nov. 11, 1945.

275 The KMT was corrupt: Ibid.

276 "The waiting area": *Da Gong Bao*, Dec. 22–25, 1945.

276 "barely a human trace": Ibid.
276 "Shanghai was bulging": Lattimore, p. 206.
276 "a raw, unheated city": Rand, p. 275.
276 "This place called Shanghai": Caughey, p. 53.
277 "the least bit of attention": Ibid., p. 61.
277 "squeeze": Ibid., p. 207.
277 "a lot of robberies": Da Gong Bao, Dec. 24, 1945.
278 "Such a spirit of daring": Ibid.

CHAPTER THIRTEEN: Everything Stalin Wanted

279 Soviet invasion of Manchuria: David M. Glantz, Soviet Operational and Tactical Combat in Manchuria, 1945, "August Storm" (Portland, OR: Frank Cass Publishers, 2003), pp. 1–2 and passim.
280 "three days of open looting": Survey of the Mukden Area Situation as It Has Developed from 16 August 1945 to 10 September 1945," NARA, RG 226 (Records of the OSS), Entry 148, Box 6.
280 "'not being normal in their minds'": Ibid.
280 "domination of the provinces": Lisle Abbott Rose, Dubious Victory: The United States and the End of World War II (Kent, OH: Kent State University Press, 1973), p. 132.
280 "The Kremlin will be careful": Davies, Dragon, pp. 406–407.
281–82 "discrediting the Chungking government": FRUS, 1945, vol. 7, p. 348.
282 "Without the support of the Soviet": FRUS, 1945, vol. 7, p. 433.
283 "One should keep Japan": Sergei N. Goncharov, John W. Lewis, and Xue Litai, Uncertain Partners: Stalin, Mao, and the Korean War (Stanford, CA: Sanford University Press, 1993), p. 3.
284 the result might be massive: Ibid., p. 5.
284 "Russia has pledged": Lohbeck, p. 405.
285 "This kicked the props": Time, Sept. 3, 1945.
285 "without hope of future help": Time, Sept. 3, 1945.
285 "minimized": New York Times, Oct. 14, 1945.
285 "because Stalin insisted": Pantsov and Levine, p. 346.
285 foment a pro-Communist uprising: Goncharov et al., pp. 8–9.
286 as a tactical move: Sheng, p. 102.
286 "very distressed and even angry": Shi Zhe, p. 215.
286 Mao argued in an interview: Mao, Collected Works, vol. 4.
287 "the talks would buy time": Goncharov et al., p. 7.
287 "beyond any measurement": Sheng, p. 100.
287 "'bourgeois influence'": Mao, "The Situation and our Policy After the Victory in the War of Resistance Against Japan," Aug. 13, 1945, in Collected Works, online at http://www.marxists.org/reference/archive/mao/selected -works/volume-4/mswv4_01.html.
287 "it should not be surprising": FRUS, 1945, vol. 7, p. 325.
288 "unanimous demand": Sheng, pp. 98–99.
289 "going to his own execution": Time, Sept. 10, 1945.

289 "weird, loud scream": Shi Zhe, p. 21.
289 "Olive oil! olive oil!": *Time*, Sept. 10, 1945.
289 "the cordial atmosphere": *Time*, Sept. 10, 1945.
290 "well-informed observers": Ibid.
290 "ten thousand years": Taylor, p. 319.
290 "I am confident": *Time*, Oct. 8, 1945.
291 "back of its hand": *Time*, Sept. 24, 1945.
291 "We must stop": Taylor, p. 321.
291 "touched the Chairman's heart": Ibid.
291 The two sides promised: Ibid., p. 319.
292 he has been justly criticized: Feis, p. 361.
292 "only words on paper": Mao, "On the Chungking Negotiations," *Collected Works*, vol. 4, online.

CHAPTER FOURTEEN: Facts on the Ground

293 "vast lost areas": *FRUS*, 1945, vol. 7, pp. 519–20.
293 "have the right to enter": Feis, pp. 340–41.
296 "It is debatable": Davies, *Dragon*, p. 406.
296 "to render to China": Feis, p. 346.
297 "The Eighth Route Army": Vladimirov, p. 26.
297 "Like everywhere in the Special Area": Ibid., p. 40.
298 "outmaneuver Stalin": Schaller, p. 256.
299 "think of the kids": David McCullough, *Truman* (New York: Simon & Schuster, 1992), p. 424.
299 "not a drop of gentleness": Melby, p. 26.
299 "There is no such thing": Schaller, p. 214.
300 Zhu De was already ordering: Taylor, p. 315.
300 Mao dispatched nine regiments: Goncharov et al., p. 9.
300 the Soviets took 925 airplanes: Taylor, p. 318.
300 "They are Red Army": Sheng, p. 106, citing Zhu Yuanshi, "Liu Shaoqi yu Kangzhan Jiesu Hou zhengduo Donbei di Zheng Dou" [Liu Shaoqi and the Struggle for Power in the Northeast After the End of the War of Resistance], *Jindaishi yanjiu* [Modern History], no. 5 (1988): pp. 124–45.
300 "The Soviet Union doesn't": Yang Kuisong, *Mao Zedong*, p. 223.
301 "The Soviets not only": Ibid.
301 "They gave high praise": Zeng Kelin, "Dadi Chongguang: Youguan Dongbei Jingun Huiyi," [Recover the Land: Recollections of Marching into the Northeast] *Renwu* [Figures] 184, no. 5 (1984): 77–78.
302 the Soviet emissary's plane: Ivan D. Yeaton, *Memoirs of Ivan D. Yeaton* (Stanford, CA: Hoover Institution on War, Revolution, and Peace, 1976), p. 116.
302 the emissary made a public statement: Sheng, pp. 106–107.
302 "We want to bore our way in": Taylor, p. 317.
303 number of Chinese Communist troops: Goncharov et al., pp. 10–11.

303 "There is a possibility": *New York Times*, Oct. 30, 1945.
303 told him that Chinese Communist troops: Yang Kuisong, *Mao Zedong*, p. 228.
303 "caught with our pants down": Yu, p. 231.
303 nearly two thousand agents: Ibid., p. 226.
304 dropped into territories: Yu, p. 232.
304 a nearby POW camp: Ibid., pp. 232–33.
304 deaths of thousands of American troops: OSS Records, NARA, RG226, Entry 148, Box 7.
304 "suddenly and unannounced": OSS "Survey of the Mukden Area," NARA, Entry 148, Box 6, Folder 87.
305 Cardinal observed the Eighth Routers: Ibid.
305 "a stabbing of a B-24 tire": Ibid.
306 "without a fight?": Ibid.
306 "support for Chinese reactionaries": Schaller, p. 266.
307 "quite capable": Benis M. Frank and Henry I. Shaw, *The History of U.S. Marine Corps Operations in World War II*, vol. 5, *Victory and Occupation* (Washington, DC: Headquarters, U.S. Marine Corps, 1968), pp. 547–48.
307 a convoy of nearly twenty-five thousand: Henri I. Shaw, *The United States Marines in North China, 1945–1949* (Washington, DC: Historical Branch, G-3, U.S. Marine Corps, 1968), p. 1.
308 "the largest troop movement": Schaller, p. 265.
309 the marines took over Qingdao: Shaw, pp. 3–4.
309 "he might have been impeached": McCullough, p. 474.
309 "the plan should be abandoned": *FRUS*, 1945, vol. 7, pp. 570–71.
311 "military necessity": Shaw, p. 10.
311 "the ports in question": *FRUS*, 1945, vol. 7, p. 571.
311 "to support undemocratic institutions": Ibid., pp. 559–62. Feis, pp. 371–73.
312 "outstanding intelligence officers": Yu, p. 235.
312 "lean, hearty, enthusiastic": Paul Fillmann and Graham Peck, *China: The Remembered Life* (Boston: Houghton Mifflin, 1968), p. 186.
312 Birch was ordered to go: W. J. Miller, "Account of the Death of Captain John Birch," OSS Headquarters, Central Command, Sept. 14, 1945, NARA retained file. Yu, pp. 235–41.
314 another American OSS team: Yu, p. 241.
315 the CCP needed industry: Steven I. Levine, *Anvil of Victory: The Communist Revolution in Manchuria* (New York: Columbia University Press, 1987), p. 26.
315 "a solid foundation": Goncharov et al., p. 9.
316 "No matter what": Sheng, p. 116.
316 "formally inform them": Ibid.
316 Communist troops opened fire: Shaw, p. 2.
317 of all the Japanese forces: *New York Times*, Oct. 8, 1945.
317 sent a message to Wedemeyer: Feis, p. 365. Sheng, pp. 116–17.

317 "with many sacrifices": Ronald H. Spector, *The Ruins of Empire: The Japanese Surrender and the Battle for Postwar Asia* (New York: Random House, 2007), p. 54.

318 "an interference": Frank and Shaw, p. 559.

318 "The decision regarding Chefoo": *New York Times*, Oct. 9, 1945.

318 "comic opera": *FRUS*, 1945, vol. 7, p. 646.

319 "every mile of track": Shaw, p. 8.

319 "the rest of the traitor army": Ibid., p. 6.

319 "an island in a Communist sea": Ibid., p. 7.

320 on a train near Guye: Ibid., p. 9.

321 "a true son": *Time*, May 30, 1960.

322 searched the KMT offices: Donald G. Gillin and Ramon H. Myers, eds., *Last Chance in Manchuria: The Diary of Chang Kia-Ngau* (Stanford, CA: Hoover Institution on War, Revolution, and Peace, 1989), pp. 88–89.

322 "filled with Soviet officers": Ibid., p. 72.

322 "On the same day": Ibid., p. 73.

322 "this issue can be negotiated": Ibid., p. 75.

323 "a sitting duck": Ibid., p. 76.

324 Chinese Communist troops were in control: Feis, pp. 384–85.

325 "It is very clear": Gillen and Myers, p. 104.

325 American actions to exclude the Soviets: Feis, pp. 390–95.

326 "these professors are distressed": *FRUS*, 1945, vol. 7, pp. 476–79.

326 Among its resolutions: Taylor, pp. 305–306.

327 plans for an airlift were dropped: Ibid., p. 324.

CHAPTER FIFTEEN: What to Do?

328 "extreme antipathy": *FRUS*, 1945, vol. 7, pp. 578–79.

328 "not an extremist": Nancy Bernkopf Tucker, *China Confidential: American Diplomats and Sino-American Relations, 1945–1996* (New York: Columbia University Press, 1996), p. 91.

329 "augment strength": *FRUS*, 1945, vol. 7, p. 601.

329 "It appears at present": Ibid., p. 602.

329 "Dissident elements": Ibid., pp. 603–604.

329 "heavy pressure": Ibid., pp. 611–12.

330 "Impasse seems to have reached": Ibid., p. 613.

330 "looting trains": Ibid., p. 618.

330 "well-entrenched": Ibid., p. 687.

330 "the darkest aspect": Ibid., p. 691.

330 "a complete victory": Ibid., p. 664.

331 "completely unprepared": Ibid., p. 652.

331 this corrosive problem: Ibid., p. 653.

333 "a momentous bearing": *FRUS*, 1945, vol. 7, p. 629.

333 "move resolutely": Ibid., p. 632.

334 "Drumright's stance": Davies, *Dragon*, p. 418.

334 "small likelihood": *FRUS*, 1945, vol. 7, p. 642.
335 "We have to recognize": *Life*, Nov. 19, 1945.
335 "It is somewhat confusing": Cited in Utley, p. 143.
335 "The political structure": *New York Times*, Feb. 25, 1945.
336 "one of the pinnacles": *Time*, Sept. 3, 1945.
336 "customary panegyrics": White, *In Search*, p. 241.
336 "Most Americans": *Life*, Nov. 19, 1945.
337 "deserted an ally": *FRUS*, 1945, vol. 7, p. 673.
337 "considered opinion": Ibid., p. 680.
337 "it's impossible for me": Ibid., p. 684.
338 "perhaps the wise course": Ibid., p. 686.
339 "the symptoms": James Forrestal, *The Forrestal Diaries*, ed. Walter Millis
     (New York: Viking, 1951), p. 111.
339 "the professional foreign service men": *New York Times*, Nov. 29, 1945.
340 "give some assurance": *New York Times*, Nov. 28, 1945.
340 "an uproar": Melby, p. 39.
340 "a victory for American people": Radio Yenan, Foreign Broadcast Infor-
     mation Service (FBIS), Nov. 28, 1945.
340 "Pat Hurley came out": *Time*, Dec. 17, 1945.
341 he called George Marshall: John Robinson Beal, *Marshall in China*
     (Garden City, NY: Doubleday, 1970), pp. 1–2.
341 "the cry of the cranes": Gillin and Myers, p. 126.
342 "speak out": Sheng, p. 113.
342 Stalin's communication with Mao: Goncharov et al., p. 15.
342 Stalin told the Communists: Sheng, p. 114.
342 posters criticizing the KMT disappeared: Gillin and Myers, p. 127.
342 he expressed the hope: Ibid., p. 135.
342 "middle and small cities": Sheng, p. 114.
343 "neutralize the United States": Ibid.
343 "a thunderous greeting": Taylor, p. 329.
343 "glorious victory": Ibid.
343 "agreed to almost all": Ibid.
344 "indicate more positive attitude": *FRUS*, 1945, vol. 7, pp. 694–95.
344 "more serious threats": Ibid., p. 700.

CHAPTER SIXTEEN: Marshall Comes Close

346 "Everybody is waiting": Melby, p. 51.
346 "He is a modest man": Beal, p. 68.
347 "the finest soldier": Forrest C. Pogue, *George C. Marshall: Statesman,
     1945–1949*, vol. 4 (New York: Viking Press, 1987), p. 27.
347 "the growing impression": Melby, p. 69.
348 "hitting him on the back": Caughey, p. 62.
349 "The murder and brutality": Melby, p. 44.
350 Vincent argued forcefully: May, pp. 139–41.
350 "failed to make reasonable concessions": *FRUS*, 1945, vol. 7, p. 768.

351 "he was not to be abandoned": Feis, p. 419.
351 two percent chance of success: Henry Byroade, "Oral History Interview with Henry Byroade," Harry S. Truman Library; online at trumanlibrary .org/oralhist/byroade.htm.
351 "You have . . . been given": Pogue, p. 29.
351 "I told General Marshall": Wedemeyer, p. 363.
352 "I am going to accomplish": Ibid.
352 "eliminating autonomous armies": Lyman P. Van Slyke, ed., *Marshall's Mission to China: The Report and Appended Document*, vol. 1 (Arlington, VA: University Publications of America, 1976), p. 6.
353 "to establish a puppet regime": Ibid., p. 11.
353 "barrier of fear": Van Slyke, *Marshall's Mission*, p. 7.
353 "All shades and grades": Melby, p. 53.
354 Stalin advised the Chinese Communists: Sheng, p. 123.
354 "My estimate": *FRUS*, 1946, vol. 9, p. 18.
354 "an expansionist force": Ibid., pp. 116–18.
355 "The position of the Communists": Ibid., pp. 41–42.
355 they would temporize on that demand: Sheng, pp. 121–22.
356 The government would be allowed: *FRUS*, 1946, vol. 9, pp. 73–104.
357 "hastening to take over": Ibid., p. 104.
357 "we can't agree to this one": Ibid.
357 "It would be a tragedy": Ibid.
357 "generously agreed to the issuance": Ibid., p. 105.
357 "I've tried to tell": Ibid., p. 40.
358 "It marks the beginning": *Liberation Daily*, monitored by FBIS, Jan. 12, 1946.
359 "the democracy to be initiated": *FRUS*, 1946, vol. 9, pp. 151–52.
359 convey an anecdote: Ibid., p. 152.
359 "The distances are great": Ibid., p. 351.
359 "We literally had a team": Byroade, oral history.
360 "impossible situation": *FRUS*, 1946, vol. 9, p. 347.
361 "It is obvious": Ibid., pp. 362–63.
361 "greatly exaggerating": Ibid., p. 373.
361 "weathered mud huts": *New York Times*, Jan. 21, 1946.
361 "The fighting did stop": Byroade, oral history.
362 "no longer any doubt": *New York Times*, Feb. 2, 1946.
362 "Affairs are progressing": A full set of carbon copies of Marshall's letters to Truman are in NARA, Joint Chiefs of Staff, records of Admiral Leahy, RG38, Entry 117, Box 2.
362 "Thousands stormed the field": Radio Yenan, monitored by FBIS, Mar. 6, 1945.
362 "I was frank to an extreme": NARA, Leahy records, RG38, Entry 117, Box 2.
362 "an amazing task": Ibid.
363 "We want unification": Sheng, p. 126.

363 "I shudder": Gillin and Myers, p. 231.
364 "undeniably outstanding": Sheng, p. 126.
364 "terminating the hostilities": *New York Times*, Mar. 17, 1946.
364 "It was very remarkable": Ibid.

CHAPTER SEVENTEEN: From Hope to Antagonism

365 "The outlook is not promising": NARA, Leahy records, RG38, entry 117, box 2.
365 "dangerous military position": Ibid.
365 "open antagonism": NARA, Leahy records, RG 218, entry 117, box 2.
365 "utter chaos": Ibid.
366 the CC clique: Taylor, p. 25.
367 "the most striking change": Fairbank, p. 131.
367 "Every night": Melby, p. 83.
368 "Now that China has paid": *New York Times*, Feb. 15, 1946.
368 "sharp criticism of Russian policy": *New York Times*, Feb. 20, 1946.
369 carried slogans: *New York Times*, Feb. 21, 1946.
369 *New China Daily* denied: Ibid.
369 "littered with crates": Gillin and Myers, p. 195.
370 When the train reached the station: Ibid., p. 223.
370 "the question of economic cooperation": Ibid., p. 222.
371 use the word "fascist": FRUS, 1946, vol. 9, pp. 513–16.
371 "Our party's policy": Sheng, pp. 133–34.
372 "the U.S. Forces Headquarters": Ibid., p. 136.
372 "All that has happened": Sheng, p. 127.
372 "spirit of cooperation": FRUS, 1946, vol. 9, p. 157.
373 vituperative attack on him: Ibid., p. 167.
373 persuasive, even impassioned rejoinder: Ibid., pp. 173–75.
373 irreconcilables were motivated: Ibid., pp. 160–61.
374 reported to Washington: Ibid., pp. 1380, 1400.
375 "a complete contrast": FRUS, 1946, vol. 10, p. 77.
375 "a decisive victory": *New York Times*, Mar. 21, 1946.
376 twenty thousand Communist troops attacked: *New York Times*, Apr. 30, 1946.
377 "shameful": *New York Times*, Apr. 20, 1946.
377 proposal for a new ceasefire: FRUS, 1946, vol. 9, pp. 791–93.
377 "excessive demands": Ibid.
379 "tantamount to supporting": Ibid
380 report from Weixian: Radio Yenan, monitored by FBIS, February 10, 1946.
380 "American planes and officers": Ibid., Apr. 2, 1946.
381 "bring disaster": Ibid., Apr. 21, 1946.
381 "an undeniable fact": Ibid., May 20, 1946.
382 "Never in the past" : Ibid, June 7, 1946.
382 "the aggravation": Pogue, p. 125.

382 "vicious Communist propaganda": Ibid., p. 127.
383 Communist forces ambushed: Van Slyke, *Marshall's Mission*, vol. 1, pp. 444–50.

EPILOGUE: The Tragedy of the Chinese Revolution

385 When the police came: Mei Zhi, *F: Hu Feng's Prison Years*, ed. and trans. Gregor Benton (London: Verso, 2013), p. 18.
385 "counterrevolutionaries are trash": Ibid., back cover.
387 the "leniency" of the party: Ibid., pp. 56–60.
387 "we are all committed": Ibid., p. 11.
389 Ma was ridiculed: Peng, p. 190.
389 "The basis of the interrogation": Wang Ruowang, *The Hunger Trilogy*, trans. Kyna Rubin (Armonk: NY: M. E. Sharpe, 1991), p. 71.
390 He went straight up the stairs: Xu Zhucheng, *Xu Zhucheng Huiyi Lu* [Memoirs of Xu Zhucheng] (Beijing: Sanlian Shudian [Sanlian Bookstore], 1998), p. 415.
393 "the Chinese people have awakened": Mao Zedong, "Farewell, Leighton Stuart," in *Selected Works*, vol. 4, online edition, www.marxists.org.
394 "idiotic": Joseph Alsop, cited in Klehr and Radosh, p. 20.
397 "To sit on the fence": Short, p. 421.

Bibliography

Abrahamson, Rudy. *Spanning the Century: The Life of W. Averell Harriman.* New York: William Morrow, 1992.

Ba Jin. *Guilin di shou-nan* [Hard Times in Guilin]. Available online at www.xiexingcun.com.

Barrett, David D. *Dixie Mission: The United States Army Observer Group in Yenan, 1944.* Berkeley: Center for Chinese Studies, University of California, 1970.

Beal, John Robinson. *Marshall in China.* Garden City, NY: Doubleday, 1970.

Beaton, Cecil. *Chinese Diary & Album.* Hong Kong: Oxford University Press, 1991.

Belden, Jack. *Still Time to Die.* New York: Harper & Brothers, 1944.

Bix, Herbert P. *Hirohito and the Making of Modern Japan.* New York: HarperCollins, 1990.

Buhite, Russell D. *Patrick J. Hurley and American Foreign Policy.* Ithaca, NY: Cornell University Press, 1973.

Byroade, Henry. "Oral History Interview with Henry Byroade." Harry S. Truman Library. Online at trumanlibrary.org/oralhist/byroade.htm.

Byron, John. *The Claws of the Dragon: Kang Sheng—the Evil Genius Behind Mao—and His Legacy of Terror in People's China.* New York; Simon & Schuster, 1992.

Caldwell, Oliver. *A Secret War: Americans in China, 1944–45.* Carbondale: Southern Illinois University Press, 1972.

Carter, Carolle J. *Mission to Yanan: American Liaison with the Chinese Communists, 1944–1947.* Lexington: University Press of Kentucky, 1997.

Caughey, John Hart. *The Marshall Mission to China, 1945–1947.* Lanham, MD: Rowman & Littlefield, 2011.

Chang, Jung, and Jon Halliday. *Mao: The Unknown Story.* New York: Alfred A. Knopf, 2005.

Chu Anping. *Chu Anping Wenyi* [Collected Essays of Chu Anping]. Shanghai: Dongfang Chuban Zhungxin [Eastern Publishing Center], 1998.

Dai Qing. *Wang Shiwei and "Wild Lilies": Rectification and Purges in the Chinese Communist Party, 1942–1944.* Armonk, NY: M. E. Sharpe, 1994.

Davies, John Paton. *China Hand: An Autobiography.* Philadelphia: University of Pennsylvania Press, 2012.

———. *Dragon by the Tail: American, British, Japanese, and Russian Encounters with China and One Another.* New York: W. W. Norton, 1972.

Deng Jiarong. *Ma Yinchu Zhuang* [The Biography of Ma Yinchu]. Shanghai: Arts and Literature Publishing House, 1986.

Dorn, Frank. *Walkout: With Stilwell in Burma.* New York: T. Y. Crowell, 1971.

Dreyer, Edward. *China at War, 1901–1949.* London: Longman, 1995.

Epstein, Israel. *My China Eye: Memoirs of a Jew and a Journalist.* San Francisco: Long River Press, 2005.

Esherick, Joseph W., ed. *Lost Chance in China: The World War II Dispatches of John S. Service.* New York: Random House, 1974.

Fairbank, John K. *Chinabound: A Fifty-Year Memoir.* New York: Harper & Row, 1982).

———. "The New China and the American Connection." *Foreign Affairs* 51, no. 1 (Oct. 1972).

Feis, Herbert. *The China Tangle: The American Effort in China from Pearl Harbor to the Marshall Mission.* Princeton, NJ: Princeton University Press, 1953.

Fillmann, Paul, and Graham Peck. *China: The Remembered Life.* Boston: Houghton Mifflin, 1968.

Forman, Harrison. *Report from Red China.* New York: Henry Holt, 1945.

Forrestal, James. *The Forrestal Diaries.* Edited by Walter Millis. New York: Viking, 1951.

Frank, Benis M., and Henry I. Shaw. *The History of U.S. Marine Corps Operations in World War II.* Vol. 5, *Victory and Occupation.* Washington, DC: Headquarters, U.S. Marine Corps, 1968.

Gaddis, John Lewis. *George F. Kennan: An American Life.* New York: Penguin Press, 2011.

Gao Hua. *Hong taiyang she tsenyang shengqi de: Yenan zhengfeng yundong de lai long qumai* [How Did the Red Sun Rise: A History of the Yenan Rectification Movement]. Hong Kong: Chinese University Press, 2000.

Gellhorn, Martha. *The Face of War.* New York: Atlantic Monthly Press, 1988.

Gillin, Donald G., and Ramon H. Myers, eds. *Last Chance in Manchuria: The Diary of Chang Kia-Ngau.* Stanford, CA: Hoover Institution on War, Revolution, and Peace, 1989.

Glantz, David M. *Soviet Operational and Tactical Combat in Manchuria, 1945, "August Storm."* Portland, OR: Frank Cass Publishers, 2003.

Goldman, Merle, *Literary Dissent in Communist China.* Cambridge, MA: Harvard University Press, 1967.

———. *China's Intellectuals: Advise and Dissent.* Cambridge, MA: Harvard University Press, 1988.

Goncharov, Sergei N., John W. Lewis, and Xue Litai. *Uncertain Partners: Sta-*

lin, Mao, and the Korean War. Stanford, CA: Stanford University Press, 1993.

Greene, Ruth Altman. Hsiang-ya Journal. Hamden, CT: Archon Press, 1977.

Gulick, Edward. Teaching in Wartime China: A Photo Memoir, 1937–1939. Amherst: University of Massachusetts Press, 1995.

Hahn, Emily. "Black and White." The New Yorker, May 5, 1945.

Han Suyin. Destination Chungking. Boston: Little, Brown, 1942.

Harbutt, Fraser J. Yalta 1945: Europe and America at the Crossroads. Cambridge: Cambridge University Press, 2010.

Harding, Harry, and Yuan Ming. Sino-American Relations, 1945–1955: A Joint Reassessment of a Critical Decade. Wilmington, DE: SR Books, 1989.

Heinzig, Dieter. The Soviet Union and Communist China, 1945–1950: The Arduous Road to the Alliance. Armonk, NY: M. E. Sharpe, 2004.

Hu Feng. Hu Feng Zizhuan [Memoirs of Hu Feng]. Beijing: People's Literary Publishing House, 1993.

Isaacson, Walter, and Evan Thomas. The Wise Men: Six Friends and the World They Made. New York: Simon & Schuster, 1986.

Jeans, Roger B., ed. The Marshall Mission to China, 1945–1947: The Letters and Diary of Colonel John Hart Caughey. New York: Rowman & Littlefield, 2011.

Joiner, Lynne. Honorable Survivor: Mao's China, McCarthy's America, and the Persecution of John S. Service. Annapolis, MD: Naval Institute Press, 2009.

Kahn, E. J., Jr. The China Hands: America's Foreign Service Officers and What Befell Them. New York: Viking Press, 1972.

Kissinger, Henry. White House Years. New York: Little, Brown, 1979.

Klehr, Harvey, and Ronald Radosh. The Amerasia Spy Case: Prelude to McCarthyism. Chapel Hill: University of North Carolina Press, 1996.

Lathrop, Alan K. "The Employment of Chinese Nationalist Troops in the First Burma Campaign." Journal of Southeast Asian Studies 12, no. 2 (Sept. 1981).

Lary, Diana. The Chinese People at War: Human Suffering and Social Transformation, 1937–1945. Cambridge: Cambridge University Press, 2010.

Lary, Diana, and Stephen R. MacKinnon, eds. Scars of War: The Impact of Warfare on Modern China. Vancouver: UBC Press, 2001.

Lattimore, Owen. China Memoir: Chiang Kai-shek and the War Against Japan. Tokyo: University of Tokyo Press, 1990.

Li, Danke. Echoes of Chungking: Women in Wartime China. Urbana: University of Illinois Press, 2010.

Liu, F. F. A Military History of Modern China, 1934–1949. Westport, CT: Greenwood Press, 1981.

Liu Heung Shing, ed. China: Portrait of a Country. Cologne: Taschen, 2009.

Lohbeck, Don. Patrick J. Hurley. Washington, DC: Henry Regnery, 1956.

Lu Ling. Qiu Ai [Night of the Chinese Victory]. Beijing: Haiyan Bookstore, 1946.

Ma Yinchu. *Complete Works.* Vol. 12. Hangzhou: Zhejiang People's Publishing House, 1999.

MacKinnon, Stephen R. *Wuhan, 1938: War, Refugees, and the Making of Modern China.* Berkeley, CA: University of California Press, 2008.

MacKinnon, Stephen R., Diana Lary, and Ezra F. Vogel, eds. *China at War: Regions of China, 1937–1945.* Palo Alto, CA: Stanford University Press, 2007.

Mackinnon, Stephen R., and Oris Friesen. *China Reporting: An Oral History of American Journalism in the 1930s and 1940s.* Berkeley: University of California Press, 1987.

May, Gary. *China Scapegoat: The Diplomatic Ordeal of John Carter Vincent.* Washington, DC: New Republic Books, 1979.

Melby, John F. *Mandate of Heaven: Records of a Civil War, China, 1945–1949.* Toronto: University of Toronto Press, 1968.

Pantsov, Alexander V., and Steven I. Levine. *Mao: The Real Story.* New York: Simon & Schuster, 2012.

Peck, Graham. *Two Kinds of Time: Life in Provincial China During the Crucial Years 1940–1941.* Boston: Houghton Mifflin, Sentry Edition, 1950.

Peng Hua. *A Biography of Ma Yinchu.* Beijing: Dangdai Zhongguo Chuban She [Contemporary China Publishing House], 2008.

Plokhy, S. M. *Yalta: The Price of Peace.* New York: Viking, 2010.

Qiao Songdu. *Qiaoguanhua yu Gong Peng: wo di fuqin muqin* [Qiao Guanhua and Gong Peng: My Father and Mother]. Beijing: Zhonghua Shu Ju, 2008.

Rand, Peter. *China Hands: The Adventures and Ordeals of the American Journalists Who Joined Forces with the Great Chinese Revolution.* New York: Simon & Schuster, 1995.

Riley, Nancy E. "China's Population: New Trends and Challenges." *Population Bulletin* 59, no. 2 (June 2004).

Romanus, Charles F., and Riley Sutherland. *United States Army in World War II: Time Runs Out in CBI.* Washington, DC: Office of the Chief of Military History, Department of the Army, 1959.

———. *The United States Army in World War II: Stilwell's Command Problems.* Washington, DC: Office of the Chief of Military History, Department of the Army, 1956.

Rose, Lisle Abbott. *Dubious Victory: The United States and the End of World War II.* Kent, OH: Kent State University Press, 1973.

Schaller, Michael. *The U.S. Crusade in China, 1938–1945.* New York: Columbia University Press, 1979.

Severeid, Eric. *Not So Wild a Dream.* New York: Alfred A. Knopf, 1947.

Shaw, Henry I. *The United States Marines in North China, 1945–1949.* Washington, DC: Historical Branch, G-3, U.S. Marine Corps, 1968.

Sheng, Michael. *Battling Western Imperialism: Mao, Stalin, and the United States.* Princeton, NJ: Princeton University Press, 1997.

Short, Philip. *Mao: A Life*. New York: Henry Holt, 1999.

Sin-Lin. *Shattered Families, Broken Dreams: Little-Known Episodes from the History of the Persecution of Chinese Revolutionaries in Stalin's Gulag*. Translated by Steven I. Levine. Portland, ME: Merwin Asia. 2012.

Spector, Ronald H. *The Ruins of Empire: The Japanese Surrender and the Battle for Postwar Asia*. New York: Random House, 2007.

Stirling, Nora B. *Pearl Buck: A Woman in Conflict*. Piscataway, NJ: New Century Publishing, 1983.

Tawney, Richard. *Land and Labor in China*. New York: Farrar, Straus, and Giroux, 1972.

Taylor, Jay. *The Generalissimo: Chiang Kai-shek and the Struggle for Modern China*. Cambridge, MA: Harvard University Press, 2009.

Tozer, Warren. "The Foreign Correspondents' Visit to Yenan in 1944: A Reassessment." *Pacific Historical Review* 14, no. 2 (May 1972).

Tsou, Tang. *America's Failure in China, 1941–1950*. Chicago: University of Chicago Press, 1968.

Tuchman, Barbara W. "If Mao Had Come to Washington," *Foreign Affairs* 51 (Oct. 1972).

———. *Stilwell and the American Experience in China, 1911–1945*. New York: Grove Press, 1970.

Tucker, Nancy Bernkopf. *China Confidential: American Diplomats and Sino-American Relations, 1945–1996*. New York: Columbia University Press, 1996.

Utley, Freda. *The China Story*. Washington, DC: Regnery, 1951.

van de Ven, Hans J. *War and Nationalism in China, 1925–1945*. London: Routledge Curzon, 2003.

Van Slyke, Lyman P., ed. *The Chinese Communist Movement: A Report of the United States War Department, July 1945*. Palo Alto, CA: Stanford University Press, 1968.

———, ed. *Marshall's Mission to China: The Report and Appended Documents*. 2 vols. Arlington, VA: University Publications of America, 1976.

Vladimirov, Pyotr. *The Vladimirov Diaries, Yenan, China, 1942–1945*. New York: Doubleday, 1975.

Wakeman, Frederic, Jr. *The Shanghai Badlands: Wartime Terrorism and Urban Crime, 1937–1941*. Cambridge: Cambridge University Press, 1996.

Waldron, Arthur. "China's New Remembering: The Case of Zhang Zhizhong." *Modern Asian Studies* 30, no. 4 (Oct. 1996): 945–978.

Wang Ruowang. *The Hunger Trilogy*. Translated by Kyna Rubin. Armonk, NY: M. E. Sharpe, 1991.

Wedemeyer, Albert C. *Wedemeyer Reports!* New York: Henry Holt, 1958.

Webster, Donovan. *The Burma Road: The Epic Story of the China-Burma-India Theater in World War II*. New York: Farrar, Straus and Giroux. 2003.

White, Theodore H. *In Search of History: A Personal Adventure*. New York: Harper & Row, 1978.

White, Theodore H., and Annalee Jacoby. *Thunder Out of China*. New York: William Sloan Associates, 1946.

Xu Zhucheng. *Xu Zhucheng Huiyi Lu* [Memoirs of Xu Zhucheng]. Beijing: Sanlian Shudian [Sanlian Bookstore], 1998.

Yang Chengyi, ed. *Feng-huo meng-yue-zhong di ji-pin: Zhejiang kangri zhanzheng kousu fangtan* [Memories in the Blaze of Wartime: Oral Interviews on the Japanese Occupation in Zhejiang]. Beijing: Beijing Library Publishing, 2007.

Yang Jianye. *Ma Yingchu*. Shijiazhuang: Huashan Wenyi Chuban She [Huashan Arts and Literature Publishing House], 1997.

Yang Kuisong. *Mao Zedong yu Mosike de enen yuanyuan* [The Love-Hate Relationship Between Mao Zedong and Moscow]. Nanchang: Jiangxi Renmin Chuban She [Jiangxi People's Publishing Co.], 1999.

———. *Zhonggong yu Mosike di Guanxi* [Relations Between the Chinese Communists and Moscow]. Nanchang: Jiangxi Renmin Chuban She [Jiangxi People's Publishing Co.], 1997.

Yeaton, Ivan D. *Memoirs of Ivan D. Yeaton*. Stanford, CA: Hoover Institution on War, Revolution, and Peace, 1976.

Yu, Maochun. *OSS in China: Prelude to Cold War*. New Haven, CT: Yale University Press, 1996.

Zhang Guotao. *Rise of the Chinese Communist Party*. Lawrence: University Press of Kansas, 1972.

Zhou Enlai. *Zhou Enlai nianpu* [Chronological Record of Zhou Enlai]. Beijing: People's Publishing Co., 1991.

Zhu Yuanshi. "Liu Shaoqi yu kangjan Jiesu Hou Zheng-duo Dongbei di Douzheng" [Liu Shaoqi and the Struggle for Power in the Northeast After the End of the War of Resistance]. *Jindaishi yanjiu* (Modern History Research), no. 5 (1988).

Index

Page numbers followed by *f* indicate a figure.

Illustration Credits

ULTIMATE JOURNEY
Retracing the Path of an Ancient Buddhist Monk
Who Crossed Asia in Search of Enlightenment

In 629, the revered Buddhist monk Hsuan Tsang set out across Asia in search of the Ultimate Truth, and to settle what he called "the perplexities of my mind." From the Tang dynasty capital at Xian through ancient Silk Road oases, over forbidding mountain passes to Tashkent, Samarkand, and the Amu Darya River, across Pakistan to the holiest cities of India and back again—his sixteen-year journey was beset with every hardship imaginable. Pilgrimage complete, Hsuan Tsang wrote an account of his trek that is still considered one of the classics of Chinese literature. In 1998, Richard Bernstein retraced the steps of Hsuan Tsang's long and sinuous route, comparing present and past. Aided by modern technology but hampered by language barriers, harried border crossings, hostile Islamic regimes, and the accidental U.S. bombing of the Chinese embassy in Belgrade, Bernstein follows the monk's path not only in physical but in contemplative ways, juxtaposing his own experiences with those of Hsuan Tsang. Inspiring and profoundly felt, *Ultimate Journey* is a marvelous amalgamation of travelogue and history, cultural critique and spiritual meditation.

Travel